Pro XML Development with Java™ Technology

Ajay Vohra and Deepak Vohra

Apress®

Pro XML Development with Java™ Technology

Copyright © 2006 by Ajay Vohra and Deepak Vohra

ISBN-13 (pbk): 978-1-59059-706-4

ISBN-10 (pbk): 1-59059-706-0

Lead Editor: Chris Mills
Technical Reviewer: Bharath Gowda
Editorial Board: Steve Anglin, Ewan Buckingham, Gary Cornell, Jason Gilmore, Jonathan Gennick, Jonathan Hassell, James Huddleston, Chris Mills, Matthew Moodie, Dominic Shakeshaft, Jim Sumser, Keir Thomas, Matt Wade
Project Manager: Elizabeth Seymour
Copy Edit Manager: Nicole LeClerc
Copy Editor: Kim Wimpsett
Assistant Production Director: Kari Brooks-Copony
Senior Production Editor: Laura Cheu
Compositor: Susan Glinert Stevens
Proofreader: Kim Burton
Indexer: Carol Burbo
Artist: Susan Glinert Stevens
Cover Designer: Kurt Krames
Manufacturing Director: Tom Debolski

Distributed to the book trade worldwide by Springer-Verlag New York, Inc., 233 Spring Street, 6th Floor, New York, NY 10013. Phone 1-800-SPRINGER, fax 201-348-4505, e-mail orders-ny@springer-sbm.com, or visit http://www.springeronline.com.

For information on translations, please contact Apress directly at 2560 Ninth Street, Suite 219, Berkeley, CA 94710. Phone 510-549-5930, fax 510-549-5939, e-mail info@apress.com, or visit http://www.apress.com.

The source code for this book is available to readers at http://www.apress.com in the Source Code section.

Dedicated to our parents

Contents at a Glance

PART 6 ▪▪▪ Web Applications and Services

Contents

PART 1 ▪▪▪ Parsing, Validating, and Addressing

PART 2 ■■■ **Object Bindings**

PART 4 ■■■ DOM Level 3.0

PART 5 ■■■ **Utilities**

PART 6 ■■■ **Web Applications and Services**

About the Authors

AJAY VOHRA is a senior solutions architect at DataSynapse (`http://www.datasynapse.com`). His current focus is service-oriented architecture based on grid-enabled virtualized application services. He has 15 years of software development experience, spanning diverse areas such as X Windows Toolkit, ATM networking, automatic conversion of COBOL to J2EE applications, and J2EE-based enterprise applications. He has a master's degree in computer science from Southern Illinois University–Carbondale and an MBA from the University of Michigan Ross School of Business in Ann Arbor, Michigan. Ajay is an avid golfer and loves swimming in Lake Michigan with his family.

DEEPAK VOHRA is an independent consultant and a founding member of NuBean (`http://www.nubean.com`). He has worked in the area of XML and Java programming for more than five years and is a Sun Certified Java Programmer and a Sun Certified Web Component Developer. He has a master's degree in mechanical engineering from Southern Illinois University–Carbondale and has published original research papers in the area of fluidized bed combustion. Currently, he is working on an automated, web-based J2EE development environment for NuBean. When not programming, Deepak likes to bike and play tennis.

About the Technical Reviewer

■**BHARATH GOWDA** works as a technical account manager (TAM) at Compuware in Michigan. In his capacity as a TAM, he is responsible for crafting development solutions based on OptimalJ in the application delivery management space. Previously, he spent most of his time building and enhancing enterprise-level J2EE solutions for organizations in the Michigan region.

Bharath earned his master's degree in computer science from the University of Southern California–Los Angeles. He lives in Ann Arbor, Michigan, with his wife, Swarupa.

Acknowledgments

First, we would like to thank all the W3C contributors who worked on numerous XML-related Drafts, Working Group Notes, and Recommendations. Second, we would like to thank all the contributors who worked on XML-related Java Specification Requests. Third, we would like to thank all the software developers who worked on creating the open source software used in this book. Fourth, we would like to thank our reviewers and editors, Bharath Gowda, Kim Wimpsett, Laura Cheu, Chris Mills, and Elizabeth Seymour.

Ajay would like to thank his mentor, Professor Kenneth J. Danhof, Ph.D., for his guidance at Southern Illinois University–Carbondale. And above all, Ajay would like to thank his wife, Pam, and their kids, Sara and Stewart, for their love and understanding during the long hours spent writing this book.

PART 1

∎∎∎

Parsing, Validating, and Addressing

CHAPTER 1

■■■

Introducing XML and Java

Extensible Markup Language (XML) is based on simple, platform-independent rules for representing structured textual information. The platform-independent nature of XML makes it an ideal format for exchanging structured textual information among disparate applications. Therefore, at the heart of it, XML is about interoperability.

XML 1.0 was made a W3C[1] Recommendation in 1998. Sun formally introduced the Java programming language in 1995, and within a few years Java had cemented its status as the preferred programming and execution platform for a dizzyingly diverse set of applications. Incidentally, both Java and XML were shaped with an eye toward the Internet. Therefore, it is not surprising that most of the XML-related W3C Recommendations have inspired corresponding Java-based application programming interfaces (APIs). Some of these Java APIs are part of the Java Platform Standard Edition (J2SE) platform; others are part of various open source or proprietary endeavors. XML-related W3C Recommendations and their corresponding Java APIs are the main focus of this book.

Scope of This Book

In this book, we have two main objectives. Our first objective is to discuss a selected subset of XML-related W3C Recommendations that have inspired corresponding Java APIs. And to that end, here is a quick synopsis of the XML-related W3C Recommendations and Java APIs that we'll cover in this book:

- XML 1.0 (`http://www.w3.org/TR/REC-xml/`) describes precise rules for crafting a well-formed XML document and describes partial rules for processing well-formed[2] documents. Java API for XML Processing (JAXP) 1.3 in J2SE 5.0 is its corresponding Java API. In addition, Streaming API for XML 1.0 (StAX) in J2SE 6.0 is relevant for processing XML documents.

- XML Schema 1.0 (`http://www.w3.org/TR/xmlschema-1/`) describes a language that can be used to specify the precise structure of an XML document and constrain its contents. JAXP 1.3 in J2SE 5.0 and Java XML Architecture for XML Binding (JAXB) 2.0 in Java 2 Enterprise Edition (J2EE)[3] 5.0 are corresponding Java APIs.

- XML Path Language (XPath) 1.0 (`http://www.w3.org/TR/xpath`) describes a language for addressing parts of an XML document. The XPath API within JAXP 1.3 is its corresponding Java API.

---

1. The World Wide Web Consortium (W3C) is dedicated to developing interoperable technologies. You can find more information about the W3C at `http://www.w3.org`.
2. Well-formed XML documents are defined as part of the XML 1.0 specification at `http://www.w3.org/TR/2004/REC-xml-20040204/#sec-well-formed`.
3. `http://java.sun.com/javaee/`

- XSL Transformations (XSLT) 1.0 (http://www.w3.org/TR/xslt) describes a language for transforming an XML document into other XML or non-XML documents. Transformation API for XML (TrAX) within JAXP 1.3 is its corresponding API.

- Document Object Model Level 3 Load and Save (http://www.w3.org/TR/DOM-Level-3-LS/) defines a platform- and language-neutral interface for bidirectional mapping between an XML document and a DOM document. The DOM Level 3 API within JAXP 1.3 is its corresponding API.

- SOAP[4] 1.1 and 1.2 (http://www.w3.org/TR/soap/) define a messaging framework for exchanging XML content across distributed processing nodes. SOAP with Attachments API for Java (SAAJ) 1.3 is its corresponding Java API.

- Web Services Description Language (WSDL) 1.1 (http://www.w3.org/TR/wsdl) is an XML-based format for describing web service endpoints. The Java API for XML Web Services (JAX-WS 2.0) in J2EE 5.0 is its corresponding Java API.

Our second objective is to discuss selected XML-related utility Java APIs that are useful in building interoperable enterprise software solutions. And to that end, here are the utility Java APIs discussed in this book:

- The XMLBeans 2.0 API, which is used for XML binding to JavaBeans. This is an alternative to JAXB 2.0 and has some pros and cons compared to JAXB 2.0.

- The XML:DB[5] group of APIs, which can be used to access and update XML documents stored in a native XML database.

- The Java Database Connectivity (JDBC) 4.0 API, which is useful for storing XML content within a relational database.

- The Apache POI[6] API, which is useful for transforming XML content into Microsoft Excel[7] spreadsheets.

- The Apache Formatting Objects Processor (FOP)[8] API, which is useful for transforming XML content into Portable Document Format (PDF).[9]

We aim to cover all this material from a pragmatic viewpoint; by that we mean we will do the following:

- Briefly explain various XML-related W3C Recommendations in simple, straightforward terms, without being imprecise.

- Discuss related Java APIs from a developer's viewpoint, without being tedious.

Based on the overall objectives of this book, we think this book is suitable for an intermediate-to advanced-level Java developer who understands introductory XML concepts and the J2SE 5.0 core APIs.

Note This book is not a comprehensive, in-depth survey of XML-related W3C Recommendations. We think all W3C Recommendations are well written and are the best source for such comprehensive information.

---

4. SOAP is not an acronym for anything anymore; it is just a name.
5. XML:DB APIs are part of the XML DB initiative at http://xmldb-org.sourceforge.net/xupdate/.
6. Apache POI defines pure Java APIs for manipulating Microsoft file formats (http://jakarta.apache.org/poi/).
7. Microsoft Excel is part of Microsoft Office (http://www.microsoft.com).
8. You can find more information about the Apache FOP project at http://xmlgraphics.apache.org/fop/.
9. PDF is a de facto standard interoperable file format from Adobe (http://www.adobe.com).

Overview of This Book's Contents

We have strived to cover a wide swath of XML-related Java APIs in this book, ranging from basic, building-block APIs used to parse XML documents to more advanced APIs used to implement interoperable XML-based web services. This book is organized in five parts. Part 1 spans Chapters 1 through 5 and covers basics of parsing, validating, addressing, and transforming XML documents. Part 2 comprises Chapters 6 and 7 and covers the binding of XML Schema to Java types. Part 3 includes Chapters 8 and 9 and focuses on XML and databases. Part 4 consists of Chapters 10 through 12 and focuses on transforming the XML document model to other document models. Part 5 consists of Chapters 13 and 14 and focuses on XML-based web applications and web services. Here is a quick synopsis of what is in each chapter:

- Chapter 1 reviews XML 1.0 and XML Schema 1.0.

- Chapter 2 discusses the parsing of XML documents using JAXP 1.3 in J2SE 5.0 and StAX 1.0 in J2SE 6.0.

- Chapter 3 discusses validating an XML document with an XML Schema, and in this context, we cover the following APIs: JAXP 1.3 APIs: SAX parser, DOM parser, and the Validation API.

- Chapter 4 reviews XPath 1.0 and discusses the JAXP 1.3 and JDOM 1.0 XPath APIs.

- Chapter 5 reviews XSLT 1.0 and discusses the TrAX API defined within JAXP 1.3.

- Chapter 6 discusses the mapping of XML Schema to Java types and covers the JAXB 1.0 and 2.0 APIs.

- Chapter 7 discusses the mapping of XML Schema to JavaBeans and covers the XMLBeans 2.0 API.

- Chapter 8 discusses native databases and covers the XML:DB APIs. We use the open source Apache Xindice native XML database as the example database in this chapter.

- Chapter 9 discusses storing an XML document in a relational database management system (RDBMS) using the JDBC 4.0 API.

- Chapter 10 discusses DOM Level 3 Load and Save and the DOM Level 3 API defined within JAXP 1.3.

- Chapter 11 discusses converting the XML document model to a Microsoft Excel spreadsheet using the Apache POI API.

- Chapter 12 discusses converting the XML document model to a PDF document model using the Apache FOP API.

- Chapter 13 discusses Asynchronous JavaScript and XML (Ajax) web programming techniques for creating highly interactive web applications.

- Chapter 14 discusses SOAP 1.1, SOAP 1.2, and WSDL 1.1 and discusses the JAX-WS 2.0 Java API, which is included in J2EE 5.0. Chapter 14 brings together a lot of the material covered in this book.

XML 1.0 Primer

XML[10] is a text-based markup language that is the de facto industry standard for exchanging data among disparate applications. XML defines precise syntactic rules for what constitutes a well-formed

---

10. XML 1.0 is a W3C Recommendation (http://www.w3.org/TR/2004/REC-xml-20040204/), and XML 1.1 is a W3C Recommendation (http://www.w3.org/TR/xml11/).

XML document. This primer is a non-normative discussion of these rules. We will gradually introduce these rules and use them to show how to incrementally build an XML document.

Before we proceed, we want to mention two central concepts that underlie all the syntactic rules defining an XML document:

- First, all syntactic constructs within an XML document are delimited by markup character sequences, which implies that within the body of any syntactic construct, the markup character sequences are not allowed. For example, a syntactic construct called a *start tag* is delimited by < and > characters, which implies that these two characters cannot appear within the body of a start tag.

- Second, if you need to get around the limitation described in the previous bulleted item, escape character sequences allow you to do that. (We do not expect this second concept to be immediately clear, but we will elaborate on this concept later in the "Elements" section.)

We will begin where most XML documents begin: XML declarations.

XML Declarations

A well-formed XML document can begin with an XML declaration. An XML declaration can be omitted, but if it appears, it should be the first thing within a document. You define an XML declaration as follows:

```
<?xml version='1.0'  ?>
```

The version attribute specifies the XML version, and it is a required attribute. The XML declaration may include additional attributes: encoding and standalone. An example XML declaration with the encoding and standalone attributes is as follows:

```
<?xml version='1.0'  encoding='UTF-8' standalone='yes' ?>
```

The encoding attribute specifies the character set used to encode data in an XML document. The default encoding is UTF-8. The standalone attribute specifies whether the XML document references external entities. If no external entities are referenced, specify the standalone attribute as yes.

Elements

The basic syntactic construct of an XML document is an element. An element in an XML document is delimited by a start tag and an end tag. An example of an XML element is as follows:

```
<journal></journal>
```

A start tag within an element is delimited by the < and > characters and has a tag name. In the previous start tag, the name is journal. The precise rules for a valid tag name are fairly complex and best left to the W3C Recommendation. However, it is useful to keep in mind that a tag name must begin with a letter and can contain hyphen (-) and underscore (_) characters. An end tag is delimited by the </ and > character sequences and also contains a tag name.

A document must have a single root element, which is also known as the *document element*. If you assume that the journal element is your root element, then your document so far looks as follows:

```
<?xml version='1.0'  encoding='UTF-8' standalone='yes' ?>
<journal></journal>
```

This is an example of a well-formed XML document, where of course the XML declaration on the first line is optional; omitting the XML declaration would still leave you with a well-formed document.

An element can contain other nested elements. So, for example, the root element may contain a nested element, as shown here:

```
<?xml version='1.0'  encoding='UTF-8' standalone='yes' ?>
<journal>
  <article></article>
</journal>
```

Elements may contain text content. So, for example, with some arbitrary text content added to the article element, the document now looks as follows:

```
<?xml version='1.0'  encoding='UTF-8' standalone='yes' ?>
<journal>
  <article>This is some arbitrary text!</article>
</journal>
```

Of course, element text content cannot contain any delimiter character sequences such as </. One way to get around that is to enclose element content within a CDATA construct, and assuming you do that for this example, your document now looks as follows:

```
 <?xml version='1.0'  encoding='UTF-8' standalone='yes' ?>
<journal>
  <article>
   <![CDATA[This is some arbitrary text <within> a CDATA!]]>
  </article>
</journal>
```

An element may of course have no nested elements or content. Such an element is termed an *empty element,* and it can be written with a special start tag that has no end tag. For example, <article/> is an empty element. If you include this empty element within your document, the document looks like this:

```
<?xml version='1.0'  encoding='UTF-8' standalone='yes' ?>
<journal>
  <article>
   <![CDATA[This is some arbitrary text <within> a CDATA!]]>
  </article>
  <article/>
</journal>
```

Elements can have attributes, which are specified in the start tag. An example of an attribute is <article title="A Tutorial on XML 1.0"></article>. An attribute is defined as a name-value pair, and in the previous example, the name of the attribute is of course title, and the value of the attribute is A Tutorial on XML 1.0. With an attribute added, the example document looks as follows:

```
<?xml version='1.0'  encoding='UTF-8' standalone='yes' ?>
<journal>
  <article title="A Tutorial on XML 1.0" >
   <![CDATA[This is some arbitrary text <within> a CDATA!]]>
  </article>
  <article/>
</journal>
```

Now let's assume you want to add another attribute named date with the value <04/12/2006>. If you recall the first central concept we mentioned at the outset of this primer, you are not allowed to include delimiter characters within an attribute value. However, the second central concept mentioned earlier comes to your rescue: you can use the < character sequence to escape <, and—yes, you guessed it—you can use the > character sequence to escape >. So, with that in place, the document now looks as follows:

```
<?xml version='1.0'  encoding='UTF-8' standalone='yes' ?>
<journal>
  <article date="&lt;04/12/2006&gt;"  title="A Tutorial on XML 1.0" >
  <![CDATA[This is some arbitrary text <within> a CDATA!]]>
  </article>
  <article/>
</journal>
```

Another mechanism for including delimiter characters within the body of a construct is to use escaped numeric references. For example, the numeric American Standard Code for Information Interchange (ASCII) value for the > character is 62, so you can use the > character sequence instead of >. Using escaped numeric references is of course the most general mechanism for including delimiter characters within a construct's body.

Comments

You can define comments in an XML document within a comment declaration as shown in the following example:

```
<!--This is a comment - ->
```

Comments can appear anywhere outside markup, which consists of start tags, end tags, empty element tags, comments, CDATA sections, escape character references, and entity references (discussed later in the "Entities" section).

Processing Instructions

Processing instructions in an XML document specify directions for applications that are expected to process the document. The semantics associated with these instructions are application specific. The syntax of a processing instruction is as follows:

```
<?target "instructions"?>
```

In a processing instruction, target specifies the target application that is expected to process the instruction, and instructions specifies the processing instructions.

DOCTYPE Declarations

An XML document can also include a document type definition (DTD).[11] A DTD defines the structure of an XML document. If the content of an XML document conforms to the structure imposed by its DTD, then such a document is termed *valid*. A DTD is defined in a DOCTYPE declaration. A DOCTYPE has three types of DTD specifications: internal, private, and public. You can specify an internal DTD within an XML document as follows:

---

11. A DTD is not an XML document and is beyond the scope of this book. However, numerous tutorials available on the Internet can quickly acquaint you with the basics of DTDs.

```
<!DOCTYPE root_element [Elements, Attributes]>
```

For example, you could have an internal DTD for the example document as shown here:

```
<!DOCTYPE journal
[
  <!ELEMENT journal (article)*>
  <!ELEMENT article (#PCDATA)>
  <!ATTLIST article title CDATA #IMPLIED>
]>
```

You can specify a private external DTD as follows:

```
<!DOCTYPE rootElement  SYSTEM "DTDLocation">
```

For example, assuming a DTD for the example document exists in a local file named journal.dtd, you can specify a private external DTD as shown here:

```
<!DOCTYPE journal  SYSTEM "journal.dtd">
```

You can specify a public external DTD as follows:

```
<!DOCTYPE rootElement  PUBLIC  "DTDName" "DTDLocation">
```

So, assuming a DTD for the example document has a public name of -//Apress.//DTD Journal Example 1.0//EN and exists at http://www.apress.com/javaxml/dtd/journal.dtd, you can specify a public external DTD as shown here:

```
<!DOCTYPE journal PUBLIC "-//Apress.//DTD Journal Example 1.0//EN"
"http://www.apress.com/javaxml/dtd/journal.dtd">
```

Entities

An entity in an XML document is a storage unit that can be referenced with an entity reference. Entities may be parsed or unparsed. Parsed entities act like replacement text, and this text replaces the entity references within the document. Unparsed entities may or may not be text, and if text, they may not be XML text. Unparsed entities are never parsed into the XML document, and they are essentially passed through to the processing application. It is up to the processing application to attach any meaning to these unparsed entities.

An entity is one of the following types: internal, parsed general entity; external, parsed general entity; or external, unparsed general entity. The syntax of an internal, parsed general entity is as follows:

```
<!ENTITY  entity_name  "entity_value">
```

The syntax of a private, external parsed general entity is as follows:

```
<!ENTITY entity_name  SYSTEM  "SYSTEM_URI">
```

The syntax of a public, external, parsed general entity is as follows:

```
<!ENTITY entity_name PUBLIC  "publicId"  "PUBLIC_URI">
```

The external, unparsed general entity is used to reference data that an XML document does not have to parse. The syntax of an external, unparsed general entity is as follows:

```
<!ENTITY entity_name SYSTEM  "SYSTEM_URI"  NDATA notation_name>
<!ENTITY entity_name PUBLIC  "publicId"  "Public_URI" NDATA notation_name>
```

All entity declarations must be within a DTD or an internal DTD declaration within a DOCTYPE. As an example, the escape sequences < and > discussed earlier are in fact entity references to implicit, internal, parsed entities. In fact, you can make these implicit entities explicit, as shown in the following example:

```
<!DOCTYPE journal [
  <!ENTITY lt '&#60;'>
  <!ENTITY gt '&#62;'>
]>
```

The XML declaration and the entity declarations form the prolog of an XML document.

Complete Example XML Document

Listing 1-1 shows the complete example XML document.

Listing 1-1. *Complete Example XML Document*

```
<?xml version='1.0'  encoding='UTF-8' ?>
<!DOCTYPE  journal  [
<!ENTITY lt '&#60;'>
<!ENTITY gt '&#62;'>
<!ELEMENT journal (article)*>
<!ELEMENT article (#PCDATA)>
<!ATTLIST article title CDATA #IMPLIED>
 ] >
<!--XML declaration must be the first thing in a document, if it appears at all -->
<!--journal is the root element -->
<journal>
  <article date="&lt;04/12/2006&gt;"  title="A Tutorial on XML 1.0" >
  <![CDATA[This is some arbitrary text <within> a CDATA!]]>
  </article>
  <!-- An empty element may of course have attributes -->
  <article title="XSLT tutorial"  />
</journal>
```

Namespaces in XML

An XML Namespace associates an element or attribute name with a specified URI and thus allows for multiple elements (or attributes) within an XML document to have the same name yet have different semantics associated with those names because they belong to different XML Namespaces. The key point to understand is that the sole purpose of associating a uniform resource indicator (URI) to a namespace is to associate a unique value with a namespace. There is absolutely no requirement that the URI should point to anything meaningful.

You specify an XML Namespace through one of two reserved attributes:

- You can specify a default XML Namespace URI using the xmlns attribute.

- You can specify a nondefault XML Namespace URI using the xmlns:prefix attribute, where prefix is a unique prefix associated with this XML Namespace.

An element or an attribute is designated to be part of an XML Namespace either by explicitly prefixing its name with an XML Namespace prefix or by implicitly nesting it within an element that has been associated with a default XML Namespace. It is important to understand that a namespace prefix is merely a syntactic device to impart brevity to a namespace reference and that the real namespace is always the associated URI. All this is best illustrated through an example, so turn your attention to the following code:

```
<?xml version='1.0'  encoding='UTF-8' ?>
<jsp:root xmlns:jsp="http://java.sun.com/JSP/Page"
      xmlns:xsi="http://www.w3.org/2001/XMLSchema-instance"
      xsi:schemaLocation=
        "http://java.sun.com/JSP/Page http://www.nubean.com/schemas/jsf_1_1.xsd"
>
  <f:view xmlns:f="http://java.sun.com/jsf/core" >
    <f:verbatim></f:verbatim>
    <html xmlns="http://www.w3.org/1999/xhtml" >
      <head><title>This was typed by hand</title></head>
      <body>
        <a href="http://www.w3.org/TR/REC-xml-names/">Namespaces in XML</a>
      </body>
    </html>
  </f:view>
</jsp:root>
```

In this example, the root element is in the http://java.sun.com/JSP/Page XML Namespace and is designated as such through the use of the associated jsp prefix in its element name, as in jsp:root. As another example, the view element is in the http://java.sun.com/jsf/core XML Namespace and is marked as such through the associated f prefix, as in the f:view element name. As an example of a default XML Namespace, the html element and all its nested elements have no prefix and are in the default XML Namespace associated with the http://www.w3.org/1999/xhtml URI.

XML Schema 1.0 Primer

The XML Schema 1.0[12] definition language specifies the structure of an XML document and constrains its content. The key concept to understand is that a schema based on the XML Schema language defines a class of valid XML documents. A document is considered valid with respect to a schema if it conforms to the structure defined by the schema. A valid XML document is formally referred to as an *instance* of the schema document. As a rough analogy, what a Java class is to a Java object, a schema is to an XML document.

One more important point to keep in mind is that a schema is also an XML document. In fact, this was one of the key motivations for the XML Schema language; the alternative structure standard, which is a DTD, is not an XML document. In case it is not already obvious, you could actually write a schema for an XML Schema–based schema document!

This is a non-normative discussion of the XML Schema language. As far as possible, we will explain various XML Schema constructs in the context of an example schema. We will show how to build an example schema incrementally as we explain various XML Schema constructs. The example schema will define a structure for the example XML document shown in Listing 1-2.

Listing 1-2. *Example XML Document*

```
<?xml version='1.0'  encoding='UTF-8' ?>
<catalog publisher="O'Reilly"  title="OnJava.com" >
 <journal date="2004-05-05" >
   <article>
    <title>Java and XML</title>
    <author>Narayanan Jayaratchagan</author>
```

---

12. See XML Schema Part 1: Structures (http://www.w3.org/TR/xmlschema-1/) and XML Schema Part 2: Datatypes (http://www.w3.org/TR/xmlschema-2/) for more information.

```
    </article>
  </journal>
</catalog>
```

Schema Declarations

The root element of a schema is schema, and it is defined in the XML Schema namespace
xmlns:xsd="http://www.w3.org/2001/XMLSchema". An example schema document with its root
element is as follows:

```
<xsd:schema xmlns:xsd="http://www.w3.org/2001/XMLSchema" >
</xsd:schema>
```

Built-in Datatypes

The XML Schema language has 44 built-in simple types that are specified in XML Schema Part 2:
Datatypes (http://www.w3.org/TR/xmlschema-2/). These datatypes of course belong to the XML
Schema namespace, so we will use them with the xsd: prefix, as in xsd:string. Table 1-1 lists the
most commonly used built-in datatypes. For a complete list of built-in datatypes, consult the W3C
Recommendation.

Table 1-1. *Commonly Used Built-in Datatypes*

Datatype	Description	Example
string	A character string	New York, NY
int	–2147483648 to 2147483647	+234, –345, 678987
double	A 64-bit floating point number	–345.e-7, NaN, –INF, INF
decimal	A valid decimal number	–42.5, 67, 92.34, +54.345
date	A date in CCYY-MM-DD format	2006-05-05
time	Time in hh:mm:ss-hh:mm format	10:27:34-05:00 (for 10:27:34 EST, which is –5 hours UTC)

Element Declarations

You define an element in an XML Schema–based schema with the element construct, as shown here:

```
<xsd:element  name="element_name"  type="element_type"/>
```

You can define an element within a schema construct. The example schema document with a
top-level catalog element declaration within a schema construct is as follows:

```
<xsd:schema xmlns:xsd="http://www.w3.org/2001/XMLSchema" >
  <xsd:element name="catalog"  type="catalogType" ></xsd:element>
  <!-- we have yet to define a catalogType -->
</xsd:schema>
```

Of course, we have not yet defined catalogType. The XML Schema language defines two main
type constructs: a simple type and a complex type. Almost no meaningful document structure is
feasible without the use of a complex type, so that is what we will cover next.

Complex Type Declarations

A complexType constrains elements and attributes in an XML document. You can specify a complexType in a schema construct or an element declaration. If you specify a complexType in a schema construct, the complexType is referenced in an element declaration with a type attribute. In the example schema, you can define the catalogType type as a complex type as shown here:

```
<xsd:schema xmlns:xsd="http://www.w3.org/2001/XMLSchema" >
  <xsd:element name="catalog"  type="catalogType" ></xsd:element>
  <xsd:complexType name="catalogType" >
  </xsd:complexType>
</xsd:schema>
```

Sequence Model Groups

You can also define an element within a sequence model group, which, as the name implies, defines an ordered list of one or more elements. In the example schema, say you want to allow a journal element in the catalogType complex type; you'd use a sequence model group as shown here:

```
<xsd:complexType name="catalogType" >
<xsd:sequence>
   <xsd:element ref="journal" />
   <!-- we have yet to define a global journal element -->
  </xsd:sequence>
</xsd:complexType>
```

The journal element declaration within the catalogType complex type uses a ref attribute to refer to a global journal element definition. Of course, we have not yet defined any global journal element, so we will do that next, using a choice model group.

Choice Model Groups

You can also define an element within a choice model group, which defines a choice of elements from which one element may be selected. In the example schema document, say you want to define a global journal element that offers a choice between article and research elements, as shown here:

```
<xsd:element name="journal" >
   <xsd:complexType>
     <xsd:choice>
       <xsd:element name="article"  type="paperType"  />
       <xsd:element name="research"  type="paperType" />
       <!-- we have yet to define a paperType type -->
     </xsd:choice>
   </xsd:complexType>
</xsd:element>
```

All Model Groups

You can also define an element within an all model group, which defines an unordered list of elements, all of which can appear in any order, but each element may be present at most once. In the example schema document, you can define the paperType complex type with an all model group, as shown here:

```
<xsd:complexType name="paperType" >
  <xsd:all>
    <xsd:element name="title"  type="titleType" />
    <xsd:element name="author"  type="authorType" />
    <!-- we have yet to define titleType and authorType -->
  </xsd:all>
</xsd:complexType>
```

Named Model Groups

You can define all the model groups you've seen so far—sequence, choice, and all—within a named model group. The named model group in turn can be referenced in complex types and in other named model groups. This promotes the reusability of model groups. For example, you could define paperGroup as a named model group and refer to it in the paperType complex type using the ref attribute, as shown in the following example:

```
<?xml version='1.0' encoding='UTF-8' ?>
<xsd:schema xmlns:xsd="http://www.w3.org/2001/XMLSchema">
  <xsd:complexType name="paperType">
    <xsd:group ref="paperGroup" />
  </xsd:complexType>
  <xsd:group name="paperGroup">
    <xsd:all>
      <xsd:element ref="title" />
      <xsd:element ref="author" />
      </xsd:all>
  </xsd:group>
</xsd:schema>
```

Cardinality

You specify the cardinality of a construct with the minOccurs and maxOccurs attributes. You can specify cardinality on an element declaration or on the sequence, choice, and all model groups, as long as these groups are specified outside a named model group. You can specify named model group cardinality when the group is referenced in a complex type. The default value for both the minOccurs and maxOccurs attributes is 1, which implies that the default cardinality of any construct is 1, if no cardinality is specified.

If you want to specify that a catalogType complex type should allow zero or more occurrences of journal elements, you can do so as shown here:

```
<xsd:complexType name="catalogType" >
 <xsd:sequence>
    <xsd:element maxOccurs="unbounded"  minOccurs="0"  ref="journal" />
  </xsd:sequence>
</xsd:complexType>
```

Attribute Declarations

You can specify an attribute declaration in a schema with the attribute construct. You can specify an attribute declaration within a schema or a complexType. For example, if you want to define the title and publisher attributes in the catalogType complex type, you can do so as shown here:

```
<xsd:complexType  name="catalogType">
  <xsd:sequence>
    <xsd:element ref="journal" minOccurs="0" maxOccurs="unbounded" />
  </xsd:sequence>
  <xsd:attribute name="title" type="xsd:string" use="required" />
  <xsd:attribute name="publisher" type="xsd:string"
    use="optional" default="Unknown" />
</xsd:complexType>
```

An attribute declaration may specify a use attribute, with a value of optional or required. The default use value for an attribute is optional. In addition, an attribute can specify a default value using the default attribute, as shown in the previous example. When an XML document instance does not specify an optional attribute with a default value, an attribute with the default value is assumed during document validation with respect to its schema. Clearly, an attribute with a default value cannot be a required attribute.

Attribute Groups

An attributeGroup construct specifies a group of attributes. For example, if you want to define the attributes for a catalogType as an attribute group, you can define a catalogAttrGroup attribute group, as shown here:

```
<xsd:attributeGroup name="catalogAttrGroup" >
  <xsd:attribute name="title"  type="xsd:string"  use="required"  />
  <xsd:attribute default="Unknown"  name="publisher"
    type="xsd:string"  use="optional" />
</xsd:attributeGroup>
```

You can specify an attributeGroup in a schema, complexType, and attributeGroup. You can specify the catalogAttrGroup shown previously within the schema element and can reference it using the ref attribute in the catalogType complex type, as shown here:

```
<xsd:complexType  name="catalogType" >
  <xsd:sequence>
    <xsd:element maxOccurs="unbounded"  minOccurs="0"  ref="journal" />
  </xsd:sequence>
  <xsd:attributeGroup ref="catalogAttrGroup" />
</xsd:complexType>
```

Simple Content

A simpleContent construct specifies a constraint on character data and attributes. You specify a simpleContent construct in a complexType construct. Two types of simple content constructs exist: an extension and a restriction.

You specify simpleContent extension with an extension construct. If you want to define an authorType as an element that allows a string type in its content and also allows an email attribute, you can do so using a simpleContent extension that adds an email attribute to a string built-in type, as shown here:

```
<xsd:complexType name="authorType" >
  <xsd:simpleContent>
   <xsd:extension base="xsd:string" >
    <xsd:attribute name="email"  type="xsd:string"  use="optional" />
   </xsd:extension>
  </xsd:simpleContent>
</xsd:complexType>
```

You specify a simpleContent restriction with a restriction element. If you want to define a titleType as an element that allows a string type in its content but restricts the length of this content to between 10 to 256 characters, you can do so using a simpleContent restriction that adds the minLength and maxLength constraining facets to a string base type, as shown here:

```
<xsd:complexType name="titleType" >
 <xsd:simpleContent>
  <xsd:restriction base="xsd:string" >
   <xsd:minLength value="10" />
   <xsd:maxLength value="256" />
  </xsd:restriction>
 </xsd:simpleContent>
</xsd:complexType>
```

Constraining Facets

Constraining facets are a powerful mechanism for restricting the content of a built-in simple type. We already looked at the use of two constraining facets in the context of a simple content construct. Table 1-2 has a complete list of the constraining facets. These facets must be applied to relevant built-in types, and most of the time the applicability of a facet to a built-in type is fairly intuitive. For complete details on the applicability of facets to built-in types, please consult XML Schema Part 2: Datatypes.

Table 1-2. *Constraining Facets*

Facet	Description	Example Value
length	Number of units of length	8
minLength	Minimum number of units of length, say m1	20
maxLength	Maximum number of units of length	200 (Greater or equal to m1)
pattern	A regular expression	[0-9]{5} (for first part of a U.S. ZIP code)
enumeration	An enumerated value	Male
whitespace	Whitespace processing	preserve (as is), replace (new line and tab with space), or collapse (contiguous sequences of space into a single space)
maxInclusive	Inclusive upper bound	255 (for a value less than or equal to 255)
maxExclusive	Exclusive upper bound	256 (for a value less than 256)
minExclusive	Exclusive lower bound	0 (for a value greater than 0)
minInclusive	Inclusive lower bound	1 (for a value greater than or equal to 1)
totalDigits	Total number of digits in a decimal value	8
fractionDigits	Total number of fractions digits in a decimal value	2

Complex Content

A complexContent element specifies a constraint on elements (including attributes). You specify a complexContent construct in a complexType element. Just like in the case of simple content, complex content has two types of constructs: an extension and a restriction.

You specify a complexContent extension with an extension element. If, for example, you want to add a webAddress attribute to a catalogType complex type using a complex content extension, you can do so as shown here:

```
<xsd:complexType name="catalogTypeExt" >
    <xsd:complexContent>
      <xsd:extension base="catalogType" >
        <xsd:attribute name="webAddress"  type="xsd:string" />
      </xsd:extension>
    </xsd:complexContent>
  </xsd:complexType>
```

You specify a complexContent restriction with a restriction element. In a complex content restriction, you basically have to repeat, in the restriction element, the part of the base model you want to retain in the restricted complex type. If, for example, you want to restrict the paperType complex type to only a title element using a complex content restriction, you can do so as shown here:

```
<xsd:complexType name="paperTypeRes" >
    <xsd:restriction base="paperType" >
      <xsd:all>
        <xsd:element name="title"  type="titleType" />
      </xsd:all>
    </xsd:restriction>
 </xsd:complexType>
```

A complex content restriction construct has a fairly limited use.

Simple Type Declarations

A simpleType construct specifies information and constraints on attributes and text elements. Since XML Schema has 44 built-in simple types, a simpleType is either used to constrain built-in datatypes or used to define a list or union type. If you wanted, you could have specified authorType as a simple type restriction on a built-in string type, as shown here:

```
<xsd:element name="authorType" >
 <xsd:simpleType>
  <xsd:restriction base="xsd:string" >
   <xsd:minLength value="10" />
   <xsd:maxLength value="256" />
  </xsd:restriction>
 </xsd:simpleType>
</xsd:element>
```

List

A list construct specifies a simpleType construct as a list of values of a specified datatype. For example, the following is a simpleType that defines a list of integer values in a chapterNumbers element:

```
<xsd:element name="chapterNumbers" >
 <xsd:simpleType>
  <xsd:list itemType="xsd:integer" />
 </xsd:simpleType>
</xsd:element>
```

The following example is an element corresponding to the `simpleType` declaration defined previously:

```
<chapterNumbers>8 12 11</chapterNumbers>
```

Union

A union construct specifies a union of `simpleTypes`. For example, if you first define `chapterNames` as a list of string values, as shown here:

```
<xsd:element name="chapterNames">
 <xsd:simpleType>
  <xsd:list itemType="xsd:string"/>
 </xsd:simpleType>
</xsd:element>
```

then you can specify a union of `chapterNumbers` and `chapterNames` as shown here:

```
<xsd:element name="chapters" >
 <xsd:simpleType>
  <xsd:union memberTypes="chapterNumbers, chapterNames" />
 </xsd:simpleType>
</xsd:element>
```

This is an example element corresponding to the `chapters` declaration defined previously:

```
<chapters>8 XSLT 11</chapters>
```

Of course, since list values may not contain any whitespace, this example is completely contrived because chapter names in real life almost always contain whitespace.

Schema Example Document

Based on the preceding discussion, Listing 1-3 shows the complete example schema document for the example XML document in Listing 1-2.

Listing 1-3. *Complete Example Schema Document*

```
<?xml version='1.0' encoding='UTF-8' ?>
<xsd:schema xmlns:xsd="http://www.w3.org/2001/XMLSchema">
  <xsd:element name="catalog" type="catalogType" />
    <xsd:complexType  name="catalogType">
      <xsd:sequence>
        <xsd:element maxOccurs="unbounded" minOccurs="0" ref="journal" />
      </xsd:sequence>
      <xsd:attribute name="title" type="xsd:string" use="required"/>
      <xsd:attribute default="Unknown" name="publisher" type="xsd:string" />
    </xsd:complexType>
```

```
<xsd:element name="journal">
  <xsd:complexType>
    <xsd:choice>
      <xsd:element name="article" type="paperType"/>
      <xsd:element name="research" type="paperType"/>
    </xsd:choice>
  </xsd:complexType>
</xsd:element>
<xsd:complexType name="paperType">
  <xsd:all>
    <xsd:element name="title" type="titleType"/>
    <xsd:element name="author" type="authorType"/>
  </xsd:all>
</xsd:complexType>
<xsd:complexType name="authorType">
  <xsd:simpleContent>
    <xsd:extension base="xsd:string">
      <xsd:attribute name="email" type="xsd:string" />
    </xsd:extension>
  </xsd:simpleContent>
</xsd:complexType>
<xsd:complexType name="titleType">
  <xsd:simpleContent>
    <xsd:restriction base="xsd:string">
      <xsd:minLength value="10"/>
      <xsd:maxLength value="256"/>
    </xsd:restriction>
  </xsd:simpleContent>
</xsd:complexType>
</xsd:schema>
```

Introducing the Eclipse IDE

We developed the Java applications in this book using the Eclipse 3.1.1 integrated development environment (IDE), which is by far the most commonly used IDE among Java developers. You can download it from http://www.eclipse.org/. The following sections are a quick introduction to Eclipse; we cover all you need to know to build and execute the Java applications included in this book. In particular, we offer a quick tutorial on how to create a Java project and how to create a Java application within a Java project.

Creating a Java Project

To create a Java project in Eclipse, select File ➤ New ➤ Project. In the New Project dialog box, select Java Project, and then click Next, as shown in Figure 1-1.

Figure 1-1. *Selecting the New Project Wizard*

On the Create a Java Project screen, specify a project name, such as Chapter1. In the Project Layout section, select Create Separate Source and Output Folders, and click Next, as shown in Figure 1-2.

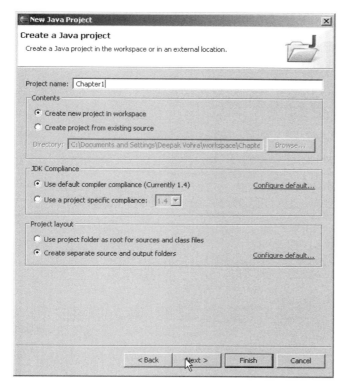

Figure 1-2. *Creating a Java project*

On the Java Settings screen, add the required project libraries under the Libraries tab, and click Finish, as shown in Figure 1-3.

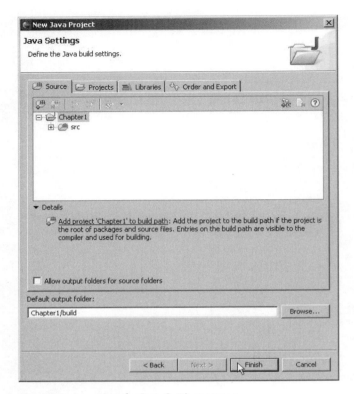

Figure 1-3. *Accessing the Java Settings screen*

This adds a Java project to the Package Explorer in Eclipse, as shown in Figure 1-4.

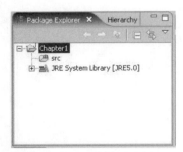

Figure 1-4. *Viewing the Java project in the Package Explorer*

Setting the Build Path

The build path of a Java project includes the JAR files and package folders required to compile various Java class files in a project. To add JAR files and package folders to a project's build path, select the project node on the Package Explorer tab, and select Project ➤ Properties. In the Properties dialog box, select the Java Build Path node, add the external JAR (external to project) files by clicking the Add External JARs button, and add the internal JAR files by clicking the Add JARs button. You can add package folders and libraries with the Add Class Folders and Add Library buttons, respectively. The JARs and package folders in the project build path appear in the Java Build Path window. As an example, it is assumed that xerces.jar is an external JAR file available at the C:\JDOM\jdom-1.0\lib path, and it is added to the Java Build Path window with the Add External JARs button, as shown in Figure 1-5.

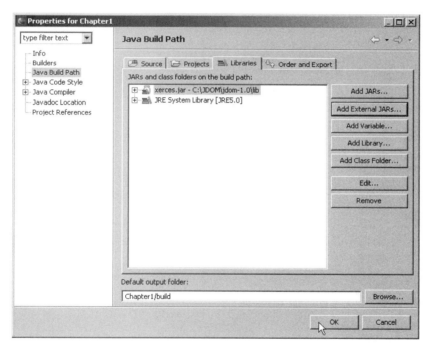

Figure 1-5. *Setting the Java build path*

Creating a Java Package

To create a Java package within a Java project, select the project node in the Package Explorer, and select File ➤ New ➤ Package. In the New Java Package dialog box, specify a package name, such as com.apress.chapter1, and click the Finish button, as shown in Figure 1-6.

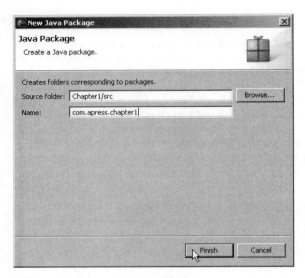

Figure 1-6. *Creating a Java package*

This adds a Java package to the Java project, as shown in Figure 1-7.

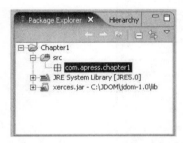

Figure 1-7. *Viewing the Java package in Package Explorer*

Creating a Java Class

To create a Java class, right-click a package node in the Package Explorer, and select New ➤ Class, as shown in Figure 1-8.

On the New Java Class screen, specify the class name, class modifiers, and interfaces implemented, and then click the Finish button, as shown in Figure 1-9.

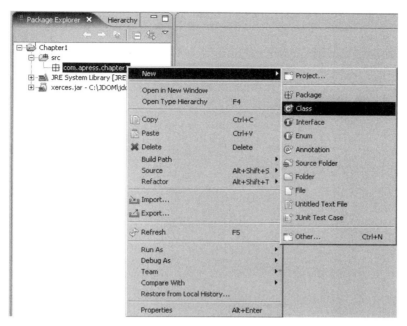

Figure 1-8. *Creating new Java class*

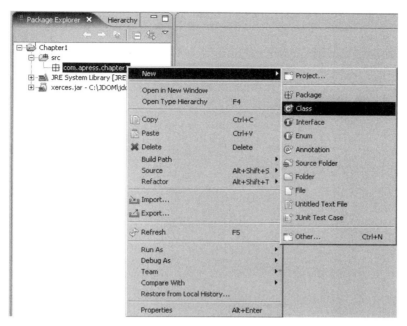

Figure 1-9. *Specifying Java class settings*

This adds a Java class to the Java project, as shown in Figure 1-10.

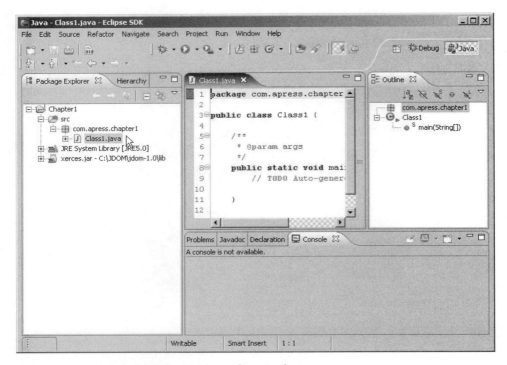

Figure 1-10. *Viewing the Java class in the Package Explorer*

Running a Java Application

To run a Java application, right-click the Java class in the Package Explorer, and select Run As ➤ Run, as shown in Figure 1-11.

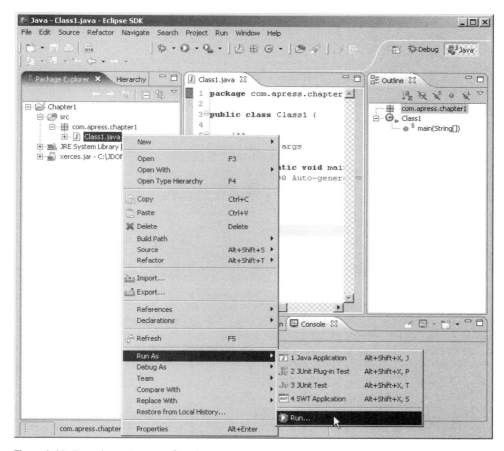

Figure 1-11. *Running a Java application*

In the Run dialog box, select a Java Application configuration, or create a new Java Application configuration by selecting Java Application ➤ New, as shown in Figure 1-12.

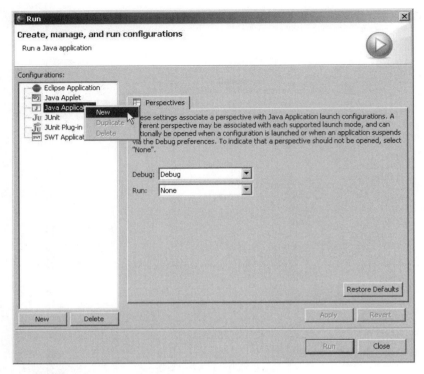

Figure 1-12. *Creating a Java Application configuration*

This creates a Java Application configuration. If any application arguments are to be set, specify the arguments on the Arguments tab. To specify the project JRE, select the JRE tab. The JAR files and packages folders in the build path are also automatically included in the Java classpath. You can add classpath JAR files and package folders on the Classpath tab. To run a Java application, click Run, as shown in Figure 1-13.

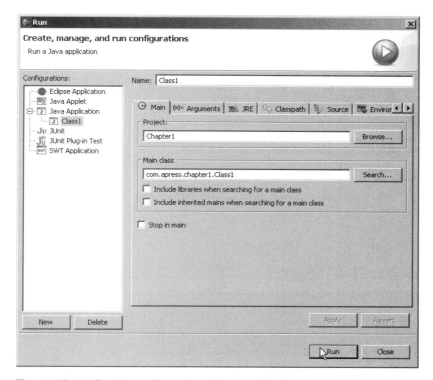

Figure 1-13. *Configuring and running a Java application*

Importing a Java Project

The Java projects for the applications in this book are available from the Apress website (http://www.apress.com). The easiest way to run these applications is to download and import these Java projects into Eclipse. Before we cover how to import the Chapter1 project, you must delete the Chapter1 project you just created, including its contents, by selecting it and hitting Delete key. Be sure to choose the option to delete the contents when prompted.

To import a Java project, select File ➤ Import. In the Import dialog box, select Existing Projects into Workspace, and click Next, as shown in Figure 1-14.

In the Import Projects dialog box, select a project directory with Browse button. Select a directory in the Browse for Folder dialog box, and click OK, as shown in Figure 1-15. Click Finish to import the project directory.

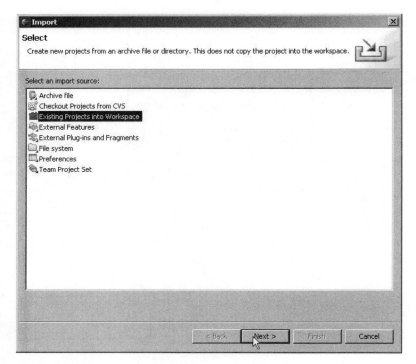

Figure 1-14. *Importing a project*

Figure 1-15. *Selecting a directory*

This imports a Java project into the Eclipse IDE, as shown in Figure 1-16.

Figure 1-16. *Viewing the project in the Package Explorer*

Summary

In this chapter, we noted the different APIs that we will cover in detail in subsequent chapters and offered quick primers on XML and XML Schema. We also introduced the Eclipse IDE, which was used to build and execute all the example applications included in this book. In the next chapter, we will discuss XML parsing in detail using the DOM, SAX, and StAX APIs.

CHAPTER 2

■■■

Parsing XML Documents

An XML document contains structured textual information. We covered the syntactic rules that define the structure of a well-formed XML document in the primer on XML 1.0 in Chapter 1. This chapter is about parsing the structure of a document to extract the content information contained in the document.

We'll start by discussing various objectives for parsing an XML document and by covering various parsing approaches compatible with these objectives. We'll discuss the advantages and disadvantages of each approach and the appropriateness of them for particular applications. We'll then discuss specific parsing APIs that implement these approaches and are defined within JAXP 1.3, which is included in J2SE 5.0, and Streaming API for XML (StAX), which is included in J2SE 6.0. We'll explain each API through code examples. Finally, we'll offer instructions on how to build and execute these code examples within the Eclipse IDE.

Objectives of Parsing XML

Parsing is the most fundamental aspect of processing an XML document. When an application parses an XML document, typically it has three distinct objectives:

- To ensure that the document is well-formed
- To check that the document conforms to the structure specified by a DTD or an XML Schema
- To access, and maybe modify, various elements and attributes specified in the document, in a manner that meets the specific needs of an application

All applications share the first objective. The second objective is not as pervasive as the first but is still fairly standard. The third objective, not surprisingly, varies from application to application. Prompted by the diverse access requirements of various applications, different parsing approaches have evolved to satisfy these requirements. To date, you can take one of three distinct approaches to parsing XML documents:

- DOM[1] parsing
- Push parsing
- Pull parsing

In the next section, we will give an overview of these three approaches and then offer a comparative analysis of them.

---

1. You can find the Document Object Model (DOM) Level 3 Core specification at http://www.w3.org/TR/ DOM-Level-3-Core/.

Overview of Parsing Approaches

In the following sections, we will give you an overview of the three major parsing approaches from a conceptual standpoint. In later sections, we will discuss specific Java APIs that implement these approaches. We will start with the DOM approach.

DOM Approach

The Document Object Model (DOM) Level 3 Core specification specifies platform- and language-neutral interfaces for accessing and manipulating content and specifies the structure of a generalized document. The DOM represents a document as a tree of Node objects. Some of these Node objects have child node objects; others are leaf objects with no children.

To represent the structure of an XML document, the generic Node type is specialized to other Node types, and each specialized node type specifies a set of allowable child Node types. Table 2-1 explains the specialized DOM Node types for representing an XML document, along with their allowable child Node types.

Table 2-1. *Specialized DOM Node Types for an XML Document*

Specialized Node Type	Description	Allowable Child Node Types
Document	Represents an XML document	DocumentType, ProcessingInstruction, Comment, Element(maximum of 1)
DocumentFragment	Represents part of an XML document	Element, ProcessingInstruction, Comment, Text, CDATASection, EntityReference
DocumentType	Represents a DTD for a document	No children
EntityReference	Represents an entity reference	Element, ProcessingInstruction, Comment, Text, CDATASection, EntityReference
Element	Represents an element	Element, ProcessingInstruction, Comment, Text, CDATASection, EntityReference
Attr	Represents an attribute	Text, EntityReference
ProcessingInstruction	Represents a processing instruction	No children
Comment	Represents a comment	No children
Text	Represents text, including whitespace	No children
CDATASection	Represents a CDATA section	No children
Entity	Represents an entity	Element, ProcessingInstruction, Comment, Text, CDATASection, EntityReference
Notation	Represents a notation	No children

The Document specialized node type is somewhat unique in that at most only one instance of this type may exist within an XML document. It is also worth noting that the Document node type is a specialized Element node type and is used to represent the root element of an XML document. Text node types, in addition to representing text, are also used to represent whitespace in an XML document.

Under the DOM approach, an XML document is parsed into a random-access tree structure in which all the elements and attributes from the document are represented as distinct nodes, with each node instantiated as an instance of a specialized node type. So, for example, under the DOM approach, the example XML document shown in Listing 2-1 would be parsed into the tree structure (annotated with specialized node types) shown in Figure 2-1.

Listing 2-1. *Example XML Document*

```
<?xml version="1.0" encoding="UTF-8"?>
<catalog title="OnJava.com" publisher="O'Reilly">
<journal date="January 2004">
   <article>
    <title>Data Binding with XMLBeans</title>
    <author>Daniel Steinberg</author>
   </article>
 </journal>
</catalog>
```

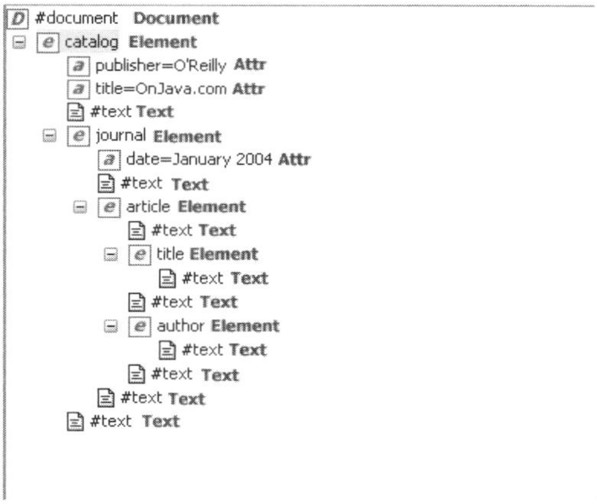

Figure 2-1. *Annotated DOM tree for example XML document*

The DOM approach has the following notable aspects:

- An in-memory DOM tree representation of the complete document is constructed before the document structure and content can be accessed or manipulated.

- Document nodes can be accessed randomly and do not have to be accessed strictly in document order.

- Random access to any tree node is fast and flexible, but parsing the complete document before accessing any node can reduce parsing efficiency.

- For large documents ranging from hundreds of megabytes to gigabytes in size, the in-memory DOM tree structure can exhaust all available memory, making it impossible to parse such large documents under the DOM approach.

- If an XML document needs to be navigated randomly or if the document content and structure needs to be manipulated, the DOM parsing approach is the most practical approach. This is because no other approach offers an in-memory representation of a document, and although such representation can certainly be created by the parsing application, doing so would be essentially replicating the DOM approach.

- An API for using the DOM parsing approach is available in JAXP 1.3.

Push Approach

Under the push parsing approach, a push parser generates synchronous events as a document is parsed, and these events can be processed by an application using a callback handler model. An API for the push approach is available as SAX[2] 2.0, which is also included in JAXP 1.3. SAX is a read-only API. The SAX API is recommended if no modification or random-access navigation of an XML document is required.

The SAX 2.0 API defines a `ContentHandler` interface, which may be implemented by an application to define a callback handler for processing synchronous parsing events generated by a SAX parser. The `ContentHandler` event methods have fairly intuitive semantics, as listed in Table 2-2.

Table 2-2. *SAX 2.0 `ContentHandler` Event Methods*

Method	Notification
startDocument	Start of a document
startElement	Start of an element
characters	Character data
endElement	End of an element
endDocument	End of a document
startPrefixMapping	Start of namespace prefix mapping
endPrefixMapping	End of namespace prefix mapping
skippedEntity	Skipped entity
ignorableWhitespace	Ignorable whitespace
processingInstruction	Processing instruction

---

2. You can find information about Simple API for XML at http://www.saxproject.org/.

In addition to the ContentHandler interface, SAX 2.0 defines an ErrorHandler interface, which may be implemented by an application to receive notifications about errors. Table 2-3 lists the ErrorHandler notification methods.

Table 2-3. *SAX 2.0 ErrorHandler Notification Methods*

Method	Notification
fatalError	Violation of XML 1.0 well-formed constraint
error	Violation of validity constraint
warning	Non-XML-related warning

An application should make no assumption about whether the endDocument method of the ContentHandler interface will be called after the fatalError method in the ErrorHandler interface has been called.

Pull Approach

Under the pull approach, events are pulled from an XML document under the control of the application using the parser. StAX is similar to the SAX API in that both offer event-based APIs. However, StAX differs from the SAX API in the following respects:

- Unlike in the SAX API, in the StAX API, it is the application rather than the parser that controls the delivery of the parsing events. StAX offers two event-based APIs: a cursor-based API and an iterator-based API, both of which are under the application's control.

- The cursor API allows a walk-through of the document in document order and provides the lowest level of access to all the structural and content information within the document.

- The iterator API is similar to the cursor API but instead of providing low-level access, it provides access to the structural and content information in the form of event objects.

- Unlike the SAX API, the StAX API can be used both for reading and for writing XML documents.

Cursor API

Key points about the StAX cursor API are as follows:

- The XMLStreamReader interface is the main interface for parsing an XML document. You can use this interface to scan an XML document's structure and contents using the next() and hasNext() methods.

- The next() method returns an integer token for the next parse event.

- Depending on the next event type, you can call specific allowed methods on the XMLStreamReader interface. Table 2-4 lists various event types and the corresponding allowed methods.

Table 2-4. *StAX Cursor API Event Types and Allowed Methods*

Event Type	Allowed Methods
Any event type	getProperty(), hasNext(), require(), close(), getNamespaceURI(), isStartElement(), isEndElement(), isCharacters(), isWhiteSpace(), getNamespaceContext(), getEventType(), getLocation(), hasText(), hasName()
START_ELEMENT	next(), getName(), getLocalName(), hasName(), getPrefix(), getAttributeXXX(), isAttributeSpecified(), getNamespaceXXX(), getElementText(), nextTag()
ATTRIBUTE	next(), nextTag(), getAttributeXXX(), isAttributeSpecified()
NAMESPACE	next(), nextTag(), getNamespaceXXX()
END_ELEMENT	next(), getName(), getLocalName(), hasName(), getPrefix(), getNamespaceXXX(), nextTag()
CHARACTERS	next(), getTextXXX(), nextTag()
CDATA	next(), getTextXXX(), nextTag()
COMMENT	next(), getTextXXX(), nextTag()
SPACE	next(), getTextXXX(), nextTag()
START_DOCUMENT	next(), getEncoding(), getVersion(), isStandalone(), standaloneSet(), getCharacterEncodingScheme(), nextTag()
END_DOCUMENT	close()
PROCESSING_INSTRUCTION	next(), getPITarget(), getPIData(), nextTag()
ENTITY_REFERENCE	next(), getLocalName(), getText(), nextTag()
DTD	next(), getText(), nextTag()

Iterator API

Key points about the StAX iterator API are as follows:

- The XMLEventReader interface is the main interface for parsing an XML document. You can use this interface to iterate over an XML document's structure and contents using the nextEvent() and hasNext() methods.
- The nextEvent() method returns an XMLEvent object.
- The XMLEvent interface provides utility methods for determining the next event type and for processing it appropriately.

The StAX API is recommended for data-binding applications, specifically for the marshaling and unmarshaling of an XML document during the bidirectional XML-to-Java mapping process. A StAX API implementation is included in J2SE 6.0.

Comparing the Parsing Approaches

Each of the three approaches discussed offers advantages and disadvantages and is appropriate for particular types of applications. Table 2-5 compares the three parsing approaches.

Table 2-5. *DOM, SAX, and StAX Comparison*

Parsing Approach	Advantages	Disadvantages	Suitable Application
DOM	Ease of use, navigation, random access, and XPath support	Must parse entire document, memory intensive	Applications that modify structure and content of an XML document, such as visual XML editors*
SAX	Low memory consumption, efficient	No navigation, no random access, no modification	Read-only XML applications, such as document validation
StAX	Ease of use, low memory consumption, application regulates parsing, filtering	No random access, no modification	Data binding, SOAP message processing

* We've written such an editor, which is available at http://www.nubean.com.

Before you see some code examples of the three parsing APIs, we'll show how to create and configure an appropriate Eclipse project.

Setting Up an Eclipse Project

In the following sections, we will show how to set up an Eclipse project and populate it with the contents needed to build and execute code examples related to the three parsing approaches discussed in this chapter. Even though in later sections we will discuss each parsing approach separately, here we will show how to prepare the Eclipse project for all three parsing approaches at once.

Example XML Document

To take any of the parsing approaches, the first element you need is an XML document. To that end, you can use the example XML document shown in Listing 2-2.

Listing 2-2. *catalog.xml*

```
<?xml version="1.0" encoding="UTF-8"?>
<catalog title="OnJava.com" publisher="O'Reilly">
<journal date="January 2004">
   <article>
    <title>Data Binding with XMLBeans</title>
    <author>Daniel Steinberg</author>
   </article>
 </journal>
```

```
<journal date="Sept 2005">
  <article>
   <title>What Is Hibernate</title>
   <author>James Elliott</author>
  </article>
</journal>
</catalog>
```

J2SE, Packages, and Classes

To build and execute these examples, you need to make sure you have the J2SE 5.0 software development kit (SDK)[3] and the J2SE 6.0 SDK (code-named Mustang[4]) installed on your machine.

Next, download the Chapter2 project from the Apress website (http://www.apress.com) and import it, as explained in detail in Chapter 1. Importing the project is the quickest way to run the example applications, because all the packages and files in the project get created automatically and the Java build path gets set automatically. Please verify that the Java build path is as shown in Figure 2-2 and the overall project structure is as shown in Figure 2-3.

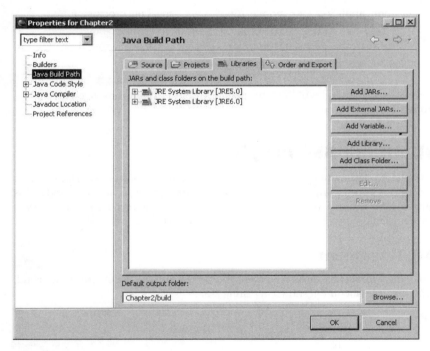

Figure 2-2. *Chapter2 project Java runtime environments (JREs)*

---

3. You can download the J2SE 5.0 SDK from http://java.sun.com/j2se/1.5.0/download.jsp.
4. You can download the snapshot release of Mustang from https://mustang.dev.java.net/.

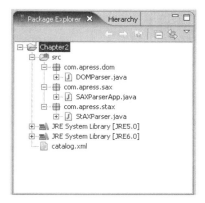

Figure 2-3. *Chapter2 project directory structure*

Parsing with the DOM Level 3 API

The DOM Level 3 API, which is part of the JAXP 1.3 API, represents an XML document as a tree of DOM nodes. Each node in this tree is a specialized Node object that is an instance of one of the specialized Node types listed in Table 2-1. The following packages and classes are essential parts of any application that uses the DOM Level 3 API:

- The classes and interfaces representing the DOM structure of an XML document are in the org.w3c.dom package, which must be imported by an application using the DOM API.

- The NodeList interface represents an ordered list of nodes. A NamedNodeMap represents an unordered set of nodes, such as attributes of an element. Both these classes are useful in traversing the DOM tree representing an XML document.

- The XML document–parsing API is in the javax.xml.parsers package. This is an essential package and must be imported by an application parsing an XML document using the DOM API.

- An application needs to import the org.xml.sax package so it can access the SAXException and SAXParseException classes, which are used in error handling. This reference to the SAX API within the DOM API may seem out of place. However, this reliance of the DOM API on the SAX API is specified by JAXP 1.3 and is basically an attempt to reuse the SAX API where appropriate.

DOM API Parsing Steps

To parse an XML document using the DOM API, you need to follow these steps:

1. Create a DOM parser factory.

2. Use the parser factory to instantiate a DOM parser.

3. Use the DOM parser to parse an XML document and create a DOM tree.

4. Access and manipulate the XML structure and content by accessing the DOM tree.

The DocumentBuilder class implements the DOM parser. The steps to instantiate a DocumentBuilder object are as follows:

1. Create a DocumentBuilderFactory object using the static method newInstance(). The DocumentBuilderFactory class is a factory API for generating DocumentBuilder objects.

2. Create a DocumentBuilder object by invoking the newDocumentBuilder() static method on the DocumentBuilderFactory object.

The DocumentBuilder parser creates an in-memory DOM structure from an XML document. If you want to handle validation errors during parsing, you need to define a class that implements the ErrorHandler interface shown in Table 2-3 and set an instance of this error handler class on the parser. Listing 2-3 shows an example class that implements the ErrorHandler interface.

Listing 2-3. *Implementing ErrorHandler*

```
class ErrorHandlerImpl implements org.xml.sax.ErrorHandler {
  public void error(SAXParseException exception)
                throws SAXException{
    // application-specific logic
  }

  public void fatalError(SAXParseException exception)
                throws SAXException{
    // application-specific logic
  }

  public void warning(SAXParseException exception)
                throws SAXException{
      // application-specific logic
    }
}
```

Listing 2-4 shows the complete code sequence for creating a DOM parser object that will validate a document and use an instance of the ErrorHandlerImpl class for error handling.

Listing 2-4. *Complete Code Sequence to Instantiate the Factory*

```
//Create a DocumentBuilderFactory
DocumentBuilderFactory factory=DocumentBuilderFactory.newInstance();
//Create a DocumentBuilder
DocumentBuilder documentBuilder=factory.newDocumentBuilder();
//Create and set an ErrorHandler
ErrorHandlerImpl errorHandler=new ErrorHandlerImpl();
documentBuilder.setErrorHandler(errorHandler);
```

A parser can parse an XML document from a File, an InputSource, an InputStream, or a URI. An example of how to parse an XML document from a File object is as follows:

```
Document document=documentBuilder.parse(new File("catalog.xml"));
```

The Document interface provides various methods to navigate the DOM structure. Table 2-6 lists some of the Document interface methods.

Table 2-6. *Document Interface Methods*

Method Name	Description
getDoctype()	Returns the DOCTYPE in the XML document
getDocumentElement()	Returns the root element
getElementById(String)	Gets an element for a specified ID
getElementsByTagName(String)	Gets a NodeList of elements

The org.w3c.dom.Element interface represents an element in the DOM structure. You can obtain element attributes and subelements from an Element object. Table 2-7 lists some of the methods in the Element interface.

Table 2-7. *Element Interface Methods*

Method Name	Description
getAttributes()	Returns a NamedNodeMap of attributes
getAttribute(String)	Gets an attribute value by attribute name
getAttributeNode(String)	Returns an Attr node for an attribute
getElementsByTagName(String)	Returns a NodeList of elements by element name
getTagName()	Gets the element tag name

The Attr interface represents an attribute node. You can obtain the attribute name and value from the Attr node. Table 2-8 lists some of the methods in the Attr node.

Table 2-8. *Attr Interface Methods*

Method Name	Description
getName()	Returns the attribute name
getValue()	Returns the attribute value

All the specialized Node interfaces, such as Document, Element and Attr, inherit methods defined by the Node interface. Table 2-9 lists some of the methods in the Node interface.

Table 2-9. *Node Interface Methods*

Method Name	Description
getAttributes()	Returns a NamedNodeMap of attributes for an element node
getChildNodes()	Returns the child nodes in a node
getLocalName()	Returns the local name from an element node and an attribute node
getNodeName()	Returns the node name
getNodeValue()	Returns the node value
getNodeType()	Returns the node type

In the example DOM application, retrieve the root element with the getDocumentElement() method, and obtain the root element name with the getTagName() method, as shown in Listing 2-5.

Listing 2-5. *Retrieving the Root Element Name*

```
Element rootElement = document.getDocumentElement();
String rootElementName = rootElement.getTagName();
```

If the root element has attributes, retrieve the attributes in the root element. The hasAttributes() method tests whether an element has attributes, and the getAttributes() method retrieves the attributes, as shown in Listing 2-6.

Listing 2-6. *Retrieving Root Element Attributes*

```
if (rootElement.hasAttributes()) {
  NamedNodeMap attributes = rootElement.getAttributes();
}
```

The getAttributes() method returns a NamedNodeMap of attributes. The NamedNodeMap method getNodeLength() returns the attribute list length, and the attributes in the attribute list are retrieved with the item(int) method. A NamedNodeMap may be iterated over to retrieve the value of attributes, as shown in Listing 2-7. The Attr object method getName() returns the attribute name, and the method getValue() returns the attribute value.

Listing 2-7. *Retrieving Attribute Values*

```
for (int i = 0; i < attributes.getLength(); i++) {
  Attr attribute = (Attr) (attributes.item(i));
  System.out.println("Attribute:" + attribute.getName()+
    " with value " + attribute.getValue());
}
```

If the root element has subnodes, you can retrieve the nodes with the getChildNodes() method. The hasChildNodes() method tests whether an element has subnodes, as shown in Listing 2-8.

Listing 2-8. *Retrieving Nodes in the Root Element*

```
if (rootElement.hasChildNodes()) {
  NodeList nodeList = rootElement.getChildNodes();
}
```

The node list includes whitespace text nodes. The NodeList method getNodeLength() returns the node list length, and you can retrieve the nodes in the node list with the item(int) method, as shown in Listing 2-9.

Listing 2-9. *Retrieving Nodes in a NodeList*

```
for (int i = 0; i < nodeList.getLength(); i++) {
  Node node = nodeList.item(i);
}
```

If a node is of type Element, a Node object may be cast to Element. The node type is obtained with the Node interface method getNodeType(). The getNodeType() method returns a short value. Table 2-10 lists the different short values and the corresponding node types.

Table 2-10. *Node Types*

Short Value	Node Type
ELEMENT_NODE	Element node
ATTRIBUTE_NODE	Attr node
TEXT_NODE	Text node
CDATA_SECTION_NODE	CDATASection node
ENTITY_REFERENCE_NODE	EntityReference node
ENTITY_NODE	Entity node
PROCESSING_INSTRUCTION_NODE	ProcessingInstruction node
COMMENT_NODE	Comment node
DOCUMENT_NODE	Document node
DOCUMENT_TYPE_NODE	DocumentType node
DOCUMENT_FRAGMENT_NODE	DocumentFragment node
NOTATION_NODE	Notation node

If a node is of type Element, cast the Node object to Element, as shown in Listing 2-10.

Listing 2-10. *Casting Node to Element*

```
if (node.getNodeType() == Node.ELEMENT_NODE) {
  Element element = (Element) (node);
}
```

If an element has a text node, you can obtain the text value with the getNodeValue() method, as shown here:

```
String textValue=node.getNodeValue();
```

DOM API Example

The Java application DOMParser.java shown in Listing 2-11 parses the XML document shown in Listing 2-2. We are assuming you have imported the XML document shown in Listing 2-2 to the Chapter2 project, as shown in Figure 2-2.

This example demonstrates how to use a DocumentBuilder object to parse the example XML document. Once you successfully parse the document, you get a Document object, which represents an in-memory tree structure for the example document. You retrieve the node representing the root element from the Document object, and you use the visitNode() method to walk down this tree and visit each node, starting at the root element.

When you get to a node while traversing the tree, you first find its node type. If the node type is Element, you traverse the child nodes of the Element node with the visitNode() method. The visitNode() method also outputs the element tag name and attributes in an element. If the node type is Text and the Text node is not an empty node, the text value of the Text node is output.

Listing 2-11. *DOM Parsing Application* DOMParser.java

```java
package com.apress.dom;

import javax.xml.parsers.DocumentBuilder;
import javax.xml.parsers.DocumentBuilderFactory;
import javax.xml.parsers.ParserConfigurationException;
import org.w3c.dom.*;
import org.xml.sax.SAXException;
import java.io.*;

public class DOMParser {

    public static void main(String argv[]) {
        try {
            // Create a DocumentBuilderFactory
            DocumentBuilderFactory factory = DocumentBuilderFactory
                    .newInstance();
            File xmlFile = new File("catalog.xml");
            // Create a DocumentBuilder
            DocumentBuilder builder = factory.newDocumentBuilder();
            // Parse an XML document
            Document document = builder.parse(xmlFile);
            // Retrieve root element
            Element rootElement = document.getDocumentElement();
            System.out.println("Root Element is: " + rootElement.getTagName());
            visitNode(null, rootElement);

        } catch (SAXException e) {
            System.out.println(e.getMessage());
```

```
        } catch (ParserConfigurationException e) {
            System.out.println(e.getMessage());

        } catch (IOException e) {
            System.out.println(e.getMessage());
        }
    }

    public static void visitNode(Element previousNode, Element visitNode) {
        // process an Element node
        if (previousNode != null) {
            System.out.println("Element " + previousNode.getTagName()
                    + " has element:");
        }
        System.out.println("Element Name: " + visitNode.getTagName());
        // list attributes for an element node
        if (visitNode.hasAttributes()) {
            System.out.println("Element " + visitNode.getTagName()
                    + " has attributes: ");
            NamedNodeMap attributes = visitNode.getAttributes();

            for (int j = 0; j < attributes.getLength(); j++) {
                Attr attribute = (Attr) (attributes.item(j));
                System.out.println("Attribute:" + attribute.getName()
                        + " with value " + attribute.getValue());

            }
        }
        // Obtain a NodeList of nodes in an Element node

        NodeList nodeList = visitNode.getChildNodes();
        for (int i = 0; i < nodeList.getLength(); i++) {
            Node node = nodeList.item(i);
            // Retrieve Element nodes
            if (node.getNodeType() == Node.ELEMENT_NODE) {
                Element element = (Element) node;
                // Recursive call to visitNode method to process
                // an Element node hierarchy
                visitNode(visitNode, element);
            } else if (node.getNodeType() == Node.TEXT_NODE) {
                String str = node.getNodeValue().trim();
                if (str.length() > 0) {
                    System.out.println("Element Text: " + str);
                }
            }
        }
    }
}
```

Listing 2-12 shows the output from running the DOM application in Eclipse. This output shows the node type and node value associated with each node visited in the tree walk.

Listing 2-12. *Output from the DOMParser Application*

```
Root Element is: catalog
Element Name: catalog
Element catalog has attributes:
Attribute:publisher with value O'Reilly
Attribute:title with value OnJava.com
Element catalog has element:
Element Name: journal
Element journal has attributes:
Attribute:date with value January 2004
Element journal has element:
Element Name: article
Element article has element:
Element Name: title
Element Text: Data Binding with XMLBeans
Element article has element:
Element Name: author
Element Text: Daniel Steinberg
Element catalog has element:
Element Name: journal
Element journal has attributes:
Attribute:date with value Sept 2005
Element journal has element:
Element Name: article
Element article has element:
Element Name: title
Element Text: What Is Hibernate
Element article has element:
Element Name: author
Element Text: James Elliott
```

Parsing with SAX 2.0

SAX 2.0[5] is an event-based API to parse an XML document. SAX 2.0 is not a W3C Recommendation. However, it is a widely used API that has become a de facto standard. To date, SAX has two major versions: SAX 1.0 and SAX 2.0. There are no fundamental differences between the two versions. The most notable difference is that the SAX 1.0 Parser interface is replaced with the SAX 2.0 XMLReader interface, which improves upon the SAX 1.0 interface by providing full support for namespaces. In this chapter, we will focus only on the SAX 2.0 API.

SAX 2.0 is a push-model API; events are generated as an XML document is parsed. Events are generated by the parser and delivered through the callback methods defined by the application. Key points pertaining to the use of the SAX 2.0 API are as follows:

- You need to import at least two packages: the org.xml.sax package for the SAX interfaces and the javax.xml.parsers package for the SAXParser and SAXParserFactory classes. In addition, you may need to import the org.xml.sax.helpers package, which has useful helper classes for using the SAX API.

---

5. You can find information about SAX at http://www.saxproject.org/.

- ContentHandler is the main interface that an application needs to implement because it provides event notification about the parsing events. The DefaultHandler class provides a default implementation of the ContentHandler interface. To handle SAX parser events, an application can either define a class that implements the ContentHandler interface or define a class that extends the DefaultHandler class.

- You use the SAXParser class to parse an XML document.

- You obtain a SAXParser object from a SAXParserFactory object. To obtain a SAX parser, you need to first create an instance of the SAXParserFactory using the static method newInstance(), as shown in the following example:

```
SAXParserFactory  factory=SAXParserFactory.newInstance();
```

JAXP Pluggability for SAX

JAXP 1.3 provides complete pluggability for the SAXParserFactory implementation classes. This means the SAXParserFactory implementation class is not a fixed class. Instead, the SAXParserFactory implementation class is obtained by JAXP, using the following lookup procedure:

1. Use the javax.xml.parsers.SAXParserFactory system property to determine the factory class to load.

2. Use the javax.xml.parsers.SAXParserFactory property specified in the lib/jaxp.properties file under the JRE directory to determine the factory class to load. JAXP reads this file only once, and the property values defined in this file are cached by JAXP.

3. Files in the META-INF/services directory within a JAR file are deemed service provider configuration files. Use the Services API, and obtain the factory class name from the META-INF/services/javax.xml.parsers.SAXParserFactory file contained in any JAR file in the runtime classpath.

4. Use the default SAXParserFactory class, included in the J2SE platform.

If validation is desired, set the validating attribute on factory to true:

```
factory.setValidating(true);
```

If the validation attribute of the SAXParserFactory object is set to true, the parser obtained from such a factory object, by default, validates an XML document with respect to a DTD. To validate the document with respect to XML Schema, you need to do more, which is covered in detail in Chapter 3.

SAX Features

SAXParserFactory features are logical switches that you can turn on and off to change parser behavior. You can set the features of a factory through the setFeature(String, boolean) method. The first argument passed to setFeature is the name of a feature, and the second argument is a true or false value. Table 2-11 lists some of the commonly used SAXParserFactory features. Some of the SAXParserFactory features are implementation specific, so not all features may be supported by different factory implementations.

Table 2-11. *SAXParserFactory Features*

Feature	Description
`http://xml.org/sax/features/namespaces`	Performs namespace processing if set to `true`
`http://xml.org/sax/features/validation`	Validates an XML document
`http://apache.org/xml/features/validation/schema`	Performs XML Schema validation
`http://xml.org/sax/features/external-general-entities`	Includes external general entities
`http://xml.org/sax/features/external-parameter-entities`	Includes external parameter entities and the external DTD subset
`http://apache.org/xml/features/nonvalidating/load-external-dtd`	Loads the external DTD
`http://xml.org/sax/features/namespace-prefixes`	Reports attributes and prefixes used for namespace declarations
`http://xml.org/sax/features/xml-1.1`	Supports XML 1.1

SAX Properties

SAX parser properties are name-value pairs that you can use to supply object values to a SAX parser. These properties affect parser behavior and can be set on a parser through the `setProperty(String, Object)` method. The first argument passed to `setProperty` is the name of a property, and the second argument is an `Object` value. Table 2-12 lists some of the commonly used SAX parser properties. Some of the properties are implementation specific, so not all properties may be supported by different SAX parser implementations.

Table 2-12. *SAX Parser Properties*

Property	Description
`http://apache.org/xml/properties/schema/external-schemaLocation`	Specifies the external schemas for validation
`http://apache.org/xml/properties/schema/external-noNamespaceSchemaLocation`	Specifies external no-namespace schemas
`http://xml.org/sax/properties/declaration-handler`	Specifies the handler for DTD declarations
`http://xml.org/sax/properties/lexical-handler`	Specifies the handler for lexical parsing events
`http://xml.org/sax/properties/dom-node`	Specifies the DOM node being parsed if SAX is used as a DOM iterator
`http://xml.org/sax/properties/document-xml-version`	Specifies the XML version of the document

SAX Handlers

To parse a document using the SAX 2.0 API, you must define two classes:

- A class that implements the ContentHandler interface (Table 2-2)
- A class that implements the ErrorHandler interface (Table 2-3)

The SAX 2.0 API provides a DefaultHandler helper class that fully implements the ContentHandler and ErrorHandler interfaces and provides default behavior for every parser event type along with default error handling. Applications can extend the DefaultHandler class and override relevant base class methods to implement their custom callback handler. CustomSAXHandler, shown in Listing 2-13, is such a class that overrides some of the base class event notification methods, including the error-handling methods.

Key points about CustomSAXHandler class are as follows:

- In the CustomSAXHandler class, in the startDocument() and endDocument() methods, the event type is output.

- In the startElement() method, the event type, element qualified name, and element attributes are output. The uri parameter of the startElement() method is the namespace uri, which may be null, for an element. The parameter localName is the element name without the element prefix. The parameter qName is the element name with the prefix. If an element is not in a namespace with a prefix, localName is the same as qName.

- The parameter attributes is a list of element attributes. The startElement() method prints the qualified element name and the element attributes. The Attributes interface method getQName() returns the qualified name of an attribute. The attribute method getValue() returns the attribute value.

- The characters() method, which gets invoked for a text event, such as element text, prints the text for a node.

- The three error handler methods—fatalError, error, and warning—print the error messages contained in the SAXParseException object passed to these methods.

Listing 2-13. *CustomSAXHandler Class*

```
import org.xml.sax.*;
import org.xml.sax.helpers.DefaultHandler;
private class CustomSAXHandler extends DefaultHandler {
    public CustomSAXHandler() {
    }

    public void startDocument() throws SAXException {
                            //Output Event Type
        System.out.println("Event Type: Start Document");
    }

    public void endDocument() throws SAXException {
                            //Output Event Type
        System.out.println("Event Type: End Document");
    }

    public void startElement(String uri, String localName, String qName,
        Attributes attributes) throws SAXException {
                            //Output Event Type and Element Name
```

```
            System.out.println("Event Type: Start Element");
            System.out.println("Element Name:" + qName);
                                    //Output Element Attributes
            for (int i = 0; i < attributes.getLength(); i++) {
               System.out.println("Attribute Name:" + attributes.getQName(i));
               System.out.println("Attribute Value:" + attributes.getValue(i));
            }

        }

        public void endElement(String uri, String localName, String qName)
            throws SAXException {
                                    //Output Event Type
            System.out.println("Event Type: End Element");
        }

        public void characters(char[] ch, int start, int length)
            throws SAXException {
                                    //Output Event Type and Text
            System.out.println("Event Type:  Text");
            String str = (new String(ch, start, length));
            System.out.println(str);
        }

//Error Handling
        public void error(SAXParseException e)
         throws SAXException{
           System.out.println("Error: "+e.getMessage());
        }

        public void fatalError(SAXParseException e)
            throws SAXException{
           System.out.println("Fatal Error: "+e.getMessage());
        }

        public void warning(SAXParseException e)
          throws SAXException{
           System.out.println("Warning: "+e.getMessage());
        }
    }
```

SAX Parsing Steps

The SAX parsing steps are as follows:

1. Create a SAXParserFactory object with the static method newInstance().

2. Create a SAXParser object from the SAXParserFactory object with the newSAXParser() method.

3. Create a DefaultHandler object, and parse the example XML document with the SAXParser method parse(File, DefaultHandler).

Listing 2-14 shows a code sequence for creating a SAX parser that uses an instance of the CustomSAXHandler class to process SAX events.

Listing 2-14. *Creating a SAX Parser*

```
SAXParserFactory  factory=SAXParserFactory.newInstance();

// create a parser
SAXParser saxParser=factory.newSAXParser();

// create and set event handler on the parser
DefaultHandler handler=new CustomSAXHandler();
saxParser.parse(new File("catalog.xml"), handler);
```

SAX API Example

The parsing events are notified through the DefaultHandler callback methods. The CustomSAXHandler class extends the DefaultHandler class and overrides some of the event notification methods. The CustomSAXHandler class also overrides the error handler methods to perform application-specific error handling. The CustomSAXHandler class is defined as a private class within the SAX parsing application, SAXParserApp.java, as shown in Listing 2-15.

Listing 2-15. *SAXParserApp.java*

```
package com.apress.sax;

import org.xml.sax.*;
import javax.xml.parsers.*;
import org.xml.sax.helpers.DefaultHandler;
import java.io.*;

public class SAXParserApp {

    public static void main(String argv[]) {

        SAXParserApp saxParserApp = new SAXParserApp();
        saxParserApp.parseDocument();

    }

    public void parseDocument() {

        try {         //Create a SAXParserFactory
           SAXParserFactory factory = SAXParserFactory.newInstance();
                                     //Create a SAXParser
           SAXParser saxParser = factory.newSAXParser();
           //Create a DefaultHandler and parser an XML document
           DefaultHandler handler = new CustomSAXHandler();
           saxParser.parse(new File("catalog.xml"), handler);
        } catch (SAXException e) {
        } catch (ParserConfigurationException e) {
        } catch (IOException e) {
        }
    }
```

```java
            //DefaultHandler class
    private class CustomSAXHandler extends DefaultHandler {
        public CustomSAXHandler() {
        }

        public void startDocument() throws SAXException {
            System.out.println("Event Type: Start Document");
        }

        public void endDocument() throws SAXException {
            System.out.println("Event Type: End Document");
        }

        public void startElement(String uri, String localName, String qName,
                Attributes attributes) throws SAXException {
            System.out.println("Event Type: Start Element");
            System.out.println("Element Name:" + qName);
            for (int i = 0; i < attributes.getLength(); i++) {
                System.out.println("Attribute Name:" + attributes.getQName(i));
                System.out.println("Attribute Value:" + attributes.getValue(i));
            }

        }

        public void endElement(String uri, String localName, String qName)
                throws SAXException {
            System.out.println("Event Type: End Element");
        }

        public void characters(char[] ch, int start, int length)
                throws SAXException {
            System.out.println("Event Type:  Text");
            String str = (new String(ch, start, length));
            System.out.println(str);
        }

        public void error(SAXParseException e)
          throws SAXException{
          System.out.println("Error "+e.getMessage());
        }

          public void fatalError(SAXParseException e)
              throws SAXException{
            System.out.println("Fatal Error "+e.getMessage());
          }

          public void warning(SAXParseException e)
            throws SAXException{
            System.out.println("Warning "+e.getMessage());
          }
    }

}
```

Listing 2-16 shows the output from SAXParserApp.java. Whitespace between elements is also output as text, because unlike in the case of the DOM API example, the SAX example does not filter out whitespace text.

Listing 2-16. *Output from the SAXParserApp Application*

```
Event Type: Start Document
Event Type: Start Element
Element Name:catalog
Attribute Name:title
Attribute Value:OnJava.com
Attribute Name:publisher
Attribute Value:O'Reilly
Event Type:  Text

Event Type:  Text


Event Type: Start Element
Element Name:journal
Attribute Name:date
Attribute Value:January 2004
Event Type:  Text


Event Type: Start Element
Element Name:article
Event Type:  Text

Event Type:  Text


Event Type: Start Element
Element Name:title
Event Type:  Text
Data Binding with XMLBeans
Event Type: End Element
Event Type:  Text


Event Type: Start Element
Element Name:author
Event Type:  Text
Daniel Steinberg
Event Type: End Element
Event Type:  Text


Event Type: End Element
Event Type:  Text
```

```
Event Type: End Element
Event Type:   Text


Event Type: Start Element
Element Name:journal
Attribute Name:date
Attribute Value:Sept 2005
Event Type:   Text

Event Type:   Text


Event Type: Start Element
Element Name:article
Event Type:   Text


Event Type: Start Element
Element Name:title
Event Type:   Text
What Is Hibernate
Event Type: End Element
Event Type:   Text


Event Type: Start Element
Element Name:author
Event Type:   Text
James Elliott
Event Type: End Element
Event Type:   Text


Event Type: End Element
Event Type:   Text


Event Type: End Element
Event Type:   Text


Event Type:   Text


Event Type: End Element
Event Type: End Document
```

To demonstrate error handling in a SAX parsing application, add an error in the example XML document, catalog.xml; remove a </journal> tag, for example. The SAX parsing application outputs the error in the XML document, as shown in Listing 2-17.

Listing 2-17. *SAX Parsing Error*

```
Fatal Error: The element type
   "journal" must be terminated by the matching end-tag "</journal>".
```

Parsing with StAX

StAX is a pull-model API for parsing XML. StAX has an advantage over the push-model SAX. In the push model, the parser generates events as the XML document is parsed. With the pull parsing in StAX, the application generates the parse events; thus, you can generate parse events as required. The StAX API (JSR-173)[6] is implemented in J2SE 6.0.

Key points about StAX API are as follows:

- The StAX API classes are in the javax.xml.stream and javax.xml.stream.events packages.

- The StAX API offers two different APIs for parsing an XML document: a cursor-based API and an iterator-based API.

- The XMLStreamReader interface parses an XML document using the cursor API.

- XMLEventReader parses an XML document using the iterator API.

- You can use the XMLStreamWriter interface to generate an XML document.

We will first discuss the cursor API and then the iterator API.

Cursor API

You can use the XMLStreamReader object to parse an XML document using the cursor approach. The next() method generates the next parse event. You can obtain the event type from the getEventType() method. You can create an XMLStreamReader object from an XMLInputFactory object, and you can create an XMLInputFactory object using the static method newInstance(), as shown in Listing 2-18.

Listing 2-18. *Creating an XMLStreamReader Object*

```
XMLInputFactory inputFactory=XMLInputFactory.newInstance();
InputStream input=new FileInputStream(new File("catalog.xml"));
XMLStreamReader  xmlStreamReader = inputFactory.createXMLStreamReader(input);
```

The next parsing event is generated with the next() method of an XMLStreamReader object, as shown in Listing 2-19.

Listing 2-19. *Obtaining a Parsing Event*

```
while (xmlStreamReader.hasNext()) {
   int event = xmlStreamReader.next();
}
```

The next() method returns an int, which corresponds to a parsing event, as specified by an XMLStreamConstants constant. Table 2-13 lists the event types returned by the XMLStreamReader object.

For a START_DOCUMENT event type, the getEncoding() method returns the encoding in the XML document. The getVersion() method returns the XML document version.

---

6. You can find this specification at http://jcp.org/aboutJava/communityprocess/final/jsr173/index.html.

Table 2-13. *XMLStreamReader Events*

Event Type	Description
START_DOCUMENT	Start of a document
START_ELEMENT	Start of an element
ATTRIBUTE	An element attribute
NAMESPACE	A namespace declaration
CHARACTERS	Characters may be text or whitespace
COMMENT	A comment
SPACE	Ignorable whitespace
PROCESSING_INSTRUCTION	Processing instruction
DTD	A DTD
ENTITY_REFERENCE	An entity reference
CDATA	CDATA section
END_ELEMENT	End element
END_DOCUMENT	End document
ENTITY_DECLARATION	An entity declaration
NOTATION_DECLARATION	A notation declaration

For a START_ELEMENT event type, the getPrefix() method returns the element prefix, and the getNamespaceURI() method returns the namespace or the default namespace. The getLocalName() method returns the local name of an element, as shown in Listing 2-20.

Listing 2-20. *Outputting the Element Name*

```
if (event == XMLStreamConstants.START_ELEMENT) {
System.out.println("Element Local Name:"+ xmlStreamReader.getLocalName());
}
```

The getAttributesCount() method returns the number of attributes in an element. The getAttributePrefix(int) method returns the attribute prefix for a specified attribute index. The getAttributeNamespace(int) method returns the attribute namespace for a specified attribute index. The getAttributeLocalName(int) method returns the local name of an attribute, and the getAttributeValue(int) method returns the attribute value. The attribute name and value are output as shown in Listing 2-21.

Listing 2-21. *Outputting the Attribute Name and Value*

```
for (int i = 0; i < xmlStreamReader.getAttributeCount(); i++) {
   //Output Attribute Name
   System.out.println("Attribute Local Name:"+
      xmlStreamReader.getAttributeLocalName(i));
   //Output Attribute Value
   System.out.println("Attribute Value:"+ xmlStreamReader.getAttributeValue(i));
}
```

The getText() method retrieves the text of a CHARACTERS event, as shown in Listing 2-22.

Listing 2-22. *Outputting Text*

```
if (event == XMLStreamConstants.CHARACTERS) {
                System.out.println("Text:" + xmlStreamReader.getText());
}
```

Listing 2-23 shows the complete StAX cursor API parsing application.

Listing 2-23. *StAXParser.java*

```
package com.apress.stax;

import javax.xml.stream.*;
import javax.xml.stream.events.*;
import javax.xml.stream.XMLInputFactory;
import java.io.*;

public class StAXParser {

    public void parseXMLDocument () {
        try {
            //Create XMLInputFactory object
            XMLInputFactory inputFactory = XMLInputFactory.newInstance();
             //Create XMLStreamReader
            InputStream input = new FileInputStream(new File("catalog.xml"));
            XMLStreamReader xmlStreamReader = inputFactory
                    .createXMLStreamReader(input);
            //Obtain StAX Parsing Events
            while (xmlStreamReader.hasNext()) {
                int event = xmlStreamReader.next();

                if (event == XMLStreamConstants.START_DOCUMENT) {
                System.out.println("Event Type:START_DOCUMENT");
                }
                if (event == XMLStreamConstants.START_ELEMENT) {
                    System.out.println("Event Type: START_ELEMENT");
                    //Output Element Local Name
                    System.out.println("Element Local Name:"
                            + xmlStreamReader.getLocalName());
                    //Output Element Attributes
                for (int i = 0; i < xmlStreamReader.getAttributeCount(); i++) {

                            System.out.println("Attribute Local Name:"
                        + xmlStreamReader.getAttributeLocalName(i));
                    System.out.println("Attribute Value:"
                        + xmlStreamReader.getAttributeValue(i));
                }

                }
```

```java
                if (event == XMLStreamConstants.CHARACTERS) {
                    System.out.println("Event Type: CHARACTERS");
                    System.out.println("Text:" + xmlStreamReader.getText());
                }

                if (event == XMLStreamConstants.END_DOCUMENT) {
                    System.out.println("Event Type:END_DOCUMENT");
                }
                if (event == XMLStreamConstants.END_ELEMENT) {
                    System.out.println("Event Type: END_ELEMENT");
                }

            }
        } catch (FactoryConfigurationError e) {
            System.out.println("FactoryConfigurationError" + e.getMessage());
        } catch (XMLStreamException e) {
            System.out.println("XMLStreamException" + e.getMessage());
        } catch (IOException e) {
            System.out.println("IOException" + e.getMessage());
        }

    }

    public static void main(String[] argv) {

        StAXParser staxParser = new StAXParser();
        staxParser.parseXMLDocument();

    }
}
```

Listing 2-24 shows the output from the StAX parsing application in Eclipse.

Listing 2-24. *Output from the StAXParser Application*

```
Event Type: START_ELEMENT
Element Local Name:catalog
Attribute Local Name:title
Attribute Value:OnJava.com
Attribute Local Name:publisher
Attribute Value:O'Reilly
Event Type: CHARACTERS
Text:

Event Type: START_ELEMENT
Element Local Name:journal
Attribute Local Name:date
Attribute Value:January 2004
Event Type: CHARACTERS
Text:

Event Type: START_ELEMENT
Element Local Name:article
Event Type: CHARACTERS
Text:
```

```
Event Type: START_ELEMENT
Element Local Name:title
Event Type: CHARACTERS
Text:Data Binding with XMLBeans
Event Type: END_ELEMENT
Event Type: CHARACTERS
Text:

Event Type: START_ELEMENT
Element Local Name:author
Event Type: CHARACTERS
Text:Daniel Steinberg
Event Type: END_ELEMENT
Event Type: CHARACTERS
Text:

Event Type: END_ELEMENT
Event Type: CHARACTERS
Text:

Event Type: END_ELEMENT
Event Type: CHARACTERS
Text:

Event Type: START_ELEMENT
Element Local Name:journal
Attribute Local Name:date
Attribute Value:Sept 2005
Event Type: CHARACTERS
Text:

Event Type: START_ELEMENT
Element Local Name:article
Event Type: CHARACTERS
Text:

Event Type: START_ELEMENT
Element Local Name:title
Event Type: CHARACTERS
Text:What Is Hibernate
Event Type: END_ELEMENT
Event Type: CHARACTERS
Text:

Event Type: START_ELEMENT
Element Local Name:author
Event Type: CHARACTERS
Text:James Elliott
Event Type: END_ELEMENT
Event Type: CHARACTERS
Text:
```

```
Event Type: END_ELEMENT
Event Type: CHARACTERS
Text:

Event Type: END_ELEMENT
Event Type: CHARACTERS
Text:


Event Type: END_ELEMENT
Event Type:END_DOCUMENT
```

Iterator API

The XMLEventReader object parses an XML document with an object event iterator and generates an XMLEvent object for each parse event. To create an XMLEventReader object, you need to first create an XMLInputFactory object with the static method newInstance() and then obtain an XMLEventReader object from the XMLInputFactory object with the createXMLEventReader method, as shown in Listing 2-25.

Listing 2-25. *Creating an XMLEventReader Object*

```
XMLInputFactory inputFactory=XMLInputFactory.newInstance();
InputStream input=new FileInputStream(new File("catalog.xml"));
XMLEventReader  xmlEventReader  = inputFactory.createXMLEventReader(input);
```

An XMLEvent object represents an XML document event in StAX. You obtain the next event with the nextEvent() method of an XMLEventReader object. The getEventType() method of an XMLEventReader object returns the event type, as shown here:

```
XMLEvent event=xmlEventReader.nextEvent();
int eventType=event.getEventType();
```

The event types listed in Table 2-13 for an XMLStreamReader object are also the event types generated with an XMLEventReader object. The isXXX() methods in the XMLEventReader interface return a boolean if the event is of the type corresponding to the isXXX() method. For example, the isStartDocument() method returns true if the event is of type START_DOCUMENT. You can use relevant XMLStreamReader methods to process event types that are of interest to the application.

Summary

You can parse an XML document using one of three methods: DOM, push, or pull.

The DOM approach provides random access and a complete ability to manipulate document elements and attributes; however, this approach consumes the most memory. This approach is best for use in situations where an in-memory model of the XML structure and content is required so that an application can easily manipulate the structure and content of an XML document. Applications that need to visualize an XML document and manipulate the document through a user interface may find this API extremely relevant to their application objectives. The DOM Level 3 API included in JAXP 1.3 implements this approach.

The push approach is based on a simple event notification model where a parser synchronously delivers parsing events so an application can handle these events by implementing a callback handler interface. The SAX 2.0 API is best suited for situations where the core objectives are as follows: quickly parse an XML document, make sure it is well-formed and valid, and extract content information contained in the document as the document is being parsed. It is worth noting that a DOM API implementation could internally use a SAX 2.0 API–based parser to parse an XML document and build a DOM tree, but it is not required to do so. The SAX 2.0 API included in JAXP 1.3 implements this approach.

The pull approach provides complete control to an application over how the document parse events are processed and provides a cursor-based approach and an iterator-based approach to control the flow of parse events. This approach is best suited for processing XML content that is being streamed over a network connection. Also, this API is useful for marshaling and unmarshaling XML documents from and to Java types. Major areas of applications for this API include web services–related message processing and XML-to-Java binding. The StAX API included in J2SE 6.0 implements this approach.

CHAPTER 3

■■■

Introducing Schema Validation

In Chapter 2, we covered how to parse XML documents, which is the most fundamental aspect of processing an XML document. During the discussion on parsing, we noted that one of the objectives of parsing an XML document is to validate the structure of an XML document with respect to a schema. The process of validating an XML document with respect to a schema is *schema validation*, and that is the subject of this chapter.

If a document conforms to a schema, it is called an *instance* of the schema. A schema defines a class of XML documents, where each document in the class is an instance of the schema. The relationship between a schema class and an instance document is analogous to the relationship between a Java class and an instance object. Several schema languages are available to define a schema. The following two schema languages are part of W3C Recommendations:

- DTD is the XML 1.0 built-in schema language that uses XML markup declarations[1] syntax to define a schema. Validating an XML document with respect to a DTD is an integral part of parsing and was covered in Chapter 2.

- W3C XML Schema[2] is an XML-based schema language. Chapter 1 offered a primer on XML Schema.

Validating an XML document with respect to a schema definition based on the XML Schema language is the focus of this chapter.

Schema Validation APIs

In this chapter, we will focus on the JAXP 1.3[3] schema validation APIs. You can classify the APIs into two groups:

- The first group includes the JAXP 1.3 SAX and DOM parser APIs. Both these APIs perform validation as an intrinsic part of the parsing process.

- The second group includes the JAXP 1.3 Validation API. The Validation API is unlike the first two APIs in that it completely decouples validation from parsing.

---

1. The complete markup declaration syntax is part of XML 1.0; you can find more information at http://www.w3.org/TR/REC-xml/#dt-markupdecl.
2. See http://www.w3.org/XML/Schema.
3. Java API for XML Processing (http://java.sun.com/webservices/jaxp/) is included in J2SE 5.0.

Clearly, if the application needs to parse an XML document and the selected parser supports schema validation, it makes sense to combine validation with parsing. However, in other scenarios, for a variety of reasons, the validation process needs to be decoupled from the parsing process. The following are some of the scenarios where an application may need to decouple validation from parsing:

- Prior to validating an XML document with a schema, an application may need to first validate the schema itself. The Validation API allows an application to separately compile and validate a schema, before it is used for validating an XML document. For example, this could be applicable if the schema were available from an external source that could not automatically be trusted to be correct.

- An application may have a DOM tree representation of an XML document, and the application may need to validate the tree with respect to a schema definition. This scenario comes about in practice if a DOM tree for an XML document is programmatically or interactively manipulated to create a new DOM tree and the new tree needs to be validated against a schema.

- An application may need to validate an XML document with respect to a schema language that is not supported by the available parser. This is generally true for less widely supported schema languages and is of course true for a new custom schema language.

- An application may need to use the same schema definition to validate multiple XML documents. Because the Validation API constructs an object representation of a schema, it is efficient to use a single schema object to validate multiple documents.

- An application may need to validate XML content that is known to be well-formed, so there is no point in first parsing such content. An example scenario for this case is when an XML document is being produced programmatically through a reliable transformation process.

We discussed guidelines for selecting the appropriate JAXP 1.3 parsing API in Chapter 2. Table 3-1 lists criteria for selecting the appropriate JAXP 1.3 validation API.

Table 3-1. *Selecting a Validation API*

Validation API	Suitable Application
SAX parser	The document is suitable for parsing with the SAX parser and requires validation, and the parser supports the schema language.
DOM parser	The document is suitable for parsing with the DOM parser and requires validation, and the parser supports the schema language.
Validation	The application needs to decouple parsing from validation; we discussed scenarios earlier.

Configuring JAXP Parsers for Schema Validation

To enable a JAXP parser for schema validation, you need to set the appropriate properties on the parser. You first need to set the Validating property to true, before any of the other schema validation properties described next will take effect. Other schema validation properties are as follows:

- You specify the schema language used in the schema definition through the `http://java.sun.com/xml/jaxp/properties/schemaLanguage` property. The value of this property must be the URI of the schema language specification, which for the W3C XML Schema language is `http://www.w3.org/2001/XMLSchema`.

- You specify the location of the schema definition source through the `http://java.sun.com/xml/jaxp/properties/schemaSource` property. The value of this property must be one of the following:

  - The URI of the schema document location as a string

  - The schema source supplied as a `java.io.InputStream` object or an `org.xml.sax.InputSource` object

  - The schema source supplied as a `File` object

  - An array of the type of objects described previously

- It is illegal to set the `schemaSource` property without setting `schemaLanguage`.

- An XML document can specify the location of a namespace-aware schema through the `xsi:schemaLocation` attribute in the document element, as shown in the following example:

```
<jsp:root xmlns:jsp="http://java.sun.com/JSP/Page"
xmlns:xsi="http://www.w3.org/2001/XMLSchema-instance"
xsi:schemaLocation=
   "http://java.sun.com/JSP/Page http://www.nubean.com/schemas/jsf_1_1.xsd" >
```

  The `schemaLocation` attribute can have one or more value pairs. In each value pair, the first value is a namespace URI, and the second value is the schema location URI for the associated namespace. The XML Schema 1.0 W3C Recommendation does not mandate that this attribute value be used to locate the schema file during the schema validation.

- An XML document can specify the location of a no-namespace schema through the `xsi:noNamespaceSchemaLocation` attribute in the document element, as shown in the following example:

```
<root xmlns:xsi="http://www.w3.org/2001/XMLSchema-instance"
   xsi:noNamespaceSchemaLocation=
     "http://www.nubean.com/schemas/jsf_1_1.xsd" >
```

  The `xsi:noNamespaceSchemaLocation` attribute specifies the schema location URI. The XML Schema 1.0 W3C Recommendation does not mandate that this attribute value be used to locate the schema file during the schema validation.

An XML document can specify a DTD and can also specify a schema location. In addition, the validating application can specify the `schemaLanguage` and `schemaSource` properties. The permutations on these options can quickly get confusing. To simplify things, Table 3-2 lists all the configuration scenarios and associated semantics. For all the scenarios in Table 3-2, we are assuming the `Validating` property is set to `true` and that whenever the `schemaLanguage` property is specified, it is set to the URI for the XML Schema specification.

Before we discuss each of the APIs in detail, you need to set up your Eclipse project so you can build and execute the code examples related to each API.

Table 3-2. *Configuration of JAXP Parsers for Validation*

DOCTYPE?	schemaLanguage?	schemaSource?	schemaLocation?	Validated Against	Schema Used
No	No	No	No	Error: Must have DOCTYPE if Validating is true	
No	No	No	Yes	Error: Schema language must be set	
No	No	Yes	No/yes	Error: Schema language must be set	
Yes/no	Yes	No	Yes	XML Schema	Schema location from the instance document
Yes/no	Yes	Yes	No	XML Schema	Schema location from the schemaSource property
Yes/no	Yes	Yes	Yes	XML Schema	Schema location from the schemaSource property
Yes	No	No	Yes/no	DTD	DTD location from DOCTYPE

Setting Up the Eclipse Project

In this chapter, we will show how to validate an example XML document, with respect to a schema definition, using the JAXP 1.3 DOM parser, SAX parser, and Validation APIs, included in J2SE 5.0. Therefore, the first step you need to take is to install J2SE 5.0.

Before you can build and run the code examples included in this chapter, you need an Eclipse project. The quickest way to create your Eclipse project is to download the Chapter3 project from the Apress website (http://www.apress.com) and import this project into Eclipse. This will create all the Java packages and files needed for this chapter automatically.

After the import, please verify that the Java build path for the Chapter3 project is as shown in Figure 3-1. You may need to click the Add Library button to add the JRE 5.0 system library to your Java build path.

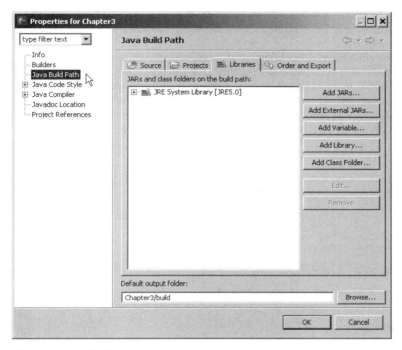

Figure 3-1. *Java build path*

We'll use the example document, catalog.xml, shown in Listing 3-1 as input in all the validation examples.

Listing 3-1. *catalog.xml*

```
<?xml version="1.0" encoding="UTF-8"?>
<catalog xmlns:xsi="http://www.w3.org/2001/XMLSchema-instance"
   xsi:noNamespaceSchemaLocation="catalog.xsd"
   title="OnJava.com" publisher="O'Reilly">
 <journal date="April 2004">
   <article>
    <title>Declarative Programming in Java</title>
    <author>Narayanan Jayaratchagan</author>
   </article>
 </journal>
 <journal date="January 2004">
   <article>
    <title>Data Binding with XMLBeans</title>
    <author>Daniel Steinberg</author>
   </article>
 </journal>
</catalog>
```

The `catalog.xml` XML document is validated with respect to the `catalog.xsd` schema definition shown in Listing 3-2. In `catalog.xml`, the attribute `xsi:noNamespaceSchemaLocation="catalog.xsd"` defines the location of the schema.

The `catalog.xml` document is an instance of the `catalog.xsd` schema definition. In this schema definition, the root `catalog` element declaration defines the `title` and `publisher` optional attributes and zero or more nested `journal` elements. Each `journal` element definition defines the optional `date` attribute and zero or more nested `article` elements. Each `article` element definition defines the nested `title` element and zero or more `author` elements. You should review this schema definition by applying the concepts covered in the XML Schema primer in Chapter 1.

Listing 3-2. *catalog.xsd*

```
<?xml version="1.0" encoding="utf-8"?>
<xs:schema xmlns:xs="http://www.w3.org/2001/XMLSchema">
  <xs:element name="catalog">
   <xs:complexType>
    <xs:sequence>
     <xs:element ref="journal" minOccurs="0" maxOccurs="unbounded"/>
    </xs:sequence>
    <xs:attribute name="title" type="xs:string"/>
    <xs:attribute name="publisher"  type="xs:string"/>
   </xs:complexType>
  </xs:element>
  <xs:element name="journal">
   <xs:complexType>
    <xs:sequence>
     <xs:element ref="article" minOccurs="0" maxOccurs="unbounded"/>
    </xs:sequence>
    <xs:attribute name="date" type="xs:string"/>
   </xs:complexType>
  </xs:element>
  <xs:element name="article">
   <xs:complexType>
    <xs:sequence>
     <xs:element name="title" type="xs:string"/>
     <xs:element ref="author" minOccurs="0" maxOccurs="unbounded"/>
    </xs:sequence>
   </xs:complexType>
  </xs:element>
  <xs:element name="author" type="xs:string"/>
</xs:schema>
```

In the following sections, we'll discuss how to validate the `catalog.xml` document with the `catalog.xsd` schema. Before we do that, though, please verify that `catalog.xml` and `catalog.xsd` appear in the `Chapter3` project, as shown in Figure 3-2.

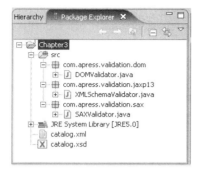

Figure 3-2. *Chapter3 project*

As noted at the outset, we will discuss schema validation using the JAXP 1.3 DOM parser, SAX parser, and Validation APIs. We will start with the JAXP 1.3 DOM parser API.

JAXP 1.3 DOM Parser API

We covered parsing with the JAXP 1.3 DOM parser API in Chapter 2. In this section, the focus is on schema validation using the JAXP 1.3 DOM parser API. The basic steps for schema validation using this API are as follows:

1. Create an instance of the DOM parser factory.

2. Configure the DOM parser factory instance to support schema validation.

3. Obtain a DOM parser from the configured DOM parser factory.

4. Configure a parser instance with an error handler so the parser can report validation errors.

5. Parse the document using the configured parser.

We will map these basic steps to specific steps using the JAXP 1.3 DOM API, which is defined in the org.w3c.dom package. In addition, the DOM API relies on the following SAX packages: org.xml.sax and org.xml.sax.helpers. The reliance on the SAX API within the DOM API is specified in JAXP 1.3 and is merely an effort to reuse classes, where appropriate. To begin, import the following classes:

```
import javax.xml.parsers.DocumentBuilderFactory;
import javax.xml.parsers.DocumentBuilder;
import javax.xml.parsers.ParserConfigurationException;
import org.xml.sax.SAXException;
import org.xml.sax.SAXParseException;
import org.xml.sax.helpers.DefaultHandler;
```

Create a DOM Parser Factory

As noted previously, the first step is to create a DOM parser factory, so you need to create a DocumentBuilderFactory, as shown here:

```
DocumentBuilderFactory factory = DocumentBuilderFactory.newInstance ();
```

The implementation class for `DocumentBuilderFactory` is pluggable. The JAXP 1.3 API loads the implementation class for `DocumentBuilderFactory` by applying the following rules, in order, until a rule succeeds:

1. Use the `javax.xml.parsers.DocumentBuilderFactory` system property to load an implementation class.

2. Use the properties file `lib/jaxp.properties` in the JRE directory. If this file exists, parse this file to check whether a property has the `javax.xml.parsers.DocumentBuilderFactory` key. If such a property exists, use the value of this property to load an implementation class.

3. Files in the `META-INF/services` directory within a JAR file are deemed service provider configuration files. Use the Services API, and obtain the factory class name from the `META-INF/services/javax.xml.parsers.DocumentBuilderFactory` file contained in any JAR file in the runtime classpath.

4. Use the platform default `DocumentBuilderFactory` instance, included in the J2SE platform being used by the application.

Configure a Factory for Validation

Before you can use a `DocumentBuilderFactory` instance to create a parser for schema validation, you need to configure the factory for schema validation. To configure a factory for validation, you may use the following options:

- To parse an XML document with a namespace-aware parser, set the `setNamespaceAware()` feature of the factory to `true`. By default, the namespace-aware feature is set to `false`.

- To make the parser a validating parser, set the `setValidating()` feature of the factory to `true`. By default, the validation feature is set to `false`.

- To validate with an XML Schema language–based schema definition, set the `schemaLanguage` attribute, which specifies the schema language for validation. The attribute name is `http://java.sun.com/xml/jaxp/properties/schemaLanguage`, and the attribute value for the W3C XML Schema language is `http://www.w3.org/2001/XMLSchema`.

- The `schemaSource` attribute specifies the location of the schema. The attribute name is `http://java.sun.com/xml/jaxp/properties/schemaSource`, and the attribute value is a URL pointing to the schema definition source.

Listing 3-3 shows the configuration of a factory instance based on these validation options.

Listing 3-3. *Setting the Validation Schema*

```
factory.setNamespaceAware (true);
factory.setValidating (true);
factory.setAttribute (
    "http://java.sun.com/xml/jaxp/properties/schemaLanguage",
    "http://www.w3.org/2001/XMLSchema");
factory.setAttribute ("http://java.sun.com/xml/jaxp/properties/schemaSource",
    "SchemaUrl");
```

Create a DOM Parser

From the `DocumentBuilderFactory` object, create a `DocumentBuilder` DOM parser:

```
DocumentBuilder builder = factory.newDocumentBuilder();
```

This returns a new DocumentBuilder with the schema validation parameters set as configured on the DocumentBuilderFactory object.

Configure a Parser for Validation

To retrieve validation errors generated during parsing, you need to first define a class that implements an ErrorHandler, and you do that by defining the Validator class, which extends the DefaultHandler SAX helper class, as shown in Listing 3-4.

Listing 3-4. *Validator Class*

```
          //ErrorHandler Class: DefaultHandler implements ErrorHandler
class Validator extends DefaultHandler {
  public boolean validationError = false;
  public SAXParseException saxParseException = null;

  public void error(SAXParseException exception) throws SAXException {
    validationError = true;
    saxParseException = exception;
  }

  public void fatalError(SAXParseException exception) throws SAXException {
    validationError = true;
    saxParseException = exception;
  }
  public void warning(SAXParseException exception) throws SAXException {
  }
}
```

A Validator instance is set as an error handler on the builder DOM parser instance, as shown here:

```
Validator handler=new Validator();
builder.setErrorHandler (handler);
```

Validate Using the Parser

To validate an XML document with a schema definition, as part of the processing process, parse the XML document with the DocumentBuilder parser using the parse(String uri) method, as shown here:

```
builder.parse (XmlDocumentUrl)
```

Validator registers validation errors generated by validation.

Complete DOM API Example

The complete example program shown in Listing 3-5 validates the catalog.xml document with respect to the catalog.xsd schema. The key method in this application is validateSchema(). In this method, a DocumentBuilderFactory instance is created, and the schema location to validate the catalog.xml document is set. A DocumentBuilder DOM parser is obtained from the factory and configured with an error handler. The private Validator class extends the DefaultHandler class and implements the error handler. Validation takes place as part of the parsing process.

Listing 3-5. *DOMValidator.java*

```java
package com.apress.validation.dom;

import javax.xml.parsers.DocumentBuilderFactory;
import javax.xml.parsers.DocumentBuilder;
import javax.xml.parsers.ParserConfigurationException;
import org.xml.sax.SAXException;
import org.xml.sax.SAXParseException;
import org.xml.sax.helpers.DefaultHandler;

public class DOMValidator {

  public void validateSchema(String SchemaUrl, String XmlDocumentUrl) {
    try {
      //Create DocumentBuilderFactory
      DocumentBuilderFactory factory = DocumentBuilderFactory
          .newInstance();

      //Set factory to be a validating factory.
      factory.setNamespaceAware(true);
      factory.setValidating(true);
       //Set schema attributes
      factory.setAttribute(
        "http://java.sun.com/xml/jaxp/properties/schemaLanguage",
          "http://www.w3.org/2001/XMLSchema");
      factory.setAttribute(
        "http://java.sun.com/xml/jaxp/properties/schemaSource",
          SchemaUrl);

      //Create a DocumentBuilder
      DocumentBuilder builder = factory.newDocumentBuilder();

       //Create a ErrorHandler and set ErrorHandler
       // on DocumentBuilderparser
      Validator handler = new Validator();
      builder.setErrorHandler(handler);

      //Parse XML Document
      builder.parse(XmlDocumentUrl);
      //Output Validation Errors
      if (handler.validationError == true)
        System.out.println("XML Document has Error:"
            + handler.validationError + " "
            + handler.saxParseException.getMessage());
      else
        System.out.println("XML Document is valid");
    } catch (java.io.IOException ioe) {
      System.out.println("IOException " + ioe.getMessage());
    } catch (SAXException e) {
      System.out.println("SAXException" + e.getMessage());
    } catch (ParserConfigurationException e) {
```

```
      System.out
          .println("ParserConfigurationException                "
              + e.getMessage());
    }
  }
            //ErrorHandler Class
  private class Validator extends DefaultHandler {
    public boolean validationError = false;

    public SAXParseException saxParseException = null;

    public void error(SAXParseException exception) throws SAXException {
      validationError = true;
      saxParseException = exception;
    }

    public void fatalError(SAXParseException exception) throws SAXException {
      validationError = true;
      saxParseException = exception;
    }

    public void warning(SAXParseException exception) throws SAXException {
    }
  }

  public static void main(String[] argv) {
    String SchemaUrl = "catalog.xsd";
    String XmlDocumentUrl = "catalog.xml";
    DOMValidator validator = new DOMValidator();
    validator.validateSchema(SchemaUrl, XmlDocumentUrl);
  }
}
```

Listing 3-6 shows the output from the DOM parser validation application.

Listing 3-6. *Output from* DOMValidator.java

```
XML Document is valid
```

To demonstrate validation error handling, add an element in catalog.xml that does not conform to the schema. For example, add a nonconforming title element to the catalog element, as shown here:

```
<title>Chapter 3: Schema Validation</title>
```

This leads to an expected validation error, as shown in Listing 3-7. Be sure to remove this error from the document, or else the remaining examples will not work correctly.

Listing 3-7. *Output with a Validation Error*

```
XML Document has Error:true cvc-complex-type.2.4.a: Invalid content was found st
arting with element 'title'. One of '{journal}' is expected.
```

JAXP 1.3 SAX Parser API

We covered parsing with the JAXP 1.3 SAX parser API in Chapter 2. In this section, the focus is on schema validation using the JAXP 1.3 SAX parser API. The basic steps for schema validation using this API are conceptually similar to the DOM parser API:

1. Create an instance of the SAX parser factory.
2. Configure the SAX parser factory instance to support schema validation.
3. Obtain a SAX parser from the SAX parser factory.
4. Configure the SAX parser instance to specify the schema location and error handler.
5. Parse the document using the configured SAX parser.

To use SAX parsing, you need the SAXParserFactory and SAXParser classes. We will show how to extend the DefaultHandler class to implement a customized error handler. So, import the following classes:

```
import javax.xml.parsers.SAXParserFactory;
import javax.xml.parsers.SAXParser;
import org.xml.sax.helpers.DefaultHandler;
```

Create a SAX Parser Factory

To create a SAX parser, you first need to create a SAXParserFactory object. You create a SAXParserFactory object using the newInstance() static method, as shown here:

```
SAXParserFactory factory = SAXParserFactory.newInstance();
```

Configure the Factory for Validation

You need to set the factory to be a namespace-aware factory and a validating factory using the setNamespaceAware() and setValidating() methods, as shown here:

```
factory.setNamespaceAware(true);
factory.setValidating(true);
```

When validating with a SAX parser, you may need to set schema validation features that are parser specific. For example, the Xerces2-j[4] SAX parser, which is the default SAX parser in JAXP 1.3, supports the following features:

- The validation feature turns on validation. This is the same as invoking setNamespaceAware(true) on the factory. In the example code, it is redundant and is purely for demonstration purposes.

- The validation/schema feature turns on XML Schema validation. This is also redundant for the example code because later you'll set the schemaLanguage and schemaSource properties on the parser.

- The validation/schema-full-checking feature turns on rigorous checking on the schema grammar. It does not affect XML document validation. Turning on this feature is both performance and memory intensive.

---

4. See http://xerces.apache.org/xerces2-j/.

For a complete list of Xerces2-j features, consult the documentation at `http://xerces.apache.`
`org/xerces2-j/features.html`. You can set the previously listed features on the SAX parser factory,
as shown in Listing 3-8.

Listing 3-8. *Setting Validation Features*

```
factory.setFeature("http://xml.org/sax/features/validation",true);
factory.setFeature("http://apache.org/xml/features/validation/schema", true);
factory.setFeature("http://apache.org/xml/features/validation/schema-full-checking",
  true);
```

Create a SAX Parser

To validate with a SAX parser, you need to create a `SAXParser` object, as shown here:

```
SAXParser parser = new SAXParser();
```

Configure the Parser

You also need to set the `schemaLanguage` and `schemaSource` properties. The `schemaLanguage` property
specifies the schema language for validation. The `schemaSource` property specifies the schema document to be used for validation, as shown in Listing 3-9.

Listing 3-9. *Setting Parser Properties*

```
parser.setProperty("http://java.sun.com/xml/jaxp/properties/schemaLanguage",
  "http://www.w3.org/2001/XMLSchema");
parser.setProperty("http://java.sun.com/xml/jaxp/properties/schemaSource",
  SchemaUrl);
```

To create a customized `ErrorHandler` class, create a class that extends the `DefaultHandler` class,
as shown in Listing 3-10.

Listing 3-10. *DefaultHandler Class*

```
private class Validator extends DefaultHandler {
    public boolean validationError = false;
    public SAXParseException saxParseException = null;

    public void error(SAXParseException exception) throws SAXException {
      validationError = true;
      saxParseException = exception;
    }
    public void fatalError(SAXParseException exception) throws SAXException {
      validationError = true;
      saxParseException = exception;
    }
    public void warning(SAXParseException exception) throws SAXException {
    }
  }
```

The `DefaultHandler` class implements the `ErrorHandler` interface and specifies an `ErrorHandler`
for the SAX parser.

Validate Using the Parser

You can use the overloaded parse methods in the SAXParser class for parsing and validating an XML document. In this example, you will use the parse(File, DefaultHandler) method, as shown here:

```
parser.parse(xmlFile, handler);
```

The validation errors generated by the parser get registered with the ErrorHandler interface and are retrieved from the ErrorHandler interface.

Complete SAX API Validator Example

Listing 3-11 lists a complete example using this API. The key method in this example is validateSchema(). In this method, a SAXParserFactory instance is created, and schema validation features are set. A SAXParser is obtained from this factory and configured with a schema source and an error handler. SAXValidator.java defines a private class Validator that extends the DefaultHandler class and implements the error hander. The example document is validated as part of the parsing process.

Listing 3-11. *SAXValidator.java*

```
package com.apress.validation.sax;

import javax.xml.parsers.SAXParserFactory;
import javax.xml.parsers.SAXParser;
import javax.xml.parsers.ParserConfigurationException;
import org.xml.sax.SAXException;
import org.xml.sax.SAXParseException;
import org.xml.sax.helpers.DefaultHandler;
import java.io.File;

public class SAXValidator {

  public void validateSchema(String SchemaUrl, File xmlFile) {
    try {
      // Create SAXParserFactory
      SAXParserFactory factory = SAXParserFactory.newInstance();

      // Set factory to be a validating factory.
      factory.setNamespaceAware(true);
      factory.setValidating(true);
      // Set schema validation features

      factory.setFeature("http://xml.org/sax/features/validation", true);
      factory.setFeature(
          "http://apache.org/xml/features/validation/schema", true);
      factory.setFeature(
        "http://apache.org/xml/features/validation/schema-full-checking",
            true);
      // Create SAXParser
      SAXParser parser = factory.newSAXParser();
```

```
    // Set schema properties
    parser.setProperty(
        "http://java.sun.com/xml/jaxp/properties/schemaLanguage",
        "http://www.w3.org/2001/XMLSchema");
    parser.setProperty(
        "http://java.sun.com/xml/jaxp/properties/schemaSource",
        SchemaUrl);
    // Create a ErrorHandler

    Validator handler = new Validator();

    // Parse XML Document
    parser.parse(xmlFile, handler);

    // Output Validation Errors
    if (handler.validationError == true)
      System.out.println("XML Document has Error:"
          + handler.validationError + " "
          + handler.saxParseException.getMessage());
    else
      System.out.println("XML Document is valid");
  } catch (java.io.IOException ioe) {
    System.out.println("IOException " + ioe.getMessage());
  } catch (SAXException e) {
    System.out.println("SAXException" + e.getMessage());
  } catch (ParserConfigurationException e) {
    System.out
        .println("ParserConfigurationException              "
            + e.getMessage());
  }
}

// ErrorHandler Class
private class Validator extends DefaultHandler {
  public boolean validationError = false;

  public SAXParseException saxParseException = null;

  public void error(SAXParseException exception) throws SAXException {
    validationError = true;
    saxParseException = exception;
  }

  public void fatalError(SAXParseException exception) throws SAXException {
    validationError = true;
    saxParseException = exception;
  }

  public void warning(SAXParseException exception) throws SAXException {
  }
}
```

```
  public static void main(String[] argv) {
    String SchemaUrl = "catalog.xsd";
    File xmlFile = new File("catalog.xml");
    SAXValidator validator = new SAXValidator();
    validator.validateSchema(SchemaUrl, xmlFile);
  }
}
```

If you run the program shown in Listing 3-11, you should see the same output as in the case of the DOM parser shown in Listing 3-6. To demonstrate validation error handling, add an element in catalog.xml that does not conform to the schema catalog.xsd. For example, add a nonconforming title element to the catalog element, as shown here:

```
<title>Chapter 3: Schema Validation</title>
```

Now run the SAXValidator.java application again. This time the program generates a validation error, as shown earlier in Listing 3-7.

JAXP 1.3 Validation API

In this section, we'll discuss the JAXP 1.3 Validation API. To recap, the key point about this API is that it completely decouples the validation process from the parsing process. The steps to use this API are as follows:

1. Create an instance of the javax.xml.validation.Validator class.

2. Set an error handler on the Validator object.

3. Validate an XML document.

Create a Validator

To validate with the Validator class, import the javax.xml.validation package, as shown here:

```
import javax.xml.validation.*;
```

To validate with an XML Schema–based schema definition, you need a Schema object representation of the schema definition. You create a Schema object from the SchemaFactory class. A SchemaFactory is a schema compiler, which is obtained from the static method newInstance(), as shown here:

```
SchemaFactory factory=SchemaFactory.newInstance(XMLConstants.W3C_XML_SCHEMA_NS_URI);
Schema schema=factory.newSchema(new File("catalog.xsd"));
```

The only argument to the newInstance() method is a schema language constant whose value is XMLConstants.W3C_XML_SCHEMA_NS_URI, which is the same as http://www.w3.org/2001/XMLSchema. The Validator class validates an XML document with respect to XML Schema, and a Validator object is obtained from a Schema object, as shown here:

```
Validator validator=schema.newValidator();
```

Set an Error Handler

To report validation errors, define an `ErrorHandler` class for `Validator`. This `ErrorHandler` class extends `DefaultHandler`, as shown in Listing 3-12.

Listing 3-12. *ErrorHandler Class*

```
private class ErrorHandlerImpl extends DefaultHandler
    {
        public boolean  validationError = false;
        public SAXParseException saxParseException=null;

        public void error(SAXParseException exception) throws SAXException
        {
            validationError = true;
            saxParseException=exception;
        }
        public void fatalError(SAXParseException exception) throws SAXException
        {
            validationError = true;
            saxParseException=exception;
        }
        public void warning(SAXParseException exception) throws SAXException
        {
        }
    }
```

An instance of an `ErrorHandlerImpl` class is set on the `validator` object with the `setErrorHandler()` method, as shown here:

```
ErrorHandlerImpl errorHandler=new ErrorHandlerImpl();
validator.setErrorHandler(errorHandler);
```

If a validation error is generated, the validation error gets registered with `errorHandler`.

Validate the XML Document

To validate an XML document, you do not need to parse the document. Instead, you create a `StreamSource` from the XML document and invoke the `validate()` method on the validator, passing it the stream source for the document, as shown here:

```
StreamSource streamSource=new StreamSource(xmlDocument);
validator.validate(streamSource);
```

Complete JAXP 1.3 Validator Example

Listing 3-13 shows a complete example using this API. The key method in this application is `validateXMLDocument()`. In this method, `SchemaFactory` creates a `Schema` object, which creates a `Validator` object. The private class `ErrorHandlerImpl` extends `DefaultHandler`, and an instance of this class is set as an error handler on the `Validator` instance. The example XML document is validated using one of the overloaded `validate()` methods defined in the `Validator` class.

Listing 3-13. *XMLSchemaValidator.java*

```java
package com.apress.validation.jdk6;

import org.xml.sax.SAXException;
import org.xml.sax.SAXParseException;
import org.xml.sax.helpers.DefaultHandler;
import java.io.*;
import javax.xml.XMLConstants;
import javax.xml.transform.stream.StreamSource;
import javax.xml.validation.*;

public class XMLSchemaValidator {
  public void validateXMLDocument(File schemaDocument, File xmlDocument) {
    try {
     //Create SchemaFactory
      SchemaFactory factory = SchemaFactory
          .newInstance("http://www.w3.org/2001/XMLSchema");
      //Create Schema object
      Schema schema = factory.newSchema(schemaDocument);
      // Create Validator and set ErrorHandler on Validator.
      Validator validator = schema.newValidator();
      ErrorHandlerImpl errorHandler = new ErrorHandlerImpl();
      validator.setErrorHandler(errorHandler);
       //Validate XML Document
      StreamSource streamSource = new StreamSource(xmlDocument);
      validator.validate(streamSource);
      //Output Validation Errors
      if (errorHandler.validationError == true) {
        System.out.println("XML Document has Error:"
            + errorHandler.validationError + " "
          + errorHandler.saxParseException.getMessage());
      } else {
        System.out.println("XML Document is valid");
      }
    } catch (SAXException e) {
    } catch (IOException e) {
    }
  }

  public static void main(String[] argv) {
    File schema = new File("catalog.xsd");
    File xmlDocument = new File("catalog.xml");
    XMLSchemaValidator validator = new XMLSchemaValidator();
    validator.validateXMLDocument(schema, xmlDocument);
  }
  //ErrorHandler class
  private class ErrorHandlerImpl extends DefaultHandler {
    public boolean validationError = false;

    public SAXParseException saxParseException = null;
```

```java
    public void error(SAXParseException exception) throws SAXException {
      validationError = true;
      saxParseException = exception;
    }

    public void fatalError(SAXParseException exception) throws SAXException {
      validationError = true;
      saxParseException = exception;
    }

    public void warning(SAXParseException exception) throws SAXException {
    }
  }
}
```

Run this validation application in Eclipse to produce the output previously shown in Listing 3-6.

Summary

In this chapter, we discussed three JAXP 1.3 schema validation APIs that can be classified into two groups:

- The first group consists of the JAXP parser APIs, and these APIs perform validation as an intrinsic part of the parsing process, if the parser is configured for schema validation.

- The second group consists of the JAXP Validation API, which decouples validation from parsing. This API instantiates an object representation of a schema and uses it to validate one or more XML documents.

When the application intent is to make sure a document being parsed is not only well-formed but also valid, then using the first group of APIs makes perfect sense. When the intent is to validate a document outside the context of parsing a document, clearly the JAXP Validation API is the way to go.

CHAPTER 4

■ ■ ■

Addressing with XPath

In Chapter 2, we discussed three approaches to parsing an XML document: the document object approach, the push approach, and the pull approach. These approaches are embodied in three APIs—DOM, SAX and StAX, respectively. To recap, you can use all three APIs to check that a document is well-formed and valid, but each provides different mechanisms for accessing document nodes. The SAX and StAX APIs allow access to document nodes only in document order[1] but offer the advantage of efficient memory use. The DOM API provides random access to document nodes but at the expense of higher processing overhead in terms of memory use.

The DOM approach creates a tree representation of an XML document that is ideally suited for use cases that require programmatic access and manipulation of document nodes. A classic example of a use case requiring programmatic access is an XML editor[2] that provides a source view and an outline view for an XML document.

Other use cases, such as the XSLT[3] template language, require imperative access instead of programmatic access to document nodes. Imperative access implies the existence of an expressive language that allows you to address the location of any document node set; XPath[4] is precisely such a language. In this chapter, we will discuss the various Java APIs that implement the XPath specification, in particular the XPath API in JAXP 1.3, which is included in J2SE 5.0,[5] and JDOM.[6]

Understanding XPath Expressions

XPath is a language for addressing node sets within an XML document. It is based on an abstract data model exclusively focused on the core information content in an XML document and ignores all information related to syntax markup. The XPath data model treats an XML document as a tree of various node types, such as an element node, an attribute node, and a text node. The XPath language provides an XPath expression as the main syntactic construct for addressing a node set within an XML document.

Simple Example

Since XPath expressions address a document node set, before you can proceed, you need an XML document to reference while we discuss XPath expressions. So, consider the following simple XML document:

---

1. Document order is the same as the depth-first order of the parse tree.
2. An example of such an editor is XMLEspresso; you can find it at http://www.nubean.com.
3. Chapter 5 covers XSLT.
4. You can find the XPath specification at http://www.w3.org/TR/xpath.
5. For more information about JDK 5.0, see http://java.sun.com/j2se/1.5.0/download.jsp.
6. For more information about JDOM, see. http://www.jdom.org/.

```
<catalog >
  <journal title="XML" />
  <journal title="Java Technology" />
</catalog>
```

Now, consider a simple XPath expression, /catalog/journal, that is based on this reference XML document. When you look at this XPath expression, you may be tempted to draw an analogy between an XPath expression and a file system path, and based on that analogy, you may intuitively interpret the expression /catalog/journal to refer to the first journal element within the document. In fact, this intuitive interpretation and the underlying analogy would both be wrong because this expression selects a node set containing both journal elements.

The reason the file system analogy does not work is simple: if /catalog/journal were a file system path, you could be assured that there would be only one journal folder under a catalog folder, but that clearly does not hold for XML document nodes. So, here is a more appropriate analogy for understanding XPath expressions: each component in an XPath expression is like a pattern that must be matched to locate the node set addressed by an XPath expression. With this basic insight in place, let's develop your intuition further by examining more XPath examples.

XPath Expression Examples

XPath expression syntax can be fairly complex, so the best way to begin understanding XPath expressions is to quickly walk through some examples. We will base these XPath examples on a slightly more complex XML document, shown in Listing 4-1, than the introductory document.

Listing 4-1. *Example XML Document:* catalog.xml

```
<?xml version="1.0" encoding="UTF-8"?>
<catalog xmlns:journal="http://www.apress.com/catalog/journal" >
  <journal:journal title="XML"  publisher="IBM developerWorks">
      <article journal:level="Intermediate"
            date="February-2003">
        <title>Design XML Schemas Using UML</title>
        <author>Ayesha Malik</author>
      </article>
  </journal:journal>
  <journal title="Java Technology"  publisher="IBM developerWorks">
      <article level="Advanced" date="January-2004">
        <title>Design service-oriented architecture
                frameworks with J2EE technology</title>
        <author>Naveen Balani</author>
      </article>
      <article level="Advanced" date="October-2003">
        <title>Advance DAO Programming</title>
        <author>Sean Sullivan </author>
      </article>
  </journal>
</catalog>
```

As we noted earlier, the XPath data model treats an XML document as a tree of nodes. Figure 4-1[7] shows the XPath data model for the example document. To fit the image within a page, not all article nodes in Figure 4-1 appear in expanded form. In Figure 4-1, the document element is designated as

---

7. This data model visualization is based on an Eclipse plug-in, available at http://www.nubean.com.

#document, element nodes are designated with their name with an "e" icon, attribute nodes are designated with their name-value pair and an "a" icon, and text nodes are designated as #text. The #text nodes in the data model correspond to the text content in element nodes, including whitespace text.

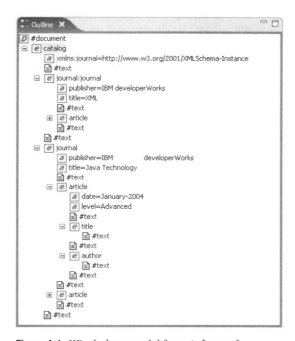

Figure 4-1. *XPath data model for* catalog.xml

Since we have not yet discussed XPath expression syntax, we will cover the following examples from an intuitive standpoint, referring to the data model shown in Figure 4-1. Later in the "Location Path" section, we will discuss XPath expression syntax in more detail.

Take a quick look at the following XPath expressions that address node sets within catalog.xml:

- /catalog/journal/article[@level='Advanced']/title is an XPath expression that evaluates to a node set containing elements named title, nested within elements named article, nested within an element named journal, nested within an element named catalog, whereby the element named article has an attribute named level (attributes are identified with the @ prefix) with a value equal to Advanced. Evaluating this expression selects the second title element, in document order.

- /catalog/journal[@title='Java Technology']/article[2] is an XPath expression that evaluates to a node set containing elements named article, nested within an element named journal, nested within an element named catalog, whereby the element named journal has an attribute named title with a value equal to Java Technology and an element named article in the second context position, in document order. The second context position of the article element is specified through the [2] suffix. Evaluating this expression selects the second article element in document order, in the journal titled Java Technology.

- `/child::catalog/child::journal/child::article[attribute::date='January-2004']/attribute::level` is an XPath expression that evaluates to a node set containing attributes named `level` that are attached to the element named `article`, nested within an element named `journal`, nested within an element named `catalog`, whereby the element named `article` has an attribute named `date` with a value equal to `January-2004`. The syntax construct `::` in an XPath expression defines a selection axis, with the name of the axis preceding this construct. So, for example, `child::` defines the child axis, and `attribute::` defines the attribute axis. If you specify no selection axis, `child::` is the implicit selection axis. So, `/` and `/child::` are equivalent constructs. Also, the `@` syntax is shorthand for the `attribute::` syntax. Evaluating this expression selects the `level` attribute of the second `article` element, in document order.

- `//article[ancestor::journal[@title='Java Technology']]` is an XPath expression that evaluates to a node set containing elements named `article`, with an ancestor element named `journal`, whereby the element named `journal` has an attribute named `title` with a value equal to `Java Technology`. The syntax construct `//` is shorthand for all descendant nodes; since it is at the beginning of the expression, it implies all the descendants of the root node. Evaluating this expression selects the second and third `article` elements, in document order.

Now that you have looked at some examples from an intuitive standpoint, we'll try to broaden your understanding of XPath syntax. Like expressions in most languages, you can compose complex XPath expressions by additively or multiplicatively combining basic expressions. Therefore, the key to understanding XPath expressions is to master the basic expressions and various datatypes that may result from evaluating an XPath expression. With that as your immediate goal, you will focus on two topics:

- XPath expression evaluation datatypes
- A basic expression construct called the *location path*

Datatypes

An XPath expression evaluation results in one of the following datatypes:

- A `boolean` value of `true` or `false`
- A `number` value (a floating-point number, as defined by the Institute of Electrical and Electronics Engineers[8] [IEEE])
- A `string` value
- A `node-set` (a set of document nodes of any type)

Location Path

Now we'll cover the syntax associated with the location path construct. A location path can be absolute, in which case it begins with a slash (/), or it can be relative, in which case it does not begin with a slash. A location path can consist of zero or more location path steps, with a slash separating adjacent steps.

Each location path step starts with an axis specifier, followed by a node test, and optionally followed by zero or more predicates:

```
Step ::= AxisSpecifier NodeTest Predicate*
```

The location path step components are as follows:

---

8. See http://www.ieee.org/portal/site.

- An *axis specifier* is basically a logical route (axis) along which you can move from the context node to find the next node set (the context node is the node where you start from).

- A *node test* is a filter that constrains the selected node set based on either a node type or a node name.

- A *predicate* is a filter that constrains the selected node set based on an XPath expression.

We will cover each of these components in more detail in the following sections. For example, the location path /child::catalog/child::journal/child::article[attribute::date= 'January-2004']/attribute::level has four steps. The first step is child::catalog, the second step is child::journal, the third step is child::article[attribute::date='January-2004'], and the fourth step is attribute::level. In the first two steps, child:: is the axis specifier, and catalog and journal are node tests. In the third step, child:: is the axis specifier, article is a node test, and [attribute::date='January-2004'] is a predicate. In the fourth step, attribute:: is the axis specifier, and level is a node test. The first, second, and fourth steps don't have any predicates.

Axis Specifier

As noted, the axis specifier specifies a logical axis along which you must move from the context node to find the next node set specified by a location path expression. An axis specifier axis is classified as a *forward axis* if by moving along it you encounter nodes that occur at or later than the context node, in document order; otherwise, an axis is classified as a *reverse axis*. In Figure 4-2, we have taken the basic XPath data model shown in Figure 4-1 and annotated it with a context node, axis labels, and associated node sets. For example, the parent:: axis label in Figure 4-2 points to its associated node set of the parent journal element. Of course, you always need to keep in mind the context node, whenever you interpret the node set for any axis value.

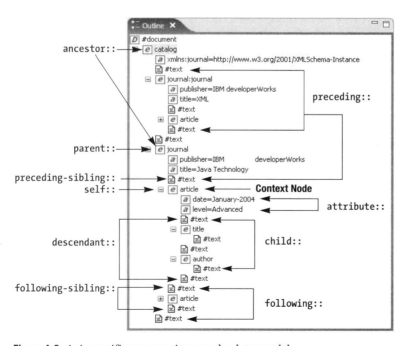

Figure 4-2. *Axis specifier annotations on the data model*

The following are possible axis specification values with examples based on the annotated data model shown in Figure 4-2:

- `self::` refers to the context node. For example, in Figure 4-2, `self::` refers to the `article` context node.

- `child::` refers to child nodes in document order. This axis applies only to element nodes. This axis is empty if the context node is an attribute, text, or namespace node. An element's attribute node is not a child node. This axis does not contain any attribute or namespace nodes. Figure 4-2 shows an example of the `child::` axis. If an axis specifier is omitted, this is the default value. This is a forward axis.

- `parent::` refers to the parent node when the context node is an element node or a text node, but it refers to the attaching element node when the context node is an attribute node. Figure 4-2 shows an example of the `parent::` axis, where the context node is an element node. If the context node were the `date` attribute of the current `article` context node, then the `parent::` axis would include only the current `article` context node. This is a reverse axis.

- `attribute::` refers to the attached attribute nodes. Figure 4-2 shows an example of the `attribute::` axis. This axis may be abbreviated with the @ character. In other words, `attribute::level` and `@level` are equivalent. This axis is empty if the context node is not an element node. This is a forward axis.

- `ancestor::` refers to all the nodes starting with the parent and continuing with the parent's parent, and so on, until it reaches the root node. If you follow this axis, you will not come across any parent siblings, attribute, or namespace nodes. Figure 4-2 shows an example of the `ancestor::` axis. This is a reverse axis.

- `descendant::` refers to all the nodes starting with all element child nodes and continuing with their descendants, in document order. This axis does not contain any attribute nodes or namespace nodes. This axis is empty if the context node is an attribute or namespace node. Figure 4-2 shows an example of the `descendant::` axis. This is a forward axis.

- `following::` refers to all the nodes that are after the context node, in document order, with the exception of those that occur along the `descendant::` axis. This axis does not contain any attribute or namespace nodes. Figure 4-2 shows an example of the `following::` axis. This is a forward axis.

- `preceding::` refers to all the nodes that are before the context node, in document order, with the exception of those that occur along the `ancestor::` axis. This axis does not contain any attribute or namespace nodes. Figure 4-2 shows an example of the `preceding::` axis. This is a reverse axis.

- `following-sibling::` refers to all the `following::` nodes that are siblings of the context node, in document order. This axis does not contain any attribute or namespace nodes. This axis is empty if the context node is an attribute or namespace node. Figure 4-2 shows an example of the `following-sibling::` axis. This is a forward axis.

- `preceding-sibling::` refers to all the `preceding::` nodes that are siblings of the context node, in reverse document order. This axis does not contain any attribute or namespace nodes. This axis is empty if the context node is an attribute or namespace node. Figure 4-2 shows an example of the `preceding-sibling::` axis. This is a reverse axis.

- `ancestor-or-self::` refers to all the nodes, including the current node and continuing with its ancestors, in reverse document order. Figure 4-2 shows an example of the `ancestor::` and `self::` nodes, and together they form the `ancestor-or-self::` axis. This is a reverse axis.

- `descendant-or-self::` refers to all the nodes, including the current node and continuing with its descendants, in document order. Figure 4-2 shows an example of the `descendant::` and `self::` nodes, and together they form the `descendant-or-self::` axis. This is a forward axis.

- `namespace::` refers to all the attached namespace nodes. This axis is empty if the context node is not an element node. For example, in Figure 4-2, if you assume that the context node is the root catalog element, then its `xmlns:journal` namespace attribute is along the `namespace::` axis. This is a forward axis.

Node Test

In a location path step, as you move along a specified axis, you will encounter nodes of different types with varying names. These nodes comprise a node set. To this base node set, you can apply a node test filter that can filter nodes based on node type or node name.

Node Type Tests

Node tests based on the node type are as follows:

- `node()` is a node test that refers to a node of any type. For example, the expression `child::node()` selects all the child nodes of the context node. As noted earlier, the attributes of an element node are not part of its child nodes.

- The axis and node test combination `self::node()` may be abbreviated with the "`.`" character. For example, the expression `./child::node()` selects all the child nodes of the context node.

- The axis and node test combination of `parent::node()` may be abbreviated as the `..` character sequence. For example, the expression `../child::node()` selects all child nodes of the parent of the context node, which may or may not include the context node. (Can you see why? Hint: The context node may be an attribute node.)

- The axis and node test combination of `/descendant-or-self::node()/` may be abbreviated as the `//` character sequence. For example, the expression `//` at the start of an XPath expression selects all the nonattribute and non-namespace nodes within a document.

- `text()` is a node test that refers to a node of type Text. For example, `descendant::text()` will evaluate to all descendant nodes of the context node that are of type Text.

- `comment()` is a node test that refers to a node of type Comment. For example, `preceding::comment()` will evaluate to all preceding nodes of the context node that are of type Comment.

- `processing-instruction()` is a node test that refers to the node of type ProcessingInstruction. For example, `following::processing-instruction()` will evaluate to all the following nodes of the context node that are of type `processing-instruction`.

Node Name Tests

A name-based node test with no namespace prefix refers to the following:

- A namespace node, if the specified axis is a namespace axis. For example, in Figure 4-2, if you assume the context node is the catalog element, then `namespace::journal` selects the `xmlns:journal` namespace node in the catalog root element.

- It refers to an attribute node that is not in any namespace (including not in the default namespace) if the specified axis is an attribute axis. For example, in Figure 4-2, `attribute::date` selects the date attribute of the article context node.

- For all other specified axes, it refers to an element node that is not in any namespace (including not in the default namespace). For example, in Figure 4-2, `following-sibling::article` selects the third `article` node, in document order.

A name-based node with a `namespace` prefix refers to the following:

- An empty set, if the specified axis is a namespace axis. For example, in Figure 4-2, if you assume the context node is the `catalog` element, then `namespace::xmlns:journal` is an empty set.

- It refers to an attribute node in the associated namespace, if the specified axis is an attribute axis. For example, in Listing 4-1, `//attribute::journal:level` selects the `level` attribute of the first `article` node, in document order.

- For all other specified axes, it refers to an element node in the associated namespace. For example, in Figure 4-2, the `preceding::journal:journal` element selects the first `journal` element, in document order.

- A node name test with * refers to an unrestricted wildcard for element nodes. For example, in Figure 4-2, `child::*` selects a node set containing all `child::` axis elements. This implies that `child::*` and `child::node()` do not have the same semantics, because the former is restricted to the `child::` axis element nodes and the later selects the `child::` axis nodes of any node type.

- A node test with the `prefix:*` name refers to a namespace-restricted wildcard for element nodes. For example, `/catalog/child::journal:*` evaluates to a node set containing all elements that are children of the `catalog` element and that belong to the `journal:` namespace, which is just the first `journal` element within the document, in document order.

Predicates

The last piece in a location path step is zero or more optional predicates. The following are the two keys to understanding predicates:

- Predicates are filters on a node set.
- Predicates are XPath expressions that are evaluated and mapped to a Boolean value through the use of a core XPath `boolean()` function, as described here:

  - A number value is mapped to `true` if and only if it is a nonzero number. For example, in Figure 4-2, the expression `//title[position()]` uses the built-in XPath `position()` function that returns the child position of the selected `title` node as a number. Since the child position of a node is always 1 or greater, this expression will select all the `title` nodes. However, the expression `//title[position() - 1]` will select only those `title` nodes that occur at a child position greater than 1. In the example, the second expression will not select any nodes since all the `title` nodes are at child position 1.

  - A string value is mapped to `true` if and only if it is a nonzero length string. For example, in Figure 4-2, the expression `//title[string()]` uses the built-in XPath `string()` function to implicitly convert the first node in a node set to its string node value. This expression will select only those title nodes that have nonzero-length text content, which for the example document means all the `title` nodes.

  - A node set is mapped to `true` if and only if it is nonempty. For example, in Figure 4-2, in the expression `//article[child::title]`, the `[child::title]` predicate evaluates to `true` only when the `child::title` node set is nonempty, so the expression selects all the `article` elements that have `title` child elements.

The output node set of a component to the left of a predicate is its input node set, and evaluating a predicate involves iterating over this input node set. As the evaluation proceeds, the current node in the iteration becomes the context node, and a predicate is evaluated with respect to this context node. If a predicate evaluates to true, this context node is added to a predicate's output node set; otherwise, it is ignored. The output node set from a predicate becomes the input node set for subsequent predicates. Multiple predicates within a location path step are evaluated from left to right.

Predicates within a location path step are evaluated with respect to the axis associated with the current step. The proximity position of a context node is defined as its position along the step axis, in document order if it is a forward axis or in reverse document order if it is a reverse axis. The proximity position of a node is defined as its context position. The size of an input node set is defined as the context size. Context node, context position, and context size comprise the total XPath context, relative to which all predicates are evaluated.

You can apply some of the concepts associated with predicates when looking at the following examples, which are based on the data model in Figure 4-2:

- /catalog/child::journal[attribute::title='Java Technology'] is an XPath expression in which the second step contains the predicate [attribute::title='Java Technology']. The input node set for this predicate consists of all non-namespace journal elements that are children of the catalog element. The input node set consists of only the second journal element, in document order, because the first journal element is part of the journal namespace. So, at the start of first iteration, the context size is 1, and the context position is also 1. As you iterate over the input node set, you make the current node, which is the journal node, the context node and then test the predicate. The predicate checks to see whether the context node has an attribute named title with a value equal to Java Technology. If the predicate test succeeds, which it should, you include this journal context node in the output set. After you iterate over all the nodes in the input set, the output node set will consist of all the journal elements that satisfy the predicate. The result of this expression will be just the second journal node in the document, in document order.

- /catalog/descendant::article[position() = 2] is an XPath expression in which the second step contains a predicate [position() = 2]. The input node set for this predicate consists of all the article elements that are descendants of the catalog element. This input node set will consist of all three article nodes in the document. So, at the start of first iteration, the context size is 3, and the context position is 1. This predicate example applies the concept of context position. As you iterate over the input node set, you make the current article element the context node and then test the predicate. The predicate checks to see whether the context position of the article element, as tested through the XPath core function position(), is equal to 2. When you apply this predicate to the data model in Figure 4-2, only the second article node that appears in expanded form will test as true. Note, the [position() = 2] predicate is equivalent to the abbreviated predicate [2].The result of this expression will be the second article node, in document order.

Having looked at XPath expressions in detail, you can now turn your attention to applying XPath expressions using the Java-based XPath APIs.

Applying XPath Expressions

Imagine a website that provides a service related to information about journal articles. Further imagine that this website receives journal content information from various publishers through some web service–based messages and that the content of these messages is an XML document that looks like the document shown earlier in Listing 4-1.

Once the web service receives this document, it needs to extract content information from this XML document, based on some criteria. Assume that you have been asked to build an application that extracts content information from this document based on some specific criteria. How would you go about it?

Your first step is to ensure the received document has a valid structure or, in other words, conforms to its schema definition. To ensure that, you will first validate the document with respect to its schema, as explained in Chapter 3.

Your next task is to devise a way for extracting relevant content information. Here, you have at two choices:

- You can retrieve document nodes using the DOM API
- You can retrieve document nodes using the XPath API.

So, this begs the obvious question, which is the better option?

Comparing the XPath API to the DOM API

Accessing element and attribute values in an XML document with an XPath expression is more efficient than using getter methods in the DOM API, because, with XPath expressions, you can select an Element node without programmatically iterating over a node list. To use the DOM API, you must first retrieve a node list with the DOM API getter method and then iterate over this node list to retrieve relevant element nodes.

These are the two major advantages of using the XPath API over the DOM API:

- You can select element nodes though an imperative XPath expression, and you do not need to iterate over a node list to select the relevant element node.
- With an XPath expression, you can select an Attr node directly, in contrast to DOM API getter methods, where an Element node needs to be accessed before an Attr node can be accessed.

As an illustration of the first advantage, you can retrieve the title element within the article context node in the example data model shown in Figure 4-2 with the XPath expression /catalog/journal/article[2]/title, and you can evaluate this XPath expression using the code shown in Listing 4-2, which results in retrieving the relevant title element. At this point, we don't expect you to understand the code in Listing 4-2. The sole purpose of showing this code now is to illustrate the comparative brevity of XPath API code, as compared to DOM API code.

Listing 4-2. *Addressing a Node with XPath*

```
Element article=(Element)(xPath.evaluate("/catalog/journal/article[2]/title",
inputSource,XPathConstants.NODE));
```

By way of contrast, if you need to retrieve the same title element with DOM API getter methods, you need to iterate over a node list, as shown in Listing 4-3.

Listing 4-3. *Retrieving a Node with the DOM*

```
NodeList nodeList=document.getElementsByTagName("journal");
Element journal=(Element)(nodeList.item(0));
NodeList nodeList2=journal.getElementsByTagName("article");
Element article=(Element)nodeList2.item(1);
```

As an illustration of the second advantage, you can retrieve the value of the level attribute for the article node with the date January-2004 directly with the XPath expression /catalog/journal/article[@date='January-2004']/@level, as shown in Listing 4-4.

Listing 4-4. *Retrieving an Attribute Node with XPath*

```
String level =
   xPath.evaluate("/catalog/journal/article[@date='January-2004']/@level",
   inputSource);
```

Suffice it to say that to achieve the same result with the DOM API, you would need to write code that is far more tedious than that shown in Listing 4-4. It would involve finding all the journal elements, finding all the article elements for each journal element, iterating over those article elements, and, retrieving the date attribute for each article element, checking to see whether the date attribute's value is January-2004, and if so, retrieving article element's level attribute.

The preceding discussion should not suggest that the DOM API is *never* useful for accessing content information. In fact, sometimes you will be interested in accessing all the nodes in a given element subtree. In such a situation, it makes perfect sense to access the relevant node through an XPath API and then access its node subtree using the DOM API.

Let's proceed with creating the XPath API–based application. To that end, you will need to first create and configure an Eclipse project.

Setting Up the Eclipse Project

Before you can build and run the code examples included in this chapter, you need an Eclipse project. The quickest way to create the Eclipse project is to download the Chapter4 project from Apress (http://www.apress.com) and import this project into Eclipse. This will create all the Java packages and files needed for this chapter automatically.

In this chapter, you will use two XPath APIs: the JAXP 1.3 XPath API included in J2SE 5.0 and the JDOM XPath API. To use J2SE 5.0's XPath API, install the J2SE 5.0[9] SDK, set its JRE system library as the JRE system library in your Eclipse project Java build path, and set the Java compiler to the J2SE 5.0 compiler under the Eclipse project's Java compiler. The Java build path in your Eclipse project should look like Figure 4-3.

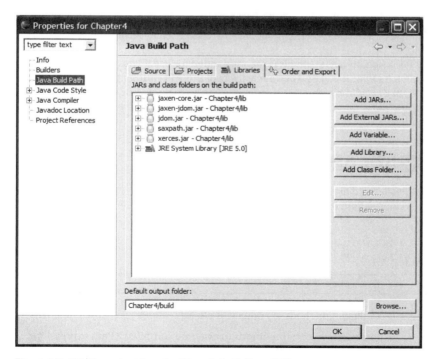

Figure 4-3. *XPath project Java build path in Eclipse IDE*

---

9. For more information about J2SE 5.0, see http://java.sun.com/j2se/1.5.0/.

The complete Eclipse project package structure should look like Figure 4-4.

Figure 4-4. *Eclipse project package structure*

Now, you are ready to proceed with the application. Since the example's goal is to impart comprehensive information about how to use the XPath APIs, we will use different XPath expressions in the sample application to illustrate various aspects of the XPath API. Overall, you will examine two specific XPath APIs:

- The first API is specified in JAXP 1.3 and is included in J2SE 5.0. It is the recommended API if you decide to base your application on the Java 5 platform. An obvious advantage of this approach is that it is completely standards based, and in our opinion, this should be the preferred approach.

- The second API is based on JDOM, and it is recommended for use if you are not yet ready to move to the J2SE 5.0 API or if you find certain aspects of this API simpler to use, compared to the J2SE 5.0 API. In our opinion, this API is simple to use and easy to understand. However, since it is currently not a standard, it may continue to change, which may affect the stability of your application.

JAXP 1.3 XPath API

The JAXP 1.3 XPath API is defined in the `javax.xml.xpath` package in J2SE 5.0. This package defines various interfaces to evaluate XPath expressions. Table 4-1 lists some of the relevant classes and interfaces in J2SE 5.0.

Table 4-1. *J2SE 5.0 XPath*

Class or Interface	Description
XPath (interface)	Provides access to the XPath evaluation environment and provides evaluate() methods to evaluate XPath expressions in an XML document
XPathExpression (interface)	Provides evaluate() methods to evaluate compiled XPath expressions in an XML document
XPathFactory (class)	Creates an XPath object

For this example, the example XML document shown in Listing 4-1 is evaluated with the `javax.xml.xpath.XPath` class, and relevant node sets are extracted with the XPath API. The `evaluate()` methods in XPath and the `XPathExpression` interfaces are used to access various document node sets, based on the relevant XPath expressions.

XPath expressions may be explicitly compiled before use, or they may be evaluated directly. The main advantage of explicitly compiling an XPath expression is to validate an expression for correctness, prior to evaluation, and to promote the reuse of an expression in multiple evaluations. Let's assume you are interested in learning about the explicit compilation of XPath expressions, so we will cover that next.

Explicitly Compiling an XPath Expression

Say you need an `XPath` object to compile an XPath expression. You can use the `XPathFactory` factory class to create XPath objects. To create an `XPath` object, first create an `XPathFactory` object with the static method `newInstance()` of the `XPathFactory` class, as shown in Listing 4-5. The `newInstance()` method uses the default object model, `DEFAULT_OBJECT_MODEL_URI`, which is based on the W3C DOM. If you're going to use an object model other than the default,[10] create an `XPathFactory` object with the `newInstance(String uri)` method. Using the specified or the default object model, create an `XPath` object from the `XPathFactory` object using the `newXPath()` method, as illustrated in Listing 4-5.

Listing 4-5. *Creating an XPath Object*

```
XPathFactory  factory=XPathFactory.newInstance();
XPath xPath=factory.newXPath();
```

Let's assume you are interested in compiling the XPath expression `/catalog/journal/article[@date='January-2004']/title`, which addresses `title` elements within all `article` elements with the `date` attribute set to `January-2004`. You can do so with the `compile()` method of the XPath object, as shown here:

```
XPathExpression  xPathExpression=
  xPath.compile("/catalog/journal/article[@date='January-2004']/title");
```

This `compile()` method returns an `XPathExpression` object. If the XPath expression has an error, an `XPathExpressionException` gets generated.

Evaluating a Compiled XPath Expression

The `XPathExpression` interface provides overloaded `evaluate()` methods to evaluate an XPath expression. Table 4-2 lists the `evaluate()` methods in the `XPathExpression` interface.

Two of the overloaded `evaluate()` methods take a `returnType` as a parameter. The return types are represented with `javax.xml.xpath.XPathConstants` class static fields. Table 4-3 lists the different return types supported by the `evaluate()` methods, and they provide the flexibility that is needed to convert the result of evaluating an expression to different return types. The default `returnType` is `javax.xml.xpath.XpathConstants.STRING`.

---

10. This feature essentially accommodates alternative document models. Currently, there is no compelling reason to use anything other than the DOM.

Table 4-2. *XPathExpression evaluate() Methods*

Evaluate Method	Description
evaluate(InputSource source)	Evaluates the compiled XPath expression in the context of the specified InputSource and returns a string. The default return type, XPathConstants.STRING, is used for evaluating the XPath expression.
evaluate(InputSource source, QName returnType)	Evaluates the compiled XPath expression in the context of the specified InputSource and returns a value of the specified return type.
evaluate(Object item)	Evaluates the compiled XPath expression in the specified context, which may be a Node or a NodeList. Returns a string.
evaluate(Object item, QName returnType)	Evaluates a compiled XPath expression in the specified context and returns a value of the specified return type.

Table 4-3. *XPath Return Types*

Return Type	Description
javax.xml.xpath.XpathConstants.BOOLEAN	XPath 1.0 boolean datatype
javax.xml.xpath.XpathConstants.NODESET	XPath 1.0 NodeSet datatype
javax.xml.xpath.XpathConstants.NODE	XPath 1.0 Node datatype
javax.xml.xpath.XpathConstants.STRING	XPath 1.0 string datatype
javax.xml.xpath.XpathConstants.NUMBER	XPath 1.0 number datatype

The evaluate() methods of the XPathExpression interface evaluate in the context of either an InputSource or a java.lang.Object that represents a DOM structure, such as an org.w3c.dom.Node object. For the sample application, you will evaluate an XPath expression in the context of an InputSource based on the XML document, as shown in Listing 4-6. In this code listing, xmlDocument is a java.io.File object that is associated with catalog.xml.

Listing 4-6. *Creating an InputSource Object*

```
File xmlDocument = new File("catalog.xml");
InputSource inputSource = new InputSource(newFileInputStream(xmlDocument));
```

Once you create an InputSource object, you can evaluate the XPath expression in the context of this InputSource object, as shown here:

```
String title =xPathExpression.evaluate(inputSource);
```

A new InputSource object is required after each invocation of evaluate() with an InputSource object. The result of evaluating the compiled /catalog/journal/article[@date='January-2004']/title XPath expression is the title: Design service-oriented architecture frameworks with J2EE technology.

Evaluating an XPath Expression Directly

As noted earlier, XPath expressions can be directly evaluated in the context of a DOM object or an InputSource object, without any compilation. The XPath interface provides overloaded evaluate() methods to evaluate an XPath expression directly. Table 4-4 lists the XPath interface evaluate() methods.

Table 4-4. *XPath Interface evaluate() Methods*

Evaluate Method	Description
evaluate(String expression,InputSource source)	Evaluates the specified XPath expression in the context of the specified InputSource and returns a string. The default return type, XPathConstants.STRING, is used for evaluating the XPath expression.
evaluate(String expression, InputSource source, QName returnType)	Evaluates the specified XPath expression in the context of the specified InputSource and returns a value of the specified return type.
evaluate(String expression, Object item)	Evaluates the specified XPath expression in the specified context, which may be a Node or a NodeList. Returns a string.
evaluate(String expression, Object item, Name returnType)	Evaluates a specified XPath expression in the specified context and returns a value of the specified return type.

The returnType values are the same as for the XPathExpression interface evaluate() methods and are listed in Table 4-3.

Assume you want to find the publishers for all the journals in your XML document. The XPath expression for addressing the node set for all publisher attributes attached to journal elements that are not in any namespace would be /catalog/journal/@publisher. You can directly evaluate this expression, without compilation, as shown here:

```
inputSource = new InputSource(new FileInputStream(xmlDocument)));
String publisher = xPath.evaluate("/catalog/journal/@publisher",inputSource);
```

The result of this XPath evaluation is the attribute value IBM developerWorks.

You can also use the evaluate() methods in the XPath class to evaluate a node set. Say you want to evaluate the XPath expression //title that selects all the title elements. To select the node set of the title element nodes in the example XML document, you need to create an XPath expression that selects the title node and invoke the evaluate() method that takes an XPath expression, a org.w3c.dom.Document object, and a returnType as parameters, as shown in Listing 4-7.

Listing 4-7. *Retrieving a NodeSet*

```
DocumentBuilder builder = DocumentBuilderFactory.newInstance().newDocumentBuilder();
Document document = builder.parse(xmlDocument);
String expression="//title";
NodeList nodes = (NodeList)xPath.evaluate(expression, document,
XPathConstants.NODESET);
```

XPathConstants.NODESET specifies the return type of a evaluate() method as a NodeSet. Because the NodeSet class implements the NodeList interface, you can cast the NodeSet object to NodeList.

Evaluating Namespace Nodes

With J2SE 5.0, you can also access namespace nodes with XPath. You can use the NamespaceContext interface for namespace context processing. To access namespace-based nodes within your application, you create an implementation class for the NamespaceContext interface. Listing 4-8 shows an example of a NamespaceContext interface implementation class with one prefix corresponding to a namespace URI. Add the NamespaceContextImpl class as an inner class in the XPathEvaluator.java class, as shown in Listing 4-10. For example, if you want to select the first journal node within the example document that is part of a namespace, you need a NamespaceContextImpl class.

Listing 4-8. *NamespaceContextImpl.java*

```java
/**
 * This is a private class for NamespaceContext
 */
private class NamespaceContextImpl implements NamespaceContext {
  public String uri;

  public String prefix;

  public NamespaceContextImpl() {
  }

  /**
   * Constructor
   * @param prefix namespace prefix
   * @param uri namespace uri
   */
  public NamespaceContextImpl(String prefix, String uri) {
    this.uri = uri;
    this.prefix = prefix;
  }

  /**
   * @param prefix namespace prefix
   * @return namespace URI
   */
  public String getNamespaceURI(String prefix) {
    return uri;
  }

  /**
   * set uri
   * @param uri namespace uri
   */
  public void setNamespaceURI(String uri) {
    this.uri = uri;
  }
```

```
/**
 * @param uri namespace uri
 * @return namespace prefix
 */
public String getPrefix(String uri) {
  return prefix;
}

/**
 * set prefix
 * @param prefix namespace prefix
 */
public void setPrefix(String prefix) {
  this.prefix = prefix;
}

/**
 * One uri may have multiple prefixes.
 * We will allow only one prefix per uri.
 * @return an iterator for all prefixes for a uri
 */
public java.util.Iterator getPrefixes(String uri) {
  if (uri == null) {
    throw new IllegalArgumentException();
  }
  java.util.ArrayList<String> li = new java.util.ArrayList<String>();
  if (this.uri == uri) {
    li.add(prefix);
  }
  return li.iterator();
}
}
```

To access namespace nodes, you need to create an instance of the NamespaceContextImpl class and set the NamespaceContext on an XPath object. To evaluate a node in the example XML document with the journal prefix in the location path, you need to create a NamespaceContextImpl object with the journal prefix and set this NamespaceContext object on the XPath object, as shown in Listing 4-9.

Listing 4-9. *Setting the Namespace Context*

```
NamespaceContext namespaceContext=new NamespaceContextImpl("journal",
"http://www.apress.com/catalog/journal");
xpath.setNamespaceContext(namespaceContext);
```

To illustrate an XPath expression evaluation with a namespace prefix, create an InputSource object, and evaluate the XPath expression /catalog/journal:journal/article/title, as shown here:

```
InputSource inputSource = new InputSource(new FileInputStream(xmlDocument));
String  title = xPath.evaluate("/catalog/journal:journal/article/title",
    inputSource);
```

The value of this title node is output to the system console as Design XML Schemas Using UML.

JAXP 1.3 XPath Example Application

This application illustrates how to use different facets of the JAXP 1.3 XPath API. In this application, you will evaluate the XPath expressions we have already discussed individually in the code snippets preceding this section.

The XPathEvaluator class, shown in Listing 4-10, implements a complete application. The key method in this application class is evaluateDocument(), which combines all the code snippets we have already discussed in detail. The main method in XPathEvaluator creates an XPathEvaluator instance and uses the the evaluateDocument() method to evaluate various XPath expressions that address node sets in catalog.xml, as shown here:

```
XPathEvaluator evaluator = new XPathEvaluator();
// create a File object based on catalog.xml
File xmlDocument = new File("catalog.xml");
evaluator.evaluateDocument(xmlDocument);
```

As the various node sets are retrieved, they are printed to the system console. Listing 4-11 shows the output from the XPathEvaluator.java application in the Eclipse IDE.

Listing 4-10. *XPathEvaluator.java*

```java
package com.apress.jdk5xpath;

import javax.xml.xpath.*;
import java.io.*;
import org.w3c.dom.*;
import javax.xml.parsers.*;
import org.xml.sax.*;
import javax.xml.namespace.NamespaceContext;

/**
 * This class illustrates executing
 * different types of XPath expressions, using JAXP 1.3
 * XPath API.
 */
public class XPathEvaluator {

  public void evaluateDocument(File xmlDocument) {

    try {
      XPathFactory factory = XPathFactory.newInstance();
      XPath xPath = factory.newXPath();

      // create input source for XML document
      InputSource inputSource = new InputSource(new FileInputStream(
          xmlDocument));

      // Find the title of the first article dated January-2004,
      // but first compile the xpath expression
      XPathExpression xPathExpression = xPath
        .compile("/catalog/journal/article[@date='January-2004']/title");
      // This returns the title value
      String title = xPathExpression.evaluate(inputSource);
      // Print title
      System.out.println("Title: " + title);
```

```
   // create input source for XML document
   inputSource = new InputSource(new FileInputStream(xmlDocument));
   // Find publisher of first journal that is not in any namespace.
   // This time we are not compiling the XPath expression.
   // Return the publisher value as a string.
   String publisher = xPath.evaluate("/catalog/journal/@publisher",
       inputSource);
   // Print publisher
   System.out.println("Publisher:" + publisher);

   // Find all titles
   String expression = "//title";
   // Reset XPath to its original configuration
   xPath.reset();
   DocumentBuilder builder = DocumentBuilderFactory.newInstance()
       .newDocumentBuilder();
   Document document = builder.parse(xmlDocument);
   // Evaluate xpath expression on a document object and
   // result as a node list.
   NodeList nodeList = (NodeList) xPath.evaluate(expression, document,
       XPathConstants.NODESET);

   // Iterate over node list and print titles
   for (int i = 0; i < nodeList.getLength(); i++) {
     Element element = (Element) nodeList.item(i);
     System.out.println(element.getFirstChild().getNodeValue());

   }

   // This is an example of using NamespaceContext
   NamespaceContext namespaceContext = new NamespaceContextImpl(
       "journal", "http://www.apress.com/catalog/journal");
   xPath.setNamespaceContext(namespaceContext);
   // Create an input source
   inputSource = new InputSource(new FileInputStream(xmlDocument));
   // Find title of first article in first
   // journal, in journal namespace
   title = xPath
       .evaluate("/catalog/journal:journal/article/title",
           inputSource);
   System.out.println("Title:" + title);

 } catch (IOException e) {
   System.out.println(e.getMessage());
 } catch (XPathExpressionException e) {
   System.out.println(e.getMessage());
 } catch (ParserConfigurationException e) {
   System.out.println(e.getMessage());
 } catch (SAXException e) {
   System.out.println(e.getMessage());
 }

}
```

```java
    public static void main(String[] argv) {

      XPathEvaluator evaluator = new XPathEvaluator();

      File xmlDocument = new File("catalog.xml");
      evaluator.evaluateDocument(xmlDocument);
    }

    /**
     * This is a private class for NamespaceContext
     */
    private class NamespaceContextImpl implements NamespaceContext {
      public String uri;

      public String prefix;

      public NamespaceContextImpl() {
      }

      /**
       * Constructor
       * @param prefix namespace prefix
       * @param uri namespace uri
       */
      public NamespaceContextImpl(String prefix, String uri) {
        this.uri = uri;
        this.prefix = prefix;
      }

      /**
       * @param prefix namespace prefix
       * @return namespace URI
       */
      public String getNamespaceURI(String prefix) {
        return uri;
      }

      /**
       * set uri
       * @param uri namespace uri
       */
      public void setNamespaceURI(String uri) {
        this.uri = uri;
      }

      /**
       * @param uri namespace uri
       * @return namespace prefix
       */
      public String getPrefix(String uri) {
        return prefix;
      }
```

```
/**
 * set prefix
 * @param prefix namespace prefix
 */
public void setPrefix(String prefix) {
  this.prefix = prefix;
}

/**
 * One uri may have multiple prefixes.
 * We will allow only one prefix per uri.
 * @return an iterator for all prefixes for a uri
 */
public java.util.Iterator getPrefixes(String uri) {
  if (uri == null) {
    throw new IllegalArgumentException();
  }
  java.util.ArrayList<String> li = new java.util.ArrayList<String>();
  if (this.uri == uri) {
    li.add(prefix);
  }
  return li.iterator();
}
}

}
```

Listing 4-11. *XPathEvaluator.java*

```
Title: Design service-oriented architecture
             frameworks with J2EE technology
Publisher:IBM developerWorks
Design XML Schemas Using UML
Design service-oriented architecture
             frameworks with J2EE technology
Advance DAO Programming
Title:Design XML Schemas Using UML
```

JDOM XPath API

The JDOM API org.jdom.xpath.XPath class supports XPath expressions to select nodes from an XML document. The JDOM XPath class is easier to use if you are going to select namespace nodes. Table 4-5 lists some of the methods in the JDOM XPath class.

In this section, you'll see how to select nodes from the example XML document in Listing 4-1 using the JDOM XPath class. Because the XPath class is in the org.jdom.xpath package, you need to import this package.

Table 4-5. *JDOM XPath Class Methods*

XPath **Class Method**	**Description**
selectSingleNode(java.lang.Object context)	Selects a single node that matches a wrapped XPath expression in the context of the specified node. If more than one node matches the XPath expression, the first node is returned.
selectSingleNode(java.lang.Object context, java.lang.String xPathExpression)	Selects a single node that matches the specified XPath expression in the context of the specified node. If more than one node matches the XPath expression, the first node is returned.
selectNodes(java.lang.Object context)	Selects nodes that match a wrapped XPath expression in the context of the specified node.
selectNodes(java.lang.Object context, java.lang.String xPathExpression)	Selects nodes that match the specified XPath expression in the context of the specified node.
addNamespace(java.lang.String prefix, java.lang.String uri)	Adds a namespace to navigate namespace nodes.

You need a context node to address an XML document with XPath. Therefore, create a SAXBuilder, and parse the XML document catalog.xml with SAXBuilder. SAXBuilder has the overloaded build() method, which takes a File, InputStream, InputSource, Reader, URL, or system ID string object as input for parsing an XML document:

```
SAXBuilder saxBuilder = new SAXBuilder("org.apache.xerces.parsers.SAXParser");
org.jdom.Document jdomDocument =saxBuilder.build(xmlDocument);
```

xmlDocument is the java.io.File representation of the XML document catalog.xml. The static method selectSingleNode(java.lang.Object context, String XPathExpression) selects a single node specified by an XPath expression. If more than one node matches the XPath expression, the first node that matches the XPath expression gets selected. As an example, select the attribute node level of the element article in a journal with the title set to Java Technology and with the article attribute date set to January-2004, with an appropriate XPath expression, as shown in Listing 4-12.

Listing 4-12. Selecting an Attribute Node

```
org.jdom.Attribute levelNode =
    (org.jdom.Attribute)(XPath.selectSingleNode(
        jdomDocument,
        "/catalog//journal[@title='JavaTechnology']" +
        "//article[@date='January-2004']/@level"));
```

The level attribute value Advanced gets selected.

You can also use the selectSingleNode(java.lang.Object context, String XPathExpression) method to select an element node within an XML document. As an example, select the title node for article with date January-2004 and with the XPath expression /catalog//journal//article[@date='January-2004']/title, as shown in Listing 4-13.

Listing 4-13. *Selecting an Element Node with the selectSingleNode() Method*

```
org.jdom.Element titleNode =
    (org.jdom.Element) XPath.selectSingleNode( jdomDocument,
  "/catalog//journal//article[@date='January-2004']/title");
```

The title node with the value Design service-oriented architecture frameworks with J2EE technology gets selected.

The static method selectNodes(java.lang.Object context, String XPathExpression) selects all the nodes specified by an XPath expression. As an example, you can select all the title nodes for non-namespace journal elements with a title attribute set to Java Technology, as shown in Listing 4-14.

Listing 4-14. *Selecting Element Nodes with the selectNodes() Method*

```
java.util.List nodeList =
    XPath.selectNodes(jdomDocument,
      "/catalog//journal[@title='Java Technology']//article/title");
```

You can iterate over the node list obtained in Listing 4-14 to output values for the title elements. This will output the title element values Design service-oriented architecture frameworks with J2EE technology and Advance DAO Programming:

```
Iterator iter = nodeList.iterator();
  while (iter.hasNext()) {
    org.jdom.Element element = (org.jdom.Element) iter.next();
    System.out.println(element.getText());
}
```

The JDOM XPath class supports the selection of nodes with namespace prefixes. To select a node with a namespace prefix, create an XPath wrapper object from an XPath expression, which has a namespace prefix node, and add a namespace to the XPath object. For example, create an XPath wrapper object with a namespace prefix expression of /catalog/journal:journal/article/@journal:level. The XPath wrapper object is created with the static method newInstance(java.lang.String path), which also compiles an XPath expression. You can add a namespace to the wrapper XPath object using the addNamespace(String prefix, String uri) method, as shown in Listing 4-15.

Listing 4-15. *Adding Namespace to an XPath Object*

```
XPath xpath = XPath.newInstance( "/catalog/journal:journal/article/@journal:level");
xpath.addNamespace("journal", "http://www.apress.com/catalog/journal ");
```

In Listing 4-15, the XPath expression, which includes a namespace prefix node, gets compiled, and a namespace with the prefix journal gets added to the XPath object. With the jdomDocument node as the context node, select the node specified in the XPath expression with the selectSingleNode(java.lang.Object context) method, as shown here:

```
org.jdom.Attribute namespaceNode =
  (org.jdom.Attribute) xpath.selectSingleNode(jdomDocument);
```

The attribute node journal:level gets selected. You can output the value of the selected namespace node. If you do so, the Intermediate value gets output.

JDOM XPath Example Application

Now let's look at a complete application where you combine all the JDOM XPath code snippets you
have examined so far into a single application. The JDomXPath class, shown in Listing 4-16, implements this complete application. We've already discussed all the code in the JDomXPath class's
parseDocument() method in detail. The main() method in the JDomXPath class creates an JDomXPath
instance and uses the parseDocument() method to evaluate various XPath expressions that address
node sets in catalog.xml, as shown here:

```
JDomXPath parser = new JDomXPath();
parser.parseDocument(new File("catalog.xml"));
```

As the various node sets are retrieved, they are printed to the system console. Listing 4-17 shows
the output from running the JDomXPath.java application in the Eclipse IDE.

Listing 4-16. *JDomXPath.java*

```java
package com.apress.jdomxpath;

import java.io.*;
import org.jdom.*;
import org.jdom.xpath.XPath;
import org.jdom.input.*;
import java.util.Iterator;

/**
 * This class illustrates executing different types of XPath expressions,
 * using JDOM 1.0 XPath API.
 */
public class JDomXPath {

  public void parseDocument(File xmlDocument) {

    try {

        // Create a SAXBuilder parser
        SAXBuilder saxBuilder = new SAXBuilder(
            "org.apache.xerces.parsers.SAXParser");
        // Create a JDOM document object
        org.jdom.Document jdomDocument = saxBuilder.build(xmlDocument);

        // select level attribute in first article dated January 2004
        // in first journal
        org.jdom.Attribute levelNode = (org.jdom.Attribute) (XPath
          .selectSingleNode(jdomDocument,
            "/catalog//journal//article[@date='January-2004']/@level"));

        System.out.println(levelNode.getValue());

        // select title attribute in first article dated January 2004
        // in first journal
        org.jdom.Element titleNode = (org.jdom.Element) XPath
          .selectSingleNode(jdomDocument,
            "/catalog//journal//article[@date='January-2004']/title");
```

```java
      System.out.println(titleNode.getText());

      // select title of all articles
      // in journal dated Java Technology
      java.util.List nodeList = XPath.selectNodes(jdomDocument,
          "/catalog/journal[@title='Java Technology']/article/title");

      Iterator iter = nodeList.iterator();

      while (iter.hasNext()) {
        org.jdom.Element element = (org.jdom.Element) iter.next();
        System.out.println(element.getText());

      }

      // Example of a xpath expression using namespace
      // Select level attribute in journal namespace
      // in first article in first journal in journal namespace
      XPath xpath = XPath
        .newInstance("/catalog/journal:journal/article/@journal:level");
      xpath.addNamespace("journal",
          "http://www.apress.com/catalog/journal");

      org.jdom.Attribute namespaceNode = (org.jdom.Attribute) xpath
          .selectSingleNode(jdomDocument);

      System.out.println(namespaceNode.getValue());

    } catch (IOException e) {
      e.printStackTrace();
    }

    catch (JDOMException e) {
      e.printStackTrace();
    }

  }

  public static void main(String[] argv) {
    JDomXPath parser = new JDomXPath();
    parser.parseDocument(new File("catalog.xml"));
  }

}
```

Listing 4-17. *Output from* `JDomXPath.java`

```
Advanced
Design service-oriented architecture
              frameworks with J2EE technology
Design service-oriented architecture
              frameworks with J2EE technology
Advance DAO Programming
Intermediate
```

Summary

The XPath language is key to addressing parts of an XML document using imperative expressions. XPath is a fundamental technology that is used in a number of other XML technologies that we will cover later in this book. Examples of technologies that use XPath include XSL Transformations (XSLT) and Java Architecture for XML Binding (JAXB), both covered in this book.

In this chapter, we covered the JAXP 1.3 XPath and JDOM XPath APIs. The JAXP 1.3 XPath API, by virtue of the fact that it is completely standards based, should be the preferred approach. However, the JDOM API is simpler to use and may eventually become part of a standard, so it's worth investigating.

CHAPTER 5

■■■

Transforming with XSLT

XSL Transformations (XSLT)[1] is part of the Extensible Stylesheet Language (XSL)[2] family of W3C Recommendations. The XSL family includes the following specifications:

- The XPath specification defines syntactic constructs for addressing various node sets within an XML document.

- The XSL Formatting Objects (XSL-FO) specification defines an XML vocabulary for expressing formatting semantics.

- The XSLT specification specifies a language for transforming XML documents into other XML documents.[3]

The original use case that prompted XSLT was this: transform a given XML document into a related XML document that specifies formatting semantics in the XSL-FO vocabulary. Even though XSLT was originally developed to address this specific use case, XSLT was also designed for transformations that have nothing to do with XSL-FO. In fact, because XSL-FO is a topic unto itself that is beyond the scope of this book, in this chapter we will focus only on XSLT transformations that are independent of XSL-FO.

XSLT language constructs are completely based on XML. Therefore, transformations written in XSLT exist as well-formed XML documents. An XML document containing XSLT transformations is commonly referred to as a *style sheet*. This is because the original use case that prompted XSLT was related to the formatting of XML documents.

An XSLT style sheet merely *specifies* a set of transformations. Therefore, you need an XSLT processor to *apply* these transformations to a given XML document. An XSLT processor takes an XML document and an XSLT style sheet as inputs, and it transforms the given XML document to its target output, according to transformations specified in the style sheet. The target output of XSLT transformations is typically an XML document but could be an HTML document or any type of text document. Two commonly used XSLT processors are Xalan-Java[4] and Saxon.[5] To use an XSLT processor, you need a set of Java APIs, and TrAX[6] is precisely such an API set. In the following sections, we will first provide an overview of XSLT and then cover TrAX.

---

1. The XSLT specification is available at http://www.w3.org/TR/xslt.
2. The XSL family of recommendations is available at http://www.w3.org/Style/XSL/.
3. As you will learn in this chapter, XSLT is applicable beyond this original specification goal.
4. Xalan-Java information is available at http://xml.apache.org/xalan-j/.
5. Saxon information is available at http://saxon.sourceforge.net/.
6. The TrAX API is part of JAXP 1.3; it has been part of JAXP since version 1.1.

Overview of XSLT

Before you look at the XSLT language syntax and semantics in detail, you will first see a simple example so you can develop an intuitive understanding of XSLT transformations.

Simple Example

Assume you have an XML document that describes a catalog of journals, as shown in Listing 5-1.

Listing 5-1. *Example Source Document*

```
<catalog>
  <journal title="XML Journal" />
  <journal title="Java Developer Journal" />
</catalog>
```

This XML document is the source document, and Figure 5-1 shows the corresponding source tree.

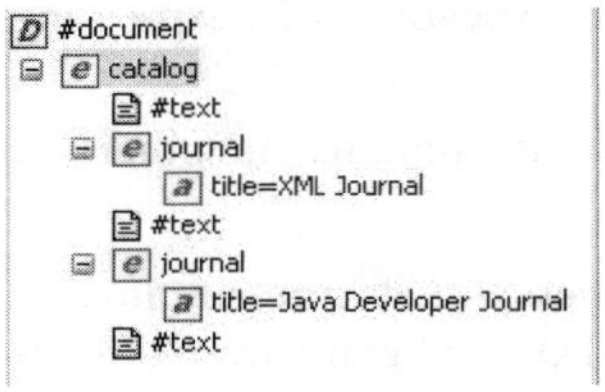

Figure 5-1. *Example source tree*

Now, further assume you want to transform this catalog document into an HTML document that displays all the magazine titles, or *journals*, in a table, as shown in Listing 5-2.

Listing 5-2. *Example Result Document*

```
<html>
  <body>
    <table>
      <tr><th>Titles</th></tr>
      <tr><td>XML Journal</td></tr>
      <tr><td>Java Developer Journal</td></tr>
    </table>
  </body>
</html>
```

This HTML document is the result document, and Figure 5-2 shows the corresponding result tree.

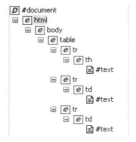

Figure 5-2. *Example result tree*

Having looked at what you want to do, the obvious question is, what XSLT style sheet will transform the source tree in Figure 5-1 to the result tree in Figure 5-2? Listing 5-3 shows one possible XSLT style sheet that will accomplish this transformation.

Listing 5-3. *Example XSLT Style Sheet*

```
<?xml version='1.0'  encoding='UTF-8' ?>
<xsl:stylesheet version="1.0"
  xmlns:xsl="http://www.w3.org/1999/XSL/Transform" >
  <xsl:output encoding="UTF-8"  method="xml"  omit-xml-declaration="yes" />
  <xsl:template match="/" >
    <html>
      <body>
        <table>
          <tr><th>Titles</th></tr>
          <xsl:for-each select="catalog/journal" >
            <tr><td>
              <xsl:apply-templates select="." ></xsl:apply-templates>
            </td></tr>
          </xsl:for-each>
        </table>
      </body>
    </html>
  </xsl:template>

  <xsl:template match="journal" >
    <xsl:value-of select="@title" />
  </xsl:template>

</xsl:stylesheet>
```

If you now examine the style sheet in Listing 5-3 from an intuitive standpoint, you may notice the following interesting facts:

- This style sheet is a well-formed XML document.

- Elements with the xsl prefix belong to the http://www.w3.org/1999/XSL/Transform namespace and are part of the XSLT language instruction set (well, you may not know that for a fact, but you may suspect that).

- Elements without the xsl prefix, such as the table element, are copied unchanged from the source tree to the result tree.

- The output method is specified as xml, but the result document is instructed not to have any xml declaration: you may intuitively infer that the `<xsl:output encoding="UTF-8" method="xml" omit-xml-declaration="yes" />` instruction in the XSLT style sheet accomplishes these objectives.

- The `xsl:template` instructions in the style sheet contain an attribute named `match`, whose value is an XPath expression. The `xsl:apply-templates` instructions in the style sheet contain an attribute named `select`, whose value is also an XPath expression. We will explain all this in detail in a moment; for now, you are just trying to develop an intuitive understanding.

- Not all nodes from the source tree appear in the result tree. In fact, only the value of the title attribute node from the source tree appears as a text node in the result tree.

- The result tree contains many elements that are not present in the source tree.

From these points, you may be able to quickly surmise that a style sheet is a well-formed XML document that contains a mix of XSLT instructions and literal XML content. With a little bit of thought, you may also be able to surmise that XSLT instructions within the style sheet use XPath expressions to address source tree nodes and then apply some transformations to these source nodes to produce the result tree. Finally, you may be able to easily infer that the literal XML content in the source tree gets copied into the result tree, unchanged; so far, so good. However, we suspect that at this point you want to know exactly how the transformations are specified and how a processor processes them. So, let's dive into those details next.

XSLT Processing Algorithm

You specify XSLT transformations through a combination of templates and instructions. A template construct is comprised of instructions and literal content in a target document. You can define instructions inside or outside a template construct. For example, the following template, from the style sheet in Listing 5-3, contains a single `<xsl:value-of select="@title" />` instruction:

```
<xsl:template match="journal" >
    <xsl:value-of select="@title" />
</xsl:template>
```

Each template is associated with a specific pattern, which is given by the value of the match attribute. The pattern for the simple template shown previously is journal. This means the template is applicable to all nodes with the name journal.

Each instruction operates on a node set selected from the source tree. When an XSLT processor is asked to transform a source document using an XSLT style sheet, the processor essentially follows this algorithm:

1. It parses the style sheet and the source document into their respective node trees.

2. It executes an implicit instruction, `<xsl:apply-templates select="/" />`. This instruction has a select attribute with an XPath expression value of /. This XPath expression evaluates to a node set containing the source tree document element. Therefore, this instruction selects the source tree document element as the current node set and scans the style sheet node tree for an `xsl:template` instruction with a match attribute that matches the source tree document element. If such a template is found, this template is instantiated as the template for the result tree root node. If no such template is found, another implicit rule continues recursive processing by selecting each child node of the root node and looking for a matching template for each selected child node (and so on, recursively), until a matching template is found. For example, in the example style sheet in Listing 5-3, the `<xsl:template match="/" >` template will match the implicit instruction.

3. From this point, as each template is instantiated in the result tree, it is in turn processed. Literal elements in the template are copied unchanged into the result tree. For each XSLT instruction found in an instantiated template, the processing continues as described in the next step. For example, in the `<xsl:template match="/" >` template in Listing 5-3, HTML elements are literal content that is copied unchanged, and `<xsl:for-each select="catalog/journal" >` is an example of an XSLT instruction that continues the processing described in the next step.

4. For each `xsl:apply-templates` instruction found in an instantiated template, the `select` attribute's XPath expression value is used to select a node set from the source tree. For each node in the selected node set, the processor scans the style sheet for a matching `xsl:template`, and if an `xsl:template` is found, it is instantiated in the result tree, and the processing continues. If more than one matching `xsl:template` is found for a node in the current node set, it is considered an error. However, the processor may choose to ignore the error and pick one of the matching templates and instantiate it. This may be a source of inconsistent behavior across different processors. Note, the algorithm for an `xsl:template` match does not require that the `select` attribute value and the `match` attribute value have to be the same. For example, in the `<xsl:apply-templates select="." >` instruction in Listing 5-3, the select value matches the `<xsl:template match="journal" >` template, as discussed in detail in the next step.

5. For each `xsl:for-each` instruction found in an instantiated template, the `select` attribute's XPath expression value is used to select a node set from the source tree. For each node in the selected node set, the body of the `xsl:for-each` instruction is instantiated into the result tree and processed. For example, the `<xsl:for-each select="catalog/journal" >` instruction in Listing 5-3 iterates over the node set of all the journal elements and executes the body of the `for` loop for each journal element. The body of the `for` loop is the `<xsl:apply-templates select="." >` instruction. The select value of this instruction matches the `<xsl:template match="journal" >` template, because this instruction gets executed in an `xsl:for-each` loop, where each iteration of the loop selects a different journal element. And the `<xsl:value-of select="@title" />` instruction within `<xsl:template match="journal" >` prints the value of each journal's title attribute.

With this basic understanding of the processing algorithm in place, you are ready to look at how transformations are specified, which you will do next.

XSLT Syntax and Semantics

The following sections highlight XSLT syntax and semantics.

xsl:stylesheet Element

The root element in an XSLT style sheet is `xsl:stylesheet`, where `xsl` is the prefix associated with the XSLT namespace URI `http://www.w3.org/1999/XSL/Transform`. You can use a prefix other than `xsl`, of course, as long as it is associated with the correct namespace URI. Attributes of the `stylesheet` element are `id`, `version`, `extension-element-prefixes`, and `exclude-result-prefixes`. The `version` attribute specifies the XSLT version, which may be either 1.0 or 1.1.[7] This attribute must be specified. We will use version 1.0, because, at this point, it is the only version that is a W3C Recommendation, and it is the version supported in the Java API for the XML (JAXP) 1.3 specification. The `extension-element-prefixes` attribute specifies namespace prefixes for extension elements. The `exclude-result-prefixes` attribute specifies namespace prefixes that are to be excluded from the output. Listing 5-4 shows an example `xsl:stylesheet` element.

---

7. Version 1.1 was abandoned as a W3C Working Draft in August 2001 (`http://www.w3.org/TR/xslt11/`).

Listing 5-4. *xsl:stylesheet*

```
<xsl:stylesheet
          xmlns:xsl="http://www.w3.org/1999/XSL/Transform"
   exclude-result-prefixes = "jaxb"
   version ="1.0" >
</xsl:stylesheet>
```

xsl:output Element

The xsl:output element, a subelement of the xsl:stylesheet element, specifies features of the result tree output. Some of the attributes of the xsl:output element are method, version, encoding, omit-xml-declaration, doctype-public, doctype-system, and indent. These attributes work as follows:

- The method attribute specifies the result tree type and may have the value xml, html, or text. You can also specify other output method types.

- The version attribute specifies the version in the XML declaration in the generated output document.

- If omit-xml-declaration is set to yes, the XML declaration is omitted from the output document.

- The encoding attribute specifies the encoding of the document generated.

- doctype-public specifies the public identifier in the DOCTYPE declaration, which was discussed in Chapter 1.

- The doctype-system attribute specifies the system identifier in the DOCTYPE declaration. If the indent attribute is set to yes, the output is indented.

Listing 5-5 shows an example xsl:output element.

Listing 5-5. *xsl:output*

```
<xsl:output
   method = "xml"
   version = "1.0"
   encoding = "utf-8"
   omit-xml-declaration = "no"
   doctype-public ="-//Sun Microsystems, Inc.//DTD Enterprise JavaBeans 2.0//EN"
   doctype-system ="http://java.sun.com/dtd/ejb-jar_2_0.dtd"
   indent = "yes"   />
```

xsl:template Element

As noted, the xsl:template element is the core of XSLT, and each xsl:template is associated with a pattern, expressed as an XPath expression. Two important attributes of the xsl:template element are match and name. The match attribute specifies the pattern to match; the name attribute identifies a template by name. The match attribute is required unless the name attribute is specified, in which case it is optional. An example of an xsl:template element is as follows:

```
<xsl:template match="journal" >
    <xsl:value-of select="@title" />
</xsl:template>
```

The XPath pattern in the match attribute in the previous example matches the node set of all the journal elements in the example source document shown in Listing 5-1. If you recall, it is the body of the xsl:for-each instruction in the Listing 5-3 loop that iterates over each journal element and, through the `<xsl:apply-templates select="." >` instruction, selects and applies the template shown previously.

xsl:apply-templates Element

You can use the xsl:apply-templates element to select a node set from the source tree. Along with the xsl:for-each instruction, it is one of the two key instructions used to change the current node set. The select attribute of the xsl:apply-templates element specifies an XPath expression that evaluates to a node set in the context of the source tree. If the XPath expression is a relative expression, it is evaluated with respect to the current processing node. If the select attribute is omitted, all the child nodes of the current processing node are processed. Listing 5-6 shows an example of an xsl:apply-templates element within an xsl:template element.

Listing 5-6. *xsl:apply-templates*

```
<xsl:template match="/" >
    <html>
      <body>
        <table>
          <tr><th>Titles</th></tr>
          <xsl:for-each select="catalog/journal" >
            <tr><td>
             <xsl:apply-templates select="." ></xsl:apply-templates>
            </td></tr>
          </xsl:for-each>
        </table>
      </body>
    </html>
  </xsl:template>
```

In Listing 5-6, the xsl:apply-templates instruction selects child journal nodes of the current catalog element, tries to find a matching template in Listing 5-3 for the selected journal node, and then applies the matched template. Earlier we discussed the matched template for this xsl:apply-templates instruction.

xsl:call-template Element

If you specify the name attribute in an xsl:template element, you can invoke the template with the xsl:call-template element. Listing 5-7 shows an example of xsl:call-template.

Listing 5-7. *xsl:call-template*

```
<xsl:template name="template1">
 </xsl:template>

<xsl:call-template name="template1">
 </xsl:call-template>
```

The difference between xsl:call-template and xsl:apply-template is that the former is an explicit call to a named xsl:template element where the match attribute is irrelevant; the latter is an implicit call that depends on a match between the select attribute in xsl:apply-template and the match attribute in xsl:template.

xsl:for-each Element

For iterating over a node set, you can use the xsl:for-each element. Listing 5-8 shows an example of xsl:for-each, which is an excerpt from Listing 5-3.

Listing 5-8. *The xsl:for-each Element*

```
<xsl:for-each select="catalog/journal" >
          <tr><td>
            <xsl:apply-templates select="." ></xsl:apply-templates>
          </td></tr>
</xsl:for-each>
```

In the example xsl:for-each element, the select attribute evaluates to a node set of journal elements in the document shown in Listing 5-1. For each node in this node set, the body of the xsl:for-each instruction is processed.

Variables

You can specify variables in XSLT with xsl:variable and xsl:param elements. The xsl:variable and xsl:param elements have the attributes name and select. You specify the value of a variable or a parameter in the select attribute or in the element. For example, you can specify a variable with the value var1 as follows:

```
<xsl:variable name="var1" select="'var1'"/>
```

or as follows:

```
<xsl:variable name="var1">var1</xsl:variable>
```

You can specify a parameter similarly:

```
<xsl:param name="param1" select="'param1'"/>
```

A difference between a parameter and a variable is that the value specified in the xsl:param element is the default value and may be overridden when a template is invoked. You can specify a parameter value with the xsl:with-param element. Listing 5-9 shows an example of overriding the default parameter value.

Listing 5-9. *Applying Templates with Parameter Values*

```
<xsl:apply-templates>
<xsl:with-param  name="param1"  select="'param1'"/>
</xsl:apply-templates>
```

You can declare xsl:variable and xsl:param elements at the top level or in a template. Another difference between xsl:param and xsl:variable is that you can declare an xsl:param element in an xsl:template element only at the beginning of the template.

Conditional Processing

The XSLT specification provides the `xsl:if` and `xsl:choose` elements for conditional processing. The attribute named `test` of the `xsl:if` element evaluates to a boolean value and controls conditional processing. Listing 5-10 shows an example of an `xsl:if` element.

Listing 5-10. *Conditional Application of the Template*

```
<xsl:if test="$param1='param1'">
   <xsl:apply-templates/>
</xsl:if>
```

The `test` attribute in Listing 5-10 compares the value of the `param` parameter with the string `param1`. If the `test` expression evaluates to `true`, `<xsl:apply-templates/>` is invoked.

xsl:copy-of Element

You can select elements in a result tree from the source tree, or you can add new elements. You can copy a source tree fragment to the result tree with the `xsl:copy-of` element. `xsl:copy-of` copies the selected element node, the attributes of the element, and the subelements of the element. The following is an example of `xsl:copy-of`:

```
<xsl:copy-of select="catalog/journal"/>
```

The `xsl:copy` element copies a selected node, but any attributes and subelements of the node are not copied.

xsl:value-of Element

The `xsl:value-of` element adds a text node in the result tree. The `xsl:value-of` element's select attribute expression evaluates to a string. The following is an example of an `xsl:value-of` element that evaluates the string value of a `title` attribute of a `journal` element:

```
<xsl:value-of select="journal/@title" />
```

Adding Elements Attributes and Text

You can add elements to a result tree with the `xsl:element` element. The following is an example of `xsl:element` that creates a `table` element:

```
<xsl:element name="table">
</xsl:element>
```

You can add attributes to a result tree with the `xsl:attribute` element. The following is an example of the `xsl:attribute` element that creates the attribute `title`:

```
<xsl:attribute name="title" >XML Journal</xsl:attribute>
```

You can add a text node to a result tree with the `xsl:text` element. The body of this element specifies the text node in the result tree.

Setting Up the Eclipse Project

In this chapter, we will show how to transform an example XML document, listed in Listing 5-11, using various XSLT style sheets; each style sheet will demonstrate a specific transformation example. In these style sheets, duplicate elements in catalog.xml will be removed, title elements will be sorted, and various nodes will be filtered.

Listing 5-11. *catalog.xml*

```
<?xml version="1.0" encoding="UTF-8"?>
<catalog  xmlns=" http://www.apress.com/catalog/journal">
  <journal title="Java Technology" publisher="IBM developerWorks">

    <article level="Intermediate" date="January-2004"
        section="Java Technology">

        <title>Service Oriented Architecture Frameworks</title>
        <author>Naveen Balani</author>
    </article>

    <article level="Advanced" date="October-2003" section="Java Technology">
      <title>Advanced DAO Programming</title>
      <author>Sean Sullivan</author>
    </article>

  <article level="Advanced" date="May-2002" section="Java Technology">
     <title>Best Practices in EJB Exception Handling</title>
     <author>Srikanth Shenoy</author>
  </article>

</journal>
</catalog>
```

Before you can build and run the code examples included in this chapter, you need an Eclipse project. The quickest way to create an Eclipse project is to download the Chapter5 project from the Apress website (http://www.apress.com) and import this project into Eclipse. This will create all the Java packages and files needed for this chapter automatically.

In this chapter, we will show how to use the JAXP 1.3 TrAX APIs included in J2SE 5.0 Therefore, you need to install the J2SE 5.0[8] SDK and set its JRE system library as the JRE system library in your Eclipse project Java build path. You can do this by right-clicking the Eclipse project name in the Package Explorer, choosing Properties, selecting the Java Build Path to Libraries tab, and clicking the Add Library button. Figure 5-3 shows all the files and folders in the Chapter5 project.

---

8. You can find information about J2SE 5.0 at http://java.sun.com/j2se/1.5.0/.

Figure 5-3. *Chapter5 project directory structure*

JAXP 1.3 Transformation APIs

TrAX is specified in JAXP 1.3 and included in J2SE 5.0. You use the TrAX APIs to transform an XML document by applying an XSLT style sheet to an input XML document. The output from a transformation application can be XML, HTML, or text. The transformation APIs are organized into the following packages:

- The generic transformation APIs are in the `javax.xml.transform` package.

- The stream- and URI-specific transformation APIs, which you use to specify stream-based input and output for a transformation application, are in the `javax.xml.transform.stream` package.

- The DOM-specific transformation APIs, which you use to specify DOM-based input and output to a transformation application, are in the `javax.xml.transform.dom` package.

- The SAX 2-specific transformation APIs, which you use to specify SAX-based input and output to a transformation application, are in the `javax.xml.transform.sax` package.

Table 5-1 lists the basic classes in the `javax.xml.transform` package.

Table 5-1. *Classes in the `javax.xml.transform` Package*

Class Name	Description
TransformerFactory	A factory class for generating `Transformer` objects
Transformer	A class to transform a source tree to a result tree
Source	An interface that defines an input source for an input XML document or an input XSLT style sheet
Result	An interface that defines a transformation result tree
OutputKeys	Specifies output properties for a `Transformer` object

With the only ordering constraint that both an input source and a result tree holder have to be ready before a transformer is applied to an input source, the conceptual steps in the use of transformation APIs are as follows:

1. Create an instance of a transformer factory.

2. Use the factory to create an instance of a transformer based on an input source for an XSLT style sheet definition.

3. Configure the transformer for error handling.

4. Create an input source from the input XML document. The input source can be based on an input stream or a document object tree.

5. Define a holder for the result tree; the holder can be a stream or a document object.

6. Apply the transformer to the input source to obtain the result tree in its holder.

The main class for transforming a source tree to a result tree is the Transformer class. You use the TransformerFactory class to generate Transformer objects. The TransformerFactory class is instantiated with the static method newInstance():

```
TransformerFactory factory=TransformerFactory.newInstance();
```

The default TransformerFactory implementation class that is instantiated is org.apache. xalan.processor.TransformerFactoryImpl. You can use the following lookup procedure to obtain a TransformerFactory implementation class:

1. Use the system property javax.xml.transform.TransformerFactory.

2. Use the javax.xml.transform.TransformerFactory property value in the lib/jaxp. properties file in the JRE directory.

3. Use the Services API to obtain the class name from the META-INF/services/javax.xml. transform.TransformerFactory file.

4. Use the platform default TransformerFactory instance.

You can obtain a Transformer object from a TransformerFactory object with the newTransformer(Source xsltSource) method. To apply an XSLT style sheet to an XML document, obtain an XSLT Source object with the StreamSource class, as shown in Listing 5-12.

Listing 5-12. *Creating a Transformer Object*

```
StreamSource xsltSource=new StreamSource(new File ("sort.xslt"));
Transformer transformer=factory.newTransformer(xsltSource);
```

You can also obtain a Transformer object from a Templates object, which is a representation of the transformations in an XSLT style sheet. To use the Templates interface to obtain a Transformer object, create a Templates object from a TransformerFactory object and create a Transformer object from the Templates object, as shown in Listing 5-13.

Listing 5-13. *Creating a Transformer Object from a Templates Object*

```
Templates templates=factory.newTemplates(xsltSource);
Transformer transformer=templates.newTransformer();
```

You can set the output properties on a Transformer object with the setOutputProperty(String name, String value) method. You specify the Transformer output properties string constants in the OutputKeys class. Table 5-2 lists the string constants specified in the OutputKeys class.

Table 5-2. *Output Properties*

Static Field	Description
DOCTYPE_PUBLIC	Specifies the public identifier for a DOCTYPE declaration.
DOCTYPE_SYSTEM	Specifies the system identifier for the DOCTYPE identifier.
ENCODING	Specifies the encoding for the XML document.
INDENT	Value can be yes or no. If the INDENT property is set to yes, the output is indented.
METHOD	Value can be xml, html, or text. Other non-namespaced values can also be specified. Specifies the method used to construct the result tree.
OMIT_XML_DECLARATION	Value can be yes or no. To omit the XML declaration from an output XML document, specify the value as yes.
VERSION	Specifies the output version. If the output method is set to xml, the default version is 1.0. If the output method is set to html, the default version is 4.0.

You can register an ErrorListener with a Transformer object to output transformation errors. To register error handling with a Transformer, create an implementation class for ErrorListener, as shown in Listing 5-14.

Listing 5-14. *ErrorListener Implementation Class*

```
private class ErrorListenerImpl implements ErrorListener {
  public TransformerException e = null;

  public void error(TransformerException exception) {
    this.e = exception;
  }

  public void fatalError(TransformerException exception) {
    this.e = exception;
  }

  public void warning(TransformerException exception) {
    this.e = exception;
  }
}
```

To register an error handler with a Transformer object, create an error handler object. With the setErrorListener(ErrorListener) method, register the error handler with a Transformer object, as shown in Listing 5-15.

Listing 5-15. *Setting* `ErrorListener`

```
ErrorListenerImpl errorHandler=new ErrorListenerImpl();
transformer.setErrorListener(errorHandler);
```

An XML source tree is transformed to a result tree with the
`transform(Source source, Result result)` method. The `Source` object can be a `DOMSource`, a
`SAXSource`, or a `StreamSource`. The `Result` object may be a `DOMResult`, a `SAXResult`, or a `StreamResult`.
To use a `DOMSource` object, obtain a `Document` object from a `DocumentBuilder` parser class, as shown in
Listing 5-16.

Listing 5-16. *Creating a* `DOMSource` *Object*

```
DocumentBuilderFactory factory = DocumentBuilderFactory.newInstance();
DocumentBuilder builder = factory.newDocumentBuilder();
Document    document = builder.parse(new File("catalog.xml"));
DOMSource  domSource=new DOMSource(document);
```

To output to a `StreamResult`, create a `StreamResult` object. Transform the input XML document
with the `transform()` method, as shown in Listing 5-17.

Listing 5-17. *Transforming the Source Tree to a Result Tree*

```
StreamResult streamResult=new StreamResult(System.out);
transformer.transform(domSource, streamResult);
```

TrAX Application

In the previous section, we discussed TrAX. In this section, we will use a transformation application
built using TrAX to demonstrate some examples of XSLT transformations. We'll use the example
XML document shown in Listing 5-11 as input for the XSLT transformations.

We'll use a generic Java application called `XSLTTransformer.java`, shown in Listing 5-18, for all
the transformation examples. `XSLTTransformer.java` takes a style sheet and an XML document as
input and transforms the XML document with the transformations specified in the style sheet. The
TrAX application, `XSLTTransformer`, parses the example XML document, `catalog.xml`, and creates a
`Document` object. It then transforms the `Document` object with a style sheet using `Transformer` object.
An `ErrorListener` is set on the `Transformer` object to output transformation errors.

You can run the TrAX application, `XSLTTransformer.java`, with different XSLT style sheets by
setting the style sheet in the `stylesheet File` object to the required XSLT. For example, to sort elements
in the input XML document, set the style sheet to `sort.xslt`, as shown here:

```
File stylesheet = new File("sort.xslt");
```

We've discussed most of the code in Listing 5-18 in the preceding sections; in addition, it is
annotated with comments.

Listing 5-18. *XSLTTransformer.java*

```
package com.apress.xslt;

import javax.xml.parsers.*;
import org.xml.sax.*;
import org.w3c.dom.*;
import javax.xml.transform.*;
import javax.xml.transform.dom.*;
```

```java
import javax.xml.transform.stream.*;
import java.io.*;

public class XSLTTransformer {

  public static void main(String argv[]) {


    try {
      //Create a DocumentBuilderFactory
      DocumentBuilderFactory factory=
            DocumentBuilderFactory.newInstance();
      //Create File object for input XSLT and
          // example XML document
      File stylesheet = new File("identityTransform.xslt");
      File datafile = new File("catalog.xml");
      //Create DocumentBuilder object
      DocumentBuilder builder = factory.newDocumentBuilder();
      //Parse example XML Document
      Document document = builder.parse(datafile);
      //Create a TransformerFactory object
      TransformerFactory tFactory = TransformerFactory.newInstance();

      //Create a Stylesource object from the stylesheet File object
      StreamSource stylesource = new StreamSource(stylesheet);

       //Create a Transformer object from the StyleSource object
      Transformer transformer = tFactory.newTransformer(stylesource);
       //Create a DOMSource object from an XML document

      DOMSource source = new DOMSource(document);
      //Create a StreamResult object to output the result of a transformation.
      StreamResult result = new StreamResult(System.out);

      //Create a ErrorListener and set the ErrorListener on the Transformer
      XSLTTransformer xsltTransformer = new XSLTTransformer();
      ErrorListenerImpl errorHandler =
                            xsltTransformer.new ErrorListenerImpl();
      transformer.setErrorListener(errorHandler);
      //Transform an XML document with an XSLT style sheet
      transformer.transform(source, result);
                               //Output transformation errors
      if (errorHandler.e != null) {
        System.out.println("Transformation Exception: "
            + errorHandler.e.getMessage());
      }

    } catch (TransformerConfigurationException e) {

      System.out.println(e.getMessage());

    } catch (TransformerException e) {
```

```java
      System.out.println(e.getMessage());
    } catch (SAXException e) {
      System.out.println(e.getMessage());

    } catch (ParserConfigurationException e) {

      System.out.println(e.getMessage());
    } catch (IOException e) {
      System.out.println(e.getMessage());
    }

  }
                //ErrorListener class
  private class ErrorListenerImpl implements ErrorListener {
    public TransformerException e = null;

    public void error(TransformerException exception) {
      this.e = exception;
    }

    public void fatalError(TransformerException exception) {
      this.e = exception;
    }

    public void warning(TransformerException exception) {
      this.e = exception;
    }
  }

}
```

In the following sections, we'll show how to apply some various XSLT transformations to the example XML document. You can apply transformations other than those discussed in these sections with the transformation application XSLTTransformer.java. Just modify the input XML document and the style sheet in the XSLTTransformer application, and run the application in Eclipse.

Transforming Identically

Identity transformation copies an input XML document to an output document without changing any of the elements or attributes. You could apply the identity transformation to modify the encoding or DOCTYPE or to add appropriate indentation. Listing 5-19 shows an example XSLT for identity transformation. The style sheet identityTransform.xslt applies a template pattern recursively to nodes in catalog.xml. The XPath expression @*|node() selects all the element and attribute nodes. In the XPath pattern, @* represents all the attribute nodes, and node() represents all the other nodes. The output from the identity transformation is the input XML document with optional modification to the document encoding, DOCTYPE, or indentation.

Listing 5-19. *identityTransform.xslt*

```xml
<xsl:stylesheet version="1.0"
xmlns:xsl="http://www.w3.org/1999/XSL/Transform">
  <xsl:output method="xml" version="1.0" indent="yes"/>
    <xsl:template match="@* | node()">
    <xsl:copy>
```

```
<xsl:apply-templates select="@* | node()"/>
    </xsl:copy>
  </xsl:template>
</xsl:stylesheet>
```

Removing Duplicates

An XML document could have duplicate elements that are required to be removed in the output. The example XML document has a duplicate `title` element. To remove any duplicate `title` elements, run the transformation application with style sheet shown in Listing 5-20, which outputs nonduplicate `article` titles. The XPath expression `//title[not(.=following::title)]` selects nonduplicate `title` elements. The XPath function `text()` in the XSLT pattern outputs the `title` element text.

Listing 5-20. *removeDuplicates.xslt*

```
<xsl:stylesheet version="1.0"
xmlns:xsl="http://www.w3.org/1999/XSL/Transform">
  <xsl:output method="xml" version="1.0" omit-xml-declaration="yes"/>
  <xsl:template match="/">
    <xsl:variable name="unique-list"
select="//title[not(.=following::title)]/text()" />
    <xsl:for-each select="$unique-list">
      <xsl:copy>
         <xsl:apply-templates/>
      </xsl:copy>
      <xsl:text disable-output-escaping="yes">
        &#13;
      </xsl:text>
    </xsl:for-each>
  </xsl:template>
</xsl:stylesheet>
```

When the output method is `xml` or `html`, certain characters are automatically escaped in the output. To disable the automatic escaping of a character, you can use the `disable-output-escaping="yes"` attribute in `xsl:text`; the body of the element contains the escaped sequence. For example, in Listing 5-20, the following instruction disables output escaping for a carriage return:

```
<xsl:text disable-output-escaping="yes">&#13; </xsl:text>
```

Before we can apply this style sheet, we need to add duplicate `title` elements to `catalog.xml`, shown in Listing 5-11. We can do so by simply copying and pasting the last `article` element, just below itself. This will add a duplicate `title` element, by virtue of the fact that there is a duplicate `article` element.

To run the transformation application with the `removeDuplicates.xslt` style sheet, specify the style sheet as input to the `File` object `stylesheet` in `XSLTTransformer.java` in the `Chapter5` project. The output is the nonduplicate article titles, as shown in Listing 5-21.

Listing 5-21. *Output in Eclipse from Removing Duplicates*

```
Service Oriented Architecture Frameworks
 Advanced DAO Programming
 Best Practices in EJB Exception Handling
```

■**Note** In subsequent sections, we'll use the XML document whose duplicate element has been removed as input, so remove the duplicate `title` element in `catalog.xml` in the Eclipse project `Chapter5`.Sorting Elements

Sorting Elements

You can use the XSLT element xsl:sort to sort a group of elements. The attribute order of the
xsl:sort element specifies the sorting order: ascending or descending. The data-type attribute
(whose value can be number or text) specifies the data type of the element to be sorted. The default
datatype value is text. The xsl:sort element is required to be in an xsl:for-each element or
xsl:apply-templates element.

For instance, try sorting the title elements in the example XML document in ascending order.
The style sheet sort.xslt, shown in Listing 5-22, sorts the title elements in ascending order and
outputs the text nodes in the title elements. To run the transformation application with sort.xslt,
set sort.xslt as the style sheet in the File object stylesheet in XSLTTransformer.java.

Listing 5-22. *sort.xslt*

```
<xsl:stylesheet  xmlns:xsl="http://www.w3.org/1999/XSL/Transform" version="1.0">
  <xsl:output method="xml" omit-xml-declaration="yes"/>
  <xsl:template match="/catalog/journal">
    <xsl:apply-templates>
      <xsl:sort select="title"
      order="ascending"/>
    </xsl:apply-templates>
  </xsl:template>

  <xsl:template match="article">
  Title:    <xsl:apply-templates select="title"/>
  </xsl:template>

</xsl:stylesheet>
```

In Listing 5-22, the **<xsl:template match="/catalog/journal">** template is matched by
the following built-in implicit XSLT instruction:

```
<xsl:template match="*|/">
  <xsl:apply-templates/>
</xsl:template>
```

The built-in rule matches the <xsl:template match="/catalog/journal"> template for each
journal node in the input source document, shown in Listing 5-11. Since the
<xsl:apply-templates> instruction within the <xsl:template match="/catalog/journal"> template
has no select attribute, this means each child of the journal node is selected and a matching
template is searched. For each article child of the journal node, the matching template that works
is of course <xsl:template match="article">, which outputs titles that get sorted by the xsl:sort
instruction in the result tree. The output is a sorted list of article titles in ascending order, as shown
in Listing 5-23.

Listing 5-23. *Output in Eclipse from Sorting*

```
Title:    Advanced DAO Programming
  Title:    Best Practices in EJB Exception Handling
  Title:    Service Oriented Architecture Frameworks
```

Converting to HTML

Data in an XML document may have to be presented as an HTML document. You can define a transformation with HTML output by setting the method attribute to html within the xsl:output element.
Listing 5-24 shows the XSLT style sheet for applying an HTML transformation.

The style sheet `htmlTransform.xslt` has HTML tags to generate an HTML file. In this style sheet, a template matches the pattern `/catalog/journal`, and the `xsl:for-each` element is used to iterate over the `article` elements in a `journal` element. Text values are output with the `xsl:value-of` element. To run the transformation application `XSLTTransformer.java` with this style sheet, set input to the `File` object `stylesheet` to `htmlTransform.xslt`, and set the output file to `catalog.html`.

Listing 5-24. *htmlTransform.xslt*

```
<?xml version="1.0" encoding="UTF-8"?>
<xsl:stylesheet version="1.0"
xmlns:xsl="http://www.w3.org/1999/XSL/Transform">
<xsl:output    method="html"/>
<xsl:template match="/catalog/journal">
<html>
  <head>
    <title>Catalog</title>
  </head>
  <body>
    <table border="1" cellspacing="0">
        <tr>
         <th>Level</th>
         <th>Date</th>
         <th>Section</th>
         <th>Title</th>
         <th>Author</th>
        </tr>
      <xsl:for-each select="article">
        <tr>
         <td><xsl:value-of select="@
           level"/></td>
         <td><xsl:value-of select="
          @date"/></td>
         <td><xsl:value-of select="@
           section"/></td>
         <td><xsl:value-of select="title"
           /></td>
         <td><xsl:value-of select="author"
           /></td>
        </tr>
      </xsl:for-each>
    </table>
  </body>
</html>
</xsl:template>
</xsl:stylesheet>
```

The output from the XSLT is an HTML document that can be displayed in a browser, as shown in Figure 5-4.

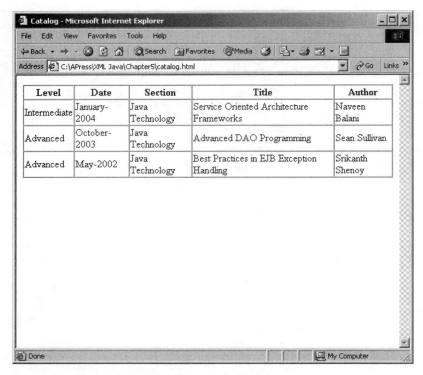

Figure 5-4. *Output in Eclipse from HTML transformation*

Merging Documents

When you merge XML documents, you create a new XML document from two XML documents. You obtain a copy of an XML document in another XML document with the document() function. As an example, combine the example XML document, catalog.xml, with the XML document, catalog2.xml, listed in Listing 5-25.

Listing 5-25. *catalog2.xml*

```
<?xml version="1.0" encoding="UTF-8"?>
<catalog xmlns="http://www.w3.org/2001/XMLSchema-Instance">
  <journal title="Java Technology"
   publisher="IBM developerWorks">
    <article level="Intermediate" date="February-2003">
     <title>Design XML Schemas Using UML</title>
        <author>Ayesha Malik</author>
    </article>
</journal>
</catalog>
```

The style sheet merge.xslt creates a copy of catalog.xml and combines the copy with a copy of catalog2.xml. To run the transformation application XSLTTransformer.java with merge.xslt, set the input XML document to catalog.xml and the input style sheet to merge.xslt, shown in Listing 5-26.

Listing 5-26. *merge.xslt*

```
<?xml version="1.0" encoding="UTF-8"?>
<xsl:stylesheet version="1.0"
xmlns:xsl="http://www.w3.org/1999/XSL/Transform">
<xsl:output method="xml" />
<xsl:template match="/">
<catalogs>
<xsl:copy-of select="*"/>
<xsl:copy-of select="document('catalog2.xml')"/>
</catalogs>
</xsl:template>
</xsl:stylesheet>
```

The style sheet combines the example XML document catalog.xml and another XML document, catalog2.xml, as shown in Listing 5-25, to produce the output shown in Listing 5-27.

Listing 5-27. *Output in Eclipse from Merging XML Documents*

```
<?xml version="1.0" encoding="UTF-8"?><catalogs>
<catalog xmlns="http://www.w3.org/2001/XMLSchema-Instance">
  <journal publisher="IBM developerWorks" title="Java Technology">
    <article date="January-2004" level="Intermediate" section="Java Technology">
        <title>Service Oriented Architecture Frameworks</title>
        <author>Naveen Balani</author>
    </article>

    <article date="October-2003" level="Advanced" section="Java Technology">
      <title>Advanced DAO Programming</title>
      <author>Sean Sullivan</author>
    </article>

  <article date="May-2002" level="Advanced" section="Java Technology">
     <title>Best Practices in EJB Exception Handling</title>
     <author>Srikanth Shenoy</author>
  </article>
</journal>
</catalog><catalog xmlns="http://www.w3.org/2001/XMLSchema-Instance">
  <journal title="Java Technology" publisher="IBM developerWorks">
    <article level="Intermediate" date="February-2003">
    <title>Design XML Schemas Using UML</title>
        <author>Ayesha Malik</author>
    </article>
</journal>
</catalog></catalogs>
```

Obtaining Node Values with XPath

XSLT node selection is based on XPath. With the xsl:value-of element, you can select the element and attribute nodes in an XML document with XPath. As an example, select the value of the date attribute for the article element with the title Advanced DAO Programming, and select the value of the title element for the article by author Srikanth Shenoy. The style sheet xpath.xslt, shown in Listing 5-28, outputs the value of the date attribute and the title element. The XPath expression article[title='Advanced DAO Programming']/@date selects the date attribute, and the XPath expression article[author='Srikanth Shenoy']/title selects the title element.

Listing 5-28. *xpath.xslt*

```
<?xml version="1.0" encoding="UTF-8"?>
<xsl:stylesheet version="1.0" xmlns:
 xsl="http://www.w3.org/1999/XSL/Transform">
<xsl:output method="xml" omit-xml-declaration="yes"/>
<xsl:template match="/catalog/journal">
Date: <xsl:value-of select="article[title='
 Advanced DAO Programming']/@date"/>
Title: <xsl:value-of select="article[author='Srikanth Shenoy']/title"/>
</xsl:template>
</xsl:stylesheet>
```

To run the transformation application with xpath.xslt, set the input style sheet in XSLTTransformer.java to xpath.xslt. Listing 5-29 shows the output from the XSLT transformation.

Listing 5-29. *Output in Eclipse with XPath Node Selection*

```
Date: October-2003
Title: Best Practices in EJB Exception Handling
```

Filtering Elements

Applying xsl:apply-templates elements to only those elements and attributes that are required in the output can filter elements in an XML document. As an example, select the article elements with the level attribute specified as Intermediate. The style sheet filter.xslt, shown in Listing 5-30, selects the article elements that have level attributes with a value of Intermediate. The XPath expression article[@level='Intermediate'] selects the article elements with the level attributes set to Intermediate.

Listing 5-30. *filter.xslt*

```
<?xml version="1.0" encoding="UTF-8"?>
<xsl:stylesheet version="1.0" xmlns:xsl="http://www.w3.org/1999/XSL/Transform">
<xsl:output method="xml" omit-xml-
 declaration="yes"/>
<xsl:template match="/catalog/journal">
<xsl:apply-templates select="article[@level='Intermediate']"/>
</xsl:template>
<xsl:template match="article">
Title: <xsl:value-of select="title"/>
Author: <xsl:value-of select="author"/>
</xsl:template>
</xsl:stylesheet>
```

To run the transformation application with filter.xslt, set the File object stylesheet input to filter.xslt in XSLTTransformer.java. The output contains only the article element with the level value of Intermediate, as shown in Listing 5-31.

Listing 5-31. *Output in Eclipse from Filtering Elements*

```
Title: Service Oriented Architecture Frameworks
Author: Naveen Balani
```

Copying Nodes

The XSLT specification provides two elements for copying nodes, `xsl-copy-of` and `xsl-copy`. The `xsl:copy-of` element copies a selected element and also copies attributes and subelements of the selected node. `xsl:copy`, a different version of the `xsl:copy-of` element, doesn't copy the subelements and attributes of the selected node. As an example, copy the second `article` element in the `journal` element in `catalog.xml` to output. The style sheet `copy.xslt` in Listing 5-32 copies the second `article` element in the `journal` node in the `catalog.xml` document to the output document. The XPath expression `journal/article[2]` selects the second `article` element in the `journal` element.

Listing 5-32. *copy.xslt*

```
<?xml version="1.0" encoding="UTF-8"?>
<xsl:stylesheet version="1.0" xmlns:xsl="http://www.w3.org/1999/XSL/Transform">
<xsl:output method="xml"/>
<xsl:template match="/catalog">
<xsl:copy-of select="journal/article[2]"/>
</xsl:template>
</xsl:stylesheet>
```

To run the transformation application with `copy.xslt`, specify `copy.xslt` as input to the `File` object `stylesheet` in `XSLTTransformer.java`. The output from the XSLT transformation consists of the second `article` element in the `journal` node from the input XML document, as shown in Listing 5-33.

Listing 5-33. *Output in Eclipse from Copying Nodes*

```
<?xml version="1.0" encoding="UTF-8"?>
<article xmlns="http://www.w3.org/2001/XMLSchema-Instance"
  date="October-2003" level="Advanced"
  section="Java Technology">
    <title>Advanced DAO Programming</title>
    <author>Sean Sullivan</author>
  </article>
```

Creating Elements and Attributes

The XSLT specification provides the `xsl:element` element to create an element and the `xsl:attribute` element to create an attribute in the resulting XML document. You specify the name of an element or an attribute in the `name` attribute, and you specify the namespace of an element or attribute in the `namespace` attribute. The style sheet `createElement.xslt` in Listing 5-34 creates an element `journal` and adds an attribute `publisher` to the `journal` element. The attribute value is specified with an `xsl:text` element in an `xsl:attribute` element.

Listing 5-34. *createElement.xslt*

```
<?xml version="1.0" encoding="UTF-8"?>
<xsl:stylesheet version="1.0" xmlns:xsl="http://www.w3.org/1999/XSL/Transform">
<xsl:output method="xml" omit-xml-declaration="yes"/>
<xsl:template match="/">
<xsl:element name="journal">
<xsl:attribute name="publisher">
<xsl:text>IBM developerWorks</xsl:text>
</xsl:attribute>
</xsl:element>
</xsl:template>
</xsl:stylesheet>
```

To run the transformation application with createElement.xslt, specify input to the File object stylesheet as createElement.xslt in XSLTTransformer.java. The output from the style sheet consists of a journal element with a publisher attribute, as shown in Listing 5-35.

Listing 5-35. *Output in Eclipse with createElement.xslt*

```
<journal publisher="IBM developerWorks"/>
```

Adding Indentation

You can format the XSLT output with the xsl:output element. You can set the indentation in the xsl:output element with the indent attribute. To add indentation, specify the xalan-indent-amount attribute and the xalan namespace attribute. The output gets indented if the XSLT processor supports indentation. Listing 5-36 shows the style sheet indent.xslt that adds indentation to the example XML document.

Listing 5-36. *indent.xslt*

```
<?xml version="1.0" encoding="UTF-8"?>
<xsl:stylesheet version="1.0" xmlns:xalan="http://xml.apache.org/xslt"
xmlns:xsl="http://www.w3.org/1999/XSL/Transform">
<xsl:output method="xml" xalan:indent-amount="3"
 indent="yes"/>
<xsl:template match="/">
<xsl:copy-of select="catalog"/>
</xsl:template>
</xsl:stylesheet>
```

Summary

XSLT is a language for transforming XML documents to other XML documents or non-XML documents such as HTML or plain-text documents. To apply transformations described in an XSLT style sheet to an XML document, you need an XSLT processor and an API to invoke the XSLT processor.

The TrAX API set available within JAXP 1.3 is ideally suited for transforming an input XML document using an XSLT style sheet. The type of target output document types produced by an XSLT style sheet is limited only by your imagination. In this chapter, we showed how to successfully transform XML documents into other XML documents, HTML documents, and plain-text documents.

PART 2

■ ■ ■

Object Bindings

■■■

CHAPTER 6

Object Binding with JAXB

XML is a simple, flexible, platform-independent language for representing structured textual information. The platform-independent nature of XML makes it an ideal vehicle for exchanging data across application components. When disparate application components exchange XML-based data, they do so because they want to process the exchanged data in some application-specific manner, such as extracting and storing the data in a database or maybe formatting and presenting the data as part of a user interface. This raises an interesting point: although XML is ideal for exchanging data, processing XML content using the various APIs we have discussed in the preceding chapters can be highly inefficient. Why is that so?

The answer is that most processing logic today resides within application components that are object oriented, whereas processing XML content is extremely procedural in nature. Each component that wants to process some XML content has to not only be concerned that the content is well-formed but also that it conforms to some specific structure (or, in other words, is valid with respect to some schema). Furthermore, once the component has verified that the XML content is well-formed and valid, it has to use an appropriate API to access the data embedded within the XML content.

Of course, it can certainly do all that—in previous chapters, we discussed how to parse and validate XML content and how to access and modify data embedded within XML content by using the appropriate APIs, but directly using these APIs within most object-oriented applications can be highly inefficient from the point of view of encapsulation and code reuse. To address the inefficiencies associated with directly processing XML content within object-oriented Java applications, you need a Java API that transparently maps XML content to Java objects and Java objects to XML content. Java Architecture for XML Binding (JAXB) is precisely such an API.

Overview

The key to understanding JAXB is to focus on the following points:

- Given an XML Schema document, an infinite number of XML documents can be constructed that would be valid with respect to the given schema.

- Given a schema and an XML document that conforms to the given schema, an element within the given XML document must conform to a type component specified within the given schema.

- What an object instance is to its corresponding class within Java, an element in an XML document is to an element declaration specified within the document's schema.

- Each type component (with some exceptions) specified within a schema can be mapped to a Java class. This Java class may already exist as part of the Java platform, or it may need to be defined as a new class.

- The process of binding schema type components to various Java class definitions is at the core of JAXB.

The JAXB API was developed as a part of the Java Community Process.[1] It is important to note that at the time of writing this book, two versions of JAXB were available:

- The first available version is JAXB 1.0, which was finalized in January 2003. An implementation of this specification is available in Java Web Services Developer Pack (JWSDP) 1.6 and also in J2EE 1.4.

- The second available version is JAXB 2.0, which was finalized in May 2006. An implementation of this specification is available in JWSDP 2.0 and also in Java Enterprise Edition 5.

The principal objectives of JAXB are unchanged from JAXB 1.0 to 2.0. However, 2.0 has a number of significant additions. So, we will first discuss JAXB 1.0 in detail and then discuss the significant additions made in JAXB 2.0.

JAXB 1.0

In the following sections, we will cover JAXB 1.0.

Architecture

Figure 6-1 shows the basic architecture of JAXB 1.0. JAXB binds a *source XML Schema* to a set of schema-derived Java content classes. A *binding compiler* (xjc) within JAXB generates Java content classes corresponding to top-level type components specified within the source schema. A runtime-binding framework API available within JAXB *marshals* and *unmarshals* an XML document *from* and *to* its corresponding Java objects.

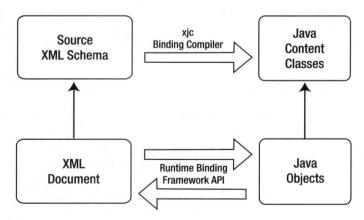

Figure 6-1. *JAXB 1.0 architecture*

---

1. Information about this process is available at http://jcp.org/en/home/index.

It is important to note that the JAXB 1.0 binding compiler does not support the mapping of every type of XML Schema component. In fact, the following XML Schema[2] components are not supported in JAXB 1.0:

- Element declarations using the `substitutionGroup` attribute, which is resolved to a predefined model group schema component (`<xs:element @substitutionGroup>`).

- Wildcard schema components (`xs:any` and `xs:anyAttribute`).

- Identity constraints used to specify uniqueness across multiple elements (`xs:key`, `xs:keyref`, and `xs:unique`).

- Redefined XML Schema components using the `redefine` declaration (`<xs:redefine>`).

- Notation XML Schema components (`<xs:notation>`).

- The following schema attributes are not supported: `complexType.abstract`, `element.abstract`, `element.substitutionGroup`, `xsi:type`, `complexType.block`, `complexType.final`, `element.block`, `element.final`, `schema.blockDefault`, and `schema.finalDefault`.

XML Schema Binding to Java Representation

JAXB 1.0 defines a default binding of the supported schema subset to Java. However, you can override this default binding through external binding declarations, which you can specify inline in the schema or in a separate XML binding declaration document. Either way, the binding declarations override the default XML Schema to Java bindings.

The detailed algorithms that bind the XML Schema subset to Java are best left to the JAXB 1.0 specification. Having said that, we will quickly add that these details will be of limited value to you if your sole interest lies in applying JAXB, not in implementing JAXB. Therefore, instead of covering all the details associated with the schema binding to Java, we will help you develop an intuitive understanding of the schema binding by presenting a simple example.

Simple Binding Example

Say you have a simple schema that specifies a structure for a postal address within the United States or Canada. It specifies the obvious elements such as name, street, city, and state. It specifies a choice of either U.S. ZIP code or Canadian postal code. It constrains the country element content to be either United States or Canada. Listing 6-1 shows an example of such a schema.

Listing 6-1. *U.S. or Canadian Address Schema:* `address.xsd`

```
<?xml version='1.0' encoding='UTF-8' ?>
<xs:schema jxb:version="1.0"
  xmlns:jxb="http://java.sun.com/xml/ns/jaxb"
  xmlns:xs="http://www.w3.org/2001/XMLSchema"
  xmlns:xsi="http://www.w3.org/2001/XMLSchema-instance"
  xsi:schemaLocation="http://www.w3.org/2001/XMLSchema
  http://www.nubean.com/schemas/schema.xsd" >
  <xs:element name="UsOrCanadaAddress" >
  <xs:complexType>
```

2. You can find detailed information about XML Schema components at `http://www.w3.org/TR/xmlschema-1/`.

```
    <xs:sequence>
      <xs:element name="name"  type="xs:string" ></xs:element>
      <xs:element name="street"  type="xs:string" ></xs:element>
      <xs:element name="city"  type="xs:string" ></xs:element>
      <xs:element name="state"  type="xs:string" ></xs:element>

      <xs:choice>
        <xs:element name="zip"  type="xs:int" ></xs:element>
        <xs:element name="postalCode"  type="xs:string" ></xs:element>
      </xs:choice>

      <xs:element name="country" >
        <xs:simpleType>
          <xs:restriction base="xs:string" >
            <xs:enumeration value="United States" ></xs:enumeration>
            <xs:enumeration value="Canada" ></xs:enumeration>
          </xs:restriction>
        </xs:simpleType>
      </xs:element>

    </xs:sequence>
  </xs:complexType>
</xs:element>
</xs:schema>
```

Now, to keep things simple, you will accept all the default XML Schema binding rules, except for one. You will override the default package name for generated Java classes and interfaces with a specific package name, com.apress.jaxb1.example, as in the external binding file shown in Listing 6-2.

Listing 6-2. *External Binding Declaration for a Package Name*

```
<?xml version='1.0' encoding='utf-8' ?>
<jxb:bindings version="1.0"
  xmlns:jxb="http://java.sun.com/xml/ns/jaxb"
  xmlns:xs="http://www.w3.org/2001/XMLSchema" >
  <jxb:bindings node="/xs:schema"  schemaLocation="address.xsd" >
    <jxb:schemaBindings>
      <jxb:package name="com.apress.jaxb1.example" ></jxb:package>
    </jxb:schemaBindings>
  </jxb:bindings>
</jxb:bindings>
```

Later in this chapter, in the "Binding the Catalog Schema to Java Classes" section, we will discuss in detail how to configure and run the xjc compiler from within Eclipse. For now, assume you know how to do that, and run the xjc compiler so it consumes the schema in Listing 6-1 and the external binding declarations in Listing 6-2. Running xjc binds the schema components to Java. For the schema shown in Listing 6-1, the xjc schema binding works as follows:

- In the com.apress.jaxb1.example package, xjc generates two Java interfaces and one Java class. The interfaces are UsOrCanadaAddressType and UsOrCanadaAddress, and the class is ObjectFactory.

- The UsOrCanadaAddressType interface is the Java representation for the <xs:complexType> component defined within the <xs:element name="UsOrCanadaAddress" > component.

- The UsOrCanadaAddress interface is the Java representation for the <xs:element name="UsOrCanadaAddress" > component.

- The UsOrCanadaAddress interface extends the UsOrCanadaAddressType interface.

- The ObjectFactory class is a typical object factory implementation that you can use to create new instances of UsOrCanadaAddress or UsOrCanadaAddressType.

- Within the com.apress.jaxb1.example.impl package, xjc generates two implementation classes: UsOrCanadaAddressTypeImpl and UsOrCanadaAddressImpl. The implementation classes implement their corresponding interfaces.

- Within the com.apress.jaxb1.example.impl.runtime package, xjc generates a number of classes that do all the low-level work associated with parsing, validating, element accessing, marshaling, and unmarshaling.

- Marshaling an XML document creates an XML document from Java classes. Unmarshaling an XML document creates a Java object tree from an XML document.

Now, let's look at the code in the Java interface UsOrCanadaAddressType. Listing 6-3 shows this generated code.

Listing 6-3. *UsOrCanadaAddressType Interface Code*

```
package com.apress.jaxb1.example;
public interface UsOrCanadaAddressType {
    java.lang.String getPostalCode();
    void setPostalCode(java.lang.String value);
    java.lang.String getState();
    void setState(java.lang.String value);
    int getZip();
    void setZip(int value);
    java.lang.String getCountry();
    void setCountry(java.lang.String value);
    java.lang.String getCity();
    void setCity(java.lang.String value);
    java.lang.String getStreet();
    void setStreet(java.lang.String value);
    java.lang.String getName();
    void setName(java.lang.String value);
}
```

When you study the code in Listing 6-3, notice that each element defined within the top-level element shown in Listing 6-1 maps to a property with get and set accessor methods. This mapping intuitively makes sense for most of the elements, but not for the two elements, zip and postalCode, that are part of a choice group. For these two elements, the obvious question is, how is the choice group reflected in the UsOrCanadaAddressType interface? The simple answer is, it is not. Under the default mapping rules, the choice group is not reflected in the interface. However, the choice is correctly implemented within the marshaling and unmarshaling logic. This is also true for the enumeration values for the country element shown in Listing 6-1.

From an intuitive standpoint, you have seen that the default binding model treats the nested elements within a top-level element as a flat list of elements, ignoring group components such as a choice group. However, an alternative binding style called *model group binding* binds each group component to its own Java interface. To understand this alternative style better, specify this in the external binding declaration file using a globalBindings element, as shown in Listing 6-4.

Listing 6-4. *External Binding Declaration with Model Group Binding Style*

```
<?xml version='1.0' encoding='utf-8' ?>
<jxb:bindings version="1.0"
  xmlns:jxb="http://java.sun.com/xml/ns/jaxb"
 xmlns:xs="http://www.w3.org/2001/XMLSchema" >
  <jxb:bindings node="/xs:schema" schemaLocation="address.xsd" >
    <jxb:globalBindings bindingStyle="modelGroupBinding">
    </jxb:globalBindings>
    <jxb:schemaBindings>
      <jxb:package name="com.apress.jaxb1.example" ></jxb:package>
    </jxb:schemaBindings>
  </jxb:bindings>
</jxb:bindings>
```

Now, if you apply the binding shown in Listing 6-4 to the schema in Listing 6-1, the results are slightly different. In particular, the interface UsOrCanadaAddressType contains the nested interface ZipOrPostalCode; in addition, the corresponding property get and set methods for the ZIP and postal code are now merged and use this new interface, as shown in Listing 6-5. (For simplicity, we have omitted the property get and set methods that are unchanged from the default binding style in Listing 6-5.)

Listing 6-5. *UsOrCanadaAddressType Derived with Model Group Binding Style*

```
package com.apress.jaxb1.example;
public interface UsOrCanadaAddressType {
    ...

    com.apress.jaxb1.example.UsOrCanadaAddressType.ZipOrPostalCode
        getZipOrPostalCode();
    void
    setZipOrPostalCode(com.apress.jaxb1.example.
UsOrCanadaAddressType.ZipOrPostalCode
                                        value);

    public interface ZipOrPostalCode {
        java.lang.String getPostalCode();
        void setPostalCode(java.lang.String value);
        boolean isSetPostalCode();
        int getZip();
        void setZip(int value);
        boolean isSetZip();
        java.io.Serializable getContent();
        boolean isSetContent();
        void unsetContent();
    }
}
```

The obvious advantage of this alternative style is that the semantics associated with various group components become apparent through the designated Java interfaces. The obvious disadvantage of this style is the proliferation of Java content interfaces, one per group component. Next, you will see an example use case that illustrates how to use the JAXB binding compiler and runtime framework.

Example Use Case

Imagine a website selling various trade journals. This website offers a web service where associated publishers can send catalog information about their journals. The website provides an XML Schema that specifies the structure of an XML document containing catalog information. This catalog schema defines a top-level `catalog` element. This `catalog` element can have zero or more `journal` elements, and each `journal` element can have zero or more `article` elements. Each of these elements defines relevant attributes. The elements are defined by reference to their associated types, which are defined separately. Listing 6-6 shows this catalog schema, `catalog.xsd`.

Listing 6-6. *catalog.xsd*

```
<xsd:schema xmlns:xsd="http://www.w3.org/2001/XMLSchema">
 <xsd:element name="catalog" type="catalogType"/>

 <xsd:complexType name="catalogType">
  <xsd:sequence>
   <xsd:element ref="journal"  minOccurs="0" maxOccurs="unbounded"/>
  </xsd:sequence>
  <xsd:attribute name="section" type="xsd:string"/>
  <xsd:attribute name="publisher" type="xsd:string"/>
 </xsd:complexType>

 <xsd:element name="journal" type="journalType"/>

 <xsd:complexType name="journalType">
  <xsd:sequence>
   <xsd:element ref="article"  minOccurs="0" maxOccurs="unbounded"/>
  </xsd:sequence>
 </xsd:complexType>

 <xsd:element name="article" type="articleType"/>

 <xsd:complexType name="articleType">
  <xsd:sequence>
   <xsd:element name="title" type="xsd:string"/>
   <xsd:element name="author" type="xsd:string"/>
  </xsd:sequence>
  <xsd:attribute name="level" type="xsd:string"/>
  <xsd:attribute name="date" type="xsd:string"/>
 </xsd:complexType>

</xsd:schema>
```

The web service client at the publisher must construct an XML document that conforms to the catalog schema shown in Listing 6-6 and must send this document in a web service message. Listing 6-7 shows an example of such a document, `catalog.xml`.

Listing 6-7. *catalog.xml*

```
<?xml version="1.0" encoding="UTF-8"?>
<catalog
        section="Java Technology"
        publisher="IBM  developerWorks">
    <journal>
       <article level="Intermediate"  date="January-2004" >
           <title>Service Oriented Architecture Frameworks </title>
            <author>Naveen Balani</author>
       </article>
      <article level="Advanced" date="October-2003"  >
          <title>Advance DAO Programming</title>
          <author>Sean Sullivan</author>
       </article>
       <article level="Advanced" date="May-2002"  >
          <title>Best Practices in EJB Exception Handling  </title>
          <author>Srikanth Shenoy     </author>
       </article>
    </journal>
</catalog>
```

The web service receiving this catalog information message needs to retrieve relevant element and attribute values from the message and store those values in a database. In this chapter, you are not concerned with the aspects of this use case that deal with storing data in a database or that deal with the mechanics of assembling and transporting a web service message. We will cover those aspects in later chapters. Your sole concern in this chapter is marshaling and unmarshaling the document shown in Listing 6-7 and subsequently retrieving the relevant element and attribute values from the mapped Java objects.

In this use case example, your objectives are as follows:

- Bind the catalog schema shown in Listing 6-6 using the xjc compiler, and generate Java content classes representing the various schema components defined within the catalog schema.

- Marshal and unmarshal the XML document shown in Listing 6-7.

- Retrieve the relevant element and attribute values from the mapped Java objects.

- Customize schema bindings using inline binding declarations.

Before presenting some Java code associated with this use case, we'll discuss how to download and install the required software and how to create and configure the Eclipse project required for this chapter.

Downloading and Installing the Software

To run the JAXB 1.0 examples, you will need to install the following software.

Installing Java Web Service Developer Pack (JWSDP)

JAXB 1.0 is included in JWSDP 1.6. Therefore, you need to download and install JWSDP 1.6.[3] Install JWSDP 1.6 in any directory. For this chapter, we will assume JWSDP is installed under the default installation directory, which on Windows is `C:\Sun\jwsdp-1.6`; assuming that is the case, JAXB is included in the `C:\Sun\jwsdp-1.6\jaxb` directory.

Installing J2SE

We recommend using J2SE 5.0 with JWSDP 1.6 because JAXB uses some `SAXParserFactory` class methods that are defined in J2SE 5.0 but are not defined in J2SE 1.4.2. With JRE 1.4.2, unmarshaling generates the following error:

```
java.lang.NoSuchMethodError: javax.xml.parsers.SAXParserFactory.
getSchema()Ljavax/xml/validation/Schema
```

You can use J2SE 1.4.2 with JWSDP 1.6 if you use the Endorsed Standards Override Mechanism (`http://java.sun.com/j2se/1.4.2/docs/guide/standards/`).[4] If you want to use J2SE 5.0, which we strongly recommend, you need to download and install it. The `xjc` compiler does not run if the `JAVA_HOME` environment variable has empty spaces in its path name. Therefore, install J2SE 5.0 in a directory with no empty spaces in its path name.

Creating and Configuring the Eclipse Project

To compile the example schema with `xjc` and to run the marshaling and unmarshaling code examples included in this project, you need to create an Eclipse Java project. The quickest way to create the Eclipse project is to download the `Chapter6` project from the Apress website (`http://www.apress.com`) and import this project into Eclipse. This creates all the Java packages and files needed for this chapter automatically.

You also need to set the `Chapter6` JRE to the J2SE 5.0 JRE. You set the JRE in the project Java build path by clicking the Add Library button. Figure 6-2 shows the `Chapter6` build path. If your JWSDP 1.6 install location is not `C:\Sun\jwsdp-1.6`, you may need to explicitly add or edit the external JARs. Either way, make sure your Java build path shows all the JWSDP 1.6 JAR files shown in Figure 6-2.

We will show how to configure the binding compiler `xjc` to generate Java content classes in the `gen_source` folder and the `gen_source_customized_bindings` folder; therefore, add these two folders to the source path under the Source tab in the Java build path area, as shown in Figure 6-3.

---

3. You can find JWSDP 1.6 at `http://java.sun.com/webservices/downloads/webservicespack.html`.
4. You can find this information at `http://java.sun.com/webservices/docs/1.6/ReleaseNotes.html#new`.

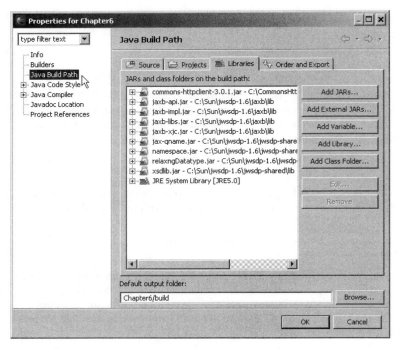

Figure 6-2. *Chapter6 Eclipse project Java build path*

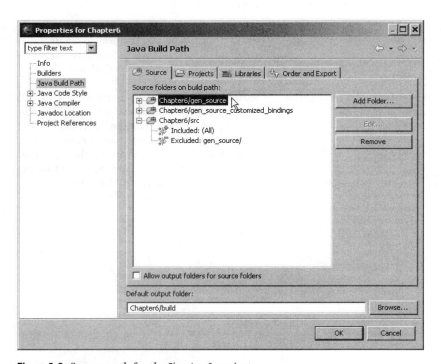

Figure 6-3. *Source path for the Chapter6 project*

Figure 6-4 shows the Chapter6 project directory structure.

Figure 6-4. *Chapter6 Eclipse project directory structure*

Binding the Catalog Schema to Java Classes

In this section, you will bind the catalog schema shown in Listing 6-6 to its Java content classes. You'll subsequently use the Java content classes to marshal and unmarshal the XML document shown in Listing 6-7. You compile the XML Schema with the JAXB binding compiler xjc, which can be run with the runtime options listed in Table 6-1.

Table 6-1. *xjc Command Options*

Option	Description
-nv	The strict validation of the input schema(s) is not performed.
-b <file>	Specifies the external binding file.
-d <dir>	Specifies the directory for generated files.
-p <pkg>	Specifies the target package.
-classpath <arg>	Specifies the classpath.
-use-runtime <pkg>	The impl.runtime package does not get generated. Instead, the runtime in the specified package is used.
-xmlschema	The input schema is a W3C XML Schema (the default).

You will run `xjc` from within Eclipse. Therefore, configure `xjc` as an external tool in Eclipse. To configure `xjc` as an external tool, select Run ➤ External Tools. In the External Tools dialog box, you need to create a new program configuration, which you do by right-clicking the Program node and selecting New. This adds a new configuration, as shown in Figure 6-5. In the new configuration, specify a name for the configuration in the Name field, and specify the path to the `xjc` batch or shell file, which resides in the `jaxb/bin` folder under the JWSDP install directory, in the Location field.

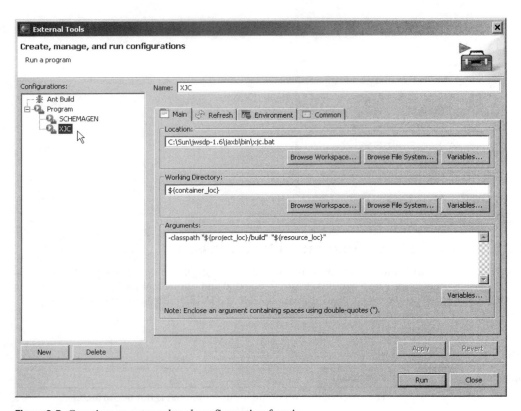

Figure 6-5. *Creating an external tool configuration for* `xjc`

You also need to set the working directory and program arguments. To set the working directory, click the Variables button for the Working Directory field, and select the `container_loc` variable. This specifies a value of `${container_loc}` in the Working Directory field. This value implies that whatever schema file is selected at the time `xjc` is run, that file's parent directory becomes the working directory for `xjc`.

In the Arguments field, you need to set the classpath and the schema that needs to be compiled with the xjc compiler. You can do that by clicking the Variables button for the Arguments field and selecting the variables project_loc and resource_loc. This specifies the values ${project_loc} and ${resource_loc} in the Arguments field. Add the –classpath option before ${project_loc}. The value ${resource_loc} means that whatever file is selected at the time xjc is run, that file becomes the schema file argument to xjc. If the directory in which Eclipse is installed has empty spaces in its path name, enclose ${project_loc} and ${resource_loc} within double quotes, as shown in Figure 6-5. To store the new configuration, click the Apply button.

You also need to set the environment variables JAVA_HOME and JAXB_HOME in the external tool configuration for xjc. On the Environment tab, add the environment variables JAVA_HOME and JAXB_HOME, as shown in Figure 6-6. Your values for these variables may of course be different.

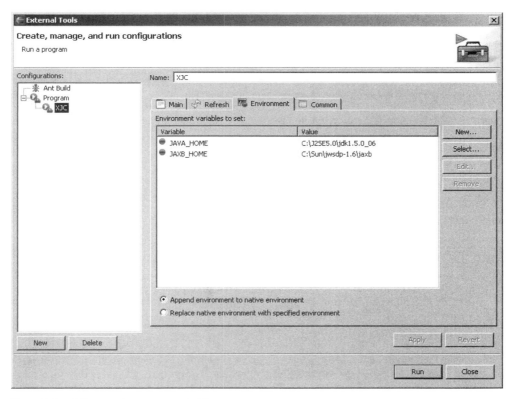

Figure 6-6. *Adding environment variables*

To add the XJC configuration to the External Tools menu, select the Common tab, and select the External Tools check box in the Display in Favorites menu area, as shown in Figure 6-7.

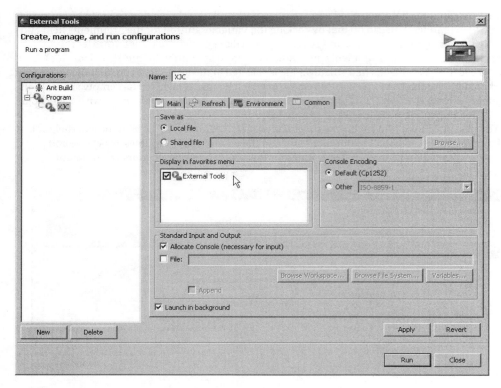

Figure 6-7. *Adding the* xjc *configuration to the external Tools menu*

To run the xjc compiler on the example schema, catalog.xsd, select the catalog.xsd file in the Package Explorer, and then select Run ➤ External Tools ➤ XJC. The Java interfaces and classes get generated in the gen_source folder, as shown in Figure 6-8.

The Java classes and interfaces are generated in the package generated, by default. The jaxb.properties file specifies an instantiation class for the javax.xml.bind.context.factory class, and the bgm.ser file contains implementation-specific serialized objects. It is important to include both these files in any JAR file containing generated classes.

For each top-level xsd:element and xsd:complexType schema component defined in the example schema shown in Listing 6-6, a Java interface is generated. For example, for the top-level <xsd:element name="catalog" type="catalogType"/> schema component, a Catalog interface gets generated (as shown in Listing 6-8), and for the <xsd:complexType name="catalogType"> component, a CatalogType interface gets generated (as shown in Listing 6-9).

Listing 6-8. *Catalog.java*

```
package generated;
public interface Catalog
  extends javax.xml.bind.Element, generated.CatalogType {
}
```

Listing 6-9. *CatalogType.java*

```
package generated;
public interface CatalogType {
    java.lang.String getSection();
    void setSection(java.lang.String value);
```

```
    java.util.List getJournal();
    java.lang.String getPublisher();
    void setPublisher(java.lang.String value);
}
```

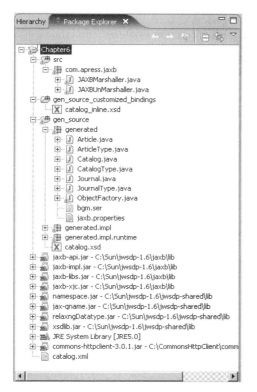

Figure 6-8. *Schema-derived Java content classes generated by* `xjc`

The `CatalogType` interface consists of getter and setter methods for each of the attributes of the `<xsd:complexType name="catalogType">` component and also a getter method for the `journal` elements in this component. A setter method is not created for the `journal` element, because the `maxOccurs` cardinality of the `journal` element is set to `unbounded`. We will explain in the next section the procedure for adding `journal` elements to the `catalog` element.

`CatalogImpl.java` and `CatalogTypeImpl.java` are the implementation Java classes generated for the `Catalog.java` and `CatalogType.java` interfaces, respectively. Similarly, the interface `Journal.java` and implementation class `JournalImpl.java` are generated for the `journal` schema element, and so on. The `jaxb.properties` file specifies an instantiation class for the `javax.xml.bind.context.factory` class, and the `bgm.ser` file contains implementation-specific serialized objects. It is important to include both these files in any JAR file containing generated classes.

Marshaling an XML Document

Marshaling a document means creating an XML document from a Java object tree. In the use case example, the web services client has to marshal the XML document shown in Listing 6-7. In this section, we will show how to marshal such a document from a Java object tree that contains objects that are instances of generated Java content classes.

To marshal the example document, you need to follow these steps:

1. Create a JAXBContext object, and use this object to create a Marshaller object.

2. Create an ObjectFactory object to create instances of the relevant generated Java content classes.

3. Using the ObjectFactory object, create an object tree with Catalog as the root object. Populate these tree objects with the relevant data using the appropriate setter methods.

An application creates a new instance of the JAXBContext class with the static method newInstance(String contextPath), where contextPath specifies a list of Java packages for the schema-derived classes. In this case, generated contains the schema-derived classes, and you create this object as follows:

```
JAXBContext jaxbContext=JAXBContext.newInstance("generated");
```

The Marshaller class converts a Java object tree to an XML document. You create a Marshaller object with the createMarshaller() method of the JAXBContext class, as shown here:

```
Marshaller marshaller=jaxbContext.createMarshaller();
```

The Marshaler class has overloaded marshal() methods to marshal into SAX 2 events, a DOM structure, an OutputStream, a javax.xml.transform.Result, or a java.io.Writer object.

To create a Java object tree for marshaling into an XML document, create an ObjectFactory, as shown here:

```
ObjectFactory factory=new ObjectFactory();
```

For each schema-derived Java class, a static factory method to create an object of that class is defined in the ObjectFactory class. The Java interface corresponding to the root element catalog is Catalog; therefore, create a Catalog object with the createCatalog() method of the ObjectFactory class:

```
Catalog catalog=factory.createCatalog();
```

The root element in the XML document to be marshaled has the attributes section and publisher. The Catalog interface provides the setter methods setSection() and setPublisher() for these attributes. You can set the section and publisher attributes with these setter methods, as shown in Listing 6-10.

Listing 6-10. *Setting the section and publisher Attributes*

```
catalog.setSection("Java Technology");
catalog.setPublisher("IBM developerWorks");
```

The Java interface for the journal element is Journal. catalog.xml has more than one journal element, which can be created from the ObjectFactory class with the createJournal() method, which returns a Journal object, as shown here:

```
Journal journal=factory.createJournal();
```

To add a journal element to a catalog element, obtain a java.util.List of Journal objects for a Catalog object, and add the journal element to this List, as shown in Listing 6-11.

Listing 6-11. *Adding a journal Element to the catalog Element*

```
java.util.List journalList=catalog.getJournal();
journalList.add(journal);
```

The Java interface for an `article` element is `Article`. You create an `Article` object with the `createArticle()` method of the `ObjectFactory` class:

```
Article article=factory.createArticle();
```

The element `article` has the attributes `level` and `date` for which the corresponding setter methods in the `Article` interface are `setLevel()` and `setDate()`. You can set the attributes `level` and `date` for an `article` element with these setter methods, as shown in Listing 6-12.

Listing 6-12. *Setting the Attributes* level *and* date

```
article.setLevel("Intermediate");
article.setDate("January-2004");
```

The element `article` has the subelements `title` and `author`. The `Article` interface has setter methods, `setTitle()` and `setAuthor()`, for setting the `title` and `author` elements, as shown in Listing 6-13.

Listing 6-13. *Setting the* title *and* author *Elements*

```
article.setTitle("Service Oriented Architecture Frameworks");
article.setAuthor("Naveen Balani");
```

To add an `article` element to a `journal` element, obtain a `java.util.List` of `Article` objects from a `Journal` object and add an `Article` object to this `List`, as shown in Listing 6-14.

Listing 6-14. *Adding an* article *Element to a* journal *Element*

```
java.util.List  articleList=journal.getArticle();
articleList.add(article);
```

To create the XML document, marshal the `Catalog` object with a `marshal()` method of class `Marshaller`. The `Catalog` object created in this section is marshaled to an XML file with an `OutputStream`, as shown here:

```
marshaler.marshal(catalog,System.out);
```

`JAXBMarshaller.java` in Listing 6-15 contains the complete program that marshals the example XML document from a Java object tree, following the steps outlined earlier. In the `JAXBMarshaller.java` application, the `generateXMLDocument()` method is where the marshaled document is generated. You can run the `JAXBMarshaller.java` application in Eclipse to marshal the example XML document.

Listing 6-15. *JAXBMarshaller.java*

```
package com.apress.jaxb;

import generated.*;
import javax.xml.bind.*;

public class JAXBMarshaller {
  public void generateXMLDocument() {
    try {

      JAXBContext jaxbContext = JAXBContext.newInstance("generated");
      Marshaller marshaller = jaxbContext.createMarshaller();
      generated.ObjectFactory factory = new generated.ObjectFactory();
```

```java
            Catalog catalog = factory.createCatalog();
            catalog.setSection("Java Technology");
            catalog.setPublisher("IBM developerWorks");

            Journal journal = factory.createJournal();
            Article article = factory.createArticle();

            article.setLevel("Intermediate");
            article.setDate("January-2004");
            article.setTitle("Service Oriented Architecture   Frameworks");
            article.setAuthor("Naveen Balani");

            java.util.List journalList = catalog.getJournal();
            journalList.add(journal);
            java.util.List articleList = journal.getArticle();
            articleList.add(article);

            article = factory.createArticle();

            article.setLevel("Advanced");
            article.setDate("October-2003");
            article.setTitle("Advance DAO Programming");
            article.setAuthor("Sean Sullivan");

            articleList = journal.getArticle();
            articleList.add(article);

            article = factory.createArticle();

            article.setLevel("Advanced");
            article.setDate("May-2002");
            article.setTitle("Best Practices in EJB   Exception Handling");
            article.setAuthor("Srikanth Shenoy");
            articleList = journal.getArticle();

            articleList.add(article);
            marshaller.setProperty("jaxb.formatted.output",Boolean.TRUE);
            marshaller.marshal(catalog, System.out);

        } catch (JAXBException e) {
          System.out.println(e.toString());

        }

    }

    public static void main(String[] argv) {
      JAXBMarshaller jaxbMarshaller = new JAXBMarshaller();
      jaxbMarshaller.generateXMLDocument();
    }
}
```

Listing 6-16 shows the output from running JAXBMarshaller.java, which shows an XML document marshaled from a Java object tree.

Listing 6-16. *Output from* JAXBMarshaller.java

```
<?xml version="1.0" encoding="UTF-8" standalone="yes"?>
<catalog publisher="IBM developerWorks" section="Java Technology">
    <journal>
        <article date="January-2004" level="Intermediate">
            <title>Service Oriented Architecture    Frameworks</title>
            <author>Naveen Balani</author>
        </article>
        <article date="October-2003" level="Advanced">
            <title>Advance DAO Programming</title>
            <author>Sean Sullivan</author>
        </article>
        <article date="May-2002" level="Advanced">
            <title>Best Practices in EJB    Exception Handling</title>
            <author>Srikanth Shenoy</author>
        </article>
    </journal>
</catalog>
```

Unmarshaling an XML Document

Unmarshaling means creating a Java object tree from an XML document. In the example use case, the website receives an XML document containing catalog information, and it needs to unmarshal this document before it can process the catalog information contained within the document. In this section, we'll first show how to unmarshal the example XML document using the JAXB API, and subsequently we'll show how to access various element and attribute values in the resulting Java object tree.

To unmarshal, you need to follow these steps:

1. The example XML document, catalog.xml (Listing 6-7), is the starting point for unmarshaling. Therefore, import catalog.xml to the Chapter6 project in Eclipse by selecting File ➤ Import.

2. Create a JAXBContext object, and use this object to create an UnMarshaller object.

3. The Unmarshaller class converts an XML document to a Java object.

As discussed in the previous section, create a JAXBContext object, which implements the JAXB binding framework operations unmarshal() and validate().

You need an Unmarshaller object to unmarshal an XML document to a Java object. Therefore, create an UnMarshaller object with the createUnmarshaller() method of the JAXBContext class, as shown here:

```
Unmarshaller unMarshaller=jaxbContext.createUnmarshaller();
```

The Unmarshaller class has overloaded unmarshal() methods for unmarshaling. To validate an XML document that is being unmarshaled, set the Unmarshaller object to be validating with the setValidating(boolean) method, as shown here:

```
unMarshaller.setValidating(true);
```

To create a Java object representation of an XML document, unmarshal the XML document to obtain a Catalog object:

```
Catalog catalog=(Catalog)(unMarshaller.unmarshal(xmlDocument));
```

xmlDocument is the File object for the XML document. The unmarshal() method also accepts an InputSource, an InputStream, a Node, a Source, or a URL as input. The unmarshal() method returns a Java object corresponding to the root element in the XML document being unmarshaled. This completes the unmarshaling of the document. Now that you have an object tree, accessing data embedded within the document is a simple matter of using the right property method on the right object.

The root element catalog has the attributes section and publisher, which you can access with the getSection() and getPublisher() methods, as shown in Listing 6-17.

Listing 6-17. *Outputting section and publisher Attributes*

```
System.out.println("Section: "+catalog.getSection());
System.out.println("Publisher: "+catalog.getPublisher());
```

You can obtain a List of Journal objects for a Catalog object with the getJournal() method of the Catalog interface:

```
java.util.List journalList=catalog.getJournal();
```

Iterate over the List to obtain the Journal objects, which correspond to the journal elements in the XML document, catalog.xml, as shown in Listing 6-18.

Listing 6-18. *Retrieving Journal Objects for a Catalog Object*

```
for(int i=0; i<journalList.size(); i++){
  Journal journal=(Journal)journalList.get(i);
}
```

You can obtain a List of Article objects with the getArticle() method of the Journal interface, as shown here:

```
java.util.List articleList=journal.getArticle();
```

To obtain Article objects in an Article List, iterate over the List, and retrieve Article objects, as shown in Listing 6-19.

Listing 6-19. *Retrieving Article Objects from a List*

```
for(int j=0; j<articleList.size(); j++){
  Article article=(Article)articleList.get(j);
}
```

An article element has the attributes level and date and the subelements title and author. You can access the values for the article element attributes and subelements with getter methods for these attributes and elements, as shown in Listing 6-20.

Listing 6-20. *Outputting article Element Attributes and Subelements*

```
System.out.println("Article Date: "+article.getDate());
System.out.println("Level: "+article.getLevel());
System.out.println("Title: "+article.getTitle());
System.out.println("Author: "+article.getAuthor());
```

The complete program, JAXBUnMarshaller.java, shown in Listing 6-21, demonstrates how to unmarshal the example XML document following the steps outlined earlier. The unmarshaling application has a method unMarshall(File), which takes a File object as input. The input file should be the document to be unmarshaled.

Listing 6-21. *JAXBUnMarshaller.java*

```java
package com.apress.jaxb;

import generated.*;
import javax.xml.bind.*;
import java.io.File;
import java.io.IOException;

public class JAXBUnMarshaller {
                      //Method to Unmarshal an XML Document
  public void unMarshall(File xmlDocument) {
    try {
      //Create a JAXBContext object
      JAXBContext jaxbContext = JAXBContext.newInstance("generated");
      //Create an Unmarshaller object
      Unmarshaller unMarshaller = jaxbContext.createUnmarshaller();
      //Set Unmarshaller to validating
      unMarshaller.setValidating(true);
      //Unmarshal an XML document to a Catalog object
      Catalog catalog = (Catalog) unMarshaller.unmarshal(xmlDocument);
      //Output the element and attribute values in XML document
      System.out.println("Section: " + catalog.getSection());
      System.out.println("Publisher: " + catalog.getPublisher());
      java.util.List journalList = catalog.getJournal();
      for (int i = 0; i < journalList.size(); i++) {

        Journal journal = (Journal) journalList.get(i);

        java.util.List articleList = journal.getArticle();
        for (int j = 0; j < articleList.size(); j++) {
          Article article = (Article) articleList.get(j);

          System.out.println("Article Date: " + article.getDate());
          System.out.println("Level: " + article.getLevel());
          System.out.println("Title: " + article.getTitle());
          System.out.println("Author: " + article.getAuthor());

        }
      }
    } catch (JAXBException e) {
      System.out.println(e.toString());
    }
  }

  public static void main(String[] argv) {
    File xmlDocument = new File("catalog.xml");
    JAXBUnMarshaller jaxbUnmarshaller = new JAXBUnMarshaller();
    jaxbUnmarshaller.unMarshall(xmlDocument);
  }
}
```

Listing 6-22 shows the output from unmarshaling the example XML document.

Listing 6-22. *Output in Eclipse from Unmarshaling* catalog.xml

```
Section: Java Technology
Publisher: IBM developerWorks
Article Date: January-2004
Level: Intermediate
Title: Service Oriented Architecture    Frameworks
Author: Naveen Balani
Article Date: October-2003
Level: Advanced
Title: Advance DAO Programming
Author: Sean Sullivan
Article Date: May-2002
Level: Advanced
Title: Best Practices in EJB    Exception Handling
Author: Srikanth Shenoy
```

Customizing JAXB Bindings

The JAXB binding compiler, xjc, provides a default binding of an XML Schema to Java classes. You can customize the schema bindings either by adding inline binding declarations to the schema or by using an external binding file. In this section, we will show how to customize JAXB bindings. You have two choices for defining JAXB customization bindings:

- The first choice for defining customization bindings is an external (to schema) bindings file. External bindings offer the advantage of applying different customizations to the same schema definition to satisfy different binding objectives. However, external bindings use XPath expressions to address binding nodes and are therefore relatively complex to define.

- Inline bindings are defined within schema definition elements; they address binding nodes implicitly. Unlike external bindings, they require no use of XPath expressions, so they are relatively easy to define.

To keep things simple, we will use inline bindings in this section. Binding declarations are of the following types:

- Global binding declarations
- Schema binding declarations
- XML-to-Java datatype binding declarations
- Class binding declarations
- Property binding declarations

We have added an example of each of the binding declaration types to the example XML Schema document, catalog_inline.xsd, as shown in Listing 6-23. We discuss these inline binding declarations in subsequent sections.

Listing 6-23. catalog_inline.xsd *with Inline Binding Declarations*

```
<?xml version="1.0" encoding="UTF-8"?>
<xsd:schema xmlns:xsd="http://www.w3.org/2001/XMLSchema"
  xmlns:jxb="http://java.sun.com/xml/ns/jaxb"
  jxb:version="1.0">
<xsd:annotation>
  <xsd:appinfo>
```

```xml
  <jxb:globalBindings
  collectionType ="java.util.ArrayList"
  fixedAttributeAsConstantProperty= "true"
  generateIsSetMethod= "false"
  enableJavaNamingConventions = "true">
    <jxb:javaType name= "java.util.Date"
     xmlType= "xsd:date"
     parseMethod= "com.apress.jaxb.DateHelper.parse"
     printMethod= "com.apress.jaxb.DateHelper.format">
     </jxb:javaType>
   </jxb:globalBindings>
   <jxb:schemaBindings>
     <jxb:package name="jaxb"/>
      <jxb:nameXmlTransform>
       <jxb:elementName suffix="Element"/>
      </jxb:nameXmlTransform>
   </jxb:schemaBindings>
  </xsd:appinfo>
</xsd:annotation>
 <xsd:element name="catalog" type="catalogType"/>
 <xsd:complexType name="catalogType">
<xsd:annotation>
  <xsd:appinfo>
   <jxb:class  name = "CatalogClass">
   </jxb:class>
  </xsd:appinfo>
</xsd:annotation>
  <xsd:sequence>
   <xsd:element ref="journal"  minOccurs="0" maxOccurs="unbounded"/>
  </xsd:sequence>
  <xsd:attribute name="section" type="xsd:string"/>
  <xsd:attribute name="publisher" type="xsd:string"/>
 </xsd:complexType>
 <xsd:element name="journal" type="journalType"/>
 <xsd:complexType name="journalType">
  <xsd:sequence>
   <xsd:element ref="article"  minOccurs="0" maxOccurs="unbounded"/>
  </xsd:sequence>
 </xsd:complexType>
 <xsd:element name="article" type="articleType"/>
 <xsd:complexType name="articleType">
  <xsd:sequence>
   <xsd:element name="title" type="xsd:string">
    <xsd:annotation>
     <xsd:appinfo>
      <jxb:property generateIsSetMethod="true" />
     </xsd:appinfo>
    </xsd:annotation>
   </xsd:element>
   <xsd:element name="author" type="xsd:string"/>
  </xsd:sequence>
  <xsd:attribute name="level" type="xsd:string"/>
  <xsd:attribute name="date" type="xsd:date"/>
 </xsd:complexType>
</xsd:schema>
```

The schema root element has a namespace declaration for the http://java.sun.com/xml/ns/ jaxb namespace. You can specify the JAXB namespace declaration with or without a prefix. If the namespace declaration has a prefix, you should add the binding declarations with the prefix. You add binding declarations with the syntax listed in Listing 6-24.

Listing 6-24. *Syntax of Binding Declaration*

```
<xs:annotation>
    <xs:appinfo>
        JAXB  Binding Declarations
    </xs:appinfo>
</xs:annotation>
```

Global Binding Declarations

Global binding declarations are declarations that apply to all the elements in the schema definition in which the declarations are specified. They also apply to any included or imported schemas. You specify global binding declarations in the root element with the globalBindings element. Listing 6-25 shows the global binding declaration in the example schema.

Listing 6-25. *Global Binding Declaration*

```
<jxb:globalBindings
    collectionType ="java.util.ArrayList"
    fixedAttributeAsConstantProperty= "true"
    generateIsSetMethod= "false"
    enableJavaNamingConventions = "true">

</jxb:globalBindings>
```

The collectionType attribute in the globalBindings element specifies a list type class, which must implement the java.util.List interface. In the example, it specifies that all lists in the generated implementations should be represented internally as java.util.ArrayList. The attribute fixedAttributeAsConstantProperty specifies that fixed attributes should be generated as constants in the Java classes. The attribute generateIsSetMethod specifies that the isSet() method should be generated corresponding to the getter and setter property methods. The attribute enableJavaNamingConventions specifies that the Java naming conventions should be enabled.

Schema Binding Declarations

You also specify schema binding declarations in the root element, with the schemaBindings element, as shown in Listing 6-26. The scope of schema declarations is all the schema elements in the target namespace of a schema. In the example schema, the schema binding declaration specifies that the Java classes be generated in the package jaxb. Also, the Java classes corresponding to the schema element declarations are generated with an Element suffix.

Listing 6-26. *Schema Binding Declaration*

```
<jxb:schemaBindings>
    <jxb:package name="jaxb"/>
        <jxb:nameXmlTransform>
            <jxb:elementName suffix="Element"/>
        </jxb:nameXmlTransform>
</jxb:schemaBindings>
```

Datatype Binding Declarations

You specify datatype binding declarations with the `javaType` element. In the example schema, the `xsd:date` datatype maps to `java.util.Date`, as shown in Listing 6-27. Because the datatype binding is specified in the `globalBindings` element, the datatype conversion applies to all the schema and included schemas. The attribute `parseMethod` specifies the method to invoke in unmarshaling an XML document, and the attribute `printMethod` specifies the method to invoke in marshaling an XML document.

Listing 6-27. *Datatype Binding Declaration*

```
<jxb:javaType name= "java.util.Date"
       xmlType= "xsd:date"
       parseMethod= "com.apress.jaxb.DateHelper.parse"
       printMethod= "com.apress.jaxb.DateHelper.format">
</jxb:javaType>
```

Class Binding Declarations

You specify class binding declarations with the `class` element in a schema element, as shown in Listing 6-28. With class binding declarations, you can map a schema element to a specified interface and implementation class. In the example schema, the complex type `catalogType` maps to `CatalogClass`. The default mapping for the complex type `catalogType` is `CatalogType`.

Listing 6-28. *Class Binding Declaration*

```
<jxb:class  name = "CatalogClass">
</jxb:class>
```

Property Binding Declarations

You specify a property binding declaration with the `property` element. A property binding declaration specifies the customization in the binding of an element to a Java interface or class. In the example schema, an `isSet()` method is generated for the `title` element. An `isSet()` method returns `true` if a default value has been specified in the schema.

```
<jxb:property generateIsSetMethod= "true" />
```

If you run the `xjc` compiler again, you will notice that the Java classes get generated in the `jaxb` package. Lists are represented internally in implementation classes with `java.util.ArrayList`. The datatype `xsd:date` maps to `java.util.Date`. Java representations generated corresponding to schema elements have an `Element` suffix. The complex type `catalogType` maps to the `CatalogClass` interface, and the `isSet()` and `unset()` methods are generated for the `title` element.

JAXB 2.0

In the following sections, we will cover JAXB 2.0 and how it differs in operation from JAXB 1.0.

Architecture

JAXB 1.0 was designed under a tight time constraint. As a result, the architects of this specification made a conscious decision to support the binding of only a subset of schema components to Java;

complete support was left to a later specification. JAXB 2.0 remedies the lack of complete schema support in JAXB 1.0 and adds binding support for missing schema components. In particular, the following schema support was added to JAXB 2.0:

- Element declarations using the substitutionGroup attribute, which is resolved to a predefined model group schema component (<xs:element @substitutionGroup>).

- Wildcard schema components (xs:any and xs:anyAttribute).

- Identity constraints used to specify uniqueness across multiple elements (xs:key, xs:keyref, and xs:unique).

- Redefined XML Schema components using the redefine declaration (<xs:redefine>).

- Notation XML Schema components (<xs:notation>).

- The following schema attributes are supported: complexType.abstract, element.abstract, element.substitutionGroup, xsi:type, complexType.block, complexType.final, element.block, element.final, schema.blockDefault, and schema.finalDefault.

The binding framework of JAXB 2.0 enhances the JAXB 1.0 unidirectional binding framework and adds support for bidirectional binding. JAXB 2.0 adds support for the binding of Java classes to XML Schema components, as shown in Figure 6-9.

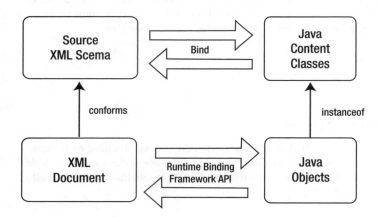

Figure 6-9. *JAXB 2.0 supports bidirectional binding.*

Annotations

JAXB 2.0 relies on J2SE 5.0 annotations[5] to support bidirectional mapping between XML Schema and Java types. Annotations are used both in generated Java content classes and in Java classes as input to generate schema definitions. These binding annotations are defined in the javax.xml.bind.annotation package. Familiarity with J2SE 5.0 is required (and is assumed) to use these annotations. Table 6-2 lists some of the more commonly used annotations defined in the javax.xml.bind.annotation package.

---

5. Annotations are a metadata facility for the Java programming language, defined as part of JSR-175 (http://www.jcp.org/aboutJava/communityprocess/review/jsr175/).

Table 6-2. *JAXB 2.0 Binding Annotations*

Annotation Type	Description	Annotation Elements
XmlAccessorType	Specifies the default serialization of fields and properties	AccessType.PUBLIC_MEMBER maps only public fields and JavaBean properties. AccessType.FIELDS maps only fields. AccessType.PROPERTIES maps only JavaBeans properties. AccessType.NONE maps neither fields nor properties.
XmlAttribute	Maps a JavaBean property to an attribute	name: Attribute name. namespace: Attribute namespace. required: Specifies whether attribute is required; the default is false.
XmlElement	Maps a JavaBean property to an element	defaultValue: The default value of element. name: The element name. namespace: Target namespace of element. nillable: Specifies whether element is nillable; the default is false. type: Element type.
XmlEnum	Maps an enum to a simple type with enumeration	value: Enumeration value
XmlList	Maps a property to a list simple type	
XmlRootElement	Maps a class to root element	name: Local name of root element. namespace: Namespace of root element.
XmlSchema	Maps a package name to a XML namespace	attributeFormDefault: Specifies the value of the attributeFormDefault attribute. elementFormDefault: Specifies the value of the attribute elementFormDefault. namespace: XML namespace. xmlns: Maps namespace prefixes to namespace URIs.
XmlType	Maps a class to an XML Schema type, which may be a simple type or a complex type	name: Target namespace of the XML Schema type. propOrder: Specifies the order of XML schema elements when a class is mapped to a complex type.
XmlValue	Maps a class to an XML Schema complex type with simpleContent or an XML Schema simple type	

XML Schema Binding to Java Representation

Just like JAXB 1.0, JAXB 2.0 specifies a default XML Schema to Java binding that can be overridden through external binding declarations. Conceptually, the JAXB 2.0 binding of XML Schema components to Java is similar to JAXB 1.0. However, since JAXB 2.0 binding is based on J2SE 5.0, its Java representation uses Java 5 annotation tags and is much more compact than the JAXB 1.0 Java representation.

Let's revisit the simple example you looked at in the context of JAXB 1.0 so you can see how the XML Schema to Java binding works under JAXB 2.0.

Simple Binding Example Revisited

Listing 6-1 shows the simple example schema. As before, to keep things simple, you will accept all the default XML Schema binding rules except for one. You will override the default package name for the generated Java content with a specific package name, com.apress.jaxb2.example, as shown in the external binding file in Listing 6-29. This file differs from Listing 6-2 in that it has a different package name and different version attribute value for the top-level jxb:bindings element, which in this case is 2.0.

Listing 6-29. *External Binding Declaration for a Package Name*

```xml
<?xml version='1.0' encoding='utf-8' ?>
<jxb:bindings version="2.0"
  xmlns:jxb="http://java.sun.com/xml/ns/jaxb"
  xmlns:xs="http://www.w3.org/2001/XMLSchema" >
  <jxb:bindings node="/xs:schema"  schemaLocation="address.xsd" >
    <jxb:schemaBindings>
      <jxb:package name="com.apress.jaxb2.example" ></jxb:package>
    </jxb:schemaBindings>
  </jxb:bindings>
</jxb:bindings>
```

Ignoring for the moment the mechanics of configuring the JAXB 2.0 binding compiler, let's assume you can run the JAXB 2.0 xjc compiler. Running xjc, of course, binds schema components to Java. For the schema shown in Listing 6-1, the JAXB 2.0 xjc schema binding works as follows:

- In the com.apress.jaxb2.example package, xjc generates two Java classes: UsOrCanadaAddress and ObjectFactory. Because the complexType in Listing 6-1 is anonymous, no separate class corresponding to an anonymous complexType is generated.

- The UsOrCanadaAddress class is the Java representation for the <xs:element name="UsOrCanadaAddress" > component.

- The ObjectFactory class is an object factory implementation.

If you compare this to the binding of the schema to Java in JAXB 1.0, as explained earlier for JAXB 1.0, you will immediately notice the compactness of the JAXB 2.0 binding, compared to the JAXB 1.0 binding. Now, take a closer look at the code for the generated Java class UsOrCanadaAddress, which is shown in Listing 6-30.

Listing 6-30. *UsOrCanadaAddress Class Code*

```java
package com.apress.jaxb2.example;

@XmlAccessorType(AccessType.FIELD)
@XmlType(name = "", propOrder = {
    "name",
    "street",
    "city",
    "state",
    "zip",
    "postalCode",
    "country"
})
@XmlRootElement(name = "UsOrCanadaAddress")
```

```java
public class UsOrCanadaAddress {

    protected String name;
    protected String street;
    protected String city;
    protected String state;
    protected Integer zip;
    protected String postalCode;
    protected String country;

    public String getName() {
        return name;
    }

    public void setName(String value) {
        this.name = value;
    }

    public String getStreet() {
        return street;
    }

    public void setStreet(String value) {
        this.street = value;
    }

    public String getCity() {
        return city;
    }

    public void setCity(String value) {
        this.city = value;
    }

    public String getState() {
        return state;
    }

    public void setState(String value) {
        this.state = value;
    }

    public Integer getZip() {
        return zip;
    }

    public void setZip(Integer value) {
        this.zip = value;
    }

    public String getPostalCode() {
        return postalCode;
    }
}
```

```
        public void setPostalCode(String value) {
            this.postalCode = value;
        }

        public String getCountry() {
            return country;
        }

        public void setCountry(String value) {
            this.country = value;
        }
    }
```

When you study the code in Listing 6-30, you'll notice that this binding is different from the one for JAXB 1.0. In the default JAXB 2.0 Java representation, instead of an interface, you have a class that is based on Java 5 and uses Java 5 annotation tags (see Table 6-2), such as @XmlAccessorType. However, you can override the default Java representation with a binding declaration such that a schema element component is mapped to an interface, instead of a class; you do this using a globalBindings element, as shown in Listing 6-31.

Listing 6-31. *External Binding Declaration with Model Group Binding Style*

```
<?xml version='1.0' encoding='utf-8' ?>
<jxb:bindings version="1.0"
xmlns:jxb="http://java.sun.com/xml/ns/jaxb"
xmlns:xs="http://www.w3.org/2001/XMLSchema" >
  <jxb:bindings node="/xs:schema"  schemaLocation="address.xsd" >
   <jxb:globalBindings generateValueClass="false">
   </jxb:globalBindings>
    <jxb:schemaBindings>
      <jxb:package name="com.apress.jaxb1.example" ></jxb:package>
     </jxb:schemaBindings>
   </jxb:bindings>
 </jxb:bindings>
```

Now, if you apply the binding shown in Listing 6-31 to the schema in Listing 6-6, the results are slightly different in that UsOrCanadaAddress is now an interface, as shown in Listing 6-32, with an associated implementation class that is not shown here.

Listing 6-32. *UsOrCanadaAddress Derived with generateValueClass Set to false*

```
package com.apress.jaxb2.example;
public interface UsOrCanadaAddress {
    String getName();
    void setName(String value);
    String getStreet();
    void setStreet(String value);
    String getCity();
    void setCity(String value);
    String getState();
    void setState(String value);
    Integer getZip();
    void setZip(Integer value);
```

```
    String getPostalCode();
    void setPostalCode(String value);
    String getCountry();
    void setCountry(String value);
}
```

Example Use Case

For JAXB 2.0, we will use the same example as for JAXB 1.0. The example schema definition is the same, catalog.xsd, listed in Listing 6-6. The example XML document is also the same, catalog.xml, listed in Listing 6-7. The example XML document will be marshaled and unmarshaled with the JAXB 2.0 API, instead of the JAXB 1.0 API, and we'll discuss the differences.

Before discussing the marshaling and unmarshaling Java applications developed with JAXB 2.0, we will show how to download and install some required software and create and configure an Eclipse project for JAXB 2.0.

Downloading and Installing Software

To run the JAXB 2.0 examples, you will need the following software.

Installing Java Web Service Developer Pack (JWSDP)

JAXB 2.0 is included in JWSDP 2.0. Therefore, you need to download and install JWSDP 2.0.[6] Install JWSDP 2.0 in any directory. We will assume JWSDP 2.0 is installed under the default installation directory, which on Windows is C:\Sun\jwsdp-2.0; assuming that is the case, JAXB is included in the C:\Sun\jwsdp-2.0\jaxb directory.

Install J2SE 5.0

In the JAXB 1.0 example, you used J2SE 5.0, because J2SE 1.4.2 does not provide some SAXParserFactory class methods. With JAXB 2.0, you need to use J2SE 5.0, because JAXB 2.0 uses parameterized types. Of course, you may have already installed J2SE 5.0 in the context of JAXB 1.0, so you may not need to install it at this point.

Creating and Configuring Eclipse Project

To compile the example schema with xjc and to run the marshaling and unmarshaling code examples for JAXB 2.0, you need to create an Eclipse Java project. The quickest way to create the Eclipse project is to download the Chapter6-JAXB2.0 project from the Apress website (http://www.apress.com) and import this project into Eclipse. This creates all the Java packages and files needed for this chapter automatically.

You also need to set the Chapter6-JAXB2.0 JRE to the J2SE 5.0 JRE. You set the JRE in the project Java build path by clicking the Add Library button. Figure 6-10 shows the Chapter6-JAXB2.0 Java build path. If your JWSDP 2.0 install location is not C:\Sun\jwsdp-2.0, you may need to explicitly add or edit the external JARs shown in Figure 6-10. Either way, make sure your Java build path shows all the JWSDP 2.0 JAR files shown in Figure 6-10.

---

6. You can find JWSDP 2.0 at http://java.sun.com/webservices/downloads/webservicespack.html.

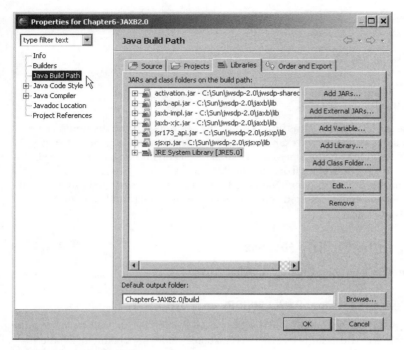

Figure 6-10. *Chapter6 Eclipse project Java build path*

We will show how to configure the binding compiler xjc to generate Java content classes in the gen_source folder; therefore, we have added the gen_source folder to the source path under the Source tab in the Java build path area, similar to the JAXB 1.0 project. Figure 6-11 shows the Chapter6-JAXB2.0 project directory structure.

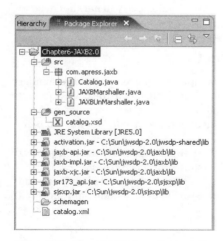

Figure 6-11. *Chapter6 Eclipse project directory structure*

Binding Catalog Schema to Java Classes

In this section, you will bind the catalog schema shown in Listing 6-6 to its Java content classes. You'll subsequently use the Java content classes to marshal and unmarshal the XML document shown in Listing 6-7. You will run xjc from within Eclipse. Therefore, configure xjc as an external tool in Eclipse, similar to the JAXB 1.0 project configuration. The only difference for the JAXB 2.0 project is that the xjc batch file Location field is set to the JAXB 2.0 xjc batch file. You set the environment variables JAVA_HOME and JAXB_HOME similar to JAXB 1.0. Set JAXB_HOME for Chapter6-JAXB2.0 to C:\Sun\jwsdp-2.0\jaxb. To add the xjc configuration to the External Tools menu, select the Common tab, and select the check box External Tools in the Display in Favorites menu area, as shown in Figure 6-7.

To run the xjc compiler on the example schema, catalog.xsd, select the catalog.xsd file in the Package Explorer and then select Run ➤ External Tools ➤ XJC. Schema-derived classes get generated in the gen_source folder, as shown in Figure 6-12.

Figure 6-12. *Schema-derived Java content classes generated by xjc*

Java classes and interfaces are generated in the package generated by default. Fewer classes are generated with JAXB 2.0 than with JAXB 1.0. For each xsd:complexType schema component, one value class gets generated, instead of an interface and an implementation class. For example, for the complex type catalogType, shown in Listing 6-33, the value class CatalogType.java gets generated.

Listing 6-33. *The Complex Type catalogType*

```
<xsd:complexType name="catalogType">
  <xsd:sequence>
   <xsd:element ref="journal"  minOccurs="0" maxOccurs="unbounded"/>
  </xsd:sequence>
  <xsd:attribute name="section" type="xsd:string"/>
  <xsd:attribute name="publisher" type="xsd:string"/>
 </xsd:complexType>
```

The CatalogType.java class consists of getter and setter methods for each of the attributes of the catalogType complex type. A getter method for the complex type journalType with the return type List<JournalType> also gets generated. Listing 6-34 shows CatalogType.java.

Listing 6-34. *CatalogType.java*

```
package generated;

import java.util.ArrayList;
import java.util.List;
import javax.xml.bind.annotation.AccessType;
import javax.xml.bind.annotation.XmlAccessorType;
import javax.xml.bind.annotation.XmlAttribute;
import javax.xml.bind.annotation.XmlType;
import generated.CatalogType;
import generated.JournalType;



@XmlAccessorType(AccessType.FIELD)
@XmlType(name = "catalogType", propOrder = {
    "journal"
})
public class CatalogType {

    protected List<JournalType> journal;
    @XmlAttribute
    protected String publisher;
    @XmlAttribute
    protected String section;


    public List<JournalType> getJournal() {
        if (journal == null) {
            journal = new ArrayList<JournalType>();
        }
        return this.journal;
    }


    public String getPublisher() {
        return publisher;
    }


    public void setPublisher(String value) {
        this.publisher = value;
    }


    public String getSection() {
        return section;
    }
```

```
    public void setSection(String value) {
        this.section = value;
    }

}
```

Similarly, the value class `JournalType.java` gets generated for the complex type `journalType`, and the value class `ArticleType.java` gets generated for the complex type `articleType`. An `ObjectFactory.java` factory class gets generated, which consists of the `create` methods for each of the complex type and element declarations in the example schema. For example, the `ObjectFactory` class method for the complex type `catalogType` is `createCatalogType()`, and its return type is `CatalogType`. The `ObjectFactory` class method for the element `catalog` is `createCatalog(CatalogType)`, and its return type is `JAXBElement<CatalogType>`. Listing 6-35 shows `ObjectFactory.java`.

Listing 6-35. *ObjectFactory.java*

```
package generated;

import javax.xml.bind.JAXBElement;
import javax.xml.bind.annotation.XmlElementDecl;
import javax.xml.bind.annotation.XmlRegistry;
import javax.xml.namespace.QName;
import generated.ArticleType;
import generated.CatalogType;
import generated.JournalType;
import generated.ObjectFactory;

@XmlRegistry
public class ObjectFactory {

    private final static QName _Article_QNAME = new QName("", "article");
    private final static QName _Journal_QNAME = new QName("", "journal");
    private final static QName _Catalog_QNAME = new QName("", "catalog");

    public ObjectFactory() {
    }
    public JournalType createJournalType() {
        return new JournalType();
    }
    public ArticleType createArticleType() {
        return new ArticleType();
    }
    public CatalogType createCatalogType() {
        return new CatalogType();
    }


    @XmlElementDecl(namespace = "", name = "article")
    public JAXBElement<ArticleType> createArticle(ArticleType value) {
        return new JAXBElement<ArticleType>
          (_Article_QNAME, ArticleType.class, null, value);
    }
```

```
    @XmlElementDecl(namespace = "", name = "journal")
    public JAXBElement<JournalType> createJournal(JournalType value) {
        return new JAXBElement<JournalType>
            (_Journal_QNAME, JournalType.class, null, value);
    }

    @XmlElementDecl(namespace = "", name = "catalog")
    public JAXBElement<CatalogType> createCatalog(CatalogType value) {
        return new JAXBElement<CatalogType>
            (_Catalog_QNAME, CatalogType.class, null, value);
    }

}
```

Marshaling an XML Document

Marshaling an XML document means creating an XML document from a Java object representation of the XML document. In the use case example, the web services client has to marshal the XML document shown in Listing 6-7. In this section, we will show how to marshal such a document from a Java object tree that contains objects that are instances of schema-derived classes, generated with JAXB 2.0.

To marshal the example document, you need to follow these steps:

- Create a JAXBContext object, and use this object to create a Marshaller object.

- Create an ObjectFactory object to create instances of the relevant generated Java content classes.

- Using the ObjectFactory object, create an object tree with CatalogType as the root object. Populate these tree objects with the relevant data using the appropriate setter methods.

- Create a JAXBElement<CatalogType> object from the CatalogType object. JAXBElement<CatalogType> represents the catalog element in XML document.

An application creates a new instance of the JAXBContext class with the static method newInstance(String contextPath), where contextPath specifies a list of Java packages for the schema-derived classes. In this case, generated contains the schema-derived classes, and you create this object as follows:

```
JAXBContext jaxbContext=JAXBContext.newInstance("generated");
```

The Marshaller class converts a Java object tree to an XML document. You create a Marshaller object with the createMarshaller() method of the JAXBContext class, as shown here:

```
Marshaller marshaller=jaxbContext.createMarshaller();
```

The Marshaller class has overloaded marshal() methods to marshal into SAX 2 events, a DOM structure, an OutputStream, a javax.xml.transform.Result, or a java.io.Writer object.

To create a Java object tree for marshaling into an XML document, create an ObjectFactory, as shown here:

```
ObjectFactory factory=new ObjectFactory();
```

For each schema-derived Java class, a static factory method to create an object of that class is defined in the ObjectFactory class. The Java value class corresponding to the root element catalog complex type catalogType is CatalogType; therefore, create a CatalogType object with the createCatalogType() method of the ObjectFactory class:

```
CatalogType catalog = factory.createCatalogType();
```

The root element in the XML document to be marshaled has the attributes section and publisher. The CatalogType value class provides the setter methods setSection() and setPublisher() for these attributes. You can set the section and publisher attributes with these setter methods, as shown in Listing 6-36.

Listing 6-36. *Setting the section and publisher Attributes*

```
catalog.setSection("Java Technology");
catalog.setPublisher("IBM developerWorks");
```

The Java value class for the journalType complex type is JournalType. You create a JournalType object with createJournalType(), as shown here:

```
JournalType journal = factory.createJournalType();
```

To add a JournalType object to a CatalogType object, obtain a parameterized type List<JournalType> object for a CatalogType object and add the JournalType object to this List, as shown in Listing 6-37.

Listing 6-37. *Adding a journal Element to the catalog Element*

```
List<JournalType> journalList = catalog.getJournal();
journalList.add(journal);
```

The Java value object for the complex type articleType is ArticleType. You create an ArticleType object with the createArticleType() method of the ObjectFactory class:

```
ArticleType article = factory.createArticleType();
```

The element article has the attributes level and date for which the corresponding setter methods in the ArticleType value object are setLevel() and setDate(). You can set the attributes level and date for an article element with these setter methods, as illustrated in Listing 6-38.

Listing 6-38. *Setting the Attributes level and date*

```
article.setLevel("Intermediate");
article.setDate("January-2004");
```

The element article has the subelements title and author. The ArticleType value object has setter methods, setTitle() and setAuthor(), for setting the title and author elements, as shown in Listing 6-39.

Listing 6-39. *Setting the title and author Elements*

```
article.setTitle("Service Oriented Architecture Frameworks");
article.setAuthor("Naveen Balani");
```

To add an ArticleType object to a JournalType object, obtain a parameterized type List<ArticleType> object from a JournalType object, and add the ArticleType object to this List, as shown in Listing 6-40.

Listing 6-40. *Adding an article Element to a journal Element*

```
List<ArticleType> articleList = journal.getArticle();
articleList.add(article);
```

To marshal the Java object representation CatalogType to an XML document, you need to create a JAXBElement object of type CatalogType with the createCatalog(CatalogType) method's

ObjectFactory.java class. Subsequently, the JAXBElement is marshaled to an output stream, as shown here:

```
JAXBElement<CatalogType> catalogElement=factory.createCatalog(catalog);
marshaller.marshal(catalogElement,System.out);
```

JAXBMarshaller.java in Listing 6-41 contains the complete program that marshals the example XML document with the JAXB 2.0 API. In the JAXBMarshaller.java application, the generateXMLDocument() method is where the marshaled document is saved. You can run the JAXBMarshaller.java application in Eclipse to marshal the example XML document. The output from JAXBMarshaller.java is the same as for JAXB 1.0, shown in Listing 6-16.

Listing 6-41. *JAXBMarshaller.java*

```java
package com.apress.jaxb;

import generated.*;

import javax.xml.bind.*;
import java.util.List;

public class JAXBMarshaller {
  public void generateXMLDocument() {
    try {

      JAXBContext jaxbContext = JAXBContext.newInstance("generated");
      Marshaller marshaller = jaxbContext.createMarshaller();
      generated.ObjectFactory factory = new generated.ObjectFactory();

      CatalogType catalog = factory.createCatalogType();
      catalog.setSection("Java Technology");
      catalog.setPublisher("IBM developerWorks");

      JournalType journal = factory.createJournalType();
      ArticleType article = factory.createArticleType();

      article.setLevel("Intermediate");
      article.setDate("January-2004");
      article.setTitle("Service Oriented Architecture    Frameworks");
      article.setAuthor("Naveen Balani");

      List<JournalType> journalList = catalog.getJournal();
      journalList.add(journal);
      List<ArticleType> articleList = journal.getArticle();
      articleList.add(article);

      article = factory.createArticleType();

      article.setLevel("Advanced");
      article.setDate("October-2003");
      article.setTitle("Advance DAO Programming");
      article.setAuthor("Sean Sullivan");

      articleList = journal.getArticle();
      articleList.add(article);
```

```
      article = factory.createArticleType();

      article.setLevel("Advanced");
      article.setDate("May-2002");
      article.setTitle("Best Practices in EJB    Exception Handling");
      article.setAuthor("Srikanth Shenoy");
      articleList = journal.getArticle();

      articleList.add(article);
      JAXBElement<CatalogType> catalogElement=factory.createCatalog(catalog);
marshaller.setProperty("jaxb.formatted.output",Boolean.TRUE);
      marshaller.marshal(catalogElement, System.out);

    } catch (JAXBException e) {
      System.out.println(e.toString());

    }

  }

  public static void main(String[] argv) {

    JAXBMarshaller jaxbMarshaller = new JAXBMarshaller();
    jaxbMarshaller.generateXMLDocument();
  }
}
```

Unmarshaling an XML Document

Unmarshaling means creating a Java object tree from an XML document. In the example use case, the website receives an XML document containing catalog information, and it needs to unmarshal this document before it can process the catalog information contained within the document. In this section, we'll show first how to unmarshal the example XML document using the JAXB 2.0 API, and subsequently we'll show how to access various element and attribute values in the resulting Java object tree.

To unmarshal, follow these steps:

1. The example XML document, catalog.xml (Listing 6-7), is the starting point for unmarshaling. Therefore, import catalog.xml to the Chapter6-JAXB2.0 project in Eclipse by selecting File ➤ Import.

2. Create a JAXBContext object, and use this object to create an UnMarshaller object.

3. The Unmarshaller class converts an XML document to a JAXBElement object of type CatalogType.

4. Create a CatalogType object from the JAXBElement object.

As discussed earlier, create a JAXBContext object, which implements the JAXB binding framework unmarshal() operation.

You need an Unmarshaller object to unmarshal an XML document to a Java object. Therefore, create an Unmarshaller object with the createUnmarshaller() method of the JAXBContext class, as shown here:

```
Unmarshaller unMarshaller=jaxbContext.createUnmarshaller();
```

JAXB 2.0 deprecates the setValidating() method to validate the XML document being unmarshaled in favor of the setSchema(Schema schema) method, whereby you can set the schema that should be used for validation during unmarshaling.

To create a Java object representation of an XML document, unmarshal the XML document to obtain a JAXBElement object of type CatalogType. Subsequently, obtain a CatalogType object from the JAXBElement object with the getValue() method, as shown in Listing 6-42.

Listing 6-42. *Unmarshaling an XML Document*

```
JAXBElement<CatalogType>
catalogElement = (JAXBElement<CatalogType>)
  unmarshaler.unmarshal(xmlDocument);
CatalogType catalog=catalogElement.getValue();
```

xmlDocument is the File object for the XML document. The unmarshal() method also accepts an InputSource, an InputStream, a Node, a Source, or a URL as input. The unmarshal() method returns a Java object corresponding to the root element in the XML document being unmarshaled. This completes the unmarshaling of the document. Now that you have an object tree, accessing data embedded within the document is a simple matter of using the right property method on the right object.

The root element catalog has the attributes section and publisher, which may be accessed with the getSection() and getPublisher() methods, as shown in Listing 6-43.

Listing 6-43. *Outputting the section and publisher Attributes*

```
System.out.println("Section: "+catalog.getSection());
System.out.println("Publisher: "+catalog.getPublisher());
```

You can obtain a List<JournalType> object of JournalType objects for a CatalogType object with the getJournal() method of the CatalogType value object:

```
List<JournalType> journalList = catalog.getJournal();
```

Iterate over the List to obtain the JournalType objects, which correspond to the journal element in the XML document, catalog.xml, as shown in Listing 6-44.

Listing 6-44. *Retrieving Journal Objects for a Catalog Object*

```
for (int i = 0; i < journalList.size(); i++) {
JournalType journal = (JournalType) journalList.get(i);
}
```

You can obtain a List of ArticleType objects with the getArticle() method of the JournalType value object, as shown here:

```
List<ArticleType> articleList = journal.getArticle();
```

To obtain ArticleType objects in an ArticleType List, iterate over the List, and retrieve ArticleType objects, as shown in Listing 6-45.

Listing 6-45. *Retrieving Article Objects from a List*

```
for (int j = 0; j < articleList.size(); j++) {
ArticleType article = (ArticleType)articleList.get(j);
}
```

An article element has the attributes level and date and the subelements title and author. You can access the values for the article element attributes and subelements with getter methods for these attributes and elements, as shown in Listing 6-46.

Listing 6-46. *Outputting* article *Element Attributes and Subelements*

```
System.out.println("Article Date: "+article.getDate());
System.out.println("Level: "+article.getLevel());
System.out.println("Title: "+article.getTitle());
System.out.println("Author: "+article.getAuthor());
```

The complete program, JAXBUnMarshaller.java, shown in Listing 6-47, demonstrates how to unmarshal the example XML document following the steps outlined earlier. The unmarshaling application has the method unMarshall(File), which takes a File object as input. The input file should be the document to be unmarshaled.

Listing 6-47. *JAXBUnMarshaller.java*

```
package com.apress.jaxb;

import generated.*;

import javax.xml.bind.*;

import java.io.File;
import java.util.List;

public class JAXBUnMarshaller {
  public void unMarshall(File xmlDocument) {
    try {

      JAXBContext jaxbContext = JAXBContext.newInstance("generated");

      Unmarshaller unMarshaller = jaxbContext.createUnmarshaller();

    JAXBElement<CatalogType> catalogElement = (JAXBElement<CatalogType>)
                                unMarshaller.unmarshal(xmlDocument);
      CatalogType catalog=catalogElement.getValue();

      System.out.println("Section: " + catalog.getSection());
      System.out.println("Publisher: " + catalog.getPublisher());
      List<JournalType> journalList = catalog.getJournal();
      for (int i = 0; i < journalList.size(); i++) {

        JournalType journal = (JournalType) journalList.get(i);

        List<ArticleType> articleList = journal.getArticle();
        for (int j = 0; j < articleList.size(); j++) {
          ArticleType article = (ArticleType)articleList.get(j);

          System.out.println("Article Date: " + article.getDate());
          System.out.println("Level: " + article.getLevel());
          System.out.println("Title: " + article.getTitle());
          System.out.println("Author: " + article.getAuthor());
```

```
        }
      }
    } catch (JAXBException e) {
      System.out.println(e.toString());
    }
  }

  public static void main(String[] argv) {
    File xmlDocument = new File("catalog.xml");
    JAXBUnMarshaller jaxbUnmarshaller = new JAXBUnMarshaller();
    jaxbUnmarshaller.unMarshall(xmlDocument);
  }
}
```

The output from unmarshaling the example XML document is the same as for the JAXB 1.0 project.

Binding Java Classes to XML Schema

JAXB 2.0 supports bidirectional mapping between the XML Schema content and Java classes. So far, you have looked at binding the XML Schema content to Java classes. In this section, you will generate XML Schema content from a Java class using the JAXB 2.0 binding annotations. Therefore, you need to define an annotated class: Catalog.java. To this class, you will apply the schemagen tool to generate a schema definition.

In the Catalog.java class, import the javax.xml.bind.annotation package that includes the binding annotation types. Define the root element with the @XmlRootElement annotation. Create a complex type using the @XmlType annotation:

```
@XmlRootElement
@XmlType(name="", propOrder={"publisher", "edition", "title", "author"})
```

You specify the annotation element name as an empty string because the complex type is defined anonymously within an element. You specify the element order using the propOrder annotation element. In the Catalog class, define constructors for the class, and define the different JavaBean properties (publisher, edition, title, author). The root element catalog has an attribute journal. Define the journal attribute using the @XmlAttribute annotation:

```
@XmlAttribute
public String journal;
```

You also need to define getter and setter methods for the different properties and the journal attribute. Listing 6-48 shows the complete Catalog.java class.

Listing 6-48. *Catalog.java*

```
import javax.xml.bind.annotation.XmlRootElement;
import javax.xml.bind.annotation.XmlAttribute;
import javax.xml.bind.annotation.XmlType;

@XmlRootElement
@XmlType(name = "", propOrder = { "publisher", "edition", "title", "author" })
public class Catalog {

  private String publisher;

  private String edition;
```

```java
private String title;

private String author;

public Catalog() {
}

public Catalog(String journal, String publisher, String edition,
    String title, String author) {

  this.journal = journal;
  this.publisher = publisher;
  this.edition = edition;
  this.title = title;
  this.author = author;
}

@XmlAttribute
public String journal;

private String getJournal() {
  return this.journal;
}

public void setJournal(String journal) {
  this.journal = journal;
}

public String getPublisher() {
  return this.publisher;
}

public void setPublisher(String publisher) {
  this.publisher = publisher;
}

public String getEdition() {
  return this.edition;
}

public void setEdition(String edition) {
  this.edition = edition;
}

public String getTitle() {
  return this.title;
}

public void setTitle(String title) {
  this.title = title;
}
```

```
  public String getAuthor() {
    return this.author;
  }

  public void setAuthor(String author) {
    this.author = author;
  }
}
```

You will use the schemagen folder to generate an XML Schema document from the annotated class Catalog.java.

To generate an XML Schema from the annotated class Catalog.java, you need to create an external tools configuration for the schemagen tool. To create an external tools configuration, select Run ➤ External Tools ➤ External Tools. Right-click the Program node, and select New. In the external tools configuration, specify a configuration name. In the Location field, specify the JAXB 2.0 schemagen.bat file, and for Working Directory, specify ${container_loc}. In the Arguments field, you need to specify the directory in which the XML Schema is generated using the -d option. Figure 6-13 shows the external tools configuration for the schemagen tool.

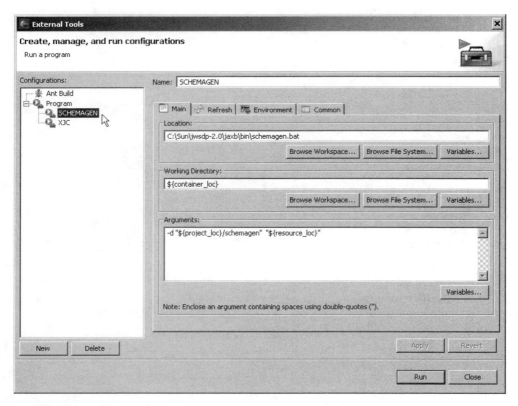

Figure 6-13. *SCHEMAGEN configuration*

To generate the XML Schema from the annotated class Catalog.java, select Catalog.java in the Package Explorer, and run the SCHEMAGEN configuration. An XML Schema gets generated from the annotated class, as shown in Figure 6-14.

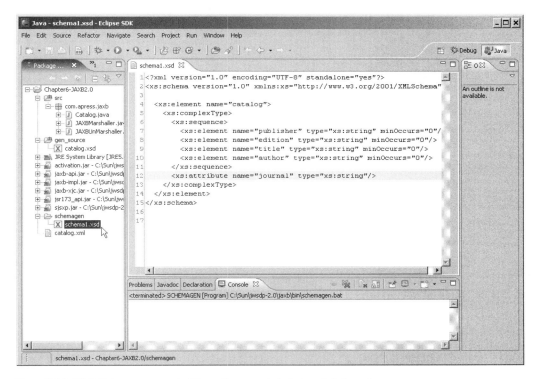

Figure 6-14. *XML Schema generated from the annotated class* `Catalog.java`

Summary

JAXB 1.0 specifies XML Schema binding to Java representation. JAXB 2.0 specifies a bidirectional XML Schema to Java representation. Both specifications provide a binding compiler for generating schema-derived Java content classes and a runtime framework for the marshaling and unmarshaling of XML documents.

You can customize the XML Schema binding to Java types through external or inline binding declarations. The external binding declarations allow the schema definition and customizations to be cleanly separated and offer the advantage of applying different customizations to the same schema definition to satisfy different binding objectives. However, external binding declarations rely on XPath expressions to address binding nodes for customizations and are therefore relatively more complex to specify than inline bindings, which are specified within the schema definition and thus address binding nodes implicitly.

JAXB 2.0 provides following advantages over JAXB 1.0:

- Support for all the schema constructs

- A relatively compact binding of a schema definition to Java content classes

- Bidirectional mapping between schema definition and Java types

We strongly recommend using JAXB 2.0, unless you explicitly need to stay with JAXB 1.0, such as for backward compatibility.

CHAPTER 7

■ ■ ■

Binding with XMLBeans

XMLBeans,[1] just like JAXB, is an XML-to-Java binding and runtime framework. You can use the binding framework to bind an XML Schema to Java types; you can use the runtime framework to unmarshal and marshal an XML document to and from its Java binding classes. If you are wondering why you are studying another XML-to-Java binding, the answer lies in the following reasons:

- XMLBeans provides full support for XML Schema binding to Java types across multiple versions of the Java platform. Even though JAXB 2.0 provides full support for XML Schema, it requires J2SE 5.0; XMLBeans is the only XML-to-Java binding with full schema support that works with J2SE 1.4.*x*, as well as with J2SE 5.0.

- XMLBeans predates JAXB, and perhaps because of that, it has found its way into many more commercial products than JAXB, although, admittedly, if JAXB 2.0 is widely adopted, this may not last into the future.

- XMLBeans defines the XmlObject API for access to XML information content through type-safe Java classes. XMLBeans also defines the XmlCursor API that provides cursor-based access to the XML InfoSet that underlies an XML document. This means by using XMLBeans, you can access and manipulate information content through type-safe Java classes, and you can do so in a manner that is related to the low-level details within the document, such as the order of elements or attributes.

- XMLBeans defines the SchemaType API that provides a schema object model for metadata contained within an XML Schema. This is useful if you want to dynamically create an XML document that conforms to a schema.

In our opinion, JAXB should be the default choice for a binding framework, because it is part of the Java Platform Standard Edition. However, in certain situations, for reasons discussed previously and summarized in Table 7-1, XMLBeans may be the more pragmatic choice.

In this chapter, we will primarily focus on the XMLBeans binding and runtime frameworks. We will also discuss the XmlCursor API related to the XML InfoSet; however, the APIs related to the schema object model are beyond the scope of this chapter, mainly because we want to keep the focus on the binding framework and because the SchemaType API is not central to this focus.

---

1. This is part of the Apache XML Project; you can find detailed information related to this project at
   `http://xmlbeans.apache.org/overview.html`.

Table 7-1. *XMLBeans vs. JAXB*

Feature	XMLBeans	JAXB
Bidirectional mapping	Does not support bidirectional mapping between the XML Schema and the Java class.	JAXB 2.0 supports bidirectional mapping between the XML Schema and the Java class.
XML Schema support	Supports all the XML Schema constructs.	JAXB 2.0 supports all the XML Schema constructs, but JAXB 1.6 does not.
XML document navigation	XMLBeans supports XML document navigation with cursors.	JAXB does not support cursors.
XQuery[a]	XMLBeans supports XQuery.	JAXB does not support XQuery.
Open source	XMLBeans is open source.	JAXB is open source.
Root class	The XMLBeans JavaBeans interfaces extend `org.apache.xmlbeans.XmlObject`.	The JAXB JavaBeans interfaces do not extend a root interface.

a.   XQuery 1.0 is an XML-based query language (`http://www.w3.org/TR/xquery/`).

Overview

The XMLBeans binding framework includes a binding compiler, which you can invoke through the scomp command. The XMLBeans runtime framework defines the XmlObject API, which you can use to marshal or unmarshal an XML document to and from the Java types corresponding to the document's schema.

In this chapter, we will first show how to use the binding compiler to bind an example schema to its Java types and then show how to use these Java types to marshal and unmarshal an example XML document. Listing 7-1 shows the example schema.

Listing 7-1. *catalog.xsd*

```
<?xml version="1.0" encoding="utf-8"?>
<xs:schema
xmlns:xs="http://www.w3.org/2001/XMLSchema">
<xs:element name="catalog">
   <xs:complexType>
    <xs:sequence>
     <xs:element ref="journal" minOccurs="0" maxOccurs="unbounded"/>
    </xs:sequence>
   </xs:complexType>
 </xs:element>
 <xs:element name="journal">
   <xs:complexType>
    <xs:sequence>
     <xs:element ref="article" minOccurs="0" maxOccurs="unbounded"/>
    </xs:sequence>
     <xs:attribute name="publisher"    type="xs:string"/>
   </xs:complexType>
 </xs:element>
```

```
<xs:element name="article">
 <xs:complexType>
  <xs:sequence>
   <xs:element name="title" type="xs:string"/>
   <xs:element name="author" type="xs:string"/>
  </xs:sequence>
  <xs:attribute name="level" type="xs:string"/>
  <xs:attribute name="date" type="xs:string"/>
  <xs:attribute name="section" type="xs:string"/>
 </xs:complexType>
</xs:element>
```

Listing 7-2 shows the example XML document we will marshal and unmarshal. The structure and content of the example XML document, of course, conforms to the example XML schema.

Listing 7-2. *catalog.xml*

```
<?xml version="1.0" encoding="UTF-8"?>
<catalog>
  <journal  publisher="IBM developerWorks">
    <article level="Intermediate" date="January-2004" section="Java Technology">
        <title>Service Oriented Architecture Frameworks</title>
        <author>Naveen Balani</author>       </article>
    <article level="Advanced" date="October-2003" section="Java Technology">
      <title>Advance DAO Programming</title>
      <author>Sean Sullivan</author>    </article>
  <article level="Advanced" date="May-2002" section="Java Technology">
     <title>Best Practices in EJB Exception Handling</title>
     <author>Srikanth Shenoy </author>   </article>
</journal>
</catalog>
```

We will show how to compile the example schema with the binding compiler. Subsequently, we will show how to unmarshal and marshal the example XML document using the Java classes generated from the schema.

Setting Up the Eclipse Project

Before you can set up your project, you need to download XMLBeans[2] 2.0 and extract it to an installation directory. You also need to download the Saxon[3] 8.1.1 XSLT and the XQuery[4] processor; you'll use the Saxon 8.1.1 API to query an XML document with the XmlCursor API. XMLBeans requires at least J2SE 1.4.*x*. We are using J2SE 5.0 because we used it for JAXB 2.0, and we think it is convenient to continue using it for XMLBeans. You may choose to follow suit or use J2SE 1.4.*x*. If you follow this choice, download and install J2SE 5.0, in case you have not already done so.

---

2. You can download the XMLBeans binary version from http://xmlbeans.apache.org/.
3. You can download this from http://sourceforge.net/project/
   showfiles.php?group_id=29872&package_id=21888.
4. We'll discuss XQuery in the "Querying XML Document with XQuery" section.

To compile and run the code examples, you will need an Eclipse project. Download the project Chapter7 from the Apress website (http://www.apress.com), and import it into your Eclipse workspace, as described in Chapter 1.

You need some XMLBeans JAR files in your project's Java build path; Figure 7-1 shows these JAR files. The JAR files required for an XMLBeans application are xbean.jar, which consists of the XMLBeans API, and jsr173_api.jar, which implements JSR-173, Streaming API for XML.[5] You also need to set the JRE system library to JRE 5.0,[6] as shown in Figure 7-1.

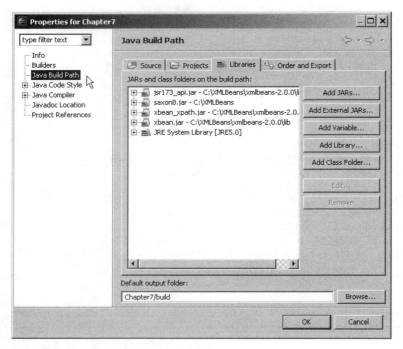

Figure 7-1. *Chapter7 project Java build path*

You will configure the binding compiler scomp to generate Java content classes in the gen_source folder; therefore, add the gen_source folder to the source path on the Source tab in the Java build path area, as shown in Figure 7-2.

Figure 7-3 shows the Chapter7 project directory structure.

---

5. JSR-173 defines the StAX API, which we covered in Chapter 2. Information about JSR 173 is available at http://www.jcp.org/en/jsr/detail?id=173.

6. As noted, you may choose to use JRE 1.4.*x*.

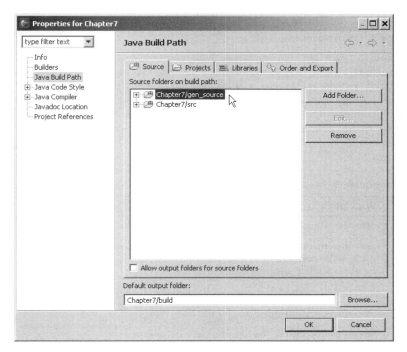

Figure 7-2. *Source path for the* Chapter7 *project*

Figure 7-3. Chapter7 *project directory structure*

Compiling an XML Schema

In this section, you will first bind the example schema (catalog.xsd, shown in Listing 7-1) to its corresponding Java types. Subsequently, you will marshal and unmarshal the example XML document (catalog.xml, shown in Listing 7-2). As noted earlier, you will use the scomp binding compiler to bind the example schema. There is a choice of syntax for scomp use, as shown in Listing 7-3.

Listing 7-3. *scomp Binding Compiler Syntax*

```
scomp [opts]  [schema.xsd]*  [config.xsdconfig]*
scomp [opts]  [directory]
```

In the first `scomp` command, `[schema.xsd]*` is zero or more schemas that are inputs for binding to their Java types, and `[config.xsdconfig]*` is zero or more configuration files that contain custom bindings that influence the binding compiler. The second command shows an alternative syntax for `scomp`, whereby `[directory]` contains input schemas and custom binding files; this is the syntax we will use in the example. In both the commands, `[opts]` denotes the `scomp` compiler options, which are listed in Table 7-2.

Table 7-2. *Scomp Compiler Options*

Option	Description
-cp [a;b;c]	Specifies the classpath.
-d [dir]	Specifies the target binary directory for the .class and .xsb files. An XSB file contains schema metainformation, which is required for tasks such as binding and validating.
-src [dir]	Specifies the target directory for the generated .java files.
-out [xmltypes.jar]	Specifies the output JAR file for the XML types.
-compiler	Specifies the path to the external Java compiler.

We will show how to run `scomp` from within Eclipse. Therefore, configure `scomp` as an external tool in Eclipse. To configure `scomp` within Eclipse, you need to execute the following steps:

1. To configure `scomp` as an external tool, select Run ➤ External Tools. In the External Tools area, create a new Program configuration by right-clicking the Program node and selecting New. This adds a new configuration, as shown in Figure 7-4.

2. An external tools configuration consists of the configuration name and location of the `scomp` compiler command file. You specify the configuration name in the Name field. The location of the `scomp` command file location is in the `bin` directory of the XMLBeans installation, which you specify in the Location field. You also need to set the working directory and program arguments. To set the working directory, click the Variables button for the Working Directory field, and select the `container_loc` variable. This specifies a value of `${container_loc}` in the Working Directory field, as shown in Figure 7-4.

3. In the Arguments field, you need to set the schema that needs to be compiled with the `scomp` compiler. You also need to specify the `scomp` compiler options `-src` and `-out`. (Table 7-2 discussed the compiler options.) In the Arguments field, specify the compiler options `-src` and `-out`, and set the schema resource using the syntax shown in Listing 7-4.

Listing 7-4. *Arguments Field*

```
-src "${resource_loc}" -out "${resource_loc}/xmltypes.jar"  "${resource_loc}"
```

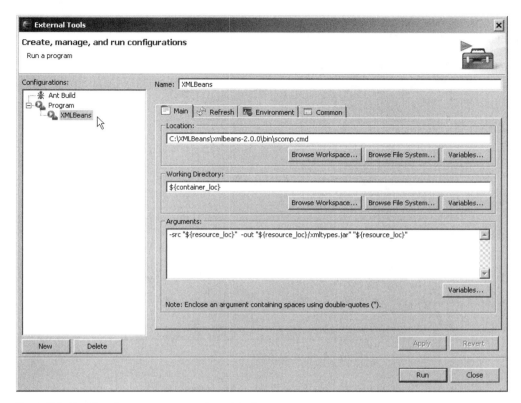

Figure 7-4. *Configuring scomp as an external tool*

The variable resource_loc specifies the location of the project folder that is selected at the time the scomp command is run, and you can add it to the Arguments field by clicking the Variables button and selecting resource_loc. If the directory in which Eclipse is installed has empty spaces in its path name, enclose ${resource_loc} in double quotes, as shown in Figure 7-4. To store the new configuration, click the Apply button.

You also need to set the environment variables JAVA_HOME, PATH, and XMLBEANS_LIB in the external tools configuration for scomp. On the Environment tab, add the environment variables JAVA_HOME, PATH, and XMLBEANS_LIB, as shown in Figure 7-5. The PATH variable needs to point to the bin directory under JAVA_HOME because scomp uses the javac compiler from the bin directory to externally compile some of the generated Java files into class files. The XMLBEANS_LIB variable's value is the directory that contains the xbean.jar file.

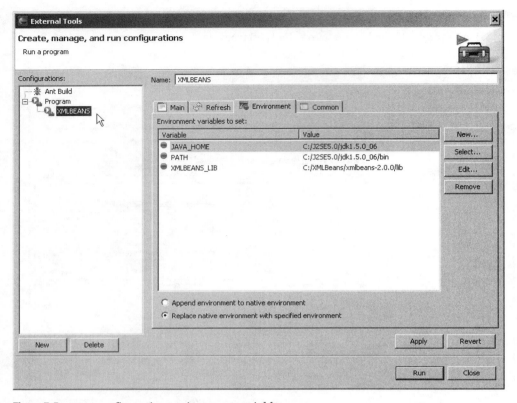

Figure 7-5. *scomp configuration environment variables*

    To add the XMLBeans configuration to the External Tools menu, select the Common tab, and select the check box External Tools in the Display in Favorites area. To run the scomp compiler on the example schema, select the gen_source folder in the Package Explorer, and then select Run ▶ External Tools ▶ XMLBeans, as shown in Figure 7-6.

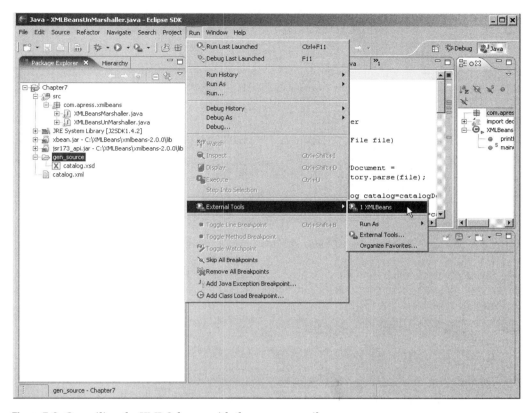

Figure 7-6. *Compiling the XML Schema with the* scomp *compiler*

Java interfaces and classes get generated in the gen_source folder, as shown in Figure 7-7. You must refresh the Chapter7 project to see the generated files. You use interfaces from the noNamespace package for marshaling and unmarshaling an XML document. Classes in the noNamespace.impl package provide an implementation of the interfaces in the noNamespace package.

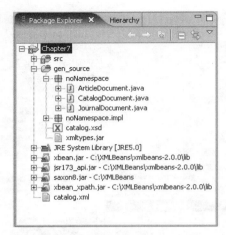

Figure 7-7. *Chapter7 directory structure with the Java classes generated from the schema[7]*

Java classes generated from the schema include a JAR file, xmltypes.jar, which you need to add to the Chapter7 Java build path, as shown in Figure 7-8.

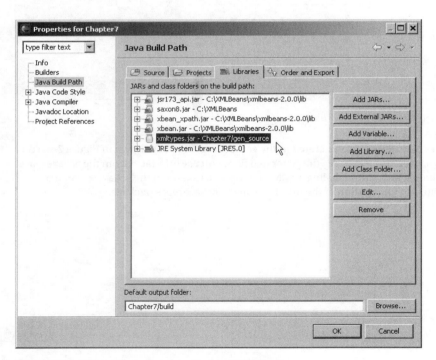

Figure 7-8. *Adding xmltypes.jar to the Java build path*

---

7. The src directory may show an error icon next to it until binding classes are generated and the Java files under the src directory are compiled.

The scomp compiler generates a Java interface and an implementation class for each of the top-level elements in the example schema. For example, for the top-level schema element catalog excerpted in Listing 7-5, the Java interface CatalogDocument.java (Listing 7-6) gets generated.

Listing 7-5. *Schema Element catalog*

```
<xs:element name="catalog">
   <xs:complexType>
    <xs:sequence>
     <xs:element ref="journal" minOccurs="0" maxOccurs="unbounded"/>
    </xs:sequence>
   </xs:complexType>
 </xs:element>
```

Listing 7-6. *CatalogDocument.java*

```
package noNamespace;
public interface CatalogDocument extends org.apache.xmlbeans.XmlObject {
  // … some code deleted
    noNamespace.CatalogDocument.Catalog getCatalog();
    void setCatalog(noNamespace.CatalogDocument.Catalog catalog);
    noNamespace.CatalogDocument.Catalog addNewCatalog();

    public interface Catalog extends org.apache.xmlbeans.XmlObject {
  // … some code deleted
        noNamespace.JournalDocument.Journal[] getJournalArray();
  // … some code deleted
        void setJournalArray(noNamespace.JournalDocument.Journal[] journalArray);
        void setJournalArray(int i, noNamespace.JournalDocument.Journal journal);
  // … some code deleted
        public static final class Factory {
            public static noNamespace.CatalogDocument.Catalog newInstance() {
              return (noNamespace.CatalogDocument.Catalog)
              org.apache.xmlbeans.XmlBeans.getContextTypeLoader().
              newInstance( type, null );
}
  // … some code deleted
            private Factory() { } // No instance of this class allowed
        }
    }

    public static final class Factory {
        public static noNamespace.CatalogDocument newInstance() {
          return (noNamespace.CatalogDocument)
          org.apache.xmlbeans.XmlBeans.
          getContextTypeLoader().
          newInstance( type, null );
        }
  // … some code deleted
        private Factory() { } // No instance of this class allowed
    }
}
```

`CatalogDocument.java` gets generated by default in the package `noNamespace`, and like all the XMLBeans compiler–generated interfaces, it extends the `org.apache.xmlbeans.XmlObject` interface. Key points about this generated interface are as follows:

- The `CatalogDocument.java` interface is the Java type mapping for the top-level `catalog` element (Listing 7-5). It consists of a nested `interface Catalog`, which is a mapping for the anonymous `complexType` definition within `catalog`.

- `Catalog` consists of getter and setter methods for retrieving and setting the `journal` element array.

- Both the `CatalogDocument` and `Catalog` interfaces define nested `Factory` classes.

- The factory class for the `Catalog` interface provides the `newInstance()` methods for creating instances of the `Catalog` interface.

- The factory class for the `CatalogDocument` interface provides the `newInstance()` methods for creating the new `CatalogDocument` objects. It also defines the `parse()` methods for parsing an XML document with catalog as its root element. The `parse()` methods return a `CatalogDocument` object.

One important concept to keep in mind is that the example schema definition (Listing 7-1) defines three top-level elements—catalog, journal, and article—so a valid XML document that conforms to this schema definition can have any one of these three elements as its root element. This is why `scomp` generates three Java types: `CatalogDocument`, `JournalDocument`, and `ArticleDocument`.

The implementation classes `CatalogDocumentImpl.java`, `JournalDocumentImpl.java`, and `ArticleDocumentImpl.java` get generated in the `noNamespace.impl` package.

Customizing XMLBeans Bindings

You can customize the XML Schema to Java types binding generated by the `scomp` compiler with an XMLBeans configuration file. Examples of customizations that can be defined in the configuration file include the addition of prefixes or suffixes to Java type names and the specification of a custom package in which the Java types are generated. The elements of a binding configuration file are defined in the `http://www.bea.com/2002/09/xbean/config` namespace.[8]

The default package in which XMLBeans classes get generated is `noNamespace`. XMLBeans classes may be generated in another package by specifying a package name in an XMLBeans configuration file; you can do this in two ways:

- If the binding schema has a target namespace, then its target namespace can be mapped to a package name. For example, the `http://xmlbeans/journal` namespace can be mapped to the `journal` package, as shown in Listing 7-7.

- If the binding schema has no target namespace, then it can be mapped to a custom package name as shown in Listing 7-8.

---

8. XMLBeans was originally developed by BEA and donated to the Apache Software Foundation in September 2003.

Listing 7-7. *catalog.xsdconfig*

```
<?xml version="1.0" encoding="UTF-8"?>
<xb:config xmlns:journal="http://xmlbeans/journal"
    xmlns:xb="http://www.bea.com/2002/09/xbean/config">
    <xb:namespace uri="http://xmlbeans/journal">
    <xb:package>journal</xb:package>
    </xb:namespace>
</xb:config>
```

Listing 7-8. *catalog.xsdconfig*

```
<?xml version="1.0" encoding="UTF-8"?>
<xb:config xmlns:xb="http://xml.apache.org/xmlbeans/2004/02/xbean/config">
  <xb:namespace>
    <xb:package>xmlbeans</xb:package>
  </xb:namespace>
</xb:config>
```

To bind the catalog.xsd schema with the configuration file catalog.xsdconfig, import catalog.xsdconfig into the gen_source folder in the Chapter7 project. To generate Java types with the configuration file, select the gen_source folder, and run the external tools configuration XMLBeans. The Java classes get generated in the xmlbeans package, as shown in Figure 7-9. You must refresh the Chapter7 project to see the new generated files.

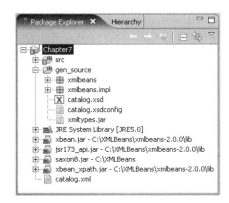

Figure 7-9. *Java classes generated in the xmlbeans package*

Marshaling an XML Document

In this section, you will marshal the example XML document (catalog.xml) from Java classes generated with XMLBeans. As the Java classes are compiled from an XML Schema, the XML document generated from the Java classes conforms to the schema. You first construct a Java object representation of an XML document, and you subsequently output the Java object as an XML document. The Java interface that represents an XML document instance is noNamespace.CatalogDocument. Therefore, create an object of type CatalogDocument, as shown here:

```
noNamespace.CatalogDocument catalogDoc =
noNamespace.CatalogDocument.Factory.newInstance();
```

The root element in an XML document instance is catalog, which is represented with the Java interface noNamespace.CatalogDocument.Catalog. You can add a Catalog object to a noNamespace. CatalogDocument object with the addNewCatalog() method, as shown here:

```
CatalogDocument.Catalog catalog=catalogDoc.addNewCatalog();
```

The XML document to be marshaled has the element journal in the element catalog. A journal element is represented with the interface noNamespace.JournalDocument.Journal. You can add a Journal object to a noNamespace.CatalogDocument.Catalog object with the addNewJournal() method, as shown in Listing 7-9. The Journal element attribute publisher's value is set with the method setPublisher().

Listing 7-9. *Adding a Journal Object and Setting the Attribute publisher*

```
noNamespace.JournalDocument.Journal journal=catalog.addNewJournal();
journal.setPublisher("IBM developerWorks");
```

An article element is represented with the Java interface noNamespace.ArticleDocument. Article. You add an Article object to a noNamespace.JournalDocument.Journal object with the addNewArticle() method, as shown in Listing 7-10. You set the level, date, and section attributes of an article element with setter methods for these attributes.

Listing 7-10. *Adding an Article Object and Setting Attributes*

```
articleDocument.Article article=journal.addNewArticle();
article.setLevel("Intermediate");
article.setDate("January-2004");
article.setSection("Java Technology");
```

You set the values for the title and author subelements of an article element with setter methods for these elements, as shown in Listing 7-11.

Listing 7-11. *Setting the title and author Values*

```
article.setTitle("Service Oriented Architecture Frameworks");
article.setAuthor("Naveen Balani");
```

Similarly, add another Article object to construct the XML document shown in Listing 7-2. Listing 7-12 shows the Java application XMLBeansMarshaller.java used to construct the example XML document. The XMLBeansMarshaller class consists of the method createCatalog(), which creates a Java object representation of an XML document. An XML document instance is represented with the CatalogDocument interface. Therefore, create a CatalogDocument object from the Factory class for CatalogDocument. You add the Java class representation CatalogDocument.Catalog of the root element catalog to the CatalogDocument object with the addNewCatalog() method. You add the Java class representation JournalDocument.Journal of the journal element to the Catalog object with the addNewJournal() method. You add the Java class representation ArticleDocument.Article of the element article to a Journal object with the method addNewArticle(). You set the values for attributes and element text with setter methods for these attributes and text nodes.

Listing 7-12. *XMLBeansMarshaller.java*

```
package com.apress.xmlbeans;

import noNamespace.*;
import noNamespace.impl.*;
```

```java
public class XMLBeansMarshaller {
            //createCatalog method
  public CatalogDocument createCatalog() {
            //Create a CatalogDocument object from Factory class
    CatalogDocument catalogDoc =CatalogDocument.Factory.newInstance();
            //Add a CatalogDocument.Catalog object to CatalogDocument object
    CatalogDocument.Catalog catalog = catalogDoc.addNewCatalog();
            //Add a JournalDocument.Journal object to CatalogDocument.Catalog object
    JournalDocument.Journal

    journal = catalog.addNewJournal();
            //Set value of publisher attribute

    journal.setPublisher("IBM developerWorks");
            //Add a ArticleDocument.Article object to JournalDocument.Journal object
    ArticleDocument.Article

    article = journal.addNewArticle();
            //Set value of Article object attributes and elements.
    article.setTitle("Service Oriented Architecture Frameworks");
    article.setAuthor("Naveen Balani");
    article.setLevel("Intermediate");
    article.setDate("January-2004");
    article.setSection("Java Technology");


            //Add another Article object
    article = journal.addNewArticle();
    article.setTitle("Advance DAO Programming");
    article.setAuthor("Sean Sullivan");
    article.setLevel("Advanced");
    article.setDate("October-2003");
    article.setSection("Java Technology");
            //Add another Article object
    article = journal.addNewArticle();
    article.setTitle("Best Practices in EJB Exception Handling");
    article.setAuthor("Srikanth Shenoy");
    article.setLevel("Advanced");
    article.setDate("May-2002");
    article.setSection("Java Technology");
            //Output CatalogDocument object
    System.out.println(catalogDoc);
    return catalogDoc;

  }

  public static void main(String[] argv) {

    XMLBeansMarshaller marshaller = new XMLBeansMarshaller();
    marshaller.createCatalog();

  }
}
```

To run the XMLBeansMarshaller.java application in Eclipse, right-click the Java file shown in Listing 7-12, and execute it by selecting Run As ➤ Java Application. Listing 7-13 shows the output from the marshaling application in Eclipse.

Listing 7-13. *Output from Marshaling an XML Document with XMLBeans*

```
<catalog>
  <journal publisher="IBM developerWorks">
    <article level="Intermediate" date="January-2004" section="Java Technology">
      <title>Service Oriented Architecture Frameworks</title>
      <author>Naveen Balani</author>
    </article>
    <article level="Advanced" date="October-2003" section="Java Technology">
      <title>Advance DAO Programming</title>
      <author>Sean Sullivan</author>
    </article>
    <article level="Advanced" date="May-2002" section="Java Technology">
      <title>Best Practices in EJB Exception Handling</title>
      <author>Srikanth Shenoy</author>
    </article>
  </journal>
</catalog>
```

Unmarshaling an XML Document

Unmarshaling is binding an XML document to Java classes and accessing XML information content through type-safe Java classes. In this section, you will unmarshal the example XML document, catalog.xml, to a Java object representation. To unmarshal the XML document catalog.xml, parse the document with one of the parse() methods in the Factory class for CatalogDocument in the CatalogDocument interface. The overloaded parse() methods return a CatalogDocument object. Listing 7-14 shows the parsing of an XML document with the parse(File) method.

Listing 7-14. *Parsing an XML Document with XMLBeans*

```
CatalogDocument catalogDocument=CatalogDocument.Factory.parse(xmlFile);
```

The variable xmlFile specifies a File object representation of the XML document to be parsed. As discussed earlier, the catalog.xsd schema element catalog is represented by the Java interface noNamespace.CatalogDocument.Catalog. Therefore, obtain a Catalog interface object from the CatalogDocument object returned by parsing catalog.xml. You can obtain a Catalog object from a CatalogDocument object with the getCatalog() method, as shown in Listing 7-15.

Listing 7-15. *Getting a Catalog Object from the CatalogDocument Object*

```
noNamespace.CatalogDocument.Catalog catalog=catalogDocument.getCatalog();
```

The element catalog has an array of journal subelements. A journal element is represented with the noNamespace.JournalDocument.Journal interface. To retrieve journal elements in the catalog element, get an array of type noNamespace.JournalDocument.Journal[] from the noNamespace.CatalogDocument.Catalog object with the getJournalArray() method, as shown here:

```
JournalDocument.Journal[] journalArray=catalog.getJournalArray();
```

The attribute publisher of the element journal may be output by iterating over the Journal[] array and retrieving the publisher attribute with the getPublisher() method, as shown in Listing 7-16.

Listing 7-16. *Retrieving the Attribute Publisher*

```
for (int i = 0; i < journalArray.length; i++) {
   System.out.println("Journal: " + i);
   System.out.println(" publisher : " + journalArray[i].getPublisher());
}
```

The schema element article is represented by the Java interface noNamespace.ArticleDocument. Article. You can obtain an array of noNamespace.ArticleDocument.Article[] from a noNamespace. JournalDocument.Journal object with the getArticleArray() method, as shown in Listing 7-17.

Listing 7-17. *Getting an Article Object Array from the Journal Object*

```
ArticleDocument.Article[] articleArray=journalArray[i].getArticleArray();
```

You can output the element and attribute values in an Article object by iterating over the Article[] array and retrieving values with getter methods for elements and attributes.

You can use the Java application XMLBeansUnMarshaller.java, listed in Listing 7-18, to unmarshal catalog.xml. XMLBeansUnMarshaller.java consists of a printElements() method, which takes a File object representing an XML document as an argument. In the printElements() method, the XML document is parsed to obtain a CatalogDocument object, from which a Catalog object is obtained. From a Catalog object, which represents the element catalog in the schema catalog.xsd, you obtain an array of Journal objects. A Journal object represents the element journal in the schema catalog.xsd. The Journal object array is iterated over to output the attribute publisher of the journal element. You obtain an array of Article objects from a Journal object. The Article array is iterated over to output article element attributes and subelements.

Listing 7-18. *XMLBeansUnMarshaller.java*

```
package com.apress.xmlbeans;

import noNamespace.*;
import java.io.File;

public class XMLBeansUnMarshaller {
         //printElements method
  public void printElements(File file) {
    try {       //Parse XML Document with Factory method parse(File)
      CatalogDocument catalogDocument = CatalogDocument.Factory
         .parse(file);
           //Obtain Catalog object from CatalogDocument object
      CatalogDocument.Catalog catalog = catalogDocument.getCatalog();
           //Obtain array of Journal objects from Catalog object
      JournalDocument.Journal[] journalArray = catalog.getJournalArray();
```

```java
            System.out.println("Catalog has " + journalArray.length
                + " journal elements");
                //Iterate over Journal object Array
            for (int i = 0; i < journalArray.length; i++) {
              System.out.println("Journal: " + i);
                //Output value of publisher Attribute
              System.out.println(" publisher : "
                + journalArray[i].getPublisher());
                //Obtain array of Article objects from Journal object
              ArticleDocument.Article[] articleArray = journalArray[i]
                .getArticleArray();
                //Iterate over Article object array
              for (int j = 0; j < articleArray.length; j++) {
                System.out.println("Article: " + j);
                //Output Article object attribute and sub element values
              System.out.println("Level : " + articleArray[j].getLevel());
                System.out.println("Date : " + articleArray[j].getDate());
                System.out.println("Section : "
                    + articleArray[j].getSection());
                System.out.println("Title : " + articleArray[j].getTitle());
                System.out.println("Author : "
                    + articleArray[j].getAuthor());

              }

            }
        } catch (org.apache.xmlbeans.XmlException e) {
        } catch (java.io.IOException e) {
        }

    }

    public static void main(String[] argv) {

      XMLBeansUnMarshaller unmarshaller = new XMLBeansUnMarshaller();
      unmarshaller.printElements(new File("catalog.xml"));

    }
}
```

Run the XMLBeansUnMarshaller.java application in Eclipse with the procedure explained in Chapter 1. Listing 7-19 shows the output from unmarshaling an XML document with XMLBeansUnMarshaller.

Listing 7-19. *Output from XMLBeansUnMarshaller.java*

```
Catalog has 1 journal elements
Journal: 0
 publisher : IBM developerWorks
Article: 0
Level : Intermediate
Date : January-2004
```

```
Section : Java Technology
Title : Service Oriented Architecture Frameworks
Author : Naveen Balani
Article: 1
Level : Advanced
Date : October-2003
Section : Java Technology
Title : Advance DAO Programming
Author : Sean Sullivan
Article: 2
Level : Advanced
Date : May-2002
Section : Java Technology
Title : Best Practices in EJB Exception Handling
Author : Srikanth Shenoy
```

In the following section, you will traverse an XML document with the XmlCursor API.

Traversing an XML Document with the XmlCursor API

XMLBeans has the provision to traverse an XML document with the XmlCursor API. An XML cursor defines a location in an XML document, where operations can be performed on the XML document. Because a cursor can be created with or without a corresponding XML Schema for an XML document, cursors are suited to navigate an XML document when a schema for the XML document is not available. By locating a cursor at some position in an XML document, you can perform operations such as getting and setting values, adding elements and attributes, selecting nodes, and querying the XML document. With XmlCursor, you can perform the following operations:

- Use the token model to navigate an XML document in small increments. Table 7-3 discusses the token model.

- Get and set values within an XML document.

- Modify the structure of an XML document by adding, removing, and moving elements and attributes.

- Select nodes with XPath.

- Query an XML document with XQuery.[9] XQuery 1.0: An XML Query Language[10] is a W3C Recommendation. It is a SQL-like language for querying XML data sources. We will cover XQuery briefly within this chapter.

In the XmlCursor API, an XML document is represented with tokens. Table 7-3 shows the token types and static int fields to represent different tokens types.

In the following sections, we will demonstrate each of these XmlCursor features with an example. XML cursors are implemented by the XmlCursor interface. Therefore, to navigate an XML document with XML cursors, import the XmlCursor interface:

```
import org.apache.xmlbeans.XmlCursor;
```

---

9. We will cover XQuery briefly within this chapter.
10. This recommendation is available at http://www.w3.org/TR/xquery/.

Table 7-3. *Token Types*

Token Type	Token Field	Description
ATTR	INT_ATTR	Attribute token type
NAMESPACE	INT_NAMESPACE	Namespace declaration token type
COMMENT	INT_COMMENT	Comment token type
PROCINST	INT_PROCINST	Processing instruction token type
END	INT_END	End element token type
TEXT	INT_TEXT	Text token type
ENDDOC	INT_ENDDOC	End document token type
NONE	INT_NONE	No-token type
START	INT_START	Start element token type
STARTDOC	INT_STARTDOC	Start document token type

Positioning the Cursor

You can create an XML cursor using the newCursor() method of the XmlObject interface. The CatalogDocument.java interface (Listing 7-6), generated with the XMLBeans compiler for the root element catalog, extends the XmlObject interface. To create a new cursor for the example XML document, catalog.xml (Listing 7-2), first create a CatalogDocument.java object from the Factory class method parse(File), as shown in Listing 7-20.

Listing 7-20. *Creating a CatalogDocument Object*

```
CatalogDocument catalogDocument = CatalogDocument.Factory.parse(xmlFile);
```

xmlFile is a File object for the XML document catalog.xml. From the CatalogDocument object, you can create a new cursor with the newCursor() method, as shown in here:

```
XmlCursor cursor = catalogDocument.newCursor();
```

The XmlCursor interface provides various methods for navigating an XML document. Table 7-4 shows some of these methods.

Table 7-4. *XmlCursor Interface Navigation Methods*

Method Name	Description
toFirstContentToken()	Moves the cursor to the first token in the content of the current START or STARTDOC. For the definition of START and STARTDOC, refer to Table 7-3.
toChild(int index)	Moves the cursor to the child element of the specified index.
toChild(String name)	Moves the cursor to the first child element of the specified element name.
toChild(String namespace, String name)	Moves the cursor to the first child element of the specified element name in the specified namespace.

Table 7-4. *XmlCursor Interface Navigation Methods*

Method Name	Description
toCursor(XmlCursor moveTo)	Moves the cursor to the position of moveCursor.
toEndDoc()	Moves the cursor to the end of the document.
toEndToken()	Moves the cursor to the END or ENDDOC token.
toFirstAttribute()	Moves the cursor to the first attribute of this element.
toFirstChild()	Moves the cursor to the first child element.
toLastAttribute()	Moves the cursor to the last attribute of this element.
toLastChild()	Moves the cursor to the last child element.
toNextAttribute()	Moves the cursor to the next attribute of this element.
toPrevToken()	Moves the cursor to the previous token.
toStartDoc()	Moves the cursor to the start of document.

In the example application XMLBeansCursor.java, you will move the cursor to the title element of the first article element and output the text of the title element. The XML declaration in a document is not considered a token; therefore, toFirstContentToken() moves the cursor to the start of the catalog element, as shown in Listing 7-21. Subsequent invocations of toFirstChild() moves the cursor to the child elements of the current element. For example, if you want to move the cursor to the start of the title element, one simple way to do that would be to invoke the toFirstChild() method three times, as shown in Listing 7-21.

Listing 7-21. *Moving the Cursor to the Start of the First title Element*

```
cursor.toFirstContentToken();
cursor.toFirstChild();
cursor.toFirstChild();
cursor.toFirstChild();
```

The text value of the title element is retrieved with the getTextValue() method, as shown in Listing 7-22. Subsequently, cursor resources may be deallocated with the dispose() method.

Listing 7-22. *Outputting the Value of the Element at the Current Cursor Location*

```
System.out.println(cursor.getTextValue());
cursor.dispose();
```

Listing 7-23 shows the output from retrieving the title element value in Eclipse. The output in Listing 7-23 may be generated by commenting out all the methods except the navigateXMLDocument() method in XMLCursor.java (Listing 7-35).

Listing 7-23. *Output in Eclipse from Navigating an XML Document*

```
Service Oriented Architecture Frameworks
```

Adding an Element

In this section, you will add a journal element to the root element catalog. As in the previous section, obtain a CatalogDocument object for the XML file catalog.xml from the Factory class, and create a cursor with the newCursor() method:

```
CatalogDocument catalogDocument = CatalogDocument.Factory.parse(xmlFile);
XmlCursor cursor = catalogDocument.newCursor();
```

Position the cursor before the start of the catalog element with the toFirstContentToken() method, and position the cursor before the start of the journal element with the toFirstChild() method, as shown in Listing 7-24.

Listing 7-24. *Moving the Cursor to the Start of the journal Element*

```
cursor.toFirstContentToken();
cursor.toFirstChild();
```

You create a new element with the beginElement(String) method, and you add a new attribute with the insertAttributeWithValue(String, String) method. As an example, add a journal element with a publisher attribute, as shown in Listing 7-25. Subsequently, deallocate cursor resources with the dispose() method.

Listing 7-25. *Adding an Element and an Attribute*

```
cursor.beginElement("journal");
cursor.insertAttributeWithValue("publisher", "IBM developerWorks");
cursor.dispose();
```

You can output the modified document with the toString() method of the CatalogDocument object, as shown here:

```
System.out.println(catalogDocument.toString());
```

Listing 7-26 shows the output from the modified XML document in Eclipse. You can generate the output in Listing 7-26 by commenting out all the methods except the addElement() method in XMLCursor.java (see Listing 7-35).

Listing 7-26. *Modified XML Document with a journal Element Added*

```
<catalog>
  <journal publisher="IBM developerWorks"/>
  <journal publisher="IBM developerWorks">
    <article level="Intermediate" date="January-2004" section="Java Technology">
      <title>Service Oriented Architecture Frameworks</title>
      <author>Naveen Balani</author>
    </article>
    <article level="Advanced" date="October-2003" section="Java Technology">
      <title>Advance DAO Programming</title>
      <author>Sean Sullivan</author>
    </article>
    <article level="Advanced" date="May-2002" section="Java Technology">
      <title>Best Practices in EJB Exception Handling</title>
      <author>Srikanth Shenoy</author>
    </article>
  </journal>
</catalog>
```

Selecting Nodes with XPath

In this section, you will select nodes in an XML file, `catalog.xml`, with XPath. The `XmlCursor` interface method `selectPath(String)` selects a list of selections or locations in an XML document that may be navigated to with the `toNextSelection()` method. The string parameter of the `selectPath()` method is an XPath expression. First you need to obtain a cursor from `CatalogDocument` object, as shown in Listing 7-27.

Listing 7-27. *Creating an XML Cursor*

```
CatalogDocument catalogDocument = CatalogDocument.Factory.parse(xmlFile);
XmlCursor cursor = catalogDocument.newCursor();
```

Move the cursor to the first child element, and save the cursor's current location by pushing the cursor onto a stack of saved locations, as shown in Listing 7-28.

Listing 7-28. *Moving the Cursor to the Start of the `catalog` Element*

```
cursor.toFirstChild();
cursor.push();
```

As an example, select all the `title` elements in the XML document, as shown in Listing 7-29. The XPath expression to select all the `title` elements is `$this//title`. The current cursor location is represented with `$this`, and `//title` selects all the `title` elements in the current token. For a reference to selecting nodes with XPath, refer to Chapter 4.

Listing 7-29. *Selecting XML Nodes with XPath*

```
cursor.selectPath("$this//title");
```

The `XmlCursor` method `toNextSelection()` moves the cursor to the next selection in the list of selections retrieved by the `selectPath()` method. The method `toNextSelection()` returns `true` if the cursor moves to the next selection. To output all the `title` elements, move the cursor to all the selections, and output the cursor value with the `getTextValue()` method, as shown in Listing 7-30.

Listing 7-30. *Outputting the `title` Element Values*

```
while (cursor.toNextSelection()) {
  System.out.println(cursor.getTextValue());
}
```

Listing 7-31 shows the output from selecting the `title` elements. You can generate the output in Listing 7-31 by commenting out all the methods except the `selectWithXPath()` method in `XMLCursor.java` (Listing 7-35).

Listing 7-31. *Output in Eclipse of the `title` Elements selected with XPath*

```
Service Oriented Architecture Frameworks
Advance DAO Programming
Best Practices in EJB Exception Handling
```

The current location of cursor can be popped off the stack as shown here:

```
cursor.pop();
```

Querying an XML Document with XQuery

In this section, you will query the XML file, catalog.xml, with XQuery.[11] XQuery[12] is an SQL-like language for querying XML data sources. The XmlCursor interface method execQuery(queryExpression) queries an XML document with an XQuery expression. First, you need to create an XML cursor with the newCursor() method of a CatalogDocument object, as shown in Listing 7-32.

Listing 7-32. *Creating an XML Cursor*

```
CatalogDocument catalogDocument = CatalogDocument.Factory.parse(xmlFile);
XmlCursor cursor = catalogDocument.newCursor();
```

As an example, query the value of the level attribute in the first article element in the journal element. You select the XQuery expression for the level attribute as shown in Listing 7-33.

Listing 7-33. *XQuery Expression to Select a level Attribute*

```
String queryExpression = "for $a in $this/catalog/journal/article[1]"
        + "return $a/@level";
```

The XQuery expression segment for $a in $this/catalog/journal/article[1] defines a variable with $a that selects the first article in the journal element in the catalog element of the current cursor position. The XQuery expression segment return $a/@level returns the level attribute of the article element. The query is run with the execQuery(String) method, and the results of the query are available at the position of resultCursor in a new XML document. You obtain a resultCursor as shown here:

```
XmlCursor resultCursor = cursor.execQuery(queryExpression);
```

You can output the ResultCursor XML fragment as shown here:

```
System.out.println(resultCursor.getObject().toString() + "\n");
```

Listing 7-34 shows the output of the resultCursor XML fragment for the example query. You can generate the output in Listing 7-34 by commenting out all the methods except the selectWithXQuery() method in XMLCursor.java (Listing 7-35).

Listing 7-34. *Output in Eclipse from Selecting an Attribute with XQuery*

```
<xml-fragment level="Intermediate"/>
```

The example application XMLBeansCursor.java, shown in Listing 7-35, consists of methods for the different operations discussed in the preceding sections. In the navigateXMLDocument(File xmlFile) method, an XML file is navigated with an XML cursor, and the value of a title element is output. In the addElement(File xmlFile) method, a new element is added to an XML file. In the selectWithXPath(File xmlFile) method, all the title elements in the example XML file are selected, and their values are output. In the selectWithXQuery(File xmlFile) method, a node in catalog.xml is selected with an XQuery expression. To run the XMLBeansCursor.java application in Eclipse, follow the procedure in Chapter 1. The outputs shown in the previous sections for the XMLBeansCursor.java application are generated by running the application with only one of the section-specific methods in the application.

---

11. You can find XQuery details at http://www.w3.org/TR/xquery/.
12. This is not to be confused with the XPath language, which is quite distinct from XQuery and is designed not for querying but for addressing parts of an XML document.

Listing 7-35. *XMLCursor.java*

```java
package com.apress.xmlbeans;

import java.io.File;
import java.io.IOException;
import org.apache.xmlbeans.XmlCursor;
import org.apache.xmlbeans.XmlException;
 import noNamespace.CatalogDocument;

public class XMLBeansCursor {
                        //Method for selecting Nodes with XPath
  public void selectWithXPath(File xmlFile) {
    try {      //Obtain an XmlObject object
      CatalogDocument catalogDocument = CatalogDocument.Factory
          .parse(xmlFile);
          //Create an XmlCursor object
      XmlCursor cursor = catalogDocument.newCursor();
          //Move cursor to first child element
      cursor.toFirstChild();
          //Push cursor onto stack
      cursor.push();
          //Select nodes with XPath
      cursor.selectPath("$this//title");
      while (cursor.toNextSelection()) {
        System.out.println(cursor.getTextValue());
      }

          //Pop cursor
      cursor.pop();
    } catch (IOException e) {
    } catch (XmlException e) {
    }
  }
          //Method to query XML document with XQuery
  public void selectWithXQuery(File xmlFile) {
    try {      //Create a cursor
      CatalogDocument catalogDocument = CatalogDocument.Factory
          .parse(xmlFile);
      XmlCursor cursor = catalogDocument.newCursor();
          //Specify XQuery expression
      String queryExpression = "for $a in $this/catalog/journal/article[1]"
          + "return $a/@level";
          //Run XQuery query
      XmlCursor resultCursor = cursor.execQuery(queryExpression);
          //Output result of XQuery
      System.out.println(resultCursor.getObject().toString() + "\n");

    } catch (IOException e) {
    } catch (XmlException e) {
    }
  }
          //Method to add an Element
  public void addElement(File xmlFile) {
```

```java
        try {        //Create a cursor
          CatalogDocument catalogDocument = CatalogDocument.Factory
              .parse(xmlFile);
          XmlCursor cursor = catalogDocument.newCursor();
              //Move cursor to start of root Element
          cursor.toFirstContentToken();
              //Move cursor to first child element
          cursor.toFirstChild();
              //Add an Element
          cursor.beginElement("journal");
                              //Add an attribute
          cursor.insertAttributeWithValue("publisher", "IBM developerWorks");
          cursor.dispose();
              //Output modified document
          System.out.println(catalogDocument.toString());

        } catch (IOException e) {
        } catch (XmlException e) {
        }
    }
          //Method to navigate an XML document
    public void navigateXMLDocument(File xmlFile) {
      try {        //Create a CatalogDocument object and create a cursor
        CatalogDocument catalogDocument = CatalogDocument.Factory
            .parse(xmlFile);
        XmlCursor cursor = catalogDocument.newCursor();
            //Move cursor to start of root Element
        cursor.toFirstContentToken();
            //Move cursor to start of first child Element
        cursor.toFirstChild();
            //Move cursor to start of article element
        cursor.toFirstChild();
            //Move cursor to start of title element
        cursor.toFirstChild();
        System.out.println(cursor.getTextValue());
            //Dispose cursor
        cursor.dispose();

      } catch (IOException e) {
      } catch (XmlException e) {
      }

    }
```

```
public static void main(String[] args) {

  XMLBeansCursor xmlBeansCursor = new XMLBeansCursor();
  File xmlFile = new File("catalog.xml");

   xmlBeansCursor.navigateXMLDocument(xmlFile);
    xmlBeansCursor.addElement(xmlFile);
    xmlBeansCursor.selectWithXPath(xmlFile);

  xmlBeansCursor.selectWithXQuery(xmlFile);

}

}
```

Summary

XMLBeans is an XML-to-Java binding and runtime framework that is similar to JAXB. You can use the binding framework to bind an XML Schema to Java types. XMLBeans offers complete support for all XML Schema constructs. You can use a binding configuration file to customize XML Schema to Java type bindings. You can use the runtime framework to unmarshal and marshal an XML document to and from Java objects that are instances of bound Java types.

In addition to marshaling and unmarshaling an XML document, XMLBeans offers low-level navigational support through the XmlCursor API. Using the XmlCursor API, you can position a cursor at a specified location and modify the document content at that location. This API also provides support for addressing document content with XPath and querying an XML document using the XQuery language.

In our opinion, JAXB 2.0 should be the default choice for an XML Schema to Java types binding framework, mainly because of the following reasons:

- It is part of the Java standards.

- It offers support for the bidirectional mapping between XML Schema content and Java types.

However, the following pragmatic reasons may indicate XMLBeans to be the more appropriate choice:

- You are looking for full XML Schema support, but you are not ready to move to J2SE 5.0.

- During the marshaling process, you want low-level control over the XML markup contained in the marshaled XML document.

- During the unmarshaling process, you want to use XPath to address specific nodes within the XML document, or you want to use the XQuery language to query the content of an XML document.

PART 3

■■■

XML and Databases

CHAPTER 8

■ ■ ■

Storing XML in Native XML Databases: Xindice

Native XML databases define a logical model for storing, retrieving, and updating an XML document. An XML document is the unit of storage in a native XML database. Native XML databases store XML documents as collections that may be queried, updated, and modified. XML documents stored in a native XML database collection are not constrained by any schema; this is unlike relational databases where data stored in a database is constrained by an underlying database schema. You can use XPath to query a native XML database; you can use the XML:DB XUpdate language to update a native XML database.

Most relational databases also support XML storage; therefore, it is pertinent to compare XML storage in a native XML database with XML storage in a relational database. Table 8-1 offers such a comparison.

Table 8-1. *Comparison of Native XML Databases with Relational XML Databases*

Feature	Native XML Database	Relational Database
Database structure	The XML document is the basic unit of storage represented by hierarchies of elements.	Data is stored in rows and columns.
Order	Elements are ordered.	Row ordering is not defined.
Schema	A schema definition is not used to constrain an XML document.	A schema may be used to constrain data structure.
Query	Querying is performed with XPath.	Querying is performed with SQL.
Application	Suitable for storing complex XML documents with attributes and subelements.	Suitable for storing XML documents that need to be stored and retrieved as a single unit.

In this chapter, we will discuss general native XML database concepts in the context of the Xindice[1] native XML database. Xindice is an open source native XML database that can be used to store, retrieve, query, and update XML documents. Since Xindice is one of many native XML databases,

---

1. Pronounced as "zeen-dee-chay," Xindice is an Apache project; you can find more information at `http://xml.apache.org/xindice/`.

it begs the obvious question, why did we choose to focus on Xindice? Well, we decided to focus on Xindice as a representative native XML database for three main reasons:

- Xindice was designed from the ground up as a native XML database, and since that is all it purports to do, it is fairly simple to understand.

- Xindice is fairly compact, easy to install, and simple to administer.

- Xindice provides command-line tools and standards-based APIs to administer, access, and modify an instance of the Xindice database.

Of course, we encourage you to explore other native XML databases, and when you do so, you can transfer the basic concepts you learn in this chapter in the context of Xindice to other native XML databases. Table 8-2 lists some of the other commonly used native XML databases.

Table 8-2. *Native XML Databases*

Database	Description	More Information
Berkeley DB XML	Open source native XML database	`http://www.sleepycat.com/`
dbXML	Open source native XML database	`http://www.dbxmlgroup.com/`

More relevant than the question of why should you focus on Xindice is the question, why do you need a native XML database? Here are some key points that can answer this pertinent question:

- A relational database is indeed sufficient if all you want to do is store and retrieve complete XML documents.

- However, if you want to query a collection of stored XML documents and retrieve parts of these documents or you want to update parts of these stored XML documents without first retrieving a complete document, changing it, and storing it back, then you need a native XML database.

- It is of course theoretically possible to map an XML document to a relational database schema. However, in practice, it is easier to marshal an XML document from a relational database than to unmarshal an XML document into a relational database. The simple reason for this asymmetry is that when the tree structure of an XML document is mapped to the grid structure of a relational database, information related to the document model is lost and any queries or updates that rely on the document model are impossible.

- The storage unit within a native XML database is a document. The model of an XML database is not concerned only with storing XML data within a document but is also concerned with retaining all the information about the document model.

- Since a native XML database retains information about the document model, it is possible to query a native XML database using the XPath language and update it using the XML:DB XUpdate[2] language, which is an XPath-based update language.

Just like working with relational databases, you need tools, query languages, and programming APIs to administer, access, and modify native XML databases. Fortunately, you have all those things available to you in Xindice, and you will explore them in detail in this chapter.

---

2. This is part of the XML:DB initiative; you can find more information at `http://xmldb-org.sourceforge.net/xupdate/xupdate-wd.html#N1f64158`.

Overview

From a logical point of view, an instance of the Xindice database is comprised of hierarchical collections, where each collection may contain nested collections and XML documents. Each query is performed over a collection, which is also referred to as a *collection context*. In a default installation of Xindice, the root collection within an instance of the Xindice database is named db, and therefore the root collection context is identified by the context path /db.

Simple Example

It is perfectly appropriate to think of collections within the Xindice database as analogous to file system folders and to think of documents stored within these collections as documents stored in folders. It is also useful to think of a reference path to a collection context as analogous to a file system path. With this intuitive understanding in place, let's look at a simple example.

Say you are an auto parts supplier and you have an XML document that stores information about windshield wiper blades for a 2006 Ford Mustang convertible, as shown in the following example document:

```
<?xml version='1.0'  encoding='UTF-8' ?>
<wipers>
  <blade location="driver" part="FMWD256783">
    <description>Driver side wiper blade</description>
    <size>22 inches</size>
  </blade>
  <blade location="passenger" part="FMWP256783">
    <description>Passenger side wiper blade</description>
    <size>20 inches</size>
  </blade>
</wipers>
```

You may decide that putting data about wiper blades for all makes and models of cars in a single collection may not be efficient so you decide to come with a more hierarchical scheme and store the example document shown previously in a collection context that looks as follows:

```
/db/parts/Ford/Mustang/2006/Convertible/
```

Now, assume you want to query this collection for information about the driver's side wiper blade. Since we have not yet talked about how you can query a collection, you will ignore the mechanics of putting together a query and instead look at an example query from a purely intuitive standpoint. Here is an example query that would extract information related to the driver's side blade using the Xindice command tool and the XPath query language:

```
xindice xpath
  -c /db/parts/Ford/Mustang/2006/Convertible/
  -q "/wipers/blade[@location='driver']"
```

Can you intuitively see what is going on? Ignore everything in this query for now except for the collection context, which is /db/parts/Ford/Mustang/2006/Convertible/, and the XPath query, which is "/wipers/blade[@location='driver']". Based on these two pieces alone, you can intuitively see that the query searches the given collection context for all the blade elements that are nested within a wipers element and that have a location attribute equal to driver. All elements that match this XPath expression no matter which document they are in are returned by this query.

It is of course entirely reasonable to assume that in addition to documents related to windshield wipers, you may choose to store other XML documents in this collection that contain data about other parts associated with this specific car. The key take-away from this simple example is that how you organize your collections and documents is entirely up to the needs of your application, as long as you keep in mind the following important points:

- Within a collection, you are allowed to store collections or XML documents.

- Xindice will not complain if objects of different types within a collection have the same name.

- You need to be aware that there is a precedence order that resolves name conflicts among different types of objects, and this order is as follows: collection and XML document. The most practical thing to do is to of course not have any name conflicts among different types of objects within a collection.

- Xindice is designed to store small- to medium-sized documents, so avoid storing large XML documents. It is recommended that you break up large documents into separate smaller documents.

Xindice database content may be accessed and modified using either the XML:DB API or the Xindice command-line tool. In this chapter, we will first discuss the command-line tool and then the XML:DB API. However, before we can do either, you need to download and install the Xindice software, which is what we will discuss next.

Installing the Xindice Software

The Xindice database is installed as a web application in a J2EE application server such as JBoss. To install an instance of the Xindice database, you need the Xindice API JAR files and the Xindice web application. Therefore, download[3] xml-xindice-1.1b4-jar.zip (version 1.1 b4 Binary (JAR)), which contains the Xindice XML:DB API JAR files, and xml-xindice-1.1b4-war.zip (version 1.1 b4 Binary (webapp)), which contains the Xindice web application. Extract the contents of the xml-xindice-1.1b4-jar.zip and xml-xindice-1.1b4-war.zip archive files to your desired Xindice installation directory, for example, C:/. There is duplication of some files in these archives, so it is all right to overwrite files while extracting files from these archives.

To run the Xindice database, you need Apache Xerces[4] or the Xerces2[5] XML parser classes in the classpath. By default, Xindice will use whatever XML parser classes are available in the JRE that you use with Xindice. Since the XML parser classes included in J2SE 1.4.2 are based on the Crimson parser, using Xindice 1.1b4 with J2SE 1.4.2 generates errors. To avoid these errors, the easiest thing to do is to use J2SE 5.0, since J2SE 5.0 includes the Xerces2 parser classes.

Before you can proceed, you need to deploy the Xindice web application within an application server. In the next section, we will cover how to deploy Xindice within the JBoss 4.0.2 application server.

---

3. You can download these Xindice zip files from http://xml.apache.org/xindice/download.cgi.
4. You can download the Xerces classes from http://xerces.apache.org/xerces-j/.
5. You can download the Xerces-2j classes from http://xerces.apache.org/xerces2-j/.

Configuring Xindice with the JBoss Server

For the purpose of this discussion, we'll assume you have access to an installation of the JBoss 4.0.2[6] application server. Assuming <jboss-4.0.2> is the JBoss 4.0.2 installation directory, you need to set the JAVA_HOME variable in the <jboss-4.0.2>\bin\run batch file to J2SE 5.0. Also, assuming <Xindice> is the Xindice installation directory, you need to rename <Xindice>/xindice-1.1b4/xindice-1.1b4.war to xindice.war and then copy the xindice.war file to the <jboss-4.0.2>\server\default\deploy directory.

The default Xindice database location is [Xindice-Web-Application-directory]/WEB-INF/db, where Xindice-Web-Application-directory is a temporary directory that is automatically created by the JBoss application server when xindice.war is deployed. Most likely, you will want to modify this default location. To modify this default database location, you have two options:

- Your first option is to edit the WEB-INF/system.xml file in the xindice.war file and set the dbroot attribute in the root-collection element to your desired location for the Xindice database. For example, the following entry in system.xml specifies the database location to be C:/xindice/db/:

  ```
  <root-collection dbroot="C:/xindice/db/"  name="db"  use-metadata="on" >
  ```

  To edit system.xml, you will of course need to expand the xindice.war archive file, edit the file, and then rebuild the archive file.

- Your second option is to set a Java system property called xindice.db.home to your desired database location. You can set this property in the <jboss-4.0.2>\bin\run batch file that is used to start the JBoss application server.

To open the default Xindice database, you need to start the JBoss server. Start the JBoss server through the <jboss-4.0.2>\bin\run batch file. When the JBoss server starts, the Xindice server web application gets deployed, and at this point the Xindice database is ready for access. Assuming the JBoss application server is listening on its default web port of 8080, the root collection context path is given by xmldb:xindice://localhost:8080/db. To check whether Xindice is running on JBoss, invoke the URL http://localhost:8080/xindice in a browser (assuming of course that your JBoss server is listening on port 8080 on the local host).

To access the Xindice database using the Xindice command-line tool and to run the Xindice Java application code examples included in this project, you need to create an Eclipse Java project, which is discussed next.

Creating an Eclipse Project

You can download the Chapter8 project from the Apress website (http://www.apress.com) and import it into your Eclipse workspace.

You need to add some Xindice JAR files to the Java build path of the Chapter8 project. Assuming <Xindice> is the Xindice installation directory, you need to add the JAR files listed in Table 8-3 to the Java build path.

---

6. You can download the JBoss 4.0.2 (or later) application server from http://www.jboss.com/.

Table 8-3. *Xindice JAR Files*

Xindice JAR File	Description
`<Xindice>/xindice-1.1b4/lib/xerces-2.6.0.jar`	Xerces XML parser
`<Xindice>/xindice-1.1b4/xindice-1.1b4.jar`	Core Server API
`<Xindice>/xindice-1.1b4/lib/commons-logging-1.0.3.jar`	Jakarta Commons Logging API
`<Xindice>/xindice-1.1b4/lib/xalan-2.5.2.jar`	XPath API

`<Xindice>/xindice-1.1b4/lib/xmldb-api-20030701.jar`
`<Xindice>/xindice-1.1b4/lib/xmldb-api-sdk-20030701.jar`
`<Xindice>/xindice-1.1b4/lib/xmldb-common-20030701.jar`
`<Xindice>/xindice-1.1b4/lib/xmldb-xupdate-20040205.jar`
	Implementations of the XML:DB API and the XUpdate API

`<Xindice>/xindice-1.1b4/lib/xmlrpc-1.1.jar`	XML-RPC API
`<Xindice>/xindice-1.1b4/lib/xml-apis.jar`	DOM API

You also need to set the `Chapter8` JRE to the J2SE 5.0 JRE. The JRE is also set in the project Java build path by clicking the Add Library button. Figure 8-1 shows the `Chapter8` Java build path.

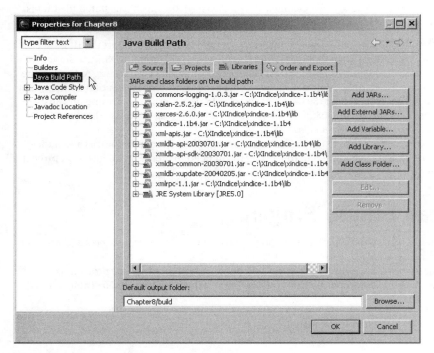

Figure 8-1. *Chapter8 project Java build path*

The XML file `catalog.xml` in the `xindice_resources` folder will be an input XML document to the `XIndiceDB.java` application; therefore, add the `xindice_resources` folder to the source path on the Source tab in the Java build path area, as shown in Figure 8-2.

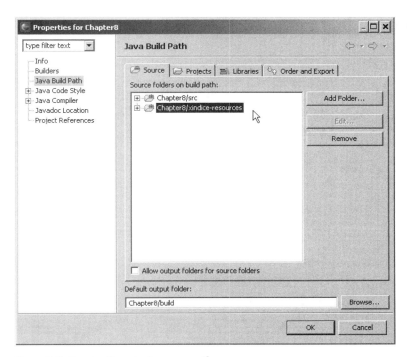

Figure 8-2. *Chapter8 project source path*

Figure 8-3 shows the `Chapter8` project directory structure.

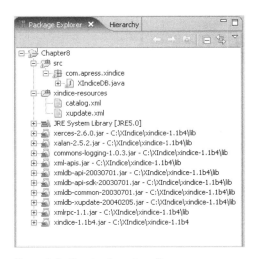

Figure 8-3. *Chapter8 project directory structure*

Before you can run the XIndiceDB application, you need to configure a Java application within Eclipse using the procedure discussed in Chapter 1. You also need to define an XINDICE_HOME environment variable with the value <Xindice>/xindice-1.1b4, as shown in Figure 8-4.

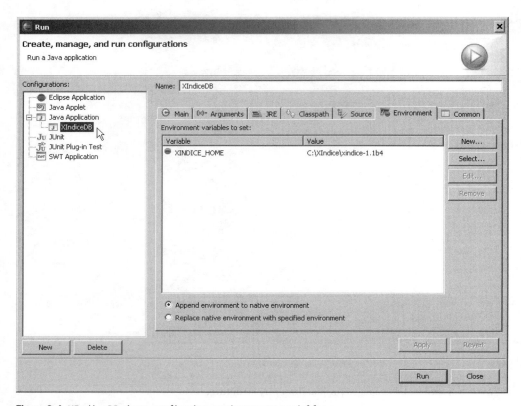

Figure 8-4. *XIndiceDB.java application environment variables*

Using the Xindice Command-line Tool

The following sections focus on details related to using the Xindice command-line tool.

Command Syntax

You access the Xindice command-line tool with the xindice command. The basic syntax of the xindice command is as follows:

```
xindice action [switch] [parameter]
```

Table 8-4 lists the commonly used xindice command action values.

Table 8-4. *Xindice Command Action Values*

Xindice Action	Description
ac	Adds a collection
dc	Deletes a collection
ad	Adds a document
dd	Deletes a document
lc	Lists the collections
rd	Retrieves a document
ld	Lists documents in a collection
xpath	Queries a document using XPath
xupdate	Updates a document using XUpdate

Table 8-5 lists frequently used xindice command switch values.

Table 8-5. *Xindice Command Switch Values*

Xindice Switch	Description
-c	Specifies a collection context. The context syntax is of the format xmldb:xindice://host:port/db.
-f	Specifies a file path.
-n	Specifies a name.
-q	Specifies an XPath query.

Command Configuration in Eclipse

You will run the xindice command in Eclipse. Therefore, configure xindice as an external tool in Eclipse. To configure xindice as an external tool, select Run ➤ External Tools. In the External Tools area, you need to create a new Program configuration, which you do by right-clicking the Program node and selecting New. This adds a new configuration, as shown in Figure 8-5. In the new configuration, specify a name for the configuration, and in the Location field, specify a path to the xindice batch or shell file, which resides in the xindice-1.1b4/bin folder.

You also need to set the working directory and program arguments. To set the working directory, click the Variables button for the Working Directory field, and select the container_loc variable. This specifies a value of ${container_loc} in the Working Directory field. This value implies that whatever file is selected at the time xindice is run, that file's parent directory becomes the working directory for xindice. Figure 8-5 shows the XINDICE external tools configuration.

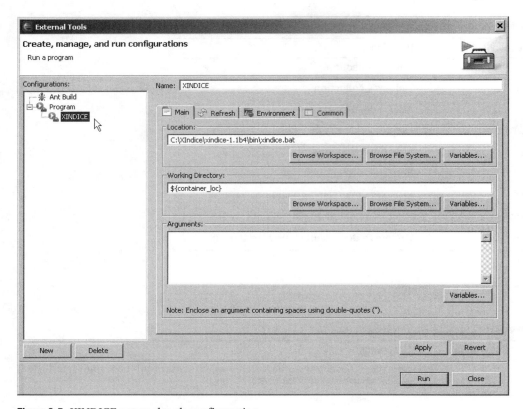

Figure 8-5. *XINDICE external tools configuration*

In the Arguments field, you need to set the arguments passed to the xindice command. You can do that by clicking the Variables button for the Arguments field and selecting the variable resource_loc. The value ${resource_loc} means that whatever file is selected at the time xindice is run, that file becomes an argument to xindice. If the directory in which Eclipse is installed has empty spaces in its path name, enclose ${resource_loc} within double quotes. Because the arguments depend on the Xindice database operation, arguments are not specified in Figure 8-5. To store the new configuration, click the Apply button. You also need to set the environment variable JAVA_HOME for the XINDICE external tools configuration. Select the Environment tab, and add the JAVA_HOME environment variable by clicking the New button, as shown in Figure 8-6.

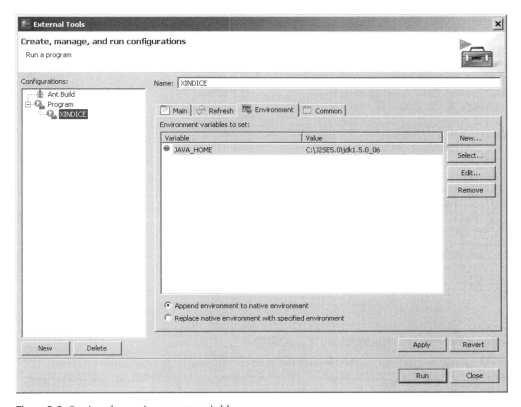

Figure 8-6. *Setting the environment variable*

Xindice Command Examples

In this section, we will demonstrate how to use the Xindice command-line tool to access the Xindice database. You will create a collection in a database instance, add an example XML document to the collection, retrieve the example XML document, query the document using XPath, update the document using XUpdate, and delete the document, all with the Xindice command-line tool. The Xindice database instance in which the collection is created is the default database, db. Listing 8-1 shows the example XML document that is added to the db database.

Listing 8-1. *catalog.xml*

```
<?xml version="1.0" encoding="UTF-8"?>
<catalog title="OnJava.com" publisher="OReilly">
 <journal date="Sept 2005">
  <article>
   <title>What Is a Portlet</title>
   <author> Sunil Patil</author>
  </article>
 </journal>
 <journal date="Sept 2005">
  <article>
   <title>What Is Hibernate</title>
   <author>James Elliott</author>
  </article>
 </journal>
 <journal date="Oct 2003">
  <article>
   <title>BCEL Maven and CSS with Swing</title>
   <author>Daniel Steinberg</author>
  </article>
 </journal>
</catalog>
```

Creating a Collection in the Xindice Database

In this section, you will create an instance of the Xindice database collection using the Xindice command-line tool. For example, to create a top-level collection named catalog, you can use the following xindice command:

```
xindice ac –c xmldb:xindice://localhost:8080/db –n catalog
```

The Xindice command action ac specifies that a collection be added, the –c switch specifies the collection context as the root context, and the –n switch specifies the collection name as catalog. Figure 8-7 shows the external tools configuration XINDICE.

You can run the XINDICE configuration with the specified arguments by clicking the Run button. The Xindice command-line tool creates the collection catalog in the db database and prints the message shown in Listing 8-2.

Listing 8-2. *Output from Adding a Collection*

```
trying to register database
Created : xmldb:xindice://localhost:8080/db/catalog
```

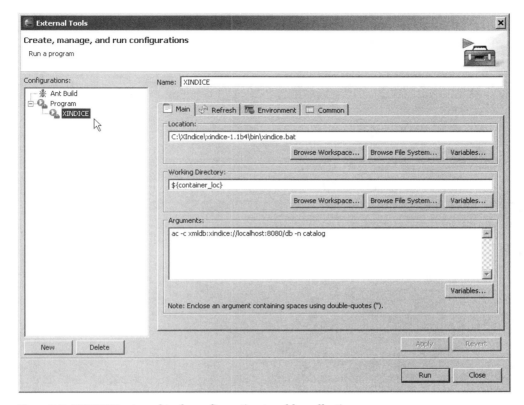

Figure 8-7. *XINDICE external tools configuration to add a collection*

Adding an XML Document to the Xindice Database

In this section, you will add your example XML document, catalog.xml (Listing 8-1), to the catalog collection. Listing 8-3 shows the Xindice command to add an XML document to a collection.

Listing 8-3. *Xindice Command to Add an XML Document*

```
xindice ad
  -c xmldb:xindice://localhost:8080/db/catalog
  -f <XML File to add> -n catalog.xml
```

The Xindice ad action specifies that an XML document be added, -c specifies the collection context as the catalog collection, the -f switch specifies the XML file to add to collection, and the -n switch specifies the XML filename in the collection.

You will run this Xindice command in Eclipse. Therefore, you need to modify the Arguments tab in the XINDICE external tools configuration and specify the arguments listed in Listing 8-3 using the Eclipse ${resource_loc} variable for <XML File to add>, as shown in Figure 8-8. To run the XINDICE configuration with the specified arguments, select the catalog.xml document in the xindice_resources folder on the Package Explorer tab of the project Chapter8 and click the Run button, as shown in Figure 8-8.

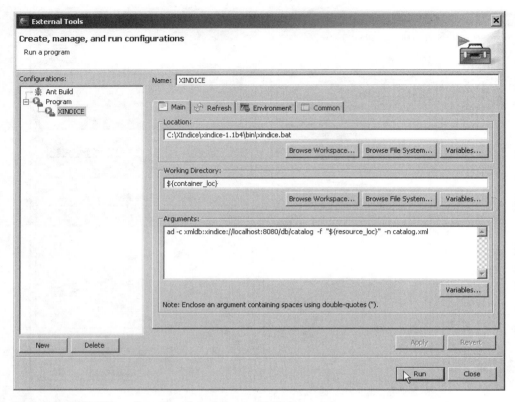

Figure 8-8. *XINDICE configuration for adding an XML document*

The XML document `catalog.xml` gets added to the `catalog` collection, as indicated by the `xindice` message in Listing 8-4.

Listing 8-4. *Output in Eclipse from Adding an XML Document*

```
trying to register database
Added document xmldb:xindice://localhost:8080/db/catalog/catalog.xml
```

Retrieving an XML Document from the Xindice Database

In this section, you will retrieve the XML document `catalog.xml` from the `catalog` collection. Listing 8-5 shows the Xindice command to retrieve an XML document from a collection.

Listing 8-5. *Xindice Command to Retrieve an XML Document*

```
xindice rd -c xmldb:xindice://localhost:8080/db/catalog  -n catalog.xml
```

The Xindice `rd` action specifies that an XML document be retrieved, the `-c` switch specifies the collection context to be the `catalog` collection, and the `-n` switch specifies the XML filename in the `catalog` collection that is to be retrieved.

You will run this Xindice command to retrieve the XML file `catalog.xml` in Eclipse. Therefore, modify the arguments in the XINDICE external tools configuration, and specify the arguments listed in Listing 8-5, as shown in Figure 8-9. To run the XINDICE configuration with the specified arguments, click the Run button, as shown in Figure 8-9.

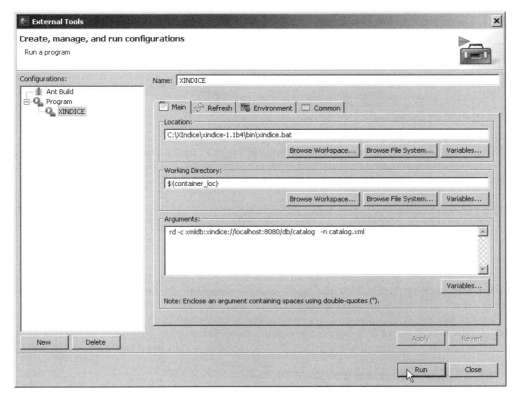

Figure 8-9. *XINDICE configuration for retrieving an XML document*

The XML document `catalog.xml` gets retrieved from the `catalog` collection, as shown in the `xindice` command output in Listing 8-6.

Listing 8-6. *Output in Eclipse from Retrieving an XML Document*

```
trying to register database
<?xml version="1.0"?>
<catalog title="OnJava.com" publisher="OReilly">
 <journal date="Sept 2005">
  <article>
   <title>What Is a Portlet</title>
   <author> Sunil Patil</author>
  </article>
 </journal>
 <journal date="Sept 2005">
  <article>
   <title>What Is Hibernate</title>
   <author>James Elliott</author>
  </article>
 </journal>
 <journal date="Oct 2003">
```

```
  <article>
   <title>BCEL Maven and CSS with Swing</title>
   <author>Daniel Steinberg</author>
  </article>
 </journal>
</catalog>
```

Querying Xindice Database Using XPath

Xindice provides an XPath query engine to query the XML document in the database using XPath. In this section, you will query the example XML document in the Xindice database using XPath. You query the XML document using the xindice xpath action. For example, Listing 8-7 shows the command to retrieve title of article in the first journal element.

Listing 8-7. *Xindice Command to Query an XML Document*

```
xindice xpath
  –c xmldb:xindice://localhost:8080/db/catalog
  -q /catalog/journal[1]/article/title
```

The Xindice xpath action specifies that an XPath query be executed, the –c switch specifies the collection context to be the catalog collection, and the -q switch specifies the XPath query to retrieve title of article in the first journal element.

You will run this Xindice command in Eclipse. Therefore, modify the arguments in the XINDICE external tools configuration to specify the arguments listed in Listing 8-7, as shown in Figure 8-10. To run the XINDICE configuration with the specified arguments, click the Run button, as shown in Figure 8-10.

Listing 8-8 shows the output from the XPath query.

Listing 8-8. *Output in Eclipse from Querying an XML Document*

```
trying to register database
<title src:col="/db/catalog" src:key="catalog.xml" xmlns:src="http://xml.apache.
org/xindice/Query">What Is a Portlet</title>
```

As another example, the command to retrieve the publisher attribute of the catalog element is as follows:

```
xindice xpath –c xmldb:xindice://localhost:8080/db/catalog -q /catalog/@publisher
```

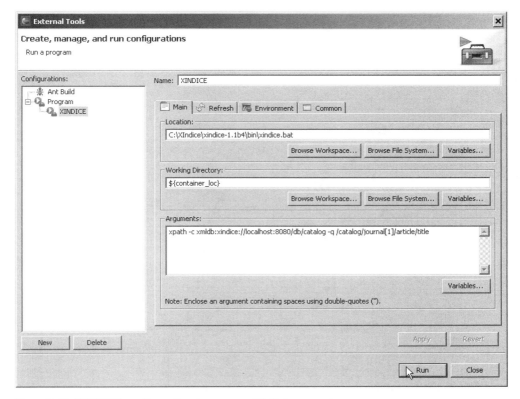

Figure 8-10. *XINDICE configuration to query an XML document*

To run the XINDICE configuration with the specified arguments, click the Run button, as shown in Figure 8-11.

Listing 8-9 shows the output from the XPath query. In this case, the XPath query output is generated as an xq:result element. The attribute value publisher="OReilly" is specified in the xq:result element.

Listing 8-9. *Output in Eclipse from Querying an XML Document*

```
trying to register database
<xq:result publisher="OReilly" xmlns:xq="http://xml.apache.org/xindice/Query" xq
:col="/db/catalog" xq:key="catalog.xml" />
```

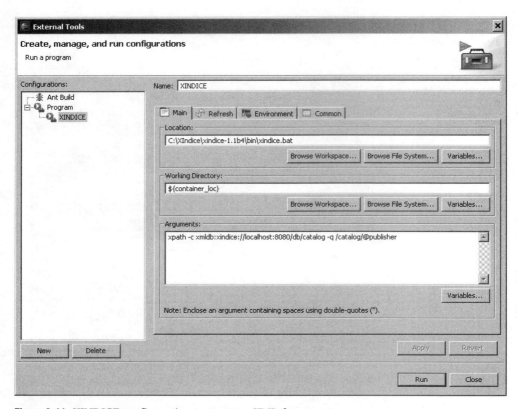

Figure 8-11. *XINDICE configuration to query an XML document*

Modifying Documents Using XUpdate Commands

Xindice implements XML:DB XUpdate commands to update an XML document; Table 8-6 lists these commands.

Table 8-6. *XUpdate Commands*

XUpdate Command	Description
xupdate:insert-after	Adds a node after the selected node
xupdate:update	Updates the selected node
xupdate:remove	Removes the selected node

Adding an Element

In this section, you'll add a journal element to the catalog.xml document in the catalog collection. You need to specify the elements and attributes to be updated in an xupdate configuration file. Therefore, you will use the xupdate.xml (Listing 8-10) configuration file to add a journal element.

Listing 8-10. *xupdate.xml*

```
<xupdate:modifications version="1.0"
  xmlns:xupdate="http://www.xmldb.org/xupdate">
 <xupdate:insert-after select="/catalog/journal[3]">
  <xupdate:element name="journal">
  <xupdate:attribute name="date">Aug 2005</xupdate:attribute>
   <article>
    <title>iBatis DAO</title>
    <author>Sunil Patil</author>
   </article>
  </xupdate:element>
 </xupdate:insert-after>
</xupdate:modifications>
```

Listing 8-11 shows the Xindice command to update the XML document catalog.xml in the catalog collection.

Listing 8-11. *Xindice Command to Update an XML Document*

```
xindice xupdate
  -c  xmldb:xindice://localhost:8080/db/catalog
  -n catalog.xml  -f  "${resource_loc}"
```

The Xindice xupdate action specifies that an XML document be updated, the -c switch specifies the collection context to be the catalog collection, the -n switch identifies the XML document to be updated, and the -f switch specifies the variable ${resource_loc} corresponding to the xupdate.xml configuration file.

The Xindice command to update the XML file catalog.xml is run in Eclipse. Therefore, modify the arguments in the XINDICE external tools configuration, and specify the arguments listed in Listing 8-11. To run the XINDICE configuration with the specified arguments, select the xupdate.xml document in the xindice_resources folder on the Package Explorer tab in the Chapter8 project, and click the Run button, as shown in Figure 8-12.

The XML document catalog.xml in the catalog collection gets updated, as shown by the output message in Listing 8-12.

Listing 8-12. *Output in Eclipse from Updating an XML Document*

```
trying to register database
1 documents updated
```

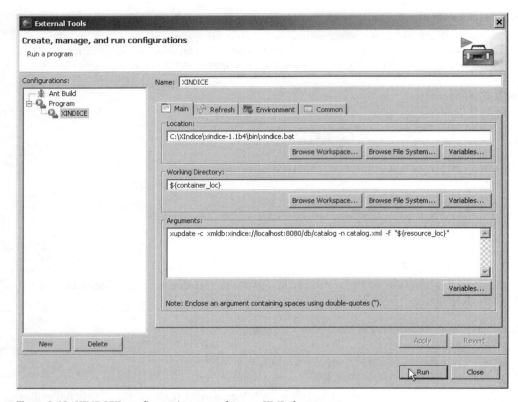

Figure 8-12. *XINDICE configuration to update an XML document*

Deleting and Modifying an Element

As another example, you will remove a journal element and modify the title attribute in another journal element. Let's remove the first journal element and modify title in the third journal element. Since the first journal element is removed before the third journal element is updated, the journal element to be updated becomes the second journal element. You use xupdate:remove to remove an element and xupdate:update to update an element. Listing 8-13 shows the XUpdate configuration file xupdate.xml for removing and modifying elements. To run the XINDICE configuration using xupdate.xml, replace the contents of the xupdate.xml file in the xindice_resources folder with Listing 8-13.

Listing 8-13. *Xupdate.xml*

```
<xupdate:modifications version="1.0"
  xmlns:xupdate="http://www.xmldb.org/xupdate">
<xupdate:remove select="/catalog/journal[1]"/>
<xupdate:update select="/catalog/journal[2]/article/title">
Maven with Swing</xupdate:update>
</xupdate:modifications>
```

Listing 8-11 shows the Xindice command to update `catalog.xml` in the `catalog` database collection using the `xupdate.xml` configuration file. To run the XINDICE configuration with the specified arguments, select the modified `xupdate.xml` document in the `xindice_resources` folder on the Package Explorer tab of the `Chapter8` project, and click the Run button. This updates the document `catalog.xml` in the `catalog` collection. The output from updating an XML document is the same as listed in Listing 8-12. To retrieve the modified XML document, run the `xindice` command to retrieve an XML document, listed in Listing 8-5. Listing 8-14 shows the modified document.

Listing 8-14. *Modified XML Document in the Xindice Database*

```
trying to register database
<?xml version="1.0"?>
<catalog title="OnJava.com" publisher="OReilly">

 <journal date="Sept 2005">
  <article>
   <title>What Is Hibernate</title>
   <author>James Elliott</author>
  </article>
 </journal>
 <journal date="Oct 2003">
  <article>
   <title>Maven with Swing</title>
   <author>Daniel Steinberg</author>
  </article>
 </journal><journal date="Aug 2005">    <article>    <title>iBatis DAO</title>
    <author>Sunil Patil</author>   </article>  </journal>
</catalog>
```

Deleting an XML Document

In this section, you will delete an XML document from a Xindice collection. Listing 8-15 shows the Xindice command to delete `catalog.xml` from the `catalog` collection.

Listing 8-15. *Xindice Command to Delete an XML Document*

```
xindice dd -c  xmldb:xindice://localhost:8080/db/catalog -n catalog.xml
```

The Xindice `dd` action specifies that an XML document be deleted. The Xindice switch `-c` specifies the collection context as `catalog`. The Xindice switch `-n` specifies the XML `catalog.xml` as the document to be deleted. The Xindice command to delete `catalog.xml` is run in Eclipse. Therefore, modify the arguments in the XINDICE external tools configuration, and specify the arguments listed in Listing 8-15. To run the XINDICE configuration with the specified arguments, click the Run button, as shown in Figure 8-13.

This deletes the document `catalog.xml` from the `catalog` collection, as indicated by the output message shown in Listing 8-16.

Listing 8-16. *Output in Eclipse from Deleting an XML Document*

```
trying to register database
DELETED: xmldb:xindice://localhost:8080/db/catalog/catalog.xml
```

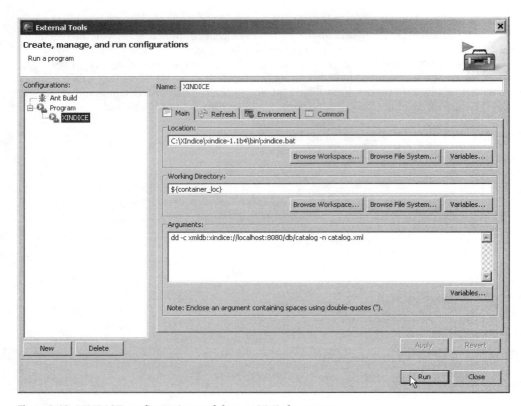

Figure 8-13. *XINDICE configuration to delete an XML document*

Deleting a Xindice Collection

In this section, you will delete the collection catalog from the Xindice database. You can delete the catalog collection using the command listed in Listing 8-17.

Listing 8-17. *Xindice Command to Delete a Collection*

```
xindice dc –c xmldb:xindice://localhost:8080/db –n catalog
```

The Xindice dc action specifies that a collection be deleted. The Xindice switch –c specifies the collection context as db. The Xindice switch –n specifies the collection to be deleted as catalog. The Xindice command to delete the collection catalog is run in Eclipse. Therefore, modify the arguments in the XINDICE external tools configuration, and specify the arguments listed in Listing 8-17. To run the XINDICE configuration with the specified arguments, click the Run button, as shown in Figure 8-14.

The Xindice collection catalog gets deleted, as indicated by the output message in Listing 8-18.

Listing 8-18. *Output in Eclipse from Deleting a Collection*

```
trying to register database
Deleted: xmldb:xindice://localhost:8080/db/catalog
```

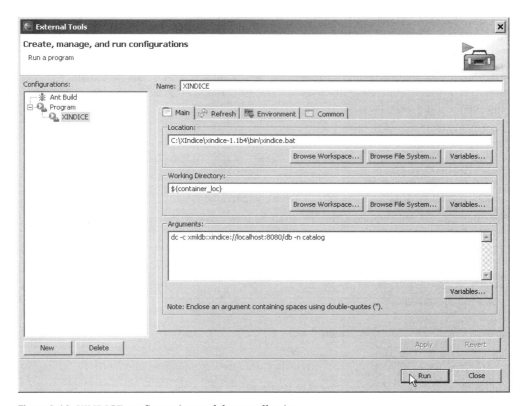

Figure 8-14. *XINDICE configuration to delete a collection*

Using XIndice with the XML:DB API

In the following sections, we will demonstrate the Xindice XML:DB API to access the Xindice database. As in the Xindice command-line section, you will create a collection in a database instance, add an example XML document to the collection, retrieve the example XML document, query the document with XPath, update the document using XUpdate, and delete the document. The Xindice database instance in which the collection is created is the default database, db. Listing 8-1 lists the example XML document, `catalog.xml`, to the `db` database. `XIndiceDB.java` in the `Chapter8` project will be used to access the Xindice database using the XML:DB API.

Creating a Collection in the Xindice Database

In this section, you will create a collection in the Xindice database using the XML:DB API. You need to import the Xindice core server classes and the XML:DB API classes listed in Listing 8-19.

Listing 8-19. *XML:DB API Packages*

```
import org.apache.xindice.client.xmldb.services.*;
import org.apache.xindice.util.XindiceException;
import org.apache.xindice.xml.dom.*;
import org.xmldb.api.*;
import org.xmldb.api.base.*;
import org.xmldb.api.modules.*;
```

First, you need to create an instance of the Xindice database engine. The XML:DB driver implementation class for the Xindice database is DatabaseImpl. To create an instance of the Xindice database, load the Xindice driver using the Class.forName() method, obtain an instance of the Xindice driver, and cast the Xindice driver instance to the database interface org.xmldb.api.base.Database. Subsequently, register the Xindice database using the org.xmldb.api.DatabaseManager class, which is used to obtain a collection from a XML:DB database. Listing 8-20 shows the code snippet to create an instance of the Xindice database.

Listing 8-20. *Creating an Instance of the Xindice Database*

```
String xindiceDriver = "org.apache.xindice.client.xmldb.DatabaseImpl";
org.xmldb.api.base.Database xindiceDatabase =  (org.xmldb.api.base.Database)
  ((Class.forName(xindiceDriver)).newInstance());
org.xmldb.api.DatabaseManager.registerDatabase(xindiceDatabase);
```

The default root collection in a Xindice database server is db. To create a new collection in db, you need a CollectionManager instance, which is obtained from a Collection object. Therefore, before you can create a CollectionManager, you need a Collection object corresponding to the db collection. You obtain a Collection object using the static method getCollection(String) of the DriverManager class. The String parameter of the getCollection() method specifies that the XML:DB URL should access the Xindice server. Listing 8-21 shows how you obtain a Collection object for the db collection.

Listing 8-21. *Creating a Collection Object*

```
String url = "xmldb:xindice://localhost:8080/db";
 org.xmldb.api.base.Collection  collection = DatabaseManager.getCollection(url);
```

From the Collection object, you need to create an org.apache.xindice.client.xmldb.services.CollectionManager object. A CollectionManager is required to create and delete collections from a database. You also need to specify a collection name and an XML configuration, which defines the structure of a collection, to create a collection. XML configurations are not very well documented in Xindice. Therefore, you will use the default XML configuration in the Xindice documentation for creating a collection. With a CollectionManager object, create a collection using the createCollection method, as shown in Listing 8-22.

Listing 8-22. *Creating a Collection from a CollectionManager Object*

```
CollectionManager collectionManagerService =
   (CollectionManager)
   collection.getService("CollectionManager", "1.0");

String collectionName = "catalog";
String collectionConfig = "<collection compressed=\"true\" " +
  "    name=\"" + collectionName + "\">" +
  " <filer class=\"org.apache.xindice.core.filer.BTreeFiler\"/>" +
  "</collection>";

org.xmldb.api.base.Collection  catalogCollection =
  collectionManagerService.createCollection (collectionName,
  DOMParser.toDocument(collectionConfig));
```

The createCollection(String path, Document configuration) method creates a new collection of the specified collection name in the database using the specified XML collection configuration. A new collection, catalog, gets created in the db collection.

Adding an XML Document to the Xindice Database

In this section, you will add an XML document to the collection created in the previous section. The example XML document will be added to the `catalog` collection; therefore, obtain the `catalog` collection from the database using the `getCollection()` method, as shown in Listing 8-23.

Listing 8-23. *Obtaining a Collection from* `DriverManager`

```
Collection collection = DatabaseManager.getCollection
  ("xmldb:xindice://localhost:8080/db/catalog");
```

An XML document resource in the Xindice database is represented with the `XMLResource` interface. You can set the content of an `XMLResource` using a DOM node or a SAX `ContentHandler`. In the example application, you will set the content of `XMLResource` using a DOM node. Therefore, obtain a `Document` object for the XML document to be added, as shown in Listing 8-24.

Listing 8-24. *Creating a* `Document` *Object*

```
DocumentBuilderFactory factory =
  DocumentBuilderFactory.newInstance();
File datafile = new File("xindice_resources/catalog.xml");
DocumentBuilder builder = factory.newDocumentBuilder();
Document document = builder.parse(datafile);
```

In Listing 8-25, you create a `File` object of the XML document to be added using the `xindice_resources/catalog.xml` file. You need to create an ID for the XML document resource to be added to collection. The ID associates the collection with an identifier. An XML document in the Xindice database is represented with the `XMLResource` interface; therefore, create an `org.xmldb.api.modules.XMLResource` object for the XML document to add to the `catalog` collection. You can set the content of the `XMLResource` from a `Document` object. To store the XML document in the database, you need to add the XML resource to the `catalog` collection using the `storeResource(XMLResource)` method. Listing 8-25 lists the procedure to create an `XMLResource` and add the resource to a collection.

Listing 8-25. *Adding an XML Resource to a Collection*

```
String  resourceID = collection.createId();
XMLResource resource = (XMLResource)
 (collection.createResource(resourceID,"XMLResource"));
resource.setContentAsDOM(document);
collection.storeResource(resource);
```

The example XML document, `catalog.xml`, gets added to the database collection.

Retrieving an XML Document from the Xindice Database

In this section, you will retrieve an example XML document from the Xindice database using the XML:DB API. An XML resource in the Xindice database is identified with a resource ID. A resource ID was created and set on the XML document to store in the previous section. With the same resource ID, obtain the XML resource from the database. You can output the XML document in the XML resource using the `getContent()` method. Listing 8-26 shows the procedure to obtain an `XMLResource` and XML document in the XML resource.

Listing 8-26. *Retrieving an XML Resource*

```
XMLResource resource = (XMLResource)
  (collection.getResource(resourceID));
System.out.println(resource.getContent());
```

The XML document added in the previous section gets retrieved.

Querying the Xindice Database Using XPath

In this section, you will query the Xindice database using the XML:DB API. You will look at a query to find title of article in the first journal element. An XPath query expression is specified as a String, as shown here:

```
String xpath = "/catalog/journal[1]/article/title";
```

The org.xmldb.api.modules.XpathQueryService service is used to query a database collection. Therefore, create an XPathQueryService object. Subsequently, query the database using the XpathQueryService.query() method. The query returns an org.xmldb.api.base.ResourceSet. A ResourceSet consists of XML resources. To retrieve an XML resource, iterate over the resource set and obtain an XML document resource org.xmldb.api.base.Resource. Listing 8-27 shows the procedure to query the Xindice database using an XPath query, iterate over the resource set returned by the query, and output XML document in a resource.

Listing 8-27. *Querying Xindice*

```
XPathQueryService queryService =
  (XPathQueryService)
  collection.getService("XPathQueryService","1.0");
ResourceSet resourceSet = queryService.query(xpath);
ResourceIterator iterator = resourceSet.getIterator();
  while (iterator.hasMoreResources()) {
      Resource resource = iterator.nextResource();
      System.out.println(resource.getContent());
 }
```

Modifying the Document Using XUpdate

In the following sections, you will update the XML document in the Xindice database using the XML:DB and XUpdate APIs. Some of XUpdate commands to update an XML document were listed in Table 8-4.

Adding an Element Using the XML:DB API

In this section, you will update the example XML document using the XML:DB API. As an example, you will add a journal element after the third journal element. You specify the XUpdate commands in an XUpdate string as in Listing 8-28. The XUpdate command xupdate:insert-after adds an element after the element specified in the select attribute.

Listing 8-28. *XUpdate Configuration String for Adding an Element*

```
String xupdate =
"<xupdate:modifications version=\"1.0\"" +
"    xmlns:xupdate=\"http://www.xmldb.org/xupdate\">" +
"    <xupdate:insert-after select=\"/catalog/journal[3]\">" +
"    <journal date=\"Aug 2005\">" + " <article>" +
"    <title>iBatis DAO</title>" +
"    <author>Sunil Patil</author>" + " </article>" +
"    </journal>" + "     </xupdate:insert-after>" +
"</xupdate:modifications>";
```

The query service class `org.xmldb.api.modules.XUpdateQueryService` is used to update the database through XUpdate. Therefore, create an `XUpdateQueryService` object from the collection to update using the `getService()` method. The Xindice database can be updated using the `update()` method of the `XUpdateQueryService` object, as shown in Listing 8-29.

Listing 8-29. *Updating a Collection Using XUpdate*

```
XUpdateQueryService queryService =
(XUpdateQueryService) collection.getService("XUpdateQueryService",
                "1.0");
queryService.update(xupdate);
```

Deleting an Element Using the XML:DB API

As another example, we will show how to remove a `journal` element from the XML document in the database using the `xupdate:remove` command. To remove the first `journal` element, create an XUpdate command `String` shown in Listing 8-30. The element to remove is specified in the `select` attribute of the `xupdate:remove` element.

Listing 8-30. *XUpdate Configuration for Deleting an Element*

```
String xupdate = "<xupdate:modifications version=\"1.0\"" +
"    xmlns:xupdate=\"http://www.xmldb.org/xupdate\">" +
"    <xupdate:remove select=\"/catalog/journal[1]\"/>" +
"</xupdate:modifications>";
queryService.update(xupdate);
```

Modifying an Element Using the XML:DB API

In this section, you will modify an element using the `xupdate:update` command. As an example, modify `title` of `article` in the second `journal` element. You need to create an XUpdate command `String` to update the XML document, as shown in Listing 8-31. The element to be modified is specified in the `select` attribute of the `xupdate:update` element.

Listing 8-31. *XUpdate Configuration for Modifying an Element*

```
String xupdate = "<xupdate:modifications version=\"1.0\"" +
"    xmlns:xupdate=\"http://www.xmldb.org/xupdate\">" +
"    <xupdate:update select=\"/catalog/journal[2]/article/title\"> +
"    Maven with Swing</xupdate:update>" +
"</xupdate:modifications>";
queryService.update(xupdate);
```

Deleting an XML Document

In this section, you will delete the XML document in the Xindice database using the XML:DB API. You need to obtain the `catalog` collection from which an XML document is to be deleted and obtain a XML resource to delete, as shown in Listing 8-32. You can obtain an XML resource with a resource ID. Subsequently, you can delete the resource using the `removeResource(XMLResource)` method.

Listing 8-32. *Deleting an XML Resource*

```
XMLResource resource = (XMLResource)
  (collection.getResource(resourceID));
collection.removeResource(resource);
```

Listing 8-33 shows `XIndiceDB.java`. Listing 8-25 showed the `XIndiceDB.java` code. You use the `XIndiceDB` class to accomplish the following:

1. Create an XML document collection in the Xindice database.

2. Add an XML document to an instance of the Xindice collection.

3. Retrieve an XML document from an instance of the Xindice collection.

4. Query an XML document using XPath.

5. Update an XML document using XUpdate.

6. Delete an XML document from the Xindice database.

Listing 8-33. *XIndiceDB.java*

```java
package com.apress.xindice;
import org.apache.xindice.client.xmldb.services.*;
import org.apache.xindice.util.XindiceException;
import org.apache.xindice.xml.dom.*;
import org.w3c.dom.Document;
import org.xml.sax.SAXException;
import org.xmldb.api.*;
import org.xmldb.api.base.*;
import org.xmldb.api.modules.*;
import java.io.*;
import javax.xml.parsers.DocumentBuilder;
import javax.xml.parsers.DocumentBuilderFactory;
import javax.xml.parsers.ParserConfigurationException;

public class XIndiceDB {
    private Collection collection;
    private Collection catalogCollection;
    String resourceID;

    public void createCollection() {
        try {
            String xindiceDriver = "org.apache.xindice.client.xmldb.DatabaseImpl";
            Database xindiceDatabase = (Database)
            ((Class.forName(xindiceDriver)).newInstance());
            DatabaseManager.registerDatabase(xindiceDatabase);
```

```
            String url = "xmldb:xindice://localhost:8080/db";
            collection = DatabaseManager.getCollection(url);

            String collectionName = "catalog";
CollectionManager collectionManagerService =
(CollectionManager)    collection.getService
("CollectionManager",
                "1.0");

            String collectionConfig = "<collection compressed=\"true\" " +
                "             name=\"" + collectionName + "\">" +
                "   <filer class=\"org.apache.xindice.core.filer.BTreeFiler\"/>" +
                "</collection>";

            catalogCollection = collectionManagerService.
            createCollection(collectionName,
                    DOMParser.toDocument(collectionConfig));
            System.out.println("XIndice Collection Created");
        } catch (XindiceException e) {
        } catch (XMLDBException e) {
        } catch (ClassNotFoundException e) {
        } catch (InstantiationException e) {
        } catch (IllegalAccessException e) {
        }
    }

    public void addDocument() {
        try {
            String xindiceDriver = "org.apache.xindice.client.xmldb.DatabaseImpl";
            Database xindiceDatabase = (Database)
              ((Class.forName(xindiceDriver)).newInstance());
            DatabaseManager.registerDatabase(xindiceDatabase);
            collection = DatabaseManager.getCollection(
                    "xmldb:xindice://localhost:8080/db/catalog");

            DocumentBuilderFactory factory = DocumentBuilderFactory.newInstance();

            File datafile = new File("xindice-resources/catalog.xml");
            DocumentBuilder builder = factory.newDocumentBuilder();
            Document document = builder.parse(datafile);

            resourceID = collection.createId();

            XMLResource resource = (XMLResource)
            (collection.createResource(resourceID,
                    "XMLResource"));
            resource.setContentAsDOM(document);

            collection.storeResource(resource);
            System.out.println("XML Document Added to Collection");
```

```
        }
        catch (SAXException e) {
        } catch (ParserConfigurationException e) {
        } catch (XMLDBException e) {
            System.out.println(e.getMessage());
        } catch (IOException e) {
            System.out.println(e.getMessage());
        } catch (ClassNotFoundException e) {
            System.out.println(e.getMessage());
        } catch (InstantiationException e) {
            System.out.println(e.getMessage());
        } catch (IllegalAccessException e) {
            System.out.println(e.getMessage());
        }
    }

    public void retrieveDocument() {
        try {
            XMLResource resource = (XMLResource)
            (collection.getResource(resourceID));

            System.out.println(resource.getContent());
        } catch (XMLDBException e) {
        }
    }

    public void queryDocument() {
        try {
            String xpath = "/catalog/journal[1]/article/title";
            XPathQueryService queryService =
             (XPathQueryService) collection.getService("XPathQueryService",
                  "1.0");
            ResourceSet resourceSet = queryService.query(xpath);
            ResourceIterator iterator = resourceSet.getIterator();
            System.out.println("XPath Query");
            while (iterator.hasMoreResources()) {
                Resource resource = iterator.nextResource();

                System.out.println(resource.getContent());
            }
        } catch (XMLDBException e) {
        }
    }

    public void updateDocument() {
        try {
            String xindiceDriver = "org.apache.xindice.client.xmldb.DatabaseImpl";
            Database xindiceDatabase = (Database)
              ((Class.forName(xindiceDriver)).newInstance());
            DatabaseManager.registerDatabase(xindiceDatabase);
            collection = DatabaseManager.getCollection(
                  "xmldb:xindice://localhost:8080/db/catalog");
```

```java
            String xupdate = "<xupdate:modifications version=\"1.0\"" +
                "   xmlns:xupdate=\"http://www.xmldb.org/xupdate\">" +
                "   <xupdate:insert-after select=\"/catalog/journal[3]\">" +
                "   <journal date=\"Aug 2005\">" + "   <article>" +
                "   <title>iBatis DAO</title>" +
                "   <author>Sunil Patil</author>" + "   </article>" +
                "   </journal>" + "   </xupdate:insert-after>" +
                "</xupdate:modifications>";

XUpdateQueryService queryService =
(XUpdateQueryService) collection.getService
("XUpdateQueryService",
                "1.0");
            queryService.update(xupdate);

            xupdate = "<xupdate:modifications version=\"1.0\"" +
                "   xmlns:xupdate=\"http://www.xmldb.org/xupdate\">" +
                "   <xupdate:remove select=\"/catalog/journal[1]\"/>" +
                "</xupdate:modifications>";

            queryService.update(xupdate);

            xupdate = "<xupdate:modifications version=\"1.0\"" +
                "   xmlns:xupdate=\"http://www.xmldb.org/xupdate\">" +
                "   <xupdate:update select=\"/catalog/journal[2]/article/title\">"+
                "Maven with Swing</xupdate:update>" +
                "</xupdate:modifications>";

            queryService.update(xupdate);

            XMLResource resource = (XMLResource)
            (collection.getResource(resourceID));
            System.out.println("Updated XML Document");
            System.out.println(resource.getContent());
        } catch (XMLDBException e) {
        } catch (ClassNotFoundException e) {
            System.out.println(e.getMessage());
        } catch (InstantiationException e) {
            System.out.println(e.getMessage());
        } catch (IllegalAccessException e) {
            System.out.println(e.getMessage());
        }
    }

    public void deleteDocument() {
        try {
            XMLResource resource = (XMLResource)
            (collection.getResource(resourceID));
            collection.removeResource(resource);
            System.out.println("XML Document Deleted");

        } catch (XMLDBException e) {
        }
    }
```

```
    public static void main(String[] argv) {
        XIndiceDB xindicedb = new XIndiceDB();
        xindicedb.createCollection();

        xindicedb.addDocument();
        xindicedb.retrieveDocument();
        xindicedb.queryDocument();
        xindicedb.updateDocument();
        xindicedb.deleteDocument();
    }
}
```

You can run the XIndiceDB.java application in Eclipse using the XIndiceDB Java application configuration. As shown in Listing 8-34, a collection is created, an XML document is added to the collection, the XML document is retrieved, and the XML document is queried, updated, and deleted.

Listing 8-34. *Output in Eclipse from Running the XIndiceDB.java Application*

```
trying to register database
XIndice Collection Created
trying to register database
XML Document Added to Collection
<?xml version="1.0"?>
<catalog publisher="OReilly" title="OnJava.com">
 <journal date="Sept 2005">
  <article>
   <title>What Is a Portlet</title>
   <author> Sunil Patil</author>
  </article>
 </journal>
 <journal date="Sept 2005">
  <article>
   <title>What Is Hibernate</title>
   <author>James Elliott</author>
  </article>
 </journal>
 <journal date="Oct 2003">
  <article>
   <title>BCEL Maven and CSS with Swing</title>
   <author>Daniel Steinberg</author>
  </article>
 </journal>
</catalog>
XPath Query
<title src:col="/db/catalog" src:key="022705cf47a9e3090000010bb028b689" xmlns:sr
c="http://xml.apache.org/xindice/Query">What Is a Portlet</title>
trying to register database
Updated XML Document
<?xml version="1.0"?>
<catalog publisher="OReilly" title="OnJava.com">
```

```
<journal date="Sept 2005">
 <article>
  <title>What Is Hibernate</title>
  <author>James Elliott</author>
 </article>
</journal>
<journal date="Oct 2003">
 <article>
  <title>Maven with Swing</title>
  <author>Daniel Steinberg</author>
 </article>
</journal><journal date="Aug 2005">   <article>    <title>iBatis DAO</title>
 <author>Sunil Patil</author>   </article>   </journal>
</catalog>
XML Document Deleted
```

Summary

Native XML databases define a model for storing and retrieving an XML document. Native XML databases store XML documents in collections and support querying with XPath and updating with the XML:DB XUpdate APIs, respectively. Native XML databases have an advantage over relational databases in that the native XML databases are specifically designed for storing, querying, and updating XML documents, whereas relational databases are designed to store atomic values within a database row-column cell. Complex XML documents with multilevel hierarchies and attributes can be easily stored, queried, and updated in a native XML database.

In this chapter, we discussed general native XML database concepts in the specific context of the Xindice open source native XML database. In addition to support for the query and update APIs, Xindice provides a command-line tool for administrating the Xindice native XML database, which was also discussed in this chapter.

CHAPTER 9

■ ■ ■

Storing XML in Relational Databases

In the previous chapter, you learned how to store an XML document in a native XML database. Native XML databases are of course limited to storing only XML documents. If you need to store an XML document along with other data, a relational database is more appropriate. In a relational database, you can store an XML document just like any other type of data, within a column in a table row.

In the absence of standards related to storing XML content in relational databases, relational database vendors started adding vendor-specific data types, utilities, and APIs to provide XML-related support within their databases. Table 9-1 discusses some of the vendor-specific tools.

Table 9-1. *Database Tools for Storing XML*

Database Tool	Database	Description
Oracle XML SQL Utility	Oracle	Stores an XML document that does not consist of subelements or attributes in a predefined database table. You can apply an XSLT to store an XML document with subelements and attributes.
IBM DB2 XML Extender	DB2 UDB	Stores an XML document either as a BLOB-like object or as a set of collection called an XML *collection*.
SQL extension and rowset function	SQL Server 2000	Stores an XML document with a rowset function and retrieves an XML document with the SQL construct FOR XML.
Result Set DTD	Sybase Adaptive Server	Stores and retrieves an XML document using a ResultSetXml class.

Clearly, a vendor-independent standard for storing and accessing XML content in relational databases was called for, so the SQL:2003[1] international standard added the new Part 14: SQL/XML (XML-Related Specifications), which is devoted to this issue.

Overview

The SQL:2003 standard provides a new XML data type for storing XML content. The XML data type is just like any other data type; using the XML data type, you can store an XML document within a column in

---

1. "SQL:2003 Has Been Published" (http://www.sigmod.org/sigmod/record/issues/0403/ E.JimAndrew-standard.pdf) is a good reference for an overview of the SQL:2003 standard.

a table row. SQL:2003 is a relatively new standard. Therefore, not all relational databases currently support this standard. You may need to research vendor-specific information to find out whether your database supports the SQL:2003 standard.

In Java, a JDBC driver is the well-established means for interacting with a relational database. The JDBC 4.0 API specification Public Review Draft (JSR-000221) proposes support for the SQL:2003 standard. It is expected that when the JDBC 4.0 specification is finalized, more and more databases will add support for the XML data type. In the JDBC 4.0 API, which is implemented in J2SE 6.0, the XML data type is mapped to the java.sql.SQLXML Java data type. The key distinguishing feature of the SQLXML Java data type is that you can use it to navigate an XML document. The JDBC 3.0 API, which is implemented in J2SE 5.0, does not define an SQLXML data type; in JDBC 3.0, you could retrieve an XML type column only as a String or as a CLOB. Unlike working with the java.sql.SQLXML type, you cannot use a String or a CLOB to navigate an XML document.

You need a JDBC 4.0 driver to retrieve an XML document from an XML data type column and map it to an object that implements the java.sql.SQLXML interface. Because the JDBC 4.0 specification is still under public review, no well-known relational database currently provides a JDBC 4.0 driver. Therefore, you can test the example application in this chapter only when a JDBC 4.0 driver becomes available. Meanwhile, we will use JDBC 3.0 drivers to build and execute the examples.

In this chapter, we will explain how to store an XML document in a relational database, retrieve an XML document from a database, and navigate an XML document using the java.sql.SQLXML interface; navigating the document using java.sql.SQLXML will of course be feasible only with a JDBC 4.0 driver. Listing 9-1 shows the example XML document we will use in the examples.

Listing 9-1. *catalog.xml*

```
<catalog title="OnJava.com" publisher="OReilly">
 <journal date="September 2005">
  <article>
   <title>What Is a Portlet</title>
   <author> Sunil Patil</author>
  </article>
  <article>
   <title>What Is Hibernate</title>
   <author>James Elliott</author>
  </article>
 </journal>
</catalog>
```

Installing the Software

The SQLXML Java type, which maps the XML database type to Java, is implemented in J2SE 6.0. Therefore, you need to install J2SE 6.0.[2] Another requirement for storing an XML document in the XML type column using the SQLXML API is a JDBC 4.0 driver. As mentioned earlier, no well-known relational database currently provides a JDBC 4.0 driver. Therefore, the best you can do at this point is to develop an application using a JDBC 3.0 driver to determine whether a database supports the XML data type. Of course, when a JDBC 4.0 driver becomes available, you can modify this application for use with a JDBC 4.0 driver.

You also need a relational database that supports the XML data type. Currently, only a few well-known databases, DB2 UDB 9.1 and SQL Server 2005, support the XML data type; however, since none of them currently supports a JDBC 4.0 driver, you won't be able to develop an SQLXML application with any

---

2. For more information about J2SE 6.0 Beta, see http://java.sun.com/javase/6/download.jsp.

of the well-known databases. Again, for a practical example that can be executed, you have to wait until JDBC 4.0 is finalized and JDBC 4.0 driver support is made available in commonly used databases.

With the caveats already noted, we will show how to develop an application with the open source database MySQL[3] using a JDBC 3.0 driver. Therefore, you need to download and install MySQL[4] 5.0. You also need to download the MySQL JDBC driver.[5] Or, if the JDBC 4.0 driver has since become available, download and install the relevant database and corresponding JDBC 4.0 driver.

Setting Up the Eclipse Project

We will show how to develop an application (XMLToSQL.java) to store and retrieve XML data in a relational database. Some of the methods of the XMLToSQL.java application are commented out and can be run when a database with support for a JDBC 4.0 driver and the XML data type becomes available.

To compile and run the example application XMLToSQL.java, you need an Eclipse project. You can download project Chapter9 from the Apress website (http://www.apress.com) and import it into your Eclipse workspace by selecting File ➤ Import.

To compile and run the XMLToSQL.java application, you need the JDBC JAR files in your project's Java build path; Figure 9-1 shows these JAR files for the MySQL driver. If you modify the XMLToSQL.java application for another database, add the JDBC JAR files for the database to the Java build path. You also need to set the JRE system library to JRE 6.0, as shown in Figure 9-1.

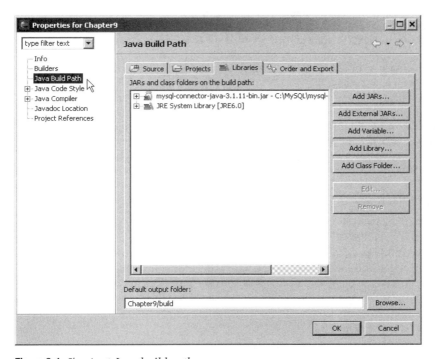

Figure 9-1. *Chapter9 Java build path*

---

3. MySQL, at the time of writing this book, did not support the XML database type. If you have access to a relational database that supports the XML database type, you can use such a database.

4. For more information about the MySQL database, see http://www.mysql.com/products/database/mysql/community_edition.html.

5. For more information about the MySQL Connector/J driver, see http://www.mysql.com/products/connector/j/.

Figure 9-2 shows the Chapter9 directory structure.

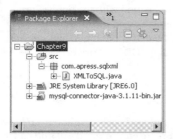

Figure 9-2. *Chapter9 directory structure*

Selecting a Database

As the String Java type is to the VARCHAR database type, the SQLXML Java type is to the XML database type. In JDBC 4.0, the java.sql.Connection interface has a new createSQLXML() method to create an SQLXML object. The SQLXML object thus created does not initially have any data. You can add data to an SQLXML object using its setString(String) method or its createXMLStreamWriter() method.

You can store an SQLXML object in a database table using PreparedStatement interface's setSQLXML(int index, SQLXML sqlXML) method or setSQLXML(String columnName, SQLXML sqlXML) method. You can retrieve an SQLXML object from a ResultSet or a CallableStatement object using the getSQLXML(int index) method or the getSQLXML(String columnName) method. The PreparedStatement and ResultSet methods for the SQLXML data type are similar to the methods for any other data type, such as String.

To develop an application using the SQLXML API, you need a relational database that supports the XML data type. Not all databases support the XML data type. To determine whether a database supports the XML data type, obtain the database metadata from a Connection object. For example, to determine whether the MySQL database supports the XML data type, load and register the com.mysql.jdbc.Driver JDBC driver, as shown in Listing 9-2. You need a connection URL to connect to the MySQL database. Listing 9-2 shows the connection URL for the MySQL database.

Listing 9-2. *Loading a JDBC Driver*

```
Class.forName("com.mysql.jdbc.Driver");
String url=" jdbc:mysql://localhost:3306/test ";
```

To obtain metadata information from the MySQL database, you first need to obtain a connection to the database. You can create a connection to the database using the static method getConnection() in the DriverManager interface, as shown in Listing 9-3. The user root does not require a password by default. Subsequently, you can obtain the database metadata from this Connection object.

Listing 9-3. *Retrieving Database Metadata*

```
Connection connection = DriverManager.getConnection(url,
                    "root", null);
DatabaseMetaData metadata= connection.getMetaData();
```

You retrieve data types supported by a database from metadata using the getTypeInfo() method, as shown in Listing 9-4. To determine whether a database supports the XML data type, iterate over the data type result set, and output the TYPE_NAME column, as shown in Listing 9-4; the complete code for this example is shown in Listing 9-23.

Listing 9-4. *Outputting Data Types*

```
ResultSet rs=metadata.getTypeInfo();
System.out.println("TYPE_NAME:"+rs.getString("TYPE_NAME"));
```

If a database supports the XML data type, XML TYPE_NAME gets output, as shown here:

```
TYPE_NAME: XML
```

The MySQL database does not yet support the XML data type. Listing 9-5 shows the data types output for the MySQL database. The data types may vary slightly for a different version of the MySQL database.

Listing 9-5. *The MySQL Database Data Types*

```
TYPE_NAME:BOOL
TYPE_NAME:TINYINT
TYPE_NAME:BIGINT
TYPE_NAME:LONG VARBINARY
TYPE_NAME:MEDIUMBLOB
TYPE_NAME:LONGBLOB
TYPE_NAME:BLOB
TYPE_NAME:TINYBLOB
TYPE_NAME:VARBINARY
TYPE_NAME:BINARY
TYPE_NAME:LONG VARCHAR
TYPE_NAME:MEDIUMTEXT
TYPE_NAME:LONGTEXT
TYPE_NAME:TEXT
TYPE_NAME:TINYTEXT
TYPE_NAME:CHAR
TYPE_NAME:NUMERIC
TYPE_NAME:DECIMAL
TYPE_NAME:INTEGER
TYPE_NAME:INT
TYPE_NAME:MEDIUMINT
TYPE_NAME:SMALLINT
TYPE_NAME:FLOAT
TYPE_NAME:DOUBLE
TYPE_NAME:DOUBLE PRECISION
TYPE_NAME:REAL
TYPE_NAME:VARCHAR
TYPE_NAME:ENUM
TYPE_NAME:SET
TYPE_NAME:DATE
TYPE_NAME:TIME
TYPE_NAME:DATETIME
TYPE_NAME:TIMESTAMP
```

Storing an XML Document

In this section, we will discuss how to store an XML document in a database table column of type XML. The key steps in this procedure are as follows:

1. Create an SQLXML object.

2. Initialize the SQLXML object with an XML document.

3. Create a database table with a column of type XML.

4. Create a PreparedStatement to store the SQLXML object in the XML type column.

5. Run the PreparedStatement to store the SQLXML object.

In the XMLToSQL.java application, you need to import the java.sql and javax.xml.stream packages, where the javax.xml.stream package has the XMLStreamWriter and XMLStreamReader interfaces that are required to work with an SQLXML object. To create an XML document to be stored in the XML type column, first you need to create an SQLXML object. You create an SQLXML object from a Connection object using the createSQLXML() method, as shown here:

```
SQLXML sqlXML=connection.createSQLXML();
```

An SQLXML object created using the createSQLXML() method does not contain any data. To add data to an SQLXML object, you need to initialize this SQLXML object. You can initialize the SQLXML object either using an XMLStreamWriter object or using the setString() method of the SQLXML interface. To add data to an SQLXML object with an XMLStreamWriter object, create an XMLStreamWriter object from this SQLXML object by first creating a StAXResult object and subsequently obtaining an XMLStreamWriter object using the getXMLStreamWriter() method of the StAXResult class, as shown here:

```
StAXResult staxResult = sqlXML.setResult(StAXResult.class);
XMLStreamWriter xmlStreamWriter = staxResult.getXMLStreamWriter();
```

You use the setResult(Class<T> resultClass) method of the SQLXML interface to create a StAXResult object. The SQLXML object becomes unwritable when the setResult(Class<T> resultClass) method is invoked.

An XMLStreamWriter object creates an XML document by adding elements and attributes. In an XMLStreamWriter object, you start an XML document using the writeStartDocument (String encoding, String version) method, as shown here:

```
xmlStreamWriter.writeStartDocument("UTF-8","1.0");
```

Encoding specified in the writeStartDocument (String encoding, String version) method sets the encoding in the XML declaration of the XML document under construction. The XMLStreamWriter interface also provides the writeStartDocument() method to create an XML document without specifying an encoding and version and provides the writeStartDocument(String version) method to create an XML document with just the version information but no encoding.

You add the root catalog element of the example XML document using the writeStartElement(String localName) method, as shown here:

```
xmlStreamWriter.writeStartElement("catalog");
```

You can create an element with a namespace prefix using the writeStartElement(String prefix, String localName, String namespaceURI) method. You can generate an empty element using the writeEmptyElement(String localName) method.

You can add the attributes `title` and `publisher` to the `XMLStreamWriter` object using the `writeAttribute(String localName, String value)` method, as shown in Listing 9-6. If an attribute has a namespace prefix, use the method `writeAttribute(String prefix, String namespaceURI, String localName, String value)`.

Listing 9-6. *Adding the* catalog *Element Attributes*

```
xmlStreamWriter.writeAttribute("title", "ONJava.com");
xmlStreamWriter.writeAttribute("publisher", "OReilly");
```

Similar to the `catalog` element, you can add the `journal` element and its `date` attribute as shown in Listing 9-7. You also add the elements `article` and `title` using the `writeStartElement(String)` method.

Listing 9-7. *Adding the Elements* journal, article, *and* title

```
xmlStreamWriter.writeStartElement("journal");
xmlStreamWriter.writeAttribute("date", "September 2005");
xmlStreamWriter.writeStartElement("article");
xmlStreamWriter.writeStartElement("title");
```

You can add the `title` element text using the `writeCharacters(String text)` method, as shown here:

```
xmlStreamWriter.writeCharacters("Managing XML data: Tag URIs");
```

You can also add text from a `char[]` array using the method `writeCharacters(char[] text, int start, int len)`.

You need to add an end element tag corresponding to each start element. You do this using the `writeEndElement()` method, as shown here:

```
xmlStreamWriter.writeEndElement();
```

The method `writeEndElement()` does not specify the element local name, because the local name is deduced implicitly. Similarly, you need to add other elements to create the example XML document shown in Listing 9-1. Finally, you need to end the document using the `writeEndDocument()` method, as shown in Listing 9-8. You also need to close the `XMLStreamWriter` object.

Listing 9-8. *Adding the End of the Document*

```
xmlStreamWriter.writeEndDocument();
xmlStreamWriter.close();
```

As mentioned earlier, you can also add an XML document to an `SQLXML` object from an XML string using the `setString(String)` method of the interface `SQLXML`, as shown in Listing 9-9. If the `setString(String)` method is invoked on an `SQLXML` object, on which the `setString(String)` method or the `createXMLStreamWriter()` method has been previously invoked, a `SQLException` gets thrown.

Listing 9-9. *Setting the XML Document As a String*

```
sqlXML.setString("<catalog title='OnJava.com' publisher='OReilly'>
 <journal date='September 2005'>
  <article>
   <title>What Is a Portlet</title>
   <author> Sunil Patil</author>
  </article>
```

```
  <article>
   <title>What Is Hibernate</title>
   <author>James Elliott</author>
  </article>
 </journal>
</catalog>");
```

You can store an SQLXML object in a database table column of type XML. Therefore, you need to create a database table with an XML type column. You can create a database table with the XML type column either with a SQL command-line tool or with the JDBC API. To create a database table with the JDBC API, create a java.sql.Statement object from the Connection object, as shown in Listing 9-10. Using the Statement object, create a database table named Catalog, with a column CatalogId of type INT and a column Catalog of type XML, as shown in Listing 9-10.

Listing 9-10. *Creating a Database Table*

```
Statement stmt=connection.createStatement();
stmt.executeUpdate("CREATE Table Catalog(CatalogId INT, Catalog XML)");
```

To store an SQLXML object in a database, create a PreparedStatement object to add values to the database table Catalog. The PreparedStatement consists of an INSERT statement with parameter markers for the INT and SQLXML values to be added to database, as shown in Listing 9-11.

Listing 9-11. *Creating a PreparedStatement*

```
PreparedStatement statement=
connection.prepareStatement
("INSERT INTO CATALOG(catalogId, catalog)
VALUES(?,?)");
```

You set the INT value using the setInt(int index, int value) method, and you set the SQLXML value using the setSQLXML(int index, SQLXML value) method of the PreparedStatement interface, as shown in Listing 9-12. If the XMLStreamWriter object has not been closed prior to invoking the setSQLXML() method, SQLException gets thrown. You can update the database using the executeUpdate() method.

Listing 9-12. *Setting an SQLXML Value*

```
statement.setInt(1, 1);
statement.setSQLXML(2, sqlXML);
statement.executeUpdate();
```

The SQLXML objects are valid for at least the duration of the transaction in which they are created. The JDBC 4.0 specification recommends freeing SQLXML object resources using the free() method, as shown here:

```
sqlXML.free();
```

JDBC 4.0 also provides update methods in the ResultSet interface to update the SQLXML values. The update methods updateSQLXML(int columnIndex, SQLXML sqlXML) and updateSQLXML(String columnName, SQLXML sqlXML) update values in the ResultSet object, which you can then use to insert a new row. For example, to add a new row, obtain a Statement object that supports an updateable ResultSet type, as shown in Listing 9-13.

Listing 9-13. *Creating a Statement Object*

```
Statement stmt = connection.createStatement(
                          ResultSet.TYPE_SCROLL_INSENSITIVE,
                          ResultSet.CONCUR_UPDATABLE);
```

Subsequently, obtain a ResultSet from the Catalog database table, as shown in Listing 9-14. To add a new row, move the ResultSet cursor to the insert row. You can update the INT column value using the updateInt() method, and you can update the SQLXML column value using the updateSQLXML() method. A new row is not inserted until the invoke insertRow() method is called, as shown in Listing 9-14.

Listing 9-14. *Adding a New Row*

```
ResultSet rs = stmt.executeQuery("SELECT * from Catalog");
rs.moveToInsertRow();
rs.updateInt(1, 2);
rs.updateSQLXML(2, xmlObject);
rs.insertRow();
```

You can also update a ResultSet from the current row in a scrollable ResultSet. To update a ResultSet from the current row in a scrollable ResultSet, move to a ResultSet row using the absolute(int) or relative(int) method. The method absolute(int) moves the cursor to the specified row; the method relative(int) moves the cursor a specified number of rows relative to the current row. You can update the SQLXML value in the ResultSet using an update method, and subsequently you can update the database row using the updateRow() method, as shown in Listing 9-15.

Listing 9-15. *Updating a Row*

```
rs.absolute(5);
rs.updateSQLXML("catalog", xmlObject);
rs.updateRow();
```

If an XMLStreamWriter object has not been closed prior to invoking the update methods, SQLException gets thrown.

Retrieving an XML Document

In this section, you will retrieve an XML document from a database table column of type XML. To obtain a ResultSet object from the Catalog database table, create a PreparedStatement using a SELECT query, as shown in Listing 9-16. The SQL statement has a parameter marker for the CatalogId value. You set the CatalogId value using the setInt(int index, int value) method. Using the PreparedStatement object, obtain a result set using the executeQuery() method, as shown in Listing 9-16.

Listing 9-16. *Retrieving a ResultSet*

```
PreparedStatement stmt=
connection.prepareStatement
("SELECT * FROM  CATALOG WHERE CatalogId=?");
stmt.setInt(1, 1);
ResultSet rs=stmt.executeQuery();
```

You can obtain the SQLXML object for the Catalog column, which is of type XML, from the ResultSet using the getSQLXML(int index) method or the getSQLXML(String columnName) method, as shown in Listing 9-17. You can output the XML document in an SQLXML object using the getString() method of the SQLXML interface.

Listing 9-17. *Retrieving the SQLXML Object*

```
SQLXML sqlXML=rs.getSQLXML("Catalog");
System.out.println(sqlXML.getString());
```

Navigating an XML Document

Instead of outputting the XML document to a String value, you can navigate a document using an XMLStreamReader object. The XMLStreamReader interface is a parse event generator. You need to create an InputStream object from the SQLXML object using the getBinaryStream() method. You also need to create an XMLInputFactory object using the static method newInstance(). From the XMLInputFactory object you need to create an XMLStreamReader object using the createXMLStreamReader(InputStream) method of the XMLInputFactory class, as shown in Listing 9-18.

Listing 9-18. *Creating an XMLStreamReader Object*

```
InputStream binaryStream = sqlXML.getBinaryStream();
XMLInputFactory factory = XMLInputFactory.newInstance();
XMLStreamReader xmlStreamReader = factory.createXMLStreamReader(binaryStream);
```

The method hasNext() determines whether parsing events are available. You obtain the next parse event using the next() method, as shown in Listing 9-19.

Listing 9-19. *Generating Parse Events*

```
while(xmlStreamReader.hasNext()){
int parseEvent=xmlStreamReader.next();
}
```

The method next() returns an int value that corresponds to an XMLStreamConstants constant and represents a parsing event. Table 9-2 lists the return values of the next() method.

Table 9-2. *Method next() Return Values*

Event Type	Description
ATTRIBUTE	Specifies an attribute
CDATA	Specifies CDATA
CHARACTERS	Specifies text
COMMENT	Specifies an XML document comment
NOTATION_DECLARATION	Specifies a notation declaration
PROCESSING_INSTRUCTION	Specifies a processing instruction
START_DOCUMENT	Specifies the start of document
START_ELEMENT	Specifies the start of an element

Table 9-2. *Method next() Return Values*

Event Type	Description
END_ELEMENT	Specifies the end of an element
ENTITY_DECLARATION	Specifies an entity declaration
ENTITY_REFERENCE	Specifies an entity reference
NAMESPACE	Specifies a namespace declaration
SPACE	Specifies ignorable whitespace
END_DOCUMENT	Specifies the end of a document
DTD	Specifies a DTD

If the return value is START_ELEMENT, the parse event indicates that an element has been parsed. You can obtain the element local name, the prefix, and the namespace using the getLocalName(), getPrefix(), and getNamespaceURI() methods, as shown in Listing 9-20.

Listing 9-20. *Outputting the Element Values*

```
if(parseEvent==XMLStreamConstants.START_ELEMENT){
System.out.println("Element Local Name: "+xmlStreamReader.getLocalName());
System.out.println("Element Prefix: "+xmlStreamReader.getPrefix());
System.out.println("Element Namespace:"+xmlStreamReader.getNamespaceURI());
}
```

You can obtain the attribute count in an element using the getAttributeCount() method. You can iterate over attributes, and you can obtain the attribute local name using the getAttributeLocalName() method, the attribute value using the getAttributeValue() method, the attribute prefix using the getAttributePrefix() method, and the attribute namespace using the getAttributeNamespace() method, as shown in Listing 9-21.

Listing 9-21. *Outputting the Attribute Values*

```
for(int i=0; i<xmlStreamReader.getAttributeCount();i++){
  System.out.println("Attribute Prefix:"+
  xmlStreamReader.getAttributePrefix(i));
  System.out.println("Attribute Namespace:"+
  xmlStreamReader.getAttributeNamespace(i));
  System.out.println("Attribute Local Name:"+
    xmlStreamReader.getAttributeLocalName(i));
  System.out.println("Attribute Value:"+
  xmlStreamReader.getAttributeValue(i));
}
```

If the parse event is of type CHARACTERS, you can obtain the text of the parse event using the getText() method, as shown in Listing 9-22.

Listing 9-22. *Outputting Text*

```
if(parseEvent==XMLStreamConstants.CHARACTERS){
    System.out.println("CHARACTERS text: "+xmlStreamReader.getText());
}
```

Complete Example Application

Listing 9-23 shows the complete XMLToSQL.java application. The XMLToSQL.java application has the methods createJDBCConnection(), storeXMLDocument(), and retrieveXMLDocument(). In the method createJDBCConnection(), you obtain a JDBC connection to a database, and the data types supported by the database are output. If the data type XML is output in data types, the database supports the SQL:2003 standard XML data type. Calls to the storeXMLDocument() and retrieveXMLDocument() methods have been commented out, because none of the databases provides a JDBC 4.0 driver at the time of publication. When a JDBC 4.0 driver becomes available, you can uncomment the methods storeXMLDocument() and retrieveXMLDocument() and use them to store an XML document in a database and retrieve an XML document from a database.

Listing 9-23. *XMLToSQL.java*

```
package com.apress.sqlxml;

import java.sql.*;
import javax.xml.stream.*;
import java.io.InputStream;
import javax.xml.transform.stax.StAXResult;


public class XMLToSQL {
  Connection connection;
               //Method to create a JDBC connection
  public void createJDBCConnection() {
    try {
              //Load JDBC driver
              Class.forName("com.mysql.jdbc.Driver");
             //Specify connection URL
                      String url = "jdbc:mysql://localhost:3306/test";
            //Get JDBC connection
            Connection connection =
              DriverManager.getConnection(url,
              "root", null);
            //Obtain database metadata
            DatabaseMetaData metadata = connection.getMetaData();
            ResultSet rs = metadata.getTypeInfo();
            rs.next();

            while (rs.next()) {
                //Output data types
                System.out.println("TYPE_NAME:" + rs.getString("TYPE_NAME"));
            }
    } catch (SQLException e) {
      System.out.println(e.getMessage());
    } catch (ClassNotFoundException e) {
      System.out.println(e.getMessage());
    }
  }
}
```

```java
//Method to store an XML document
public void storeXMLDocument() {

   try {
           //Create an SQLXML object
           SQLXML sqlXML = connection.createSQLXML();

            //Create an XMLStreamWriter
           StAXResult staxResult =
                   sqlXML.setResult(StAXResult.class);
           XMLStreamWriter xmlStreamWriter =
                   staxResult.getXMLStreamWriter();

            //Create XML document
            xmlStreamWriter.writeStartDocument("UTF-8", "1.0");
            xmlStreamWriter.writeStartElement("catalog");
            xmlStreamWriter.writeAttribute("title", "ONJava.com");
            xmlStreamWriter.writeAttribute("publisher", "OReilly");

            xmlStreamWriter.writeStartElement("journal");
            xmlStreamWriter.writeAttribute("date", "September 2005");
            xmlStreamWriter.writeStartElement("article");

            xmlStreamWriter.writeStartElement("title");
            xmlStreamWriter.writeCharacters("What Is a Portlet");
            xmlStreamWriter.writeEndElement();

            xmlStreamWriter.writeStartElement("author");
            xmlStreamWriter.writeCharacters("Sunil Patil");
            xmlStreamWriter.writeEndElement();

            xmlStreamWriter.writeEndElement();

            xmlStreamWriter.writeStartElement("article");

            xmlStreamWriter.writeStartElement("title");
            xmlStreamWriter.writeCharacters("What Is Hibernate");
            xmlStreamWriter.writeEndElement();

           xmlStreamWriter.writeStartElement("author");
           xmlStreamWriter.writeCharacters("James Elliott");
           xmlStreamWriter.writeEndElement();

           xmlStreamWriter.writeEndElement();
           xmlStreamWriter.writeEndElement();

           xmlStreamWriter.writeEndElement();

        xmlStreamWriter.writeEndDocument();
        xmlStreamWriter.close();
```

```java
          //Create database table
        Statement stmt = connection.createStatement();
        stmt.executeUpdate("CREATE Table Catalog(CatalogId int, Catalog XML)");

        //Create PreparedStatement
        PreparedStatement statement =
         connection.prepareStatement
         ("INSERT INTO CATALOG(catalogId, catalog)
         VALUES(?,?)");

         //Set values in PreparedStatement
         statement.setInt(1, 1);
         statement.setSQLXML(2, sqlXML);

         //Update database
        statement.executeUpdate();
        sqlXML.free();

   } catch (SQLException e) {
   } catch (XMLStreamException e) {
   }

}
          //Retrieve XML document
public void retrieveXMLDocument() {

  try {//Create PreparedStatement
  PreparedStatement stmt =
   connection.prepareStatement
   ("SELECT * FROM  CATALOG WHERE catalogId=?");
   stmt.setInt(1, 1);
                                    //Obtain ResultSet
    ResultSet rs = stmt.executeQuery();
                                    //Obtain SQLXML object
    SQLXML sqlXML = rs.getSQLXML("catalog");
    System.out.println(sqlXML.getString());
         //Create XMLStreamReader object
    InputStream binaryStream = sqlXML.getBinaryStream();
    XMLInputFactory factory = XMLInputFactory.newInstance();
    XMLStreamReader xmlStreamReader =
      factory.createXMLStreamReader(binaryStream);
    //Generate parse events
    while (xmlStreamReader.hasNext()) {
      int parseEvent = xmlStreamReader.next();
      if (parseEvent == XMLStreamConstants.ATTRIBUTE) {
        System.out.println("ATTRIBUTE");
        System.out.println("Attribute Local Name: "
        + xmlStreamReader.getAttributeLocalName(0));
        System.out.println("Attribute Namespace: "
        + xmlStreamReader.getAttributeNamespace(0));
        System.out.println("Attribute Prefix: "
        + xmlStreamReader.getAttributePrefix(0));
        System.out.println("Attribute Value: "
          + xmlStreamReader.getAttributeValue(0));
```

```
      }
    if (parseEvent == XMLStreamConstants.CDATA) {
      System.out.println("CDATA");
    System.out.println("Text: " + xmlStreamReader.getText());
      }
    if (parseEvent == XMLStreamConstants.CHARACTERS) {
      System.out.println("CHARACTERS");
    System.out.println("Text: " + xmlStreamReader.getText());
      }
    if (parseEvent == XMLStreamConstants.COMMENT) {
      System.out.println("COMMENT");
    System.out.println("Text: " + xmlStreamReader.getText());
      }
  if (parseEvent == XMLStreamConstants.NOTATION_DECLARATION) {
      System.out.println("NOTATION_DECLARATION");
      }
    if (parseEvent == XMLStreamConstants.START_DOCUMENT) {
      System.out.println("START_DOCUMENT");
      }
    if (parseEvent == XMLStreamConstants.START_ELEMENT) {
      System.out.println("START_ELEMENT");
      System.out.println("Local Name: "
        + xmlStreamReader.getLocalName());
      System.out.println("Text: "
        + xmlStreamReader.getElementText());
      System.out
      .println("Prefix: " + xmlStreamReader.getPrefix());
      System.out.println("Namespace: "
        + xmlStreamReader.getNamespaceURI());
      }
    if (parseEvent == XMLStreamConstants.END_ELEMENT) {
      System.out.println("END_ELEMENT");
      System.out.println("Local Name: "
        + xmlStreamReader.getLocalName());
      }
  if (parseEvent == XMLStreamConstants.ENTITY_DECLARATION) {
      System.out.println("ENTITY_DECLARATION");
      }
    if (parseEvent == XMLStreamConstants.ENTITY_REFERENCE) {
      System.out.println("ENTITY_REFERENCE");
      System.out.println("Text: "
        + xmlStreamReader.getElementText());
      }
    if (parseEvent == XMLStreamConstants.NAMESPACE) {
      System.out.println("NAMESPACE");
      System.out.println("Prefix: "
      + xmlStreamReader.getNamespacePrefix(0));
      System.out.println("NamespaceURI: "
        + xmlStreamReader.getNamespaceURI(0));

      }
    if (parseEvent == XMLStreamConstants.SPACE) {
      System.out.println("SPACE");
    System.out.println("Text: " + xmlStreamReader.getText());
```

```
        }
      if (parseEvent == XMLStreamConstants.END_DOCUMENT) {
         System.out.println("END_DOCUMENT");
      }
       if (parseEvent == XMLStreamConstants.DTD) {
         System.out.println("DTD");
      }

    }

    sqlXML.free();

  } catch (SQLException e) {
  }

}

public static void main(String[] argv) {
  XMLToSQL sqlXMLApp = new XMLToSQL();
  sqlXMLApp.createJDBCConnection();

  /*
   * sqlXMLApp.storeXMLDocument();
   * sqlXMLApp.retrieveXMLDocument();
   */
  }
}
```

Summary

The SQL:2003 standard provides a new database data type, XML. JDBC 4.0 provides a Java data type, SQLXML, for the database data type XML. The JDBC 4.0 API is included in the upcoming J2SE 6.0. To store an XML document in a database table column of type XML, the database is required to support the XML database type. At the time of writing this book, the databases DB2 UDB 9.1 and SQL Server 2005 support the XML data type. To retrieve an XML document from an XML type column using the SQLXML Java data type, you need a JDBC 4.0 driver for the relevant database. At the time of writing this book, the JDBC 4.0 specification is not yet finalized.

You can use the example application in this chapter when a JDBC 4.0 driver becomes available. In this chapter, we explained the procedure to create an SQLXML object, initialize the SQLXML object, and store the SQLXML object using the JDBC 4.0 API. We also discussed the procedure to retrieve an SQLXML object from a ResultSet and navigate an XML document.

PART 4

DOM Level 3.0

■ ■ ■

CHAPTER 10

Loading and Saving with the DOM Level 3 API

The DOM Level 3 Core specification, which builds upon the DOM Level 2 and Level 1 Core specifications, defines platform- and language-neutral interfaces for accessing and manipulating the content and structure of a generalized document, represented as a document tree. In addition to the interfaces for a generalized document, the DOM Level 3 Core specification contains specific interfaces for manipulating XML documents. (Chapter 2 discussed the DOM Level 3 Core specification.)

The DOM Level 3 Load and Save[1] specification provides a set of interfaces for loading and saving (*serializing* and *deserializing*) an XML document. Loading an XML document means mapping the XML document model to a DOM document model. Saving an XML document implies converting a DOM document model to an XML document model. DOM Load and Save Level 3 is a platform- and language-neutral specification. Beside its language- and platform-neutral status, the key features that motivated this specification are as follows:

- The ability to filter content during the loading and saving process
- The ability to load and save selected nodes within a document, as opposed to the whole document
- The ability to serialize a document to a string, rather than a file
- The facility for event handling during document loads and saves

The myriad reasons for filtering content, or loading and saving selected nodes, are too numerous to enumerate, but some common reasons for filtering content, or loading and saving selected nodes, are as follows:

- Filtering confidential information from a document, before it is communicated to a third party
- Adding or removing application-specific annotations or processing instructions to a document
- Adapting a template document for a specific purpose

In this chapter, we will discuss the DOM 3 Load and Save specification as implemented by JAXP 1.3, which is included in J2SE 5.0. In addition to providing the loading and saving of an XML document and the filtering of content during loading and saving, the DOM 3 Load and Save API provides event handling as the document is loaded or serialized. In this chapter, we will cover all these features of the DOM Level 3 Load and Save API.

---

1. The DOM Level 3 Load and Save specification is a W3C Recommendation available at http://www.w3.org/TR/DOM-Level-3-LS/.

Overview

The DOM 3 Load and Save specification provides an interface for bidirectional mapping between a DOM document model and an XML document model. The mapping is implemented by a set of interfaces that we will discuss briefly in the following sections; we explain the interfaces in greater detail in subsequent sections.

The DOMImplementationLS interface extends the DOM Level 3 Core DOMImplementation interface and provides factory methods for creating objects required for loading and saving an XML document. Using a DOMImplementationLS object, you can create an LSParser, LSSerializer, LSInput, or LSOutput object.

Introducing the Load API

The following are the key points of the Load API:

- LSParser is an interface to parse data into a DOM document model.
- The LSInput interface represents a data source. You can set a data source on an LSInput object using a character stream, a byte stream, a string, a system ID, or a public ID. LSParser uses an LSInput object to determine how to read data. You can set multiple input sources on an LSParser object, and LSParser uses the first input that is not null and not an empty string. The LSParser object scans the different input sources in the following order to select one to read from:

  a. LSInput.characterStream

  b. LSInput.byteStream

  c. LSInput.stringData

  d. LSInput.systemId

  e. LSInput.publicId

- The LSResourceResolver interface resolves external resources, such as external entities, and creates an LSInput object from an external resource.
- LSParserFilter filters nodes as data is parsed.

Introducing the Save API

The following are the key points of the Save API:

- The LSSerializer interface is for serializing (saving) a DOM document model to an XML document model.
- The LSOutput interface represents output for serializing a DOM document model. The LSSerializer will use an LSOutput object to determine the output destination. You can set multiple outputs on an LSSerializer object, and LSSerializer uses the first output that is not null and not an empty string. The LSSerializer object scans the different outputs in the following order to determine which one to output to:

  a. LSOutput.characterStream

  b. LSOutput.byteStream

  c. LSOutput.systemId

- The LSSerializerFilter interface filters nodes as a DOM document model is saved.

Comparing JAXP's DocumentBuilder and Transformer APIs

The DOM Level 3 Load and Save specification was influenced by earlier versions of JAXP. It turns out that prior to the DOM Level 3 Load and Save specification, JAXP defined APIs that you can use for serializing and deserializing an XML document. The JAXP DocumentBuilder class provides a standard method to map an XML document to a DOM object, and the JAXP Transformer class provides a method for serializing a DOM document model to an XML document model. Of course, JAXP is a Java-specific API. The DOM Level 3 Load and Save specification built upon ideas from JAXP and defined platform- and language-neutral interfaces for loading and saving an XML document and also added features such as event handling and filtering. And to bring things full circle, JAXP 1.3 now provides a Java binding of the DOM Level 3 Load and Save specification.

If you don't require the filtering, event handling, or loading and saving of selected nodes, you can use JAXP's DocumentBuilder and Transformer APIs for loading and saving an XML document. The DOM 3 Load and Save specification interfaces offer the following features over and above what the JAXP DocumentBuilder and Transformer classes offer:

- DOM Level 3 Load and Save supports the registration of an event listener with a parser. When the loading of an XML document using the DOM 3 parser is complete, the generated load event indicates that the document loading has completed.

- You can filter nodes as a DOM 3 parser loads them or as they are serialized.

- You can save a selected node in a DOM document model instead of the complete document.

- You can save a Document node or an Element node as a java.lang.String object, instead of a file. Exchanging XML documents in a web service sometimes requires an XML document as a String type.

In this chapter, we will explain the procedure to load and save an XML document using the DOM Level 3 specification. We will demonstrate how to filter content at load time and at serialization time using the DOM Level 3 Load and Save specification. This chapter uses the DOM Level 3 Load and Save implementation provided by JAXP 1.3, which is included in J2SE 5.0.

Creating an Eclipse Project

The DOM Level 3 specification is implemented in several API distributions such as Xerce2-j and JAXP 1.3. In this chapter, you will use the JAXP 1.3 API distribution included in J2SE 5.0. You will use JAXP 1.3, because JAXP 1.3 is a Java Specification Requests (JSR) specification. Before you can set up your project, you need to download Xerces[2] version 2.7.1 and extract the zip file to an installation directory. The Xerces2-j.zip file is required, because an implementation class in the xercesImpl.jar file is required to set a DOMImplementationRegistry property. You also need to download and install J2SE version 5.0, which includes the JAXP 1.3 implementation of the DOM Level 3 Load and Save specification.

To compile and run the code examples, you need an Eclipse project. You can download project Chapter10 from the Apress website (http://www.apress.com) and import it into your Eclipse workspace.

To compile and run your DOM Level 3 Load and Save code examples, you need a Xerces2-J JAR file in your project's Java build path; Figure 10-1 shows the JAR files. The JAR file required for a DOM 3 Load and Save application is xercesImpl.jar, which consists of the Xerces implementation API. You also need to set the JRE system library to JRE 5.0, as shown in Figure 10-1.

---

2. For more information about Xerces2-j, see http://xerces.apache.org/xerces2-j/.

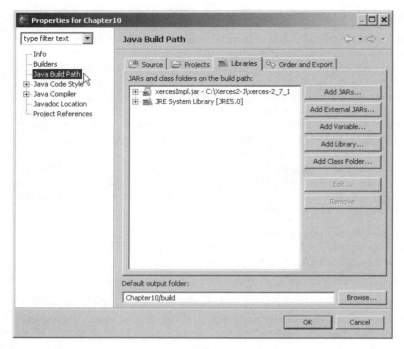

Figure 10-1. *Chapter10 project Java build path*

Figure 10-2 shows the Chapter10 project directory structure.

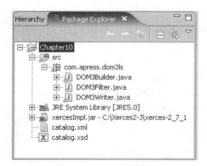

Figure 10-2. *Chapter10 project directory structure*

Loading an XML Document

Let's first look at how to load an XML document. You use the interfaces and classes in the org.w3c. dom.ls package to load, save, and filter an XML document. You use the LSParser interface in this package to load an XML document, parse an XML document, and obtain a Document object. The procedure to load an XML document is as follows:

1. Set the system property DOMImplementationRegistry.PROPERTY.

2. Create a DOMImplementationRegistry object.

3. Create a `DOMImplementationLS` object.

4. Create an `LSParser` object.

5. Create a `DOMConfiguration` object.

6. Create an error handler class, and set the `error-handler` parameter.

7. Set the `validate`, `schema-type`, `validate-if-schema`, and `schema-location` parameters.

8. Parse the XML document.

Listing 10-1 shows the example document loaded, `catalog.xml`.

Listing 10-1. *catalog.xml*

```xml
<?xml version="1.0" encoding="UTF-8"?>
<catalog  title="dev2dev">
 <journal  date="May 2005">
  <article section="WebLogic Server">
    <title>Session Management for Clustered Applications</title>
    <author> Jon Purdy</author>
   </article>
  </journal>

 <journal  date="April 2005">
  <article section="WebLogic Platform">
    <title>Integrating WebLogic Platform 8.1 with the
     Stellent Web Content Management System</title>
    <author>Munish Gandhi</author>
   </article>
  </journal>
</catalog>
```

You can also validate the document that is loaded by an `LSParser` object with an XML Schema. Listing 10-2 shows the example XML Schema, `catalog.xsd`, with which the example XML document is validated.

Listing 10-2. *catalog.xsd*

```xml
<?xml version="1.0" encoding="utf-8"?>
<xs:schema
xmlns:xs="http://www.w3.org/2001/XMLSchema">
  <xs:element name="catalog">
   <xs:complexType>
    <xs:sequence>
     <xs:element ref="journal" minOccurs="0"
maxOccurs="unbounded"/>
    </xs:sequence>
    <xs:attribute name="title" type="xs:string"/>
   </xs:complexType>
  </xs:element>
  <xs:element name="journal">
   <xs:complexType>
    <xs:sequence>
     <xs:element ref="article" minOccurs="0"
       maxOccurs="unbounded"/>
    </xs:sequence>
```

```
     <xs:attribute name="date" type="xs:string"/>
   </xs:complexType>
 </xs:element>
 <xs:element name="article">
  <xs:complexType>
   <xs:sequence>
    <xs:element name="title" type="xs:string"/>
    <xs:element ref="author" minOccurs="0"
       maxOccurs="unbounded"/>
   </xs:sequence>
  <xs:attribute name="section" type="xs:string"/>
   </xs:complexType>
 </xs:element>
 <xs:element name="author" type="xs:string"/>
</xs:schema>
```

The following code is the standard way in which to retrieve a DOM implementation, which you can then use to parse an XML document. As you will see, most of the code is simply used to initialize registries and properties so as to extract the final parser. To parse an XML document, first you need to import the org.w3c.dom.ls package. Next, you need to set the DOMImplementationRegistry.PROPERTY system property, as shown here:

```
System.setProperty(DOMImplementationRegistry.PROPERTY,
  "org.apache.xerces.dom.DOMImplementationSourceImpl");
```

A DOMImplementationRegistry is a factory that enables applications to obtain instances of a DOMImplementation. To obtain a DOMImplementation, first create a DOMImplementationRegistry object using the static method newInstance(). Subsequently, obtain a DOMImplementation instance from the DOMImplementationRegistry object, as shown in Listing 10-3.

Listing 10-3. *Creating a DOMImplementation*

```
DOMImplementationRegistry registry =DOMImplementationRegistry.newInstance();
DOMImplementation domImpl = registry.getDOMImplementation("LS 3.0");
```

Specifying LS 3.0 in the features list ensures that the DOMImplementation object implements the Load and Save features of the DOM 3.0 specification. Some of the other features that may be included are XML 1.0 Traversal and Events 2.0. You need to cast the DOMImplementation object to DOMImplementationLS, which provides methods to create an LSParser. The LSParser interface loads an XML document. Therefore, create an LSParser instance from the DOMImplementationLS type object, as shown in Listing 10-4.

Listing 10-4. *Creating an LSParser*

```
DOMImplementationLS implLS = (DOMImplementationLS)domImpl;
LSParser parser =
implLS.createLSParser(DOMImplementationLS.MODE_SYNCHRONOUS,
  "http://www.w3.org/2001/XMLSchema");
```

You can set the mode of parsing to MODE_SYNCHRONOUS or MODE_ASYNCHRONOUS. If the mode is MODE_SYNCHRONOUS, the parse() and parseURI() methods of the LSParser object return an org.w3c. dom.Document object. If the mode is MODE_ASYNCHRONOUS, the parse() and parseURI() methods return null. The schemaType, http://www.w3.org/2001/XMLSchema, specifies the type of schema used to load an XML document. To set the configuration parameters of an LSParser object, obtain a DOMConfiguration object from LSParser, as shown here:

```
DOMConfiguration config=parser.getDomConfig();
```

To set the error-handler parameter of the DOMConfiguration, you need to create a class that implements the DOMErrorHandler interface. Listing 10-5 shows a DOMErrorHandler implementation class.

Listing 10-5. *Error Handler Class*

```
private class DOMErrorHandlerImpl implements DOMErrorHandler{
    public boolean handleError(DOMError error){
        System.out.println("Error Message:"+error.getMessage());
        if(error.getSeverity()==DOMError.SEVERITY_WARNING)
            return true;
        else
            return false;
    }
}
```

To add error handling to the LSParser object, create an instance of the DOMErrorHandlerImpl class, and set the error-handler parameter of the DOMConfiguration object, as shown in Listing 10-6.

Listing 10-6. *Setting Error Handling*

```
DOMErrorHandlerImpl errorHandler=new DOMErrorHandlerImpl();
config.setParameter("error-handler", errorHandler);
```

You can configure an LSParser object to be a schema-validating parser by setting the validate, schema-type, validate-if-schema, and schema-location parameters, as shown in Listing 10-7.

Listing 10-7. *Setting the Schema Validation*

```
config.setParameter("validate" , Boolean.TRUE);
config.setParameter("schema-type" , "http://www.w3.org/2001/XMLSchema");
config.setParameter("validate-if-schema" , Boolean.TRUE);
config.setParameter("schema-location"  ,"catalog.xsd");
```

Finally, parse the XML document using the LSParser, as shown here:

```
Document document = parser.parseURI("catalog.xml");
```

If the XML document schema validation has any errors, the error handler specified with the error-handler parameter registers the errors. Having loaded the XML document, you can update the XML document using the DOM Level 3 Core API. Previous to the DOM Level 3 Load and Save specification, XML document loading varied with the parser used to load and parse an XML document. With the DOM Level 3 specification, the loading and saving mechanism is standardized.

The JAXP 1.3 implementation of the DOM 3 Load and Save specification has a limitation: the org.w3c.dom.ls package does not provide an implementation class for the LSParser interface that also implements the EventTarget interface. Without an implementation class for the LSParser interface that also implements the EventTarget interface, event handling is not feasible without creating a custom class that implements the LSParser interface and the EventTarget interface. Because we are not using a custom class that implements the LSParser interface, we have not included event handling in the example application.

Listing 10-8 shows the application DOM3Builder.java, which loads an XML document. The application consists of a method loadDocument() that loads an XML document. In the loadDocument() method, first set the system property for DOMImplementationRegistry, and subsequently create a DOMImplementationRegistry object. From the DOMImplementationRegistry object, create a DOMImplementation object, and cast the DOMImplementation object to DOMImplementationLS. From the DOMImplementationLS object, create an LSParser object. From the LSParser object, obtain a DOMConfiguration object, and set the error-handler parameter on the DOMConfiguration object. Also, set the schema validation parameters on the DOMConfiguration object. The example XML document is parsed using the parseURI() method.

Listing 10-8. *DOM3Builder.java*

```java
package com.apress.dom3ls;
import org.w3c.dom.*;
import org.w3c.dom.bootstrap.*;
import org.w3c.dom.ls.*;


public class DOM3Builder {
                                        //Method to load an XML document
  public void loadDocument() {
    try {
      //Setting system property for DOMImplementationRegistry
      System.setProperty(DOMImplementationRegistry.PROPERTY,
        "org.apache.xerces.dom.DOMImplementationSourceImpl");

      //Creating a DOMImplementationRegistry
      DOMImplementationRegistry registry = DOMImplementationRegistry
          .newInstance();

      //Creating a DOMImplementation object
      DOMImplementation domImpl = registry.getDOMImplementation("LS 3.0");

      //Casting DOMImplementation to DOMImplementationLS
      DOMImplementationLS implLS = (DOMImplementationLS) domImpl;

      //Creating an LSParser object
      LSParser parser = implLS.createLSParser(
          DOMImplementationLS.MODE_SYNCHRONOUS,
          "http://www.w3.org/2001/XMLSchema");

      //Obtaining a DOMConfiguration object
      DOMConfiguration config = parser.getDomConfig();

      //Setting the error handler
      DOMErrorHandlerImpl errorHandler = new DOMErrorHandlerImpl();
      config.setParameter("error-handler", errorHandler);

      //Setting schema validation parameters
      config.setParameter("validate", Boolean.TRUE);
      config.setParameter("schema-type",
          "http://www.w3.org/2001/XMLSchema");

      config.setParameter("validate-if-schema", Boolean.TRUE);
      config.setParameter("schema-location", "catalog.xsd");
                                        //Parsing an XML document
      Document document = parser.parseURI("catalog.xml");
      System.out.println("XML document loaded");
```

```
    } catch (DOMException e) {
      System.out.println("DOMException " + e.getMessage());
    } catch (ClassNotFoundException e) {
      System.out.println("ClassNotFoundException " + e.getMessage());
    } catch (InstantiationException e) {
      System.out.println("InstantiationException " + e.getMessage());
    } catch (IllegalAccessException e) {
      System.out.println("IllegalAccessException " + e.getMessage());
    }
  }

  public static void main(String[] args) {
    DOM3Builder dom3Builder = new DOM3Builder();
    dom3Builder.loadDocument();
  }
              //Error handler class
  private class DOMErrorHandlerImpl implements DOMErrorHandler {
    public boolean handleError(DOMError error) {
      System.out.println("Error Message:" + error.getMessage());

      if (error.getSeverity() == DOMError.SEVERITY_WARNING) {
        return true;
      } else {
        return false;
      }
    }
  }
}
```

Run the DOM3Builder.java application in Eclipse with the procedure explained in Chapter 1. The output from the application indicates the XML document has been loaded, as shown in Listing 10-9.

Listing 10-9. *Output from DOM3Builder.java*

```
XML document loaded
```

Saving an XML Document

Let's now look at saving a DOM document model as an XML document model. With the DOM Level 3 API, you can save an XML document to an XML file or a String. The DOM Level 3 API has the added feature of being able to serialize only a selected node in a DOM document model. You use the LSSerializer interface to save a DOM document model to an XML document model. The procedure to save an XML document is as follows:

1. Create an XML document to save.

2. Set the system property DOMImplementationRegistry.PROPERTY.

3. Create a DOMImplementationRegistry object.

4. Create a DOMImplementationLS object.

5. Create an LSSerializer object.

6. Create an LSOutput object.

7. Output the XML document.

The following code is the standard way in which to retrieve a DOM implementation, which you can then use to save an XML document. As earlier in the chapter, import the org.w3c.dom.ls package.

We will demonstrate the LSSerializer interface by creating an XML document, adding elements and attributes to the XML document, and serializing the XML document. As earlier in the chapter, set the system property DOMImplementationRegistry.PROPERTY, as shown here:

```
System.setProperty(DOMImplementationRegistry.PROPERTY,
    "org.apache.xerces.dom.DOMImplementationSourceImpl");
```

To create an LSSerializer object, you need to create a DOMImplementationRegistry object. You create a DOMImplementationRegistry object using the static method newInstance(). Subsequently, create a DOMImplementation object from the registry, and cast the DOMImplementation instance to DOMImplementationLS. From the DOMImplementationLS object, create an LSSerializer object, as shown in Listing 10-10.

Listing 10-10. *Creating an LSSerializer Object*

```
DOMImplementationRegistry registry =DOMImplementationRegistry.newInstance();
DOMImplementation domImpl =registry.getDOMImplementation("LS 3.0");
DOMImplementationLS implLS = (DOMImplementationLS)domImpl;
LSSerializer dom3Writer = implLS.createLSSerializer();
```

To output the XML document generated, create an LSOutput object. You need to set an OutputStream, to which an XML document is output, on the LSOutput object. Also, you can specify an output encoding. You can output an XML document using the write(Node, LSOutput) method, as shown in Listing 10-11.

Listing 10-11. *Outputting an XML Document*

```
LSOutput output=implLS.createLSOutput();
output.setByteStream(System.out);
output.setEncoding("UTF-8");
dom3Writer.write(document,output);
```

The DOM Level 3 specification has a feature to output a selected node in a DOM document model instead of the complete document. For example, say you need to save the journal element node. To output the journal node, specify the journal node as an argument to the write(Node, LSOutput) method, as shown in Listing 10-12.

Listing 10-12. *Outputting the journal Node*

```
output.setByteStream(System.out);
dom3Writer.write(journal,output);
```

With the DOM Level 3 API, you can output a DOM document model to a String. Simply use the writeToString(Node) method, as shown here:

```
String nodeString = dom3Writer.writeToString(journal);
```

Listing 10-13 shows DOM3Writer.java, which is a Java class used to output an XML document. The application DOM3Writer.java consists of a method saveDocument(). In the saveDocument() method, create an XML document to save. Set the DOMImplementationRegistry system property, and create a DOMImplementationRegistry object. Create a DOMImplementation object, and cast to DOMImplementationLS. Create an LSSerializer object from the DOMImplementationLS object. Using an LSOutput object, output the XML document to System.out. You can also output a selected node in the DOM document model instead of the complete document. You can output a DOM document model to a String instead of a file.

Listing 10-13. *DOM3Writer.java*

```java
package com.apress.dom3ls;

import org.w3c.dom.*;
import org.w3c.dom.bootstrap.DOMImplementationRegistry;
import org.w3c.dom.ls.*;

import javax.xml.parsers.*;

public class DOM3Writer {

                                    //Method to save an XML document
  public void saveDocument() {
    try {      //Create an XML Document
      DocumentBuilderFactory factory = DocumentBuilderFactory
          .newInstance();
      DocumentBuilder builder = factory.newDocumentBuilder();

      Document document = builder.newDocument();
      Element catalog = document.createElement("catalog");

      catalog.setAttribute("publisher", "IBM developerWorks");

      document.appendChild(catalog);

      Element journal = document.createElement("journal");

      journal.setAttribute("edition", "October 2005");

      journal.setAttribute("section", "XML");

      catalog.appendChild(journal);

      Element article = document.createElement("article");
      journal.appendChild(article);

      Element title = document.createElement("title");

      title.appendChild(document.createTextNode("JAXP Validation"));
      article.appendChild(title);

      Element author = document.createElement("author");

      author.appendChild(document.createTextNode("Brett McLaughlin"));
      article.appendChild(author);
              //Set system property for DOMImplementationRegistry

  System.setProperty(DOMImplementationRegistry.PROPERTY,
      "org.apache.xerces.dom.DOMImplementationSourceImpl");
                              //Create a DOMImplementationRegistry object
    DOMImplementationRegistry registry = DOMImplementationRegistry
        .newInstance();
```

```
                                        //Create a DOMImplementation object
      DOMImplementation domImpl = registry.getDOMImplementation("LS 3.0");

      DOMImplementationLS implLS = (DOMImplementationLS) domImpl;
                                        //Create an LSSerializer object
      LSSerializer dom3Writer = implLS.createLSSerializer();
                                        //Create an LSOutput object
      LSOutput output = implLS.createLSOutput();

      System.out.println("Outputting XML Document");
      output.setByteStream(System.out);

      output.setEncoding("UTF-8");
                                        //Output the XML document
      dom3Writer.write(document, output);

      System.out.println("\n\n"+"Outputting the journal Node"+"\n");
                                        //Output a node
      dom3Writer.write(journal, output);
                                        //Output a node to String
      String nodeString = dom3Writer.writeToString(journal);


    } catch (ParserConfigurationException e) {
    } catch (ClassNotFoundException e) {
    } catch (InstantiationException e) {
    } catch (IllegalAccessException e) {
    }
  }

  public static void main(String[] argv) {

    DOM3Writer dom3Writer = new DOM3Writer();
    dom3Writer.saveDocument();
  }
}
```

You can run the DOM3Writer.java application in Eclipse with the procedure explained in Chapter 1. Listing 10-14 shows the output from the application.

Listing 10-14. *Output in Eclipse from the DOM3Writer.java Application*

```
Outputting XML Document
<?xml version="1.0" encoding="UTF-8"?>
<catalog publisher="IBM developerWorks"><journal edition="October 2005" section=
"XML"><article><title>JAXP Validation</title><author>Brett McLaughlin</author></
article></journal></catalog>

Outputting the journal Node

<?xml version="1.0" encoding="UTF-8"?>
<journal edition="October 2005" section="XML"><article><title>JAXP Validation</t
itle><author>Brett McLaughlin</author></article></journal>
```

Filtering an XML Document

You can filter an XML document model as the XML document model is parsed, and you can filter a DOM document model as the DOM document model is stored. In this section, we will show how to filter an XML document model. We will show how to filter an input XML document model using an input filter and save the parsed DOM document model using an output filter. In filtering a document model, you can remove some of the nodes from the document. The LSParserFilter interface allows the filtering of input, while the LSSerializerFilter interface allows the filtering of output. For our example, the procedure to filter input is as follows:

1. Create an input filter, a class that implements the LSParserFilter interface.

2. In the input filter class, show the element nodes to filter. Nodes that are not shown to the filter are added to the Document object without the filter selecting the nodes to add to the Document object.

3. Accept all the nodes that are shown to the filter.

4. Create an LSParser object.

5. Create an LSInput object for the XML document to filter.

6. Set the input filter on the LSParser object.

7. Parse an XML document using the LSInput object.

For our example, the procedure to filter the output is as follows:

1. Create an output filter, a class that implements the LSSerializerFilter interface.

2. In the output filter class, show the element nodes to filter. Nodes that are not shown to the filter are output without the filter selecting the nodes to output.

3. As an example, accept all the nodes that are shown to the filter except the journal node with the date attribute set to April 2005.

4. Create an LSSerializer object.

5. Create an LSOutput object for the filter output.

6. Set the output filter on the LSSerializer object.

7. Filter the Document object.

As when loading and saving, import the DOM 3 org.w3c.dom.ls package. For input filtering, create an LSParser implementation and an LSParser parser, as shown in Listing 10-15. The procedure to create a filter is same as in the loading section: create a DOMImplementationRegistry object, obtain a DOMImplementation object from the registry object, cast DOMImplementation to DOMImplementationLS, and create an LSParser from the DOMImplementationLS object.

Listing 10-15. *Creating an LSParser*

```
System.setProperty(DOMImplementationRegistry.PROPERTY,
"org.apache.xerces.dom.DOMImplementationSourceImpl");
DOMImplementationRegistry registry =DOMImplementationRegistry.newInstance();
DOMImplementation domImpl = registry.getDOMImplementation("LS 3.0");
DOMImplementationLS implLS = (DOMImplementationLS)domImpl;
LSParser parser =
implLS.createLSParser(DOMImplementationLS.MODE_SYNCHRONOUS,
  "http://www.w3.org/2001/XMLSchema");
```

In the loading section, an XML document was parsed from a URI. In this section, we will show how to parse the example XML document from an LSInput object. Therefore, create an LSInput object, and set an InputStream for the LSInput, as shown in Listing 10-16.

Listing 10-16. *Creating an LSInput Object*

```
LSInput input = impl.createLSInput();
 InputStream inputStream = new FileInputStream(new File("catalog.xml"));
 input.setByteStream(inputStream);
```

You need to create an input filter for input filtering. In the input filter, you will print the Element nodes as they are parsed without filtering any nodes. An input filter is required to implement the LSParserFilter interface. Therefore, define a filter class that implements the LSParserFilter interface and implements the acceptNode(), startElement(), and getWhatToShow() methods of the LSParserFilter interface. The acceptNode() method returns a short that indicates whether a node is to be accepted, rejected, or skipped. Table 10-1 lists the values that can be returned by the acceptNode() method.

Table 10-1. *Return Values for the acceptNode() Method*

Return Value	Description
FILTER_ACCEPT	Accepts the node
FILTER_INTERRUPT	Interrupts document filtering
FILTER_REJECT	Rejects the node
FILTER_SKIP	Skips the node

If a node is accepted using FILTER_ACCEPT, the node is included in the Document object returned by a parser. If a node is skipped using FILTER_SKIP, only the specified node is skipped; the children of the node are parsed and included in the DOM document. If a node is rejected using FILTER_REJECT, the node and its children are rejected. The startElement() method specifies whether an Element node is to be accepted, rejected, or skipped. Table 10-1 also lists the return values of the startElement() method. Only an Element and the Element's attributes are input to the startElement() method. You can use the startElement() method to modify attributes of an element. The differences between the acceptNode() method and the startElement() method are as follows:

- Only Element nodes are input to the startElement() method as compared to the acceptNode() method in which all nodes except the Document, DocumentType, Notation, Entity, DocumentFragment, and Attribute nodes may be input to the method. Attribute nodes may be input to the acceptNode() method of the LSSerializerFilter interface.

- The element node input to startElement() will include all the Element's attributes but none of the children nodes. Nodes input to the acceptNode() method of LSParserFilter include all the children nodes but none of the attribute nodes. Nodes input to the acceptNode() method of LSSerializerFilter include all the children nodes and may include the attribute nodes.

The getWhatToShow() method specifies nodes that are input to the LSParserFilter.acceptNode() method. Table 10-2 shows the return values of the getWhatToShow() method. Nodes that are not input to the acceptNode() method of a filter are included in the DOM document model being built without filtering. Nodes that are input to the acceptNode() method of a filter are accepted, skipped, or rejected as specified in the method.

Table 10-2. *Return Values for the getWhatToShow() Method*

Return Value	Description
NodeFilter.SHOW_ALL	Shows all nodes
NodeFilter.SHOW_ELEMENT	Shows Element nodes
NodeFilter.SHOW_TEXT	Shows Text nodes
NodeFilter.SHOW_COMMENT	Shows Comment nodes
NodeFilter.SHOW_PROCESSING_INSTRUCTION	Shows ProcessingInstruction nodes
NodeFilter.SHOW_CDATA_SECTION	Shows CDATASection section nodes
NodeFilter.SHOW_ENTITY_REFERENCE	Shows EntityReference nodes

In the example input filter class, InputFilter, the filtering application shows element nodes to the acceptNode() method. Therefore, specify the return type of the getWhatToShow() method as NodeFilter.SHOW_ELEMENT. The return type of the acceptNode() and startElement() methods is LSParser.FILTER_ACCEPT. Listing 10-17 shows the input filter class.

Listing 10-17. *InputFilter Class*

```
private class InputFilter implements LSParserFilter {
    public short acceptNode(Node node) {
      return NodeFilter.FILTER_ACCEPT;
    }

    public int getWhatToShow() {
      return NodeFilter.SHOW_ELEMENT;
    }

    public short startElement(Element element) {
      System.out.println("Element Parsed " + element.getTagName());
      return NodeFilter.FILTER_ACCEPT;
    }
}
```

The example input filter inputs only Element nodes to the filter's acceptNode() method; other nodes are included in the DOM document model without filtering. The acceptNode() method of the filter accepts all nodes that are input. The startElement() method prints element nodes as element nodes are parsed and accepts all element nodes that are parsed. To set filtering on input, create an instance of the InputFilter class, and set the filter on the LSParser, as shown in Listing 10-18. Subsequently, parse the example XML document using the parse(LSInput) method of the LSParser interface.

Listing 10-18. *Filtering Input*

```
InputFilter inputFilter=new InputFilter();
parser.setFilter(inputFilter);
Document document=parser.parse(input);
```

Next, we will demonstrate output filtering. For output filtering, create an output filter. As an example, we will filter a journal node from Document using an output filter. An output filter class is required to implement the LSSerializerFilter interface. Therefore, create an output filter class,

OutputFilter, that implements the LSSerializerFilter interface. In addition to returning the values listed in Table 10-2, the getWhatToShow() method of the LSSerializerFilter interface may also return SHOW_ATTRIBUTE. In the example, the OutputFilter class specifies the return type of the getWhatToShow() method as NodeFilter.SHOW_ELEMENT and the return type of the acceptNode() method as FILTER_ACCEPT for journal nodes other than the journal node with the date attribute April 2005. In the example output filter, only element nodes are input to the filter's acceptNode() method, and the acceptNode() method accepts all nodes except the journal node with the date April 2005. Listing 10-19 shows the output filter class OutputFilter.

Listing 10-19. *Output Filter Class*

```
private class OutputFilter implements LSSerializerFilter {
    public short acceptNode(Node node) {
        Element element = (Element) node;

        if (element.getTagName().equals("journal")) {
            if (element.getAttribute("date").equals("April 2005")) {
                return NodeFilter.FILTER_REJECT;
            }
        }

        return NodeFilter.FILTER_ACCEPT;
    }

    public int getWhatToShow() {
        return NodeFilter.SHOW_ELEMENT;
    }
}
```

To set filtering on the LSSerializer object, create an instance of OutputFilter, and set the filter on the LSSerializer, as shown in Listing 10-20.

Listing 10-20. *Setting Filtering on LSSerializer*

```
LSSerializer domWriter = impl.createLSSerializer();
OutputFilter outputFilter = new OutputFilter();
domWriter.setFilter(outputFilter);
```

To output a filtered XML document, create an LSOutput object, and set an OutputStream for the LSOutput object. Then output the filtered XML document using the write(Node, LSOutput) method, as shown in Listing 10-21.

Listing 10-21. *Outputting Filtered XML Document*

```
LSOutput lsOutput = impl.createLSOutput();
lsOutput.setByteStream(System.out);
domWriter.write( document, lsOutput);
```

Listing 10-22 lists DOM3Filter.java, the Java class used to filter an XML document. The filtering application consists of a method filter() to filter input from an XML document and output to an XML document. DOM3Filter.java also defines the filter classes InputFilter and OutputFilter for input filtering and output filtering. You can filter the input by setting an InputFilter object on an LSParser object and subsequently parsing an XML document. You can filter the output by setting an OutputFilter object on an LSSerializer object and subsequently serializing an XML document.

Listing 10-22. *DOM3Filter.java*

```
package com.apress.dom3ls;

import org.w3c.dom.*;
import org.w3c.dom.bootstrap.DOMImplementationRegistry;
import org.w3c.dom.ls.*;
import org.w3c.dom.traversal.*;

import java.io.*;

public class DOM3Filter {

  // Method to filter an input document and an output document.
  public void filter() {
    try {
        //Set DOMImplementationRegistry object
        System.setProperty(DOMImplementationRegistry.PROPERTY,
         "org.apache.xerces.dom.DOMImplementationSourceImpl");

        //Create  a DOMImplementationRegistry object
        DOMImplementationRegistry registry =
            DOMImplementationRegistry.newInstance();

          //Create a DOMImplementation object
          DOMImplementation domImpl =
            registry.getDOMImplementation("XML 3.0");

          //Create a DOMImplementationLS object
          DOMImplementationLS impl = (DOMImplementationLS) domImpl;

          //Create an LSParser object
          LSParser parser = impl.createLSParser(
            DOMImplementationLS.MODE_SYNCHRONOUS, null);

          //Filter Input
          LSInput input = impl.createLSInput();
          InputStream inputStream =
             new FileInputStream(new File("catalog.xml"));
          input.setByteStream(inputStream);

          InputFilter inputFilter = new InputFilter();
          parser.setFilter(inputFilter);

          Document document = parser.parse(input);

          //Create an LSSerializer object
          LSSerializer domWriter = impl.createLSSerializer();

          //Set an output filter
          OutputFilter outputFilter = new OutputFilter();
          domWriter.setFilter(outputFilter);
```

```java
        LSOutput lsOutput = impl.createLSOutput();

        lsOutput.setByteStream(System.out);
        System.out.println("\n"+"Filtered Document"+"\n");

        //Filter output
        domWriter.write(document, lsOutput);
    } catch (IOException e) {
      System.err.println(e);
    } catch (ClassNotFoundException e) {
    } catch (InstantiationException e) {
    } catch (IllegalAccessException e) {
    }
  }

  public static void main(String[] args) {
    DOM3Filter dom3Filter = new DOM3Filter();
    dom3Filter.filter();
  }
                    //Input filter class
  private class InputFilter implements LSParserFilter {
    public short acceptNode(Node node) {
      return NodeFilter.FILTER_ACCEPT;
    }

    public int getWhatToShow() {
      return NodeFilter.SHOW_ELEMENT;
    }

    public short startElement(Element element) {
      System.out.println("Element Parsed " + element.getTagName());

      return NodeFilter.FILTER_ACCEPT;
    }
  }
                    //Output filter class
  private class OutputFilter implements LSSerializerFilter {
    public short acceptNode(Node node) {
      Element element = (Element) node;

      if (element.getTagName().equals("journal")) {
        if (element.getAttribute("date").equals("April 2005")) {
          return NodeFilter.FILTER_REJECT;
        }
      }

      return NodeFilter.FILTER_ACCEPT;
    }

    public int getWhatToShow() {
      return NodeFilter.SHOW_ELEMENT;
    }
  }
}
```

You can run the filtering application in Eclipse with the procedure explained in Chapter 1. An input filter lists elements as they are parsed. An output filter filters a `journal` node from the XML document. Listing 10-23 shows the output from the output filter.

Listing 10-23. *Output in Eclipse from the* `DOM3Filter.java` *Application*

```
Element Parsed journal
Element Parsed article
Element Parsed title
Element Parsed author
Element Parsed journal
Element Parsed article
Element Parsed title
Element Parsed author

Filtered Document

<?xml version="1.0" encoding="UTF-8"?>
<catalog title="dev2dev">
 <journal date="May 2005">
  <article section="WebLogic Server">
    <title>Session Management for Clustered Applications</title>
    <author> Jon Purdy</author>
  </article>
  </journal>


</catalog>
```

As illustrated in the output, the `journal` node with `date="April 2005"` has been removed from the XML document.

Summary

The DOM Level 3 specification provides a set of interfaces for the following:

- Loading and saving an XML document
- Filtering content during XML document loads and saves
- Saving selected nodes within a document, as opposed to the whole document
- Serializing a complete document, or selected document nodes, to a string, as opposed to a file

The DOM Level 3 Load and Save interfaces offer some advantages over the JAXP `DocumentBuilder` and `Transformer` classes. The DOM Level 3 Load and Save features that are not included in the JAXP `DocumentBuilder` and `Transformer` classes are as follows:

- Event handling during document loads and saves
- Filtering content during document loads and saves
- Loading and saving selected nodes, instead of the complete document
- Saving `Document` object to a `String`, as opposed to a file

In this chapter, we offered code examples to illustrate the DOM Level 3 Load and Save interfaces, specifically, loading an XML document (with schema validation), saving an XML document or a selected node to a file or a string, and filtering content during the loading and saving process. All code examples are based on the DOM Level Load and Save implementation within JAXP 1.3, which is included in J2SE 5.0.

PART 5

■■■

Utilities

CHAPTER 11

Converting XML to Spreadsheet, and Vice Versa

Often it is useful for XML data to be presented as a spreadsheet. A typical spreadsheet (for example, a Microsoft Excel spreadsheet) consists of cells represented in a grid of rows and columns, containing textual data, numeric data, or formulas. An Excel spreadsheet defines some standard functions such as SUM and AVERAGE that you can specify in cells. The Apache Jakarta POI project provides the HSSF API to create an Excel spreadsheet from an XML document or to go the opposite way, parsing an Excel spreadsheet and converting to XML. The HSSF API has provisions for setting the layout, border settings, and fonts of an Excel document. In this chapter, you'll learn how to generate an example Excel spreadsheet by parsing an XML document and adding data from the XML document to a spreadsheet. Subsequently, you'll convert the Excel spreadsheet to an XML document.

Overview

The Jakarta POI HSSF API provides classes to create an Excel workbook and add spreadsheets to the workbook. With the POI API, the HSSFWorkbook class represents a workbook, and you set the spreadsheet fonts, sheet order, and cell styles in the HSSFWorkbook class. You can represent the spreadsheet using the HSSFSheet class. Specifically, you set the sheet layout, including the column widths, margins, header, footer, and print setup using the HSSFSheet class. You can represent a spreadsheet row using the HSSFRow class, and you set the row height using the HSSFRow class. The HSSFCell class represents a cell in a spreadsheet row, and you set the cell style using the HSSFCell class. The indexing of spreadsheets in a workbook, of rows in a spreadsheet, and of cells in a row is zero based. In this chapter, we'll show how to convert an example XML document to an Excel spreadsheet and then convert the spreadsheet to an XML document. Listing 11-1 shows the example document, incomestatements.xml.

Listing 11-1. *incomestatements.xml*

```
<?xml version="1.0" encoding="UTF-8"?>
<incmstmts>
<stmt>
<year>2005</year>
<revenue>11837</revenue>
<costofrevenue>2239</costofrevenue>
<researchdevelopment>1591</researchdevelopment>
<salesmarketing>2689</salesmarketing>
<generaladmin>661</generaladmin>
<totaloperexpenses>7180</totaloperexpenses>
```

```
<operincome>4657</operincome>
<invincome>480</invincome>
<incbeforetaxes>5137</incbeforetaxes>
<taxes>1484</taxes>
<netincome>3653</netincome>
</stmt>

<stmt>
<year>2004</year>
<revenue>10818</revenue>
<costofrevenue>1875</costofrevenue>
<researchdevelopment>1421</researchdevelopment>
<salesmarketing>2122</salesmarketing>
<generaladmin>651</generaladmin>
<totaloperexpenses>6069</totaloperexpenses>
<operincome>4749</operincome>
<invincome>420</invincome>
<incbeforetaxes>5169</incbeforetaxes>
<taxes>1706</taxes>
<netincome>3463</netincome>
</stmt>
<incmstmts>
```

Creating an Eclipse Project

In this chapter, we'll show how to create and parse an Excel spreadsheet using the Apache POI HSSF API. Before you can set up your project, you need to download Apache POI[1] 2.5.1 and extract the zip file to an installation directory. You also need to download and install JDK 5.0. (You can also use another version of JDK such as 1.4 or 6.0.)

To compile and run the code examples, you will need an Eclipse project. You can download project Chapter11 from the Apress website (http://www.apress.com) and import it into your Eclipse workspace by selecting File ➤ Import.

To compile and run the Apache POI code examples, you need some JAR files in your project's Java build path; Figure 11-1 shows these JAR files. The JAR file required for an Apache POI application is poi-2.5.1-final-20040804.jar, which consists of the Apache POI API. You also need to set the JRE system library to JRE 5.0, as shown in Figure 11-1.

Figure 11-2 shows the Chapter11 project directory structure.

If you haven't got a copy of Excel handy, you can instead open the Excel spreadsheet generated from the example XML document using Excel Viewer.[2]

---

1. For more information about Apache POI, see http://jakarta.apache.org/poi/.
2. For more information about Excel Viewer, see http://www.microsoft.com/downloads/
   details.aspx?FamilyID=c8378bf4-996c-4569-b547-75edbd03aaf0&displaylang=EN.

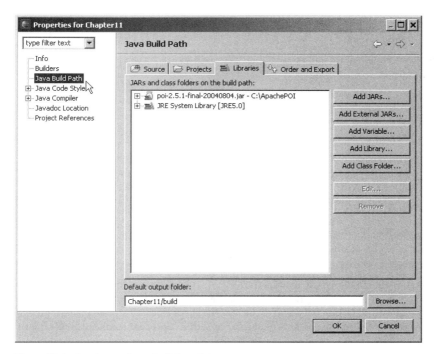

Figure 11-1. *Chapter11 Java build path*

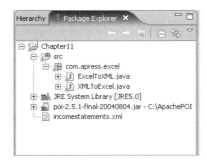

Figure 11-2. *Chapter11 directory structure*

Converting an XML Document to an Excel Spreadsheet

In this section, we will show how to convert the example XML document in Listing 11-1 to an Excel document using the Apache POI HSSF API. Specifically, you will parse the example XML document, retrieve values from the document, and construct an Excel spreadsheet. The procedure to create a spreadsheet is as follows:

1. Create an Excel spreadsheet workbook and an empty spreadsheet.

2. Define a cell style.

3. Set the spreadsheet column width.

4. Add a header row to the spreadsheet.

5. Parse the XML document.

6. Add statement columns to the spreadsheet.

7. Output the spreadsheet.

You need to import the Apache POI HSSF package, `org.apache.poi.hssf.usermodel`. You can create an Excel workbook using a no-arguments constructor for `HSSFWorkbook`, as shown in Listing 11-2. You create a spreadsheet, represented with the `HSSFSheet` class, by using the `createSheet(String sheetName)` method of the `HSSFWorkbook` class.

Listing 11-2. *Creating an Excel Workbook and Spreadsheet*

```
HSSFWorkbook wb=new HSSFWorkbook();
HSSFSheet spreadSheet=wb.createSheet("spreadSheet");
```

You can represent a cell in a spreadsheet using the `HSSFCell` class. You set the cell style using the `HSSFCellStyle` class. To set the cell style in the example spreadsheet being generated, create a cell style object using the `createCellStyle()` method of the `HSSFWorkbook` class, as shown in Listing 11-3. The example cell style defines a cell border and is used for cells that represent totals for a column or subcolumn. You can set the border settings for an `HSSFCellStyle` object using the setter methods `setBorderTop(short)`, `setBorderLeft(short)`, `setBorderBottom(short)`, and `setBorderRight(short)`.

Listing 11-3. *Setting the Cell Style*

```
HSSFCellStyle cellStyle=wb.createCellStyle();
cellStyle.setBorderRight(HSSFCellStyle.BORDER_MEDIUM);
cellStyle.setBorderTop(HSSFCellStyle.BORDER_MEDIUM);
cellStyle.setBorderLeft(HSSFCellStyle.BORDER_MEDIUM);
cellStyle.setBorderBottom(HSSFCellStyle.BORDER_MEDIUM);
```

You can represent a border type with a short value, as shown in Listing 11-3. Table 11-1 lists some of the commonly used types of borders.

Table 11-1. *Border Types*

Short	Description
BORDER_DASH_DOT	Dash-dot border
BORDER_DASHED	Dashed border
BORDER_DOUBLE	Double-line border
BORDER_MEDIUM	Medium border
BORDER_NONE	No border
BORDER_THICK	Thick border
BORDER_THIN	Thin border

You can set the border color using the setter methods setBottomBorderColor(short color), setLeftBorderColor(short color), setRightBorderColor(short color), and setTopBorderColor(short color). You can represent spreadsheet color using the HSSFColor subclasses. For example, the class HSSFColor.BLUE represents the color blue. You can obtain a short value corresponding to a color using the field index. The following is an example of setting a color:

```
short blue= HSSFColor.BLUE.index;
cellStyle.setRightBorderColor(blue);
```

You can set background color and foreground color using the methods setFillBackgroundColor(short fg) and setFillForegroundColor(short bg). You can set text indentation using the setIndention(short indent) method. You can wrap cell text using the setWrapText(boolean wrapped) method. For example, you can set cell-style indentation to 4 and add text wrapping, as shown here:

```
cellStyle.setIndention((short)4);
cellStyle.setWrapText(true);
```

Further, you can add text rotation to cell text using the setRotation(short rotation) method. You specify rotation in degrees using values from –90 to +90. You can horizontally align cell text using the setAlignment(short) method. You represent cell alignment using a short value. Some of the commonly used cell alignment types are ALIGN_CENTER, ALIGN_RIGHT, ALIGN_LEFT, and ALIGN_FILL. You can set vertical alignment using the setVerticalAlignment(short align) method. Vertical alignment short values are VERTICAL_TOP, VERTICAL_CENTER, VERTICAL_BOTTOM, and VERTICAL_JUSTIFY. You define the spreadsheet font using the HSSFFont class. Listing 11-4 shows an example of creating an italicized font using font height 24 and font name Courier New. As shown in the listing, a font is created using the method createFont() of the HSSFWorkbook class.

Listing 11-4. *Setting the Font*

```
HSSFFont font = wb.createFont();
    font.setFontHeightInPoints((short)24);
    font.setFontName("Courier New");
    font.setItalic(true);
    cellStyle.setFont(font);
```

A row in the spreadsheet created from the example XML document has cells corresponding to each of the elements in the stmt tag of the example XML document. You set the column width in a spreadsheet at column level using the HSSFSheet method setColumnWidth(short column, short width). For example, you specify the column width of the first column of a spreadsheet as shown here:

```
spreadSheet.setColumnWidth((short)0,  (short)(256*25));
```

A spreadsheet has a header row that specifies headers for the columns in the spreadsheet. Therefore, add a header row to the HSSFSheet class. A header row is just like any other row and is created using the createRow(int rowNumber) method, as shown in Listing 11-5.

You add column headers to the header row using the createCell(short) method, as shown in Listing 11-5. You set the cell value using the setCellValue(String) method. For example, add a column header for the Year 2005 column.

Listing 11-5. *Adding the Spreadsheet Header Row*

```
HSSFRow row = spreadSheet.createRow(0);
HSSFCell cell = row.createCell((short) 0);
cell.setCellValue("Year 2005");
```

You can add the column header for the Year 2004 column similarly. You need to parse the example XML document using a DocumentBuilder to navigate an XML document and retrieve the values from the document. (Chapter 2 discussed the procedure to parse an XML document.) You need to create a DocumentBuilderFactory from which you will create a DocumentBuilder parser, as shown in Listing 11-6. Subsequently, parse the example XML document, and obtain a Document object.

Listing 11-6. *Parsing an XML Document*

```
DocumentBuilderFactory factory =DocumentBuilderFactory.newInstance();
DocumentBuilder builder = factory.newDocumentBuilder();
Document  document = builder.parse(xmlDocument);
```

You can obtain a node list that consists of stmt nodes from the Document object using the getElementsByTagName(String) method as shown in Listing 11-7. Each stmt node represents a column in a spreadsheet. The subelements in an stmt element represent the row values for a column. In the spreadsheet, add 11 rows corresponding to the subelements of an stmt element. For example, the following code shows how to add row 1:

```
HSSFRow row1 = spreadSheet.createRow(1);
```

To construct a spreadsheet, iterate over the node list, and add a column to the spreadsheet corresponding to each of the stmt nodes in the node list, as shown in Listing 11-7. You add a spread-sheet column using the HSSFRow object. The node list of stmt elements has two nodes corresponding to the two stmt elements in the example XML document. Using a switch statement, you'll add row labels and row values for two columns. For example, to add a row labeled Revenue, create a row label, and create row cells for the two nodes in the stmt element node list, as shown in Listing 11-7. A column consists of cells corresponding to each of the elements in the stmt element. You create a cell using the createCell(short) method of the HSSFRow object, as shown in Listing 11-7. You set the cell value using the setCellValue(String) method.

Listing 11-7. *Constructing a Spreadsheet*

```
NodeList nodeList = document.getElementsByTagName("stmt");
for (int i = 0; i < nodeList.getLength(); i++) {

switch(i){
case 0:
HSSFCell cell = row1.createCell((short) 0);
cell.setCellValue("Revenue ($)");
cell = row1.createCell((short) 1);

cell.setCellValue(((Element)
(nodeList.item(0))).
getElementsByTagName
("revenue").item(0).getFirstChild()
.getNodeValue());

break;
case 1:
```

```
HSSFCell cell = row1.createCell((short) 2);
cell.setCellValue(((Element)
(nodeList.item(1))).
getElementsByTagName("revenue").
item(0).getFirstChild().getNodeValue());
break;

}

}
```

The first cell in a row has index 0. Earlier in the section, you defined a cell style. The cell style is set at the cell level using the setCellStyle() method of the HSSFCell object, as shown here:

```
cell.setCellStyle(cellStyle);
```

Similarly, you need to set row values for other cells in a column. HSSFSheet provides some methods to set different characteristics of a spreadsheet. Table 11-2 discusses some of these methods.

Table 11-2. *HSSFSheet Methods*

Method Name	Description
setColumnBreak(short column)	Sets a page break at the specified column
setDefaultColumnWidth(short width)	Sets the default column width, if the width is not specified at the column level
setDefaultRowHeight(short height)	Sets the default row height, if the height is not specified at the row level
setFitToPage(boolean b)	Sets it to fit to the page
setHorizontallyCenter(boolean value)	Sets the output to be horizontally centered
setMargin(short margin,double size)	Sets the style sheet margin
setRowBreak(int row)	Sets a page break at the specified row
setZoom(int numerator, int denominator)	Sets the zoom magnification for the style sheet

To output the Excel workbook to an .xls file, create a FileOutputStream object, as shown in Listing 11-8. You can output the Excel workbook using the write(HSSFWorkbook) method, and you can close the FileOutputStream object using the close() method.

Listing 11-8. *Outputting the Excel Workbook*

```
FileOutputStream output=new FileOutputStream(new File("IncomeStatements.xls"));
 wb.write(output);
 output.flush();
 output.close();
```

Listing 11-9 shows the Java application, XMLToExcel.java, used to convert an XML document to an Excel spreadsheet. The application consists of a method generateExcel(File) that generates an Excel spreadsheet from an XML document. In the generateExcel() method, an Excel workbook is created and a spreadsheet is added to the workbook. The cell style is added using an HSSFCellStyle object. An XML document is parsed, and the stmt element node list is iterated over to retrieve node values. A spreadsheet column is added corresponding to each of the stmt nodes in the example XML document. A column header value is set from the year element in an stmt element. A spreadsheet row is added corresponding to each of the subelements in an stmt element. A switch statement is used to set row values for a column. Subsequently, the Excel workbook is output using a FileOutputStream.

Listing 11-9. *XMLToExcel.java*

```java
package com.apress.excel;

import org.apache.poi.hssf.usermodel.*;
import org.w3c.dom.*;
import java.io.*;
import javax.xml.parsers.DocumentBuilder;
import javax.xml.parsers.DocumentBuilderFactory;
import javax.xml.parsers.ParserConfigurationException;
import org.xml.sax.SAXException;

public class XMLToExcel {
  public void generateExcel(File xmlDocument) {
    try {// Creating a Workbook
      HSSFWorkbook wb = new HSSFWorkbook();
      HSSFSheet spreadSheet = wb.createSheet("spreadSheet");

      spreadSheet.setColumnWidth((short) 0, (short) (256 * 25));
      spreadSheet.setColumnWidth((short) 1, (short) (256 * 25));
      // Parsing XML Document
      DocumentBuilderFactory factory = DocumentBuilderFactory
          .newInstance();
      DocumentBuilder builder = factory.newDocumentBuilder();
      Document document = builder.parse(xmlDocument);
      NodeList nodeList = document.getElementsByTagName("stmt");
      // Creating Rows
      HSSFRow row = spreadSheet.createRow(0);

      HSSFCell cell = row.createCell((short) 1);
      cell.setCellValue("Year 2005");
      cell = row.createCell((short) 2);
      cell.setCellValue("Year 2004");

      HSSFRow row1 = spreadSheet.createRow(1);
      HSSFRow row2 = spreadSheet.createRow(2);
      HSSFRow row3 = spreadSheet.createRow(3);
      HSSFRow row4 = spreadSheet.createRow(4);
      HSSFRow row5 = spreadSheet.createRow(5);
      HSSFRow row6 = spreadSheet.createRow(6);
      HSSFRow row7 = spreadSheet.createRow(7);
      HSSFRow row8 = spreadSheet.createRow(8);
      HSSFRow row9 = spreadSheet.createRow(9);
      HSSFRow row10 = spreadSheet.createRow(10);
      HSSFRow row11 = spreadSheet.createRow(11);

      for (int i = 0; i < nodeList.getLength(); i++) {
```

```java
HSSFCellStyle cellStyle = wb.createCellStyle();
cellStyle.setBorderRight(HSSFCellStyle.BORDER_MEDIUM);
cellStyle.setBorderTop(HSSFCellStyle.BORDER_MEDIUM);
cellStyle.setBorderLeft(HSSFCellStyle.BORDER_MEDIUM);
cellStyle.setBorderBottom(HSSFCellStyle.BORDER_MEDIUM);

switch (i) {
// Creating column1 (Row label) and column 2 (Year 2005 stmt)
case 0:

  cell = row1.createCell((short) 0);
  cell.setCellValue("Revenue ($)");

  cell = row1.createCell((short) 1);
  cell.setCellValue(((Element) (nodeList.item(0)))
      .getElementsByTagName("revenue").item(0)
      .getFirstChild().getNodeValue());

  cell = row2.createCell((short) 0);
  cell.setCellValue("Cost of Revenue ($)");

  cell = row2.createCell((short) 1);
  cell.setCellValue(((Element) (nodeList.item(0)))
      .getElementsByTagName("costofrevenue").item(0)
      .getFirstChild().getNodeValue());

  cell = row3.createCell((short) 0);
  cell.setCellValue("Research and Development ($)");

  cell = row3.createCell((short) 1);
  cell.setCellValue(((Element) (nodeList.item(0)))
      .getElementsByTagName("researchdevelopment")
      .item(0).getFirstChild().getNodeValue());

  cell = row4.createCell((short) 0);
  cell.setCellValue("Sales and Marketing ($)");

  cell = row4.createCell((short) 1);
  cell.setCellValue(((Element) (nodeList.item(0)))
      .getElementsByTagName("salesmarketing").item(0)
      .getFirstChild().getNodeValue());

  cell = row5.createCell((short) 0);
  cell.setCellValue("General and Administrative ($)");

  cell = row5.createCell((short) 1);
  cell.setCellValue(((Element) (nodeList.item(0)))
      .getElementsByTagName("generaladmin").item(0)
      .getFirstChild().getNodeValue());

  cell = row6.createCell((short) 0);
  cell.setCellValue("Total Operating Expenses ($)");
  cell.setCellStyle(cellStyle);
```

```
cell = row6.createCell((short) 1);
cell.setCellValue(((Element) (nodeList.item(0)))
    .getElementsByTagName("totaloperexpenses").item(0)
    .getFirstChild().getNodeValue());

cell.setCellStyle(cellStyle);

cell = row7.createCell((short) 0);
cell.setCellValue("Operating Income ($)");

cell = row7.createCell((short) 1);
cell.setCellValue(((Element) (nodeList.item(0)))
    .getElementsByTagName("operincome").item(0)
    .getFirstChild().getNodeValue());

cell = row8.createCell((short) 0);
cell.setCellValue("Investment Income ($)");

cell = row8.createCell((short) 1);
cell.setCellValue(((Element) (nodeList.item(0)))
    .getElementsByTagName("invincome").item(0)
    .getFirstChild().getNodeValue());

cell = row9.createCell((short) 0);
cell.setCellValue("Income Before Taxes ($)");
cell.setCellStyle(cellStyle);

cell = row9.createCell((short) 1);
cell.setCellValue(((Element) (nodeList.item(0)))
    .getElementsByTagName("incbeforetaxes").item(0)
    .getFirstChild().getNodeValue());

cell.setCellStyle(cellStyle);

cell = row10.createCell((short) 0);
cell.setCellValue("Taxes ($)");

cell = row10.createCell((short) 1);
cell.setCellValue(((Element) (nodeList.item(0)))
    .getElementsByTagName("taxes").item(0)
    .getFirstChild().getNodeValue());

cell = row11.createCell((short) 0);
cell.setCellValue("Net Income ($)");
cell.setCellStyle(cellStyle);

cell = row11.createCell((short) 1);
cell.setCellValue(((Element) (nodeList.item(0)))
    .getElementsByTagName("netincome").item(0)
    .getFirstChild().getNodeValue());

cell.setCellStyle(cellStyle);

break;
```

```
// Creating column 3 (Year 2004 stmt)
case 1:

  cell = row1.createCell((short) 2);
  cell.setCellValue(((Element) (nodeList.item(1)))
      .getElementsByTagName("revenue").item(0)
      .getFirstChild().getNodeValue());

  cell = row2.createCell((short) 2);
  cell.setCellValue(((Element) (nodeList.item(1)))
      .getElementsByTagName("costofrevenue").item(0)
      .getFirstChild().getNodeValue());

  cell = row3.createCell((short) 2);
  cell.setCellValue(((Element) (nodeList.item(1)))
      .getElementsByTagName("researchdevelopment")
      .item(0).getFirstChild().getNodeValue());

  cell = row4.createCell((short) 2);
  cell.setCellValue(((Element) (nodeList.item(1)))
      .getElementsByTagName("salesmarketing").item(0)
      .getFirstChild().getNodeValue());

  cell = row5.createCell((short) 2);
  cell.setCellValue(((Element) (nodeList.item(1)))
      .getElementsByTagName("generaladmin").item(0)
      .getFirstChild().getNodeValue());

  cell = row6.createCell((short) 2);
  cell.setCellValue(((Element) (nodeList.item(1)))
      .getElementsByTagName("totaloperexpenses").item(0)
      .getFirstChild().getNodeValue());

  cell.setCellStyle(cellStyle);

  cell = row7.createCell((short) 2);
  cell.setCellValue(((Element) (nodeList.item(1)))
      .getElementsByTagName("operincome").item(0)
      .getFirstChild().getNodeValue());

  cell = row8.createCell((short) 2);
  cell.setCellValue(((Element) (nodeList.item(1)))
      .getElementsByTagName("invincome").item(0)
      .getFirstChild().getNodeValue());

  cell = row9.createCell((short) 2);
  cell.setCellValue(((Element) (nodeList.item(1)))
      .getElementsByTagName("incbeforetaxes").item(0)
      .getFirstChild().getNodeValue());

  cell.setCellStyle(cellStyle);
```

```
        cell = row10.createCell((short) 2);
        cell.setCellValue(((Element) (nodeList.item(1)))
            .getElementsByTagName("taxes").item(0)
            .getFirstChild().getNodeValue());

        cell = row11.createCell((short) 2);
        cell.setCellValue(((Element) (nodeList.item(1)))
            .getElementsByTagName("netincome").item(0)
            .getFirstChild().getNodeValue());
        cell.setCellStyle(cellStyle);
        break;

      default:
        break;
      }


    }
    // Outputting to Excel spreadsheet
    FileOutputStream output = new FileOutputStream(new File(
        "IncomeStatements.xls"));
    wb.write(output);
    output.flush();
    output.close();
  } catch (IOException e) {
    System.out.println("IOException " + e.getMessage());
  } catch (ParserConfigurationException e) {
    System.out
        .println("ParserConfigurationException " + e.getMessage());
  } catch (SAXException e) {
    System.out.println("SAXException " + e.getMessage());
  }


}

public static void main(String[] argv) {

  File xmlDocument = new File("incomestatements.xml");

  XMLToExcel excel = new XMLToExcel();
  excel.generateExcel(xmlDocument);
  }
}
```

You can run the XMLToExcel.java application in Eclipse as explained in Chapter 1. This generates an Excel spreadsheet. IncomeStatements.xls, the example spreadsheet generated from the example XML document, gets added to the Chapter11 project, as shown in Figure 11-3.

Figure 11-4 shows the Excel spreadsheet generated with the Apache POI HSSF API.

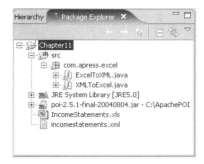

Figure 11-3. *The Excel spreadsheet* IncomeStatements.xls *in the* Chapter11 *project*

	A	B	C	D	E
1		Year 2005	Year 2004		
2	Revenue ($)	11837	10818		
3	Cost of Revenue ($)	2239	1875		
4	Research and Development ($	1591	1421		
5	Sales and Marketing ($)	2689	2122		
6	General and Administrative ($)	661	651		
7	Total Operating Expenses ($)	7180	6069		
8	Operating Income ($)	4657	4749		
9	Investment Income ($)	480	420		
10	Income Before Taxes ($)	5137	5169		
11	Taxes ($)	1484	1706		
12	Net Income ($)	3653	3463		
13					
14					
15					
16					
17					
18					

Figure 11-4. IncomeStatements.xls *spreadsheet*

Converting an Excel Spreadsheet to an XML Document

In the previous section, you learned how to generate an Excel document from an XML document. In this section, you'll convert the Excel document to an XML document. The procedure to generate an XML document from a spreadsheet is as follows:

1. Create an empty XML document using DocumentBuilder.

2. Add top-level stmt elements.

3. Create an HSSFSheet object from the Excel file.

4. Iterate over the spreadsheet, and add subelements to the XML document.

5. Output the XML document using the Transformer API.

You can use the Apache POI HSSF API to parse an Excel spreadsheet and retrieve cell values from the spreadsheet. As in the previous section, first you need to import the Apache POI package `org.apache.poi.hssf.usermodel`.

The root element of the XML document (Listing 11-1) that you will generate is `incmstmts`, and you'll add an `stmt` element corresponding to each of the columns of the Excel spreadsheet. Therefore, generate an XML document using a `DocumentBuilder` object as shown in Listing 11-10, and add the root element of the document. You can obtain the `DocumentBuilder` object from a `DocumentBuilderFactory` object, as shown in Listing 11-10.

Listing 11-10. *Creating an XML Document*

```
DocumentBuilderFactory factory =DocumentBuilderFactory.newInstance();
 DocumentBuilder builder = factory.newDocumentBuilder();
Document document = builder.newDocument();
Element rootElement=document.createElement("incmstmts");
document.appendChild(rootElement);
```

You can read the XLS spreadsheet that is to be converted to an XML document using an `InputStream`, as shown in Listing 11-11. Subsequently, obtain a workbook from the `InputStream` object, and obtain the spreadsheet in the Excel workbook.

Listing 11-11. *Obtaining Spreadsheet*

```
InputStream input=new FileInputStream(new File("IncomeStatements.xls") );
HSSFWorkbook workbook=new HSSFWorkbook(input);
HSSFSheet spreadsheet=workbook.getSheetAt(0);
```

To construct an XML document, add an `stmt` element for each of the columns in the spreadsheet. You also need to add an element, `year`, corresponding to the column header, to each of the `stmt` elements, as shown in Listing 11-12.

Listing 11-12. *Adding stmt Elements*

```
Element stmtElement1 = document.createElement("stmt");
rootElement.appendChild(stmtElement1);
Element year1 = document.createElement("year");
stmtElement1.appendChild(year1);
year1.appendChild(document.createTextNode("2005"));
```

To add subelements to `stmt` elements, iterate over spreadsheet rows and, using a `switch` statement, retrieve row cell values; use these row cell values to create the subelements. Because the first row(corresponding to index 0)) is a header row, iterate from the second row. For example, to add a revenue element, retrieve the second spreadsheet row, which corresponds to index 1, using the `getRow(int)` method of the `HSSFSheet` class. You can retrieve a row cell value using the `HSSFRow` method `getCell(short)` and a row cell value using the method `getStringCellValue()`, as shown in Listing 11-13. You can obtain the number of rows in a spreadsheet using the `HSSFSheet` class method `getLastRowNum()`.

Listing 11-13. *Adding Elements to the XML Document*

```
for (int i = 1; i <= spreadsheet.getLastRowNum(); i++) {
      switch (i) {
      case 1:
      HSSFRow row1 = spreadsheet.getRow(1);
      Element revenueElement1 =
      document.createElement("revenue");
```

```
                stmtElement1.appendChild(revenueElement1);
                    revenueElement1.appendChild
                    (document.createTextNode
                    (row1.getCell((short)1).
                     getStringCellValue()));
                     Element revenueElement2 = document.createElement("revenue");
                     stmtElement2.appendChild(revenueElement2);
                     revenueElement2.appendChild
                    (document.createTextNode
                     (row1.getCell((short)  2).
                     getStringCellValue()));

                    break;
                    }

}
```

Similarly, other cell values are retrieved from the spreadsheet and specified in the XML document. You can generate the XML document using the Transformer API. You obtain a `Transformer` object from a `TransformerFactory` object, as shown in Listing 11-14. You can output the XML document using the `transform(DOMSource, StreamResult)` method with a `DOMSource` object as input and a `StreamResult` object as output, as shown in Listing 11-14.

Listing 11-14. *Outputting an XML Document*

```
TransformerFactory tFactory = TransformerFactory.newInstance();
Transformer transformer = tFactory.newTransformer();
DOMSource source = new DOMSource(document);
StreamResult result = new StreamResult(new File(System.out));
transformer.transform(source, result);
```

Listing 11-15 shows the Java application, ExcelToXML.java, used to convert an Excel spreadsheet to an XML document. The application consists of a method generateXML(File excelFile) that converts a spreadsheet to an XML document. An XML document is created using a DocumentBuilder object. A spreadsheet is parsed, and an XML document element, stmt, is added corresponding to each of the columns in the spreadsheet. Elements are added to the stmt element that corresponds to the rows in a column. The XML document is output using the Transformer API.

Listing 11-15. *ExcelToXML.java*

```
package com.apress.excel;

import org.apache.poi.hssf.usermodel.*;
import org.w3c.dom.*;

import java.io.*;
import javax.xml.parsers.*;
import javax.xml.transform.*;
import javax.xml.transform.dom.DOMSource;
import javax.xml.transform.stream.StreamResult;
```

```java
public class ExcelToXML {
  public void generateXML(File excelFile) {
    try {         //Initializing the XML document
      DocumentBuilderFactory factory = DocumentBuilderFactory
          .newInstance();
      DocumentBuilder builder = factory.newDocumentBuilder();
      Document document = builder.newDocument();
      Element rootElement = document.createElement("incmstmts");
      document.appendChild(rootElement);
                                //Creating top-level elements
      Element stmtElement1 = document.createElement("stmt");
      rootElement.appendChild(stmtElement1);

      Element stmtElement2 = document.createElement("stmt");
      rootElement.appendChild(stmtElement2);
                                //Adding first subelements
      Element year1 = document.createElement("year");
      stmtElement1.appendChild(year1);

      year1.appendChild(document.createTextNode("2005"));

      Element year2 = document.createElement("year");
      stmtElement2.appendChild(year2);
      year2.appendChild(document.createTextNode("2004"));
       //Creating an HSSFSpreadsheet object from an Excel file
      InputStream input = new FileInputStream(excelFile);
      HSSFWorkbook workbook = new HSSFWorkbook(input);
      HSSFSheet spreadsheet = workbook.getSheetAt(0);

      for (int i = 1; i <= spreadsheet.getLastRowNum(); i++) {
        switch (i) {
    //Iterate over spreadsheet rows to create stmt element
    //subelements.
        case 1:
          HSSFRow row1 = spreadsheet.getRow(1);

      Element revenueElement1 = document.createElement("revenue");
         stmtElement1.appendChild(revenueElement1);

         revenueElement1.appendChild
         (document.createTextNode
          (row1.getCell((short) 1).
         getStringCellValue()));

      Element revenueElement2 = document.createElement("revenue");
      stmtElement2.appendChild(revenueElement2);

         revenueElement2.appendChild
          (document.createTextNode
         (row1.getCell((short) 2).
          getStringCellValue()));
```

```
      break;
    case 2:
      HSSFRow row2 = spreadsheet.getRow(2);

      Element costofrevenue1 = document
          .createElement("costofrevenue");
      stmtElement1.appendChild(costofrevenue1);
      costofrevenue1.appendChild
      (document.createTextNode
      (row2.getCell((short)1).
      getStringCellValue()));

  Element costofrevenue2 = document.createElement("costofrevenue");
      stmtElement2.appendChild(costofrevenue2);

      costofrevenue2.appendChild
      (document.createTextNode
      (row2.getCell((short) 2).
      getStringCellValue()));
      break;
    case 3:
      HSSFRow row3 = spreadsheet.getRow(3);

Element researchdevelopment1 = document.createElement("researchdevelopment");
      stmtElement1.appendChild(researchdevelopment1);

    researchdevelopment1.appendChild
    (document.createTextNode
    (row3.getCell((short) 1)
              .getStringCellValue()));

        Element researchdevelopment2 =
      document.createElement("researchdevelopment");
       stmtElement2.appendChild(researchdevelopment2);

      researchdevelopment2.appendChild
       (document.createTextNode
       (row3.getCell((short) 2).
      getStringCellValue()));
        break;
    case 4:
      HSSFRow row4 = spreadsheet.getRow(4);

      Element salesmarketing1 = document
          .createElement("salesmarketing");
      stmtElement1.appendChild(salesmarketing1);

    salesmarketing1.appendChild(document.createTextNode(row4
        .getCell((short) 1).getStringCellValue()));

      Element salesmarketing2 = document
          .createElement("salesmarketing");
      stmtElement2.appendChild(salesmarketing2);
```

```java
          salesmarketing2.appendChild(document.createTextNode(row4
            .getCell((short) 2).getStringCellValue()));
          break;
        case 5:
          HSSFRow row5 = spreadsheet.getRow(5);

          Element generaladmin1 = document
              .createElement("generaladmin");
          stmtElement1.appendChild(generaladmin1);

          generaladmin1.appendChild(document.createTextNode(row5
            .getCell((short) 1).getStringCellValue()));

          Element generaladmin2 = document
              .createElement("generaladmin");
          stmtElement2.appendChild(generaladmin2);

          generaladmin2.appendChild(document.createTextNode(row5
            .getCell((short) 2).getStringCellValue()));
          break;
        case 6:
          HSSFRow row6 = spreadsheet.getRow(6);

          Element totaloperexpenses1 = document
              .createElement("totaloperexpenses");
          stmtElement1.appendChild(totaloperexpenses1);

          totaloperexpenses1.appendChild(document.createTextNode(row6
            .getCell((short) 1).getStringCellValue()));

          Element totaloperexpenses2 = document
              .createElement("totaloperexpenses");
          stmtElement2.appendChild(totaloperexpenses2);

          totaloperexpenses2.appendChild(document.createTextNode(row6
            .getCell((short) 2).getStringCellValue()));
          break;
        case 7:
          HSSFRow row7 = spreadsheet.getRow(7);

      Element operincome1 = document.createElement("operincome");
          stmtElement1.appendChild(operincome1);

          operincome1.appendChild(document.createTextNode(row7
            .getCell((short) 1).getStringCellValue()));

      Element operincome2 = document.createElement("operincome");
          stmtElement2.appendChild(operincome2);

          operincome2.appendChild
          (document.createTextNode
          (row7.getCell((short) 2).
           getStringCellValue()));
          break;
```

```java
      case 8:
        HSSFRow row8 = spreadsheet.getRow(8);

      Element invincome1 = document.createElement("invincome");
        stmtElement1.appendChild(invincome1);

        invincome1.appendChild
        (document.createTextNode
        (row8.getCell((short) 1).
        getStringCellValue()));

Element invincome2 = document.createElement("invincome");
stmtElement2.appendChild(invincome2);

        invincome2.appendChild
        (document.createTextNode
        (row8.getCell((short) 2).
        getStringCellValue()));
        break;
      case 9:
        HSSFRow row9 = spreadsheet.getRow(9);

        Element incbeforetaxes1 = document
            .createElement("incbeforetaxes");
        stmtElement1.appendChild(incbeforetaxes1);

        incbeforetaxes1.appendChild
         (document.createTextNode
        (row9.getCell((short) 1).
         getStringCellValue()));

       Element incbeforetaxes2 =
        document.createElement("incbeforetaxes");
        stmtElement2.appendChild(incbeforetaxes2);

        incbeforetaxes2.appendChild
        (document.createTextNode
       (row9.getCell((short)2).
        getStringCellValue()));
        break;
      case 10:
        HSSFRow row10 = spreadsheet.getRow(10);

        Element taxes1 = document.createElement("taxes");
        stmtElement1.appendChild(taxes1);

        taxes1.appendChild(document.createTextNode(row10.getCell(
            (short) 1).getStringCellValue()));

        Element taxes2 = document.createElement("taxes");
        stmtElement2.appendChild(taxes2);
```

```java
        taxes2.appendChild(document.createTextNode(row10.getCell(
            (short) 2).getStringCellValue()));
        break;

      case 11:
        HSSFRow row11 = spreadsheet.getRow(11);

      Element netincome1 = document.createElement("netincome");
        stmtElement1.appendChild(netincome1);

      netincome1.appendChild(document.createTextNode(row11
          .getCell((short) 1).getStringCellValue()));

      Element netincome2 = document.createElement("netincome");
        stmtElement2.appendChild(netincome2);

        netincome2.appendChild(document.createTextNode(row11
          .getCell((short) 2).getStringCellValue()));
        break;

      default:
        break;
      }

    }

    TransformerFactory tFactory = TransformerFactory.newInstance();

    Transformer transformer = tFactory.newTransformer();
      //Add indentation to output
     transformer.setOutputProperty
    (OutputKeys.INDENT, "yes");
    transformer.setOutputProperty(
        "{http://xml.apache.org/xslt}indent-amount", "2");

    DOMSource source = new DOMSource(document);
    StreamResult result = new StreamResult(System.out);
    transformer.transform(source, result);
  } catch (IOException e) {
    System.out.println("IOException " + e.getMessage());
  } catch (ParserConfigurationException e) {
    System.out
      .println("ParserConfigurationException " + e.getMessage());
  } catch (TransformerConfigurationException e) {
    System.out.println("TransformerConfigurationException "
        + e.getMessage());
  } catch (TransformerException e) {
    System.out.println("TransformerException " + e.getMessage());
  }
}
```

```
  public static void main(String[] argv) {
    ExcelToXML excel = new ExcelToXML();
    File input = new File("IncomeStatements.xls");
    excel.generateXML(input);
  }
}
```

You can run the application ExcelToXML.java in Eclipse with the procedure explained in Chapter 1. Listing 11-16 shows the output from the ExcelToXML.java application.

Listing 11-16. *Output from ExcelToXML.java*

```
<?xml version="1.0" encoding="UTF-8"?>
<incmstmts>
<stmt>
<year>2005</year>
<revenue>11837</revenue>
<costofrevenue>2239</costofrevenue>
<researchdevelopment>1591</researchdevelopment>
<salesmarketing>2689</salesmarketing>
<generaladmin>661</generaladmin>
<totaloperexpenses>7180</totaloperexpenses>
<operincome>4657</operincome>
<invincome>480</invincome>
<incbeforetaxes>5137</incbeforetaxes>
<taxes>1484</taxes>
<netincome>3653</netincome>
</stmt>
<stmt>
<year>2004</year>
<revenue>10818</revenue>
<costofrevenue>1875</costofrevenue>
<researchdevelopment>1421</researchdevelopment>
<salesmarketing>2122</salesmarketing>
<generaladmin>651</generaladmin>
<totaloperexpenses>6069</totaloperexpenses>
<operincome>4749</operincome>
<invincome>420</invincome>
<incbeforetaxes>5169</incbeforetaxes>
<taxes>1706</taxes>
<netincome>3463</netincome>
</stmt>
</incmstmts>
```

Summary

The Apache POI API provides a useful mechanism for converting data between XML and spreadsheets. In this chapter, you learned how to convert an example XML document to an Excel spreadsheet and then convert the spreadsheet to an XML document. With XML being a universal format, there really is no limit to what you can do with it!

CHAPTER 12

Converting XML to PDF

In the previous chapter, we discussed the procedure to convert an XML document to a Microsoft Excel spreadsheet. In this chapter, we will show how to convert an XML document to a PDF document. The open source Apache Formatting Objects Processor (FOP) project provides an API to convert an XML document to PDF or other formats such as Printer Control Language (PCL), PostScript (PS), Scalable Vector Graphics (SVG), XML, Print, Abstract Window Toolkit (AWT), Maker Interchange Format (MIF), or TXT. You can also set the layout and font with the Apache FOP API. The Apache FOP takes an XSL formatting object (an XSL-FO object) as input and produces a PDF (or other format) document as output. XSL-FO is defined in the XSL 1.0 specification.[1] Therefore, to convert XML to PDF, you first need to convert XML to XSL-FO and subsequently convert XSL-FO to PDF.

Installing the Software

Before you can set up your project, you need to download the Apache FOP[2] zip file fop-0.20.5-bin.zip and extract the zip file to a directory. Assuming <FOP> is the directory in which you extracted the FOP zip file, you need the JAR files listed in Table 12-1 for developing an XML to PDF conversion application.

Table 12-1. *Apache FOP JAR Files*

JAR File	Description
<FOP>/build/fop.jar	FOP API classes
<FOP>/lib/avalon-framework-cvs-20020806.jar	Logger classes
<FOP>/lib/batik.jar	Graphics classes
<FOP>/lib/xercesImpl-2.2.1.jar	The Xerces API
<FOP>/lib/xml-apis.jar	The XML API
<FOP>/lib/xalan-2.4.1.jar	The XSLT API

You also need to download JDK 5.0. (You can also use another version of the JDK such as 1.4 or 6.0.)

---

1. See http://www.w3.org/TR/xsl/.
2. For more information about Apache FOP, see http://xmlgraphics.apache.org/fop/.

Setting Up the Eclipse Project

To compile and run the code examples, you will need an Eclipse project. You can download project Chapter12 from the Apress website (http://www.apress.com) and import it into your Eclipse workspace by selecting File ➤ Import. The Chapter12 project consists of a com.apress.pdf package and the Java class XMLToPDF.java in the package. The XMLToPDF.java application performs the XML to PDF conversion. The Chapter12 project also consists of an example XML document (catalog.xml in Listing 12-1) and an example XSLT style sheet (catalog.xslt in Listing 12-2).

To compile and run the XML to PDF code example, you need some Apache FOP JAR files in your project's Java build path; Figure 12-1 shows these JAR files. You also need to set the JRE system library to JRE 5.0, as shown in Figure 12-1.

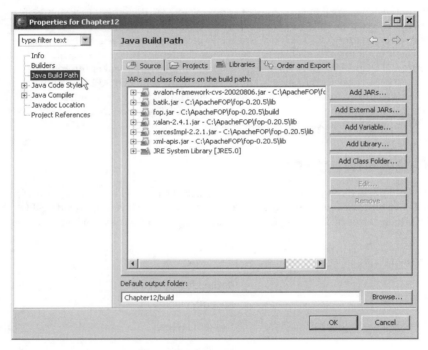

Figure 12-1. *Chapter12 Java build path*

Figure 12-2 shows the Chapter12 project directory structure.

Figure 12-2. *Chapter12 Project directory structure*

Converting an XML Document to XSL-FO

An XSL-FO formatting object includes formatting information about the data to be presented in a PDF document, the layout and fonts used in the document, and the tables in the document. To convert an XML document to a PDF document, first you need to convert the XML document to an XSL-FO document. The procedure to convert an XML document to an XSL-FO document is as follows:

1. Create an XSLT to transform XML to XSL-FO.

2. Set the parser and transformer system properties.

3. Create a Document object from the XML document.

4. Create a Transformer object.

5. Transform the XML document to an XSL-FO document.

An XSL-FO document is in the FO namespace. Therefore, an XSL-FO document includes a namespace declaration, xmlns:fo=http://www.w3.org/1999/XSL/Format, in the root element fo:root. Table 12-2 lists some of commonly used elements in an XSL-FO document.

Table 12-2. *XSL-FO Elements*

Element	Attributes	Subelements	Description
fo:root	xmlns:fo	fo-layout-master-set, fo-page-sequence	Root element in an XSL-FO document
fo:layout-master-set		fo:simple-page-master	Consists of a set of page masters (at least one page master is required)
fo:simple-page-master	margin-right, margin-left, margin-bottom, margin-top, page-width, page-height, master-name	fo:region-body	Specifies page layout

Table 12-2. *XSL-FO Elements (Continued)*

Element	Attributes	Subelements	Description
fo:page-sequence	master-reference	fo:title, fo:static-content, fo:flow	Specifies the order of page masters
fo:flow	flow-name	fo:block	Page content
fo:block	space-before, space-after, font-weight, font-size	fo:table, fo:list-block	Base element for page content; includes formatting information.
fo:list-block	provisional-distance-between-starts, provisional-label-separation	fo:list-item	Specifies a block that includes a list
fo:list-item	text-indent	fo:list-item-label, fo:list-item-body	Specifies a list item
fo:table	border-spacing, table-layout	fo:table-column, fo:table-header, fo:table-body	Specifies a table in a page
fo:table-column	column-number, column-width		Column in a table
fo:table-header		fo:table-row	Table header
fo:table-body	table-layout	fo:table-row	Table rows
fo:table-row	font-weight	fo:table-cell	Row in a table
fo:table-cell	column-number	fo:block	Row cell that has the text of a row cell

The DTD for the XSL-FO object is available from http://www.renderx.com/Tests/validator/fo2000.dtd.html. In this section, we will show how to convert an example XML document, catalog.xml, to an XSL-FO document using XSLT. Listing 12-1 shows the example XML document, catalog.xml.

Listing 12-1. *catalog.xml*

```
<?xml version="1.0" encoding="UTF-8"?>
<catalog>
<journal>
<section>Java Technology</section>
<publisher>IBM developerWorks</publisher>
<level>Introductory</level>
<edition>Nov-2004</edition>
<title>Getting started with enumerated types</title>
<author>Brett McLaughlin</author>
  </journal>
<journal>
<section>Java Technology</section>
```

```
<publisher>IBM developerWorks</publisher>
<level>Intermediate</level>
<edition>Sep-2004</edition>
<title>Migrating to Eclipse</title>
<author>David Gallardo</author>
  </journal>
    <journal>
<section>Java Technology</section>
<publisher>IBM developerWorks</publisher>
<level>Intermediate</level>
<edition>Jan-2004</edition>
<title>Design service-oriented architecture frameworks with J2EE technology</title>
<author>Naveen Balani</author>
  </journal>
</catalog>
```

The Apache FOP API generates a PDF document from an XSL-FO document. The PDF document presents the XML document data in the form of a table. Therefore, you first need to convert the example XML document to an XSL-FO document using XSLT. An XSLT style sheet that converts XML to XSL-FO retrieves data from the XML document and, using elements in the XSL-FO namespace, creates a formatting object representation of the XML data. (Table 12-2 discussed the XSL-FO namespace elements.) Listing 12-2 shows the example XSLT document, catalog.xslt, to convert the example document to an XSL-FO document.

Listing 12-2. *catalog.xslt*

```
<?xml version="1.0" encoding="UTF-8"?>
<xsl:stylesheet version="1.1" xmlns:xsl="http://www.w3.org/1999/XSL/Transform"
    xmlns:fo="http://www.w3.org/1999/XSL/Format" exclude-result-prefixes="fo">
  <xsl:output method="xml" version="1.0" omit-xml-declaration="no" indent="yes"/>
  <!-- ========================= -->
  <!-- root element: catalog -->
  <!-- ========================= -->
  <xsl:template match="/catalog">
    <fo:root xmlns:fo="http://www.w3.org/1999/XSL/Format">
<!--Setting up the Font and the Pages -->
      <fo:layout-master-set>
        <fo:simple-page-master master-name="simpleA4" page-height="29.7cm"
        page-width="75cm" margin-top="2cm" margin-bottom="2cm"
         margin-left="5cm" margin-right="5cm">
          <fo:region-body/>
        </fo:simple-page-master>
      </fo:layout-master-set>
      <fo:page-sequence master-reference="simpleA4">
        <fo:flow flow-name="xsl-region-body">
         <fo:block font-size="40pt"
          font-weight="bold" text-align="center"
        space-after="5mm">
              Catalog
          </fo:block>
          <fo:block font-size="25pt">
```

```
<fo:table table-layout="fixed">
              <fo:table-column column-width="10cm"/>
              <fo:table-column column-width="10cm"/>
              <fo:table-column column-width="10cm"/>
              <fo:table-column column-width="10cm"/>
              <fo:table-column column-width="10cm"/>
              <fo:table-column column-width="10cm"/>
<!--Setting up the header  -->

            <fo:table-header>
<fo:table-row font-weight="bold"><fo:table-cell>
        <fo:block>
          <xsl:text>Section</xsl:text>
        </fo:block>
      </fo:table-cell>
 <fo:table-cell>
        <fo:block>
          <xsl:text>Publisher</xsl:text>
        </fo:block>
      </fo:table-cell>
<fo:table-cell>
        <fo:block>
          <xsl:text>Level</xsl:text>
        </fo:block>
      </fo:table-cell>
<fo:table-cell>
        <fo:block>
          <xsl:text>Edition</xsl:text>
        </fo:block>
      </fo:table-cell>
<fo:table-cell>
        <fo:block>
          <xsl:text>Title</xsl:text>
        </fo:block>
      </fo:table-cell>
<fo:table-cell>
        <fo:block>
          <xsl:text>Author</xsl:text>
        </fo:block>
      </fo:table-cell>
 </fo:table-row>

</fo:table-header>

  <fo:table-body>
<!--Calling template to add data from XML document to XSL-FO Table -->
            <xsl:apply-templates select="journal"/>
            </fo:table-body>
          </fo:table>
        </fo:block>
      </fo:flow>
    </fo:page-sequence>
<!--End of root element of XSL-FO document -->
    </fo:root>
```

```
    </xsl:template>
  <!--Template to add data to XSL-FO document -->
  <xsl:template match="journal">

<fo:table-row>
        <fo:table-cell>
        <fo:block>
          <xsl:value-of select="section"/>
        </fo:block>
      </fo:table-cell>
      <fo:table-cell>
        <fo:block>
          <xsl:value-of select="publisher"/>
        </fo:block>
      </fo:table-cell>
      <fo:table-cell>
        <fo:block>
          <xsl:value-of select="level"/>
        </fo:block>
      </fo:table-cell>
<fo:table-cell>
        <fo:block>
          <xsl:value-of select="edition"/>
        </fo:block>
      </fo:table-cell>
<fo:table-cell>
        <fo:block>
          <xsl:value-of select="title"/>
        </fo:block>
      </fo:table-cell>
<fo:table-cell>
        <fo:block>
          <xsl:value-of select="author"/>
        </fo:block>
      </fo:table-cell>
    </fo:table-row>

  </xsl:template>
</xsl:stylesheet>
```

Setting the System Properties

You perform the XML to XSL-FO transformation using the Transformation API for XML, which was discussed in Chapter 5. You will parse the example XML document using a `DocumentBuilder` parser and transform it using a `Transformer` object. So, you need to set the system properties `javax.xml.parsers.DocumentBuilderFactory` and `javax.xml.transform.TransformerFactory`, as shown in Listing 12-3. You use `DocumentBuilderFactory` to create a `DocumentBuilder` object and `TransformerFactory` to create a `Transformer` object.

Listing 12-3. *Setting System Properties*

```
System.setProperty("javax.xml.parsers.DocumentBuilderFactory",
"org.apache.xerces.jaxp.DocumentBuilderFactoryImpl");
System.setProperty
("javax.xml.transform.TransformerFactory",
"org.apache.xalan.processor.TransformerFactoryImpl");
```

Creating a Document

You can create a Document object by parsing an XML document with a DocumentBuilder object. You obtain a DocumentBuilder object from a DocumentBuilderFactory object. Therefore, you need to create a DocumentBuilderFactory object using the static method newInstance(). Subsequently, create a DocumentBuilder object from the DocumentBuilderFactory object using the method newDocumentBuilder(), as shown in Listing 12-4. You can parse an XML document using one of the overloaded parse() methods from an InputStream, an InputSource, or a File. The example application parses the XML document from a File object, as shown in Listing 12-4. The parse(File) object returns a Document object.

Listing 12-4. *Parsing an XML Document*

```
DocumentBuilderFactory factory = DocumentBuilderFactory.newInstance();
DocumentBuilder builder = factory.newDocumentBuilder();
Document document = builder.parse(new File("catalog.xml"));
```

Creating a Transformer

You also need to create a Transformer object to transform the Document object obtained with a DocumentBuilder object. You can obtain a Transformer object from a TransformerFactory object. Therefore, create a TransformerFactory object using the static method newInstance(), as shown in Listing 12-5. To set a stylesheet on the Transformer object obtained from the TransformerFactory object, create a StreamSource object from the example style sheet. Subsequently, create a Transformer object using the method newTransformer(StyleSource).

Listing 12-5. *Creating a Transformer Object*

```
TransformerFactory tFactory = TransformerFactory.newInstance();
StreamSource stylesource = new StreamSource(new File("catalog.xslt"));
Transformer transformer = tFactory.newTransformer(stylesource);
```

Transforming the XML Document to XSL-FO

The Transformer class provides the method transform(Source, Result) to transform XML input to output. You can specify the input as DOMSource, SAXSource, or StreamSource. You can specify the output as DOMResult, SAXResult, or StreamResult. In the example application, input is specified as DOMSource, and output is specified as StreamResult. Therefore, create a DOMSource object from the Document object, and create a StreamResult object from a catalog.fo file, as shown in Listing 12-6. Subsequently, transform the example XML document using the transform(DOMSource, SAXResult) object, as shown in Listing 12-6.

Listing 12-6. *Transforming an XML Document to XSL-FO*

```
DOMSource source = new DOMSource(document);
StreamResult result = new StreamResult("catalog.fo");
transformer.transform(source, result);
```

The XSL-FO document, catalog.fo, presents the XML document data in the form of a table. The layout-master-set element specifies the page layout and page characteristics such as the page margins, page width, and page height. The element page-sequence defines an XSL-FO page. Fo-block elements specify the page content. The fo-table element defines a table. Listing 12-7 shows the XSL-FO document generated from the transformation.

Listing 12-7. *catalog.fo*

```
<?xml version="1.0" encoding="UTF-8"?>
<fo:root xmlns:fo="http://www.w3.org/1999/XSL/Format">
<fo:layout-master-set>
<fo:simple-page-master margin-right="5cm"
margin-left="5cm" margin-bottom="2cm"
margin-top="2cm" page-width="75cm"
page-height="29.7cm" master-name="simpleA4">
<fo:region-body/>
</fo:simple-page-master>
</fo:layout-master-set>
<fo:page-sequence master-reference="simpleA4">
<fo:flow flow-name="xsl-region-body">
<fo:block space-after="5mm" text-align="center" font-weight="bold" font-size="40pt">
            Catalog
        </fo:block>
<fo:block font-size="25pt">
<fo:table table-layout="fixed">
<fo:table-column column-width="10cm"/>
<fo:table-column column-width="10cm"/>
<fo:table-column column-width="10cm"/>
<fo:table-column column-width="10cm"/>
<fo:table-column column-width="10cm"/>
<fo:table-column column-width="10cm"/>
<fo:table-header>
<fo:table-row font-weight="bold">
<fo:table-cell>
<fo:block>Section</fo:block>
</fo:table-cell>
<fo:table-cell>
<fo:block>Publisher</fo:block>
</fo:table-cell>
<fo:table-cell>
<fo:block>Level</fo:block>
</fo:table-cell>
<fo:table-cell>
<fo:block>Edition</fo:block>
</fo:table-cell>
<fo:table-cell>
<fo:block>Title</fo:block>
</fo:table-cell>
<fo:table-cell>
```

```
<fo:block>Author</fo:block>
</fo:table-cell>
</fo:table-row>
</fo:table-header>
<fo:table-body>
<fo:table-row>
<fo:table-cell>
<fo:block>Java Technology</fo:block>
</fo:table-cell>
<fo:table-cell>
<fo:block>IBM developerWorks</fo:block>
</fo:table-cell>
<fo:table-cell>
<fo:block>Introductory</fo:block>
</fo:table-cell>
<fo:table-cell>
<fo:block>Nov-2004</fo:block>
</fo:table-cell>
<fo:table-cell>
<fo:block>Getting started with enumerated types</fo:block>
</fo:table-cell>
<fo:table-cell>
<fo:block>Brett McLaughlin</fo:block>
</fo:table-cell>
</fo:table-row>
<fo:table-row>
<fo:table-cell>
<fo:block>Java Technology</fo:block>
</fo:table-cell>
<fo:table-cell>
<fo:block>IBM developerWorks</fo:block>
</fo:table-cell>
<fo:table-cell>
<fo:block>Intermediate</fo:block>
</fo:table-cell>
<fo:table-cell>
<fo:block>Sep-2004</fo:block>
</fo:table-cell>
<fo:table-cell>
<fo:block>Migrating to Eclipse</fo:block>
</fo:table-cell>
<fo:table-cell>
<fo:block>David Gallardo</fo:block>
</fo:table-cell>
</fo:table-row>
<fo:table-row>
<fo:table-cell>
<fo:block>Java Technology</fo:block>
</fo:table-cell>
<fo:table-cell>
<fo:block>IBM developerWorks</fo:block>
</fo:table-cell>
<fo:table-cell>
<fo:block>Intermediate</fo:block>
```

```
</fo:table-cell>
<fo:table-cell>
<fo:block>Jan-2004</fo:block>
</fo:table-cell>
<fo:table-cell>
<fo:block>Design service-oriented architecture
frameworks with J2EE technology</fo:block>
</fo:table-cell>
<fo:table-cell>
<fo:block>Naveen Balani</fo:block>
</fo:table-cell>
</fo:table-row>
</fo:table-body>
</fo:table>
</fo:block>
</fo:flow>
</fo:page-sequence>
</fo:root>
```

Generating a PDF Document

In the following sections, you will generate a PDF document from the XSL-FO document, `catalog.fo`, with the Apache FOP API. The procedure to generate a PDF document from an XSL-FO document is as follows:

1. Create a FOP driver.

2. Set the FOP driver renderer to the PDF renderer.

3. Specify the input for the XSL-FO document and the output for the PDF document.

4. Run the FOP driver to generate the PDF document.

You need to import the Apache FOP packages `org.apache.fop.apps` and `org.apache.avalon.framework.logger` to the `XMLToPDF.java` application.

Creating a FOP Driver

To convert the XSL-FO document to a PDF document, you need to create a FOP driver object, as shown in Listing 12-8. You also need to create a console logger with the level setting `LEVEL_INFO` and set the logger on the FOP driver and `MessageHandler`. You can also set the logger level to `LEVEL_DEBUG`, `LEVEL_DISABLED`, `LEVEL_ERROR`, `LEVEL_FATAL`, or `LEVEL_WARN`. `ConsoleLogger` outputs to the standard output stream. You can also use a `BufferedLogger`, which outputs to a `StringBuffer`. The `MessageHandler` class generates the message output. By default, `MessageHandler` outputs to the screen. You can also configure the `MessageHandler` class to output to a file. The `setScreenLogger(Logger)` method sets the screen logger of the `MessageHandler` class.

Listing 12-8. *Creating a FOP Driver*

```
Driver driver=new Driver();
Logger logger=new ConsoleLogger(ConsoleLogger.LEVEL_INFO);
driver.setLogger(logger);
org.apache.fop.messaging.MessageHandler.setScreenLogger(logger);
```

You can render an XSL-FO document to various output types using the corresponding renderer. Table 12-3 lists the different rendering types supported by the FOP driver.

Table 12-3. *Renderer Types*

Render Type	Description
RENDER_PDF	Renders to a PDF document
RENDER_AWT	Renders to a GUI window
RENDER_MIF	Renders to MIF
RENDER_XML	Renders to an XML document
RENDER_PCL	Renders to a PCL document
RENDER_PS	Renders to a Postscript document
RENDER_TXT	Renders to a text document
RENDER_SVG	Renders to SVG

Converting XSL-FO to PDF

Because you will be converting an XSL-FO document to a PDF document, set the renderer type to Driver.RENDER_PDF, as shown here:

```
driver.setRenderer(Driver.RENDER_PDF);
```

You need to specify the input XSL-FO document for the FOP driver, as shown next. You set the XSL-FO document as input using the setInputSource(InputSource) method.

```
InputStream input=new FileInputStream(new File("catalog.fo")));
driver.setInputSource(new InputSource(input));
```

You also need to set the output for the PDF document generated with the FOP driver. You set the output using the method setOutputStream(OutputStream), as shown here:

```
OutputStream output=new FileOutputStream(new File("catalog.pdf")));
driver.setOutputStream(output);
```

To generate a PDF document from the XSL-FO document, run the FOP driver using the method run(), as shown next. Subsequently, close the Driver object using the close() method.

```
driver.run();
output.flush();
output.close();
```

Viewing the Complete Example

Listing 12-9 shows the Java application, XMLToPDF.java, for converting an XML document to a PDF document. The application consists of the methods generateXSLFO(File xmlFile, File xsltFile) and generatePDF(). In the generateXSLFO() method, a DocumentBuilder parses an XML document to obtain a Document object, and a Transformer transforms the Document object to an XSL-FO file using a stylesheet. In the generatePDF() method, a FOP driver converts the XSL-FO file to a PDF document.

Listing 12-9. *XMLToPDF.java*

```java
package com.apress.pdf;

import org.apache.fop.apps.*;
import org.apache.avalon.framework.logger.*;
import java.io.*;
import org.xml.sax.InputSource;
import javax.xml.parsers.*;
import org.xml.sax.*;
import org.w3c.dom.*;
import javax.xml.transform.*;
import javax.xml.transform.dom.*;
import javax.xml.transform.stream.*;

public class XMLToPDF {
  public void generateXSLFO(File xmlFile, File xsltFile) {
    try {
    System.setProperty
       ("javax.xml.parsers.DocumentBuilderFactory",
       "org.apache.xerces.jaxp.DocumentBuilderFactoryImpl");
System.setProperty("javax.xml.transform.TransformerFactory",
       "org.apache.xalan.processor.TransformerFactoryImpl");
      // Create a DocumentBuilderFactory
      DocumentBuilderFactory factory = DocumentBuilderFactory
          .newInstance();

      // Create DocumentBuilder object
      DocumentBuilder builder = factory.newDocumentBuilder();
      // Parse example XML Document
      Document document = builder.parse(xmlFile);
      // Create a TransformerFactory object
    TransformerFactory tFactory = TransformerFactory.newInstance();

      // Create a Stylesource object from the style sheet File object
      StreamSource stylesource = new StreamSource(xsltFile);

      // Create a Transformer object from the StyleSource object
    Transformer transformer = tFactory.newTransformer(stylesource);
      // Create a DOMSource object from an XML document

      DOMSource source = new DOMSource(document);
      // Create a StreamResult object to output the result of a
      // transformation
      StreamResult result = new StreamResult("catalog.fo");

      // Transform an XML document with an XSLT style sheet
      transformer.transform(source, result);

    } catch (TransformerConfigurationException e) {

      System.out.println(e.getMessage());
```

```java
      } catch (TransformerException e) {

        System.out.println(e.getMessage());
      } catch (SAXException e) {
        System.out.println(e.getMessage());

      } catch (ParserConfigurationException e) {

        System.out.println(e.getMessage());
      } catch (IOException e) {
        System.out.println(e.getMessage());
      }

  }

  public void generatePDF() {
    try {      //Create a FOP driver
      Driver driver = new Driver();
                                    //Create and set a logger on the driver
      Logger logger = new ConsoleLogger(ConsoleLogger.LEVEL_INFO);
      driver.setLogger(logger);
      org.apache.fop.messaging.MessageHandler.setScreenLogger(logger);
                                    //Set renderer type
      driver.setRenderer(Driver.RENDER_PDF);
      //Set input and output
      InputStream input = new FileInputStream(new File("catalog.fo"));
      driver.setInputSource(new InputSource(input));
    OutputStream output = new FileOutputStream(new File("catalog.pdf"));
      driver.setOutputStream(output);
                                    //Run FOP driver
      driver.run();
      output.flush();
      output.close();
    } catch (IOException e) {
    } catch (org.apache.fop.apps.FOPException e) {
      System.out.println(e.getMessage());
    }

  }

  public static void main(String[] argv) {

    XMLToPDF xmlToPDF = new XMLToPDF();
    File xmlFile = new File("catalog.xml");
    File xsltFile = new File("catalog.xslt");


    xmlToPDF.generateXSLFO(xmlFile, xsltFile);
    xmlToPDF.generatePDF();

  }
}
```

You can run the application XMLToPDF.java in Eclipse with the procedure explained in Chapter 1. Listing 12-10 shows the output generated from the application. As shown in the output, org.pache. xerces.parsers.SAXParser parses the XSL-FO object.

Listing 12-10. *Output from Converting XSL-FO to PDF*

```
[INFO] Using org.apache.xerces.parsers.SAXParser as SAX2 Parser
[INFO] building formatting object tree
[INFO] setting up fonts
[INFO] [1]
[INFO] Parsing of document complete, stopping renderer
```

The PDF document catalog.pdf gets generated and added to the Chapter12 project, as shown in Figure 12-3.

Figure 12-3. *Chapter12 project directory structure including* catalog.pdf

Summary

In this chapter, you learned how to convert an example XML document to a PDF document. You can also generate other output types such as AWT, MIF, XML, PCL, PS, TXT, and SVG using the corresponding renderer. To convert an XML document to a PDF document, first you convert the XML document to an XSL-FO document, and subsequently you convert the XSL-FO document to a PDF document. You convert the XML document to an XSL-FO document using an XSLT stylesheet and the Transformer API. You can convert the XSL-FO document to a PDF document using the FOP driver.

PART 6

Web Applications and Services

CHAPTER 13

■ ■ ■

Building Web Applications with Ajax

Asynchronous JavaScript and XML (Ajax) is a term, coined by Jesse James Garrett of Adaptive Path,[1] used to describe a web technique that allows you to create asynchronous web applications using JavaScript, the Document Object Model (DOM), and `XMLHttpRequest` technologies. Using this technique, a browser-based user interface can interact with the server to update selected parts of a web page without having to reload the web page.

This web technique decreases the amount of data exchanged between a browser and the back end, which in turn decreases latency and makes a browser-based user interface much more interactive; and this makes it more like a conventional desktop application.

Ajax has numerous useful applications; some of the more common ones are as follows:

Dynamic form data validation: While a user fills in a form that requires a unique identifier in a field, a form field can be validated without the complete form being submitted.

Autocompletion: While a user types data in a form field, the form field gets autocompleted based on data fetched from the server.

Data refreshes on a page: Some web pages require that parts of the web page be refreshed frequently; a weather website, for example, has this requirement. Using Ajax techniques, a web page can poll a server for the latest data and refresh selected parts of the web page, without reloading the page.

JavaScript and DOM scripting are basic web technologies; therefore, we won't discuss them in detail here. We will, however, cover how the `XMLHttpRequest` object works.

■**Note** If you want to read more about JavaScript, DOM scripting, and general Ajax techniques, check out *Beginning JavaScript with DOM Scripting and Ajax* by Christian Heilmann (Apress, 2006). For a lot more on Ajax programming with Java, check out *Pro Ajax with Java Frameworks* by Nathaniel T. Schutta and Ryan Asleson (Apress, 2006).

---

1. The seminal article on Ajax is available at `http://adaptivepath.com/publications/essays/archives/000385.php`.

What Is XMLHttpRequest?

The XMLHttpRequest object provides asynchronous communication between a browser-based user interface and web[2] server–based business services. Using the XMLHttpRequest object, clients can submit and retrieve XML data to and from a web server without reloading the web page. You can convert XML data to HTML on the client side using the DOM and XSLT.

Microsoft introduced XMLHttpRequest within Internet Explorer (IE) 5 as ActiveXObject.[3] Most browsers support XMLHttpRequest; however, the implementations are not interoperable. For example, you can create an instance of the XMLHttpRequest object in IE 6 with the following code:

```
var req = new ActiveXObject("Microsoft.XMLHTTP");
```

In IE 7, XMLHttpRequest is available as a window object property. You create an instance of the XMLHttpRequest object in IE 7 as shown here:

```
var req = new XMLHttpRequest();
```

Recently, the W3C introduced a Working Draft[4] of the XMLHttpRequest object, which will standardize the implementations of it. The XMLHttpRequest object provides various properties for implementing HTTP client functionality, which are discussed in Table 13-1.

Table 13-1. *XMLHttpRequest Properties*

Property	Description
onreadystatechange	Sets the callback method for asynchronous requests.
readyState	Retrieves the current state of a request. 0: the XMLHttpRequest object has been created. 1: the object has been created, and the open() method has been invoked. 2: the send() method has been called, but the response has not been received. 3: some data has been received that is available in the responseText property. The property responseXML produces null, and response headers and status are not completely available. 4: the response has been received.
responseText	Retrieves the text of the response from the server.
responseXML	Retrieves the XML DOM of the response from the server.
status	Retrieves the HTTP status code of the request. For status code definitions, refer to http://www.w3.org/Protocols/rfc2616/rfc2616-sec10.html.
statusText	Retrieves the status text of the HTTP request.

The XMLHttpRequest object methods are used to open an HTTP request, send the request, and receive a response. Table 13-2 describes the XMLHttpRequest methods.

---

2. It can be a web container within an application server, which is what we will use. In this chapter, we will use the terms *web server* and *application server* interchangeably.
3. The ActiveXObject API is available at http://msdn2.microsoft.com/en-us/library/6958xykx.aspx.
4. You can find the W3C Working Draft for the XMLHttpRequest object at http://www.w3.org/TR/XMLHttpRequest/.

Table 13-2. *XMLHttpRequest Methods*

Method	Description
abort()	Cancels the current HTTP request.
getAllResponseHeaders()	Gets all the response headers. readyState is required to be 3 or 4 to retrieve the response headers.
getResponseHeader(string header)	Gets a specified response header. readyState is required to be 3 or 4 to retrieve a response header.
open(string method, string url, boolean asynch, string username, string password)	Opens an HTTP request but does not send a request. The readyState property gets set to 1. The responseText, responseXML, status, and statusText properties get reset to their initial values. The HTTP method and server URL, which may be relative or absolute, are required parameters. The boolean parameter asynch specifies whether the HTTP request is asynchronous; the default value is true. The parameters username and password are optional.
send(data)	Sends an HTTP request to the server, including data, which can be a string, an array of unsigned bytes, an XML DOM object, or null. This method is synchronous or asynchronous, corresponding to the value of the asynch parameter to the open() method. If synchronous, the method does not return until the request is completely loaded and the entire response has been received. If asynchronous, the method returns immediately. The readyState property gets set to 2 after invoking the send() method. The readyState property gets set to 4 after the request has completed loading.
setRequestHeader(string headerName, string headerValue)	Sets HTTP request headers.

Now that you've looked at some of the theory behind Ajax and seen what it can do, you'll implement a working example—dynamic form validation.

Installing the Software

Ajax, being a web technique rather than a technology, does not require any additional software other than a browser that supports the XMLHttpRequest object. If not already installed, you need to install a web browser, such as IE 7 or 6 or Netscape 6+.

To develop and deploy an Ajax web application, you need an application server that supports J2EE 1.4. Therefore, download and install JBoss 4.0.2. You could also use any other application server that supports J2EE 1.4, such as BEA WebLogic, IBM WebSphere, Oracle Application Server, or Sun One Application Server.

You also need to download and install the J2EE 1.4 SDK and J2SE 5.0 so you can compile the example application.

The Ajax application you will develop retrieves data from a database using a JDBC[5] driver. Therefore, you need to install a relational database along with a compatible JDBC driver. We use the open source relational database MySQL in this chapter; if you choose to do the same, download and install the MySQL 5.0[6] database and a compatible MySQL Connector/J JDBC driver. You may, of course, use any other JDBC-supported relational database, such as Oracle, IBM DB2, or Microsoft SQL Server.

Configuring JBoss with the MySQL Database

After installing the MySQL database, you need to create a MySQL database user. To create a user, log in to the MySQL database using the following command:

```
mysql --user=root mysql
```

You can add a new user to the user table with a GRANT statement, as shown in the following example, where you create the user mysql with the password mysql:

```
GRANT ALL PRIVILEGES ON test TO 'mysql'@'localhost' IDENTIFIED BY 'mysql' ;
```

You also need to create an example table in the MySQL database. To create the example table, log in to the database as the mysql user and run the SQL script shown in Listing 13-1.

Listing 13-1. *SQL Script catalog.sql*

```
CREATE TABLE Catalog(CatalogId VARCHAR(25),
Journal VARCHAR(25), Publisher Varchar(25),
Edition VARCHAR(25), Title Varchar(45),
Author Varchar(25));
INSERT INTO Catalog VALUES
('catalog1', 'XML Zone',  'IBM developerWorks', 'Jan 2006',
'Managing XML data: Tag URIs', 'Elliotte Harold');
INSERT INTO Catalog VALUES
('catalog2', 'XML Zone',   'IBM developerWorks',
'Jan 2006', 'Practical data binding', 'Brett McLaughlin');
```

You also need to configure the JBoss application server with the MySQL database. Assuming < jboss-4.0.2> as the root of the JBoss 4.0.2 install directory, you can proceed as follows:

1. To use the JBoss 4.0.2 application server with MySQL, you first need to copy the MySQL driver classes to the JBoss server classpath. So, copy mysql-connector-java-3.1.11-bin.jar to the < jboss-4.0.2>/server/default/lib directory.

2. To use a MySQL data source, copy < jboss-4.0.2>/docs/examples/jca/mysql-ds.xml to the < jboss-4.0.2>/server/default/deploy directory. Modify the mysql-ds.xml configuration file by setting the <driver-class> XML element to com.mysql.jdbc.Driver and the <connection-url> XML element to jdbc:mysql://localhost:3306/test. In mysql-ds.xml, specify user-name as mysql and password as mysql. The jndi-name is set to MySqlDS by default. Listing 13-2 shows the fully configured mysql-ds.xml file.

---

5. Information about JDBC technology is available at http://java.sun.com/javase/technologies/database.jsp.
6. MySQL 5.0 is available at http://www.mysql.com.

Listing 13-2. *Mysql-ds.xml*

```
<?xml version="1.0" encoding="UTF-8"?>

<datasources>
  <local-tx-datasource>
    <jndi-name>MySqlDS</jndi-name>
    <connection-url>jdbc:mysql://localhost:3306/test</connection-url>
    <driver-class>com.mysql.jdbc.Driver</driver-class>
    <user-name>mysql</user-name>
    <password>mysql</password>

  </local-tx-datasource>
</datasources>
```

3. You also need to modify `<jboss-4.0.2>/server/default/conf/login-config.xml` by adding the `<application-policy>` XML element shown in Listing 13-3 to `login-config.xml`.

Listing 13-3. *login-config.xml*

```
<application-policy name = "MySqlDbRealm">
   <authentication>
      <login-module code =
  "org.jboss.resource.security.ConfiguredIdentityLoginModule"
                          flag = "required">
         <module-option name ="principal"></module-option>
         <module-option name ="userName">mysql</module-option>
         <module-option name ="password">mysql</module-option>
         <module-option name ="managedConnectionFactoryName">
             jboss.jca:service=LocalTxCM,name=MySqlDS
         </module-option>
      </login-module>
   </authentication>
</application-policy>
```

Modifying the `mysql-ds.xml` and `login-config.xml` files, as described previously, configures the JBoss 4.0.2 server for use with an instance of the MySQL database.

Setting Up the Eclipse Project

In this chapter, you will develop a web application using Ajax techniques. To compile and run the code examples, you will need an Eclipse project. You can download project `Chapter13` from `http://www.apress.com` and import it into your Eclipse workspace by selecting File ➤ Import.

In the Eclipse project `Chapter13`, you will compile and deploy an Ajax application using an Apache Ant `build.xml` file. If you are not familiar with Apache Ant, refer to the Apache Ant website[7] or read *Pro Apache Ant* by Matthew Moodie (Apress 2005).[8]

---

7. See `http://ant.apache.org/`.
8. See `http://www.apress.com/book/bookDisplay.html?bID=10038`.

The example build.xml file has four targets: init, compile, webapp, and clean. These targets act as follows:

1. The init target creates the directories required for the Ajax application.

2. The compile target compiles a Java servlet[9] in the Ajax application.

3. The webapp target generates a J2EE 1.4–compliant web application archive (WAR) file and deploys the WAR file to the JBoss application server.

4. Optional: The clean target deletes the project directories.

Listing 13-4 shows the build.xml file.

Listing 13-4. *build.xml*

```
<project name="ajax" default="webapp" basedir=".">
<property name="build" value="build"/>
<property name="src" value="." />
<property name="jboss.deploy"
 value="C:\JBoss\jboss-4.0.2\server\default\deploy"/>
<property name="dist" value="dist"/>
<property name="j2sdkee" value="C:\J2sdkee1.4"/>
<property name="mysql" value="C:\MySQL\mysql-connector-java-3.1.11"/>
<target name="init">
    <tstamp/>
  <mkdir dir="${build}" />
  <mkdir dir="${dist}" />
  <mkdir dir="${build}/WEB-INF" />

  <mkdir dir="${build}/WEB-INF/classes" />
</target>
<target name="compile" depends="init">
  <javac debug="true" classpath=
"${j2sdkee}/lib/j2ee.jar:${mysql}
/lib/mysql-connector-java-3.1.11-bin.jar"
  srcdir="${src}/WEB-INF/classes"
  destdir="${src}/WEB-INF/classes">
    <include name="**/*.java" />
  </javac>
  <copy todir="${build}/WEB-INF">
    <fileset dir="WEB-INF" >
      <include name="web.xml" />
    </fileset>
  </copy>

 <copy todir="${build}/WEB-INF/classes">
    <fileset dir="${src}/WEB-INF/classes" >
      <include name="**/FormServlet.class" />
    </fileset>
  </copy>
```

<hr/>

9. See http://java.sun.com/products/servlet/.

```
  <copy todir="${build}">
    <fileset dir="${src}" >
      <include name="inputForm.jsp" />
    </fileset>
  </copy>
</target>
<target name="webapp" depends="compile">
 <war basedir="${build}" includes="**/*.class,inputForm.jsp"
 destfile="${dist}/ajax.war"  webxml="WEB-INF/web.xml"/>
 <copy file="${dist}/ajax.war" todir="${jboss.deploy}"/>
  </target>

  <target name="clean">
    <delete dir="${dist}"/>
    <delete dir="${build}"/>

  </target>

</project>
```

In the Chapter13 Eclipse project, you need to set the JRE system library to JRE 5.0, as shown in Figure 13-1.

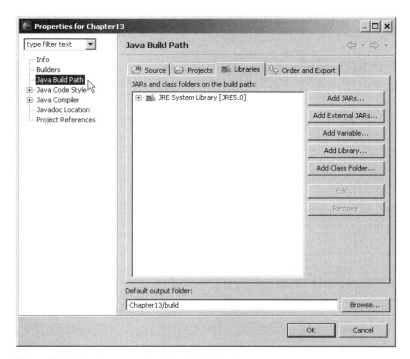

Figure 13-1. *Chapter13 project Java build path*

Figure 13-2 shows the directory structure of the Chapter13 project.

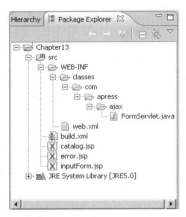

Figure 13-2. *Chapter13 project directory structure*

You need to select the build targets in the Ant build.xml file that will compile and deploy the Ajax web application. Right-click the build.xml file, select Run As, and select the second Ant Build item.

Select the Targets tab in the Chapter13 build.xml dialog box. Select the boxes for the init, compile, and webapp targets, and click the Apply button, as shown in Figure 13-3.

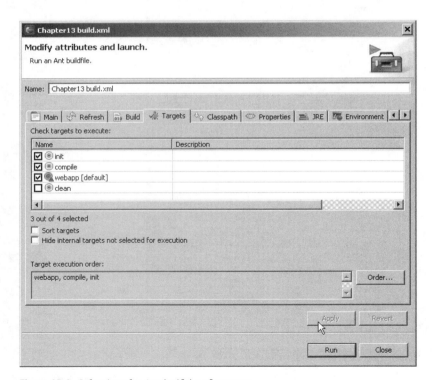

Figure 13-3. *Selecting the Ant build.xml targets*

Next, you need to run the Ant `build.xml` file to compile the Ajax web application and deploy it to the JBoss application server. Right-click `build.xml` in the Package Explorer, and select Run As and the first Ant `build.xml` file. The Ant `build.xml` script runs, compiles, and deploys the Ajax web application, as shown in Listing 13-5. We will discuss the details of the Ajax web application in the next section.

Listing 13-5. *Output of Ant Build File*

```
Buildfile: C:\Documents and Settings\Deepak Vohra\workspace\Chapter13\src\build.
xml
init:
    [mkdir] Created dir: C:\Documents and Settings\Deepak Vohra\workspace\Chapte
r13\src\build
    [mkdir] Created dir: C:\Documents and Settings\Deepak Vohra\workspace\Chapte
r13\src\dist
    [mkdir] Created dir: C:\Documents and Settings\Deepak Vohra\workspace\Chapte
r13\src\build\WEB-INF
    [mkdir] Created dir: C:\Documents and Settings\Deepak Vohra\workspace\Chapte
r13\src\build\WEB-INF\classes
compile:
     [copy] Copying 1 file to C:\Documents and Settings\Deepak Vohra\workspace\C
hapter13\src\build\WEB-INF
     [copy] Copying 1 file to C:\Documents and Settings\Deepak Vohra\workspace\C
hapter13\src\build\WEB-INF\classes
     [copy] Copying 1 file to C:\Documents and Settings\Deepak Vohra\workspace\C
hapter13\src\build
webapp:
      [war] Building war: C:\Documents and Settings\Deepak Vohra\workspace\Chapt
er13\src\dist\ajax.war
     [copy] Copying 1 file to C:\JBoss\jboss-4.0.2\server\default\deploy
init:
compile:
init:
BUILD SUCCESSFUL
```

Developing an Ajax Application

Now that you have put together the Eclipse project, you can start constructing the actual functionality of the Ajax application. In this section, you will create the functionality to validate data input in an HTML form.

The input form requires a unique catalog ID to create a catalog entry. Therefore, you will validate catalog ID input in the form against data in the database to check whether the catalog ID is already specified in the database. Data typed in the HTML form is sent to a servlet URL using the GET method. On the server side, an HTTP servlet's `doGet()` method gets invoked. In the `doGet()` method, the input value is compared with data in the database. The HTTP servlet returns an XML response that contains information about the validity of the input data.

In the client application, the XML response from the server is processed, and if the instructions indicate that the data input is valid, the message "Catalog ID is Valid" displays. An `XMLHttpRequest` request is sent to the server with each modification in the input field. Without Ajax, you would have to submit the complete input form to the server and then reload the browser web page after a response is received from the server.

The procedure to send an XMLHttpRequest request to the server involves the following steps:

1. Invoke a JavaScript function from an event handler in response to an HTML event.

2. Create an XMLHttpRequest object in the JavaScript function.

3. Open an XMLHttpRequest request, which specifies the URL and the HTTP method.

4. Register a callback event handler that gets invoked when the request state changes.

5. Send an XMLHttpRequest request asynchronously.

6. Retrieve the XML response, and modify the HTML page.

Next, you will examine the browser-side processing involved in the example application.

Browser-Side Processing

To initiate an XMLHttpRequest request, register a JavaScript function as an event handler for the onkeyup event generated from the HTML form input field, catalogId, which is required to be validated. In the example application, a JavaScript function, validateCatalogId(), is invoked on the onkeyup event, as shown in Listing 13-6.

Listing 13-6. *Input Form*

```
<form name="validationForm" action="validateForm" method="post">
<table>
<tr>
  <td>Catalog ID:</td>
  <td><input    type="text"
           size="20"
           id="catalogId"
           name="catalogId"
           autocomplete="off"
          onkeyup="validateCatalogId()"></td>
    <td><div id="validationMessage"></div></td>
</tr>
….
</table>
</form>
```

In the JavaScript function validateCatalogId(), you need to create a new XMLHttpRequest object. If a browser supports the XMLHttpRequest object as an ActiveXObject object, the procedure to create an XMLHttpRequest object is different when the XMLHttpRequest object is a window object property. IE 7 and Netscape support XMLHttpRequest as a window property, and IE 6 supports the XMLHTTPRequest object as an ActiveXObject object. Therefore, you check to see whether the XMLHttpRequest object is a window object property and act accordingly, as shown in Listing 13-7.

Listing 13-7. *Creating an XMLHttpRequest Object*

```
<script type="text/javascript">
function validateCatalogId(){

var xmlHttpRequest=init();
```

```
function init(){
    if (window.XMLHttpRequest) {
            return new XMLHttpRequest();
    } else if (window.ActiveXObject) {
            return new ActiveXObject("Microsoft.XMLHTTP");
    }
}
</script>
```

Next, you need to construct a URL to which the XMLHttpRequest will be sent. In the example application, you will invoke a servlet, FormServlet. Within the web server, FormServlet is mapped to the servlet URL pattern /validateForm, as specified in the web.xml deployment descriptor shown in Listing 13-8.

Listing 13-8. *web.xml*

```
<?xml version="1.0" ?>
<!DOCTYPE  web-app  PUBLIC '-//Sun Microsystems, Inc.//DTD Web Application 2.3//EN'
  'http://java.sun.com/dtd/web-app_2_3.dtd'>
<web-app>

  <servlet>
    <servlet-name>FormServlet</servlet-name>
    <servlet-class>com.apress.ajax.FormServlet</servlet-class>
  </servlet>

  <servlet-mapping>
    <servlet-name>FormServlet</servlet-name>
    <url-pattern>/validateForm</url-pattern>
  </servlet-mapping>

</web-app>
```

Therefore, you specify the URL as validateForm?catalogId=encodeURIComponent(catalogId.value), whereby the parameter catalogId specifies the value of the catalog ID input in the HTML form, and you use the encodeURIComponent(string) method to encode the catalog ID value. The HTTP method specified is GET, because form data is encoded into the URL as shown in Listing 13-9.

Listing 13-9. *Opening an HTTP Request*

```
var catalogId=document.getElementById("catalogId");
xmlHttpRequest.open("GET",
  "validateForm?catalogId="+
  encodeURIComponent(catalogId.value), true);
```

You need to register a callback event handler with the XMLHttpRequest object using the onreadystatechange property. In the example application, the callback method is the JavaScript function processRequest(), as shown here:

```
xmlHttpRequest.onreadystatechange=processRequest;
```

Next, you need to send an HTTP request using the send() method, as shown here:

```
xmlHttpRequest.send(null);
```

Because the HTTP method is GET, data sent with the send() method is set to null. Because the callback event handler is processRequest(), the processRequest() function gets invoked when the value of the readyState property changes. In the processRequest() function, the readyState property value is retrieved. If the request has loaded completely, which is denoted by the readyState value 4, and the HTTP status is "OK", you invoke the processResponse() JavaScript function to process the response from the server, as shown in Listing 13-10.

Listing 13-10. *Event Handler for the onreadystatechange Property Change Event*

```
function processRequest(){
    if(xmlHttpRequest.readyState==4){
        if(xmlHttpRequest.status==200){
            processResponse();
        }
    }
}
```

Next, we will discuss the server-side processing of the XMLHttpRequest request.

Web Server–Side Processing

The XMLHttpRequest object is sent to the relative URL validateForm?catalogId=encodeURIComponent(catalogId.value), which invokes the FormServlet servlet. Because the XMLHttpRequest method is GET, the doGet() method of the servlet gets invoked.
In the doGet() method, first you retrieve the value of the catalogId parameter, as shown here:

```
String catalogId = request.getParameter("catalogId");
```

Next, you obtain data from the database to check whether a catalog ID value is already specified in the database. Connecting to a database is a two-step process:

1. First, you discover the database through a lookup process that is akin to looking up a phone number in a phone directory, based on a name. This lookup process involves creating a JNDI[10] InitialContext object and invoking the lookup("java:MySqlDS") method on the object. The lookup() method returns a DataSource object.

2. From the DataSource object, you create a Connection object, as shown in Listing 13-11.

Listing 13-11. *Creating a Connection Object*

```
InitialContext initialContext = new InitialContext();
javax.sql.DataSource ds = (javax.sql.DataSource)
initialContext.lookup("java:MySqlDS");
java.sql.Connection conn = ds.getConnection();
```

Subsequently, you create a Statement object to run a SQL query. Using the catalog ID value specified in the input form, you create a SQL query to retrieve data from the database. You run the SQL query using the executeQuery(String) method, which returns a ResultSet object, as shown in Listing 13-12.

---

10. The JNDI API is part of J2EE 1.4.

Listing 13-12. *Obtaining a ResultSet Object*

```
Statement stmt = conn.createStatement();
            String query = "SELECT * from .Catalog WHERE catalogId=" + "'" +
                catalogId + "'";
ResultSet rs = stmt.executeQuery(query);
```

Before you check the data obtained from the database to see whether the form input is valid, you need to set the content type of the HttpServletResponse to text/xml and the cache-control header to no-cache, as shown here:

```
response.setContentType("text/xml");
response.setHeader("Cache-Control", "no-cache");
```

The FormServlet servlet sends a response in the form of an XML string. Therefore, you need to construct an XML DOM object that contains instructions about the validity of the catalog ID field value.

An empty ResultSet object implies that the catalog ID field value is not defined in the database table Catalog; thus, the catalog ID field value is valid. A ResultSet object that contains data implies that the catalog ID value is already defined in the database; thus, the catalog ID field value is not valid.

For a nonvalid catalog ID, you construct an XML string that includes the contents of a catalog ID under the root element catalog. The first child element of the catalog root element is the <valid>false</valid> element, which denotes that the catalog ID is not valid.

For the case where the catalog ID is valid, you construct an XML string that simply includes a <valid>true</valid> element.

Listing 13-13 shows the XML response.

Listing 13-13. *Returning an XML Response*

```
if (rs.next()) {
    out.println("<catalog>" + "<valid>false</valid>" + "<journal>" +
    rs.getString(2) + "</journal>" + "<publisher>" +
    rs.getString(3) + "</publisher>" + "<edition>" +
    rs.getString(4) + "</edition>" + "<title>" +
    rs.getString(5) + "</title>" + "<author>" +
    rs.getString(6) + "</author>" + "</catalog>");
} else {
    out.println("<valid>true</valid>");
}
```

If the catalog ID field value is valid, the input form can be posted to the server using the HTTP POST method, which on the server side invokes the doPost() method in the FormServlet servlet. In the doPost() method, you create a database Connection and add a catalog entry with the INSERT statement.

Listing 13-14 shows the complete FormServlet.

Listing 13-14. *FormServlet.java*

```
package com.apress.ajax;
import java.io.*;
import java.sql.*;
import javax.naming.InitialContext;
import javax.servlet.*;
import javax.servlet.http.*;
```

```java
public class FormServlet extends HttpServlet {
public void doGet(HttpServletRequest request, HttpServletResponse response)
    throws ServletException, IOException {
    try {
      // Obtain value of Catalog Id field to ve validated.
      String catalogId = request.getParameter("catalogId");
      // Obtain Connection
      InitialContext initialContext = new InitialContext();
      javax.sql.DataSource ds = (javax.sql.DataSource) initialContext
          .lookup("java:MySqlDS");
      java.sql.Connection conn = ds.getConnection();
      // Obtain result set
      Statement stmt = conn.createStatement();
      String query = "SELECT * from Catalog WHERE catalogId=" + "'"
          + catalogId + "'";
      ResultSet rs = stmt.executeQuery(query);
      // set headers before accessing the Writer
      response.setContentType("text/xml");
      response.setHeader("Cache-Control", "no-cache");
      PrintWriter out = response.getWriter();
      // then write the response
      // If result set is empty set valid element to true
      if (rs.next()) {
      out.println("<catalog>" + "<valid>false</valid>" + "<journal>"
          + rs.getString(2) + "</journal>" + "<publisher>"
          + rs.getString(3) + "</publisher>" + "<edition>"
          + rs.getString(4) + "</edition>" + "<title>"
          + rs.getString(5) + "</title>" + "<author>"
          + rs.getString(6) + "</author>" + "</catalog>");
      } else {
        out.println("<valid>true</valid>");
      }
          //Close the ResultSet, Statement,
          //and Connection objects.
      rs.close();
      stmt.close();
      conn.close();
    } catch (javax.naming.NamingException e) {
    } catch (SQLException e) {
    }
  }

  public void doPost(HttpServletRequest request, HttpServletResponse response)
      throws ServletException, IOException {
    try {
      // Obtain Connection
      InitialContext initialContext = new InitialContext();
      javax.sql.DataSource ds = (javax.sql.DataSource) initialContext
          .lookup("java:MySqlDS");
      java.sql.Connection conn = ds.getConnection();
      String catalogId = request.getParameter("catalogId");
      String journal = request.getParameter("journal");
      String publisher = request.getParameter("publisher");
      String edition = request.getParameter("edition");
```

```
        String title = request.getParameter("title");
        String author = request.getParameter("author");
        Statement stmt = conn.createStatement();
        String sql = "INSERT INTO Catalog VALUES(" + "\'" + catalogId
            + "\'" + "," + "\'" + journal + "\'" + "," + "\'"
            + publisher + "\'" + "," + "\'" + edition + "\'" + ","
            + "\'" + title + "\'" + "," + "\'" + author + "\'" + ")";
        stmt.execute(sql);
        response.sendRedirect("catalog.jsp");
        stmt.close();
        conn.close();
    } catch (javax.naming.NamingException e) {
        response.sendRedirect("error.jsp");
    } catch (SQLException e) {
        response.sendRedirect("error.jsp");
    }
  }
}
```

On the browser side, in the processRequest() JavaScript function, if the HTTP request has loaded completely, which corresponds to the readyState property value 4 and the status property value 200, the processResponse() JavaScript function gets invoked. In the processResponse() function, you need to obtain the value of the responseXML property. The responseXML property contains the response XML string that was set in the doGet() method of the FormServlet servlet:

```
var xmlMessage=xmlHttpRequest.responseXML;
```

The responseXML property contains instructions in XML form about the validity of the catalog ID value specified in the input form. You need to obtain the value of the <valid> element using the getElementsByTagName(string) method, as shown here:

```
var valid=xmlMessage.getElementsByTagName("valid")[0].firstChild.nodeValue;
```

If the <valid> element content is set to true, set the HTML validationMessage div to "Catalog ID is Valid", and enable the submitForm button in the input form, as shown in Listing 13-15.

Listing 13-15. *Setting the Validation Message*

```
if(valid=="true"){
    var validationMessage=document.getElementById("validationMessage");
    validationMessage.innerHTML = "Catalog ID is Valid";
    document.getElementById("submitForm").disabled = false;
}
```

If the <valid> element value is set to false, set the HTML of validationMessage div in the catalog ID field row to "Catalog ID is not Valid", and disable the submitForm button. You can also set the values of the other input fields, as shown in Listing 13-16.

Listing 13-16. *Setting the Validation Message for the Nonvalid Catalog ID*

```
if(valid=="false"){
    var validationMessage=document.getElementById("validationMessage");
    validationMessage.innerHTML = "Catalog ID is not Valid";
    document.getElementById("submitForm").disabled = true;
}
```

Listing 13-17 shows the inputForm.jsp page.

Listing 13-17. *inputForm.jsp*

```
<html>
<head>
<script type="text/javascript">
function validateCatalogId(){

var xmlHttpRequest=init();

  function init(){

if (window.XMLHttpRequest) {
        return new XMLHttpRequest();
    } else if (window.ActiveXObject) {

        return new ActiveXObject("Microsoft.XMLHTTP");
    }

}
var catalogId=document.getElementById("catalogId");
xmlHttpRequest.open("GET", "validateForm?catalogId="+
encodeURIComponent(catalogId.value), true);
xmlHttpRequest.onreadystatechange=processRequest;
xmlHttpRequest.send(null);

function processRequest(){

if(xmlHttpRequest.readyState==4){
   if(xmlHttpRequest.status==200){

     processResponse();

   }
 }
}

function processResponse(){

var xmlMessage=xmlHttpRequest.responseXML;

var valid=xmlMessage.getElementsByTagName("valid")[0].firstChild.nodeValue;

if(valid=="true"){
```

```
var validationMessage=document.getElementById("validationMessage");
validationMessage.innerHTML = "Catalog ID is Valid";
document.getElementById("submitForm").disabled = false;

var journalElement=document.getElementById("journal");
journalElement.value = "";

var publisherElement=document.getElementById("publisher");
publisherElement.value = "";

var editionElement=document.getElementById("edition");
editionElement.value = "";

var titleElement=document.getElementById("title");
titleElement.value = "";

var authorElement=document.getElementById("author");
authorElement.value = "";
}
if(valid=="false"){

var validationMessage=document.getElementById("validationMessage");
validationMessage.innerHTML = "Catalog ID is not Valid";
document.getElementById("submitForm").disabled = true;

var journal=xmlMessage.getElementsByTagName("journal")[0].firstChild.nodeValue;
var publisher=xmlMessage.getElementsByTagName("publisher")[0].firstChild.nodeValue;
var edition=xmlMessage.getElementsByTagName("edition")[0].firstChild.nodeValue;
var title=xmlMessage.getElementsByTagName("title")[0].firstChild.nodeValue;
var author=xmlMessage.getElementsByTagName("author")[0].firstChild.nodeValue;

var journalElement=document.getElementById("journal");
journalElement.value = journal;

var publisherElement=document.getElementById("publisher");
publisherElement.value = publisher;

var editionElement=document.getElementById("edition");
editionElement.value = edition;

var titleElement=document.getElementById("title");
titleElement.value = title;

var authorElement=document.getElementById("author");
authorElement.value = author;
  }
 }
}
```

```
</script>

</head>
<body>
<h1>Form for Catalog Entry</h1>
<form name="validationForm" action="validateForm" method="post">
<table>
<tr><td>Catalog ID:</td><td><input     type="text"
          size="20"
           id="catalogId"
          name="catalogId"
    autocomplete="off"
        onkeyup="validateCatalogId()"></td>
        <td><div id="validationMessage"></div></td>
</tr>


<tr><td>Journal:</td><td><input     type="text"
          size="20"
           id="journal"
          name="journal"></td>
</tr>

<tr><td>Publisher:</td><td><input     type="text"
          size="20"
           id="publisher"
          name="publisher"></td>
</tr>

<tr><td>Edition:</td><td><input     type="text"
          size="20"
           id="edition"
          name="edition"></td>
</tr>
<tr><td>Title:</td><td><input     type="text"
          size="20"
           id="title"
          name="title"></td>
</tr>

<tr><td>Author:</td><td><input     type="text"
          size="20"
           id="author"
          name="author"></td>
</tr>

<tr><td><input     type="submit"
          value="Create Catalog"
           id="submitForm"
          name="submitForm"></td>
```

```
</tr>
</table>

</form>

</body>
</html>
```

Listing 13-18 shows the page to which inputForm.jsp is forwarded when there is no error when updating the database.

Listing 13-18. *catalog.jsp*

```
<html>
<head>

</head>
<body>
<%out.println("Database Updated");%>

</body>
</html>
```

Listing 13-19 shows the page to which inputForm.jsp is forwarded where there is an error when updating the database.

Listing 13-19. *error.jsp*

```
<html>
<head>

</head>
<body>
<%out.println("Error in updating Database");%>

</body>
</html>
```

You need to deploy the Ajax web application to the JBoss application server and access the application from your browser.

When the build.xml script is run in Eclipse, an ajax.war web application gets copied to the deploy directory of the JBoss application server. We showed how to run the build.xml file in Eclipse in the "Setting Up the Eclipse Project" section.

Now you are ready to start the JBoss application server using the < jboss-4.0.2>/bin/run.bat (or run.sh for Unix and Linux) file. The ajax.war web application gets deployed in the JBoss application server. To test the web application, you need to go to http://localhost:8080/ajax/inputForm.jsp in your browser. The inputForm.jsp returns the web page shown in Figure 13-4.

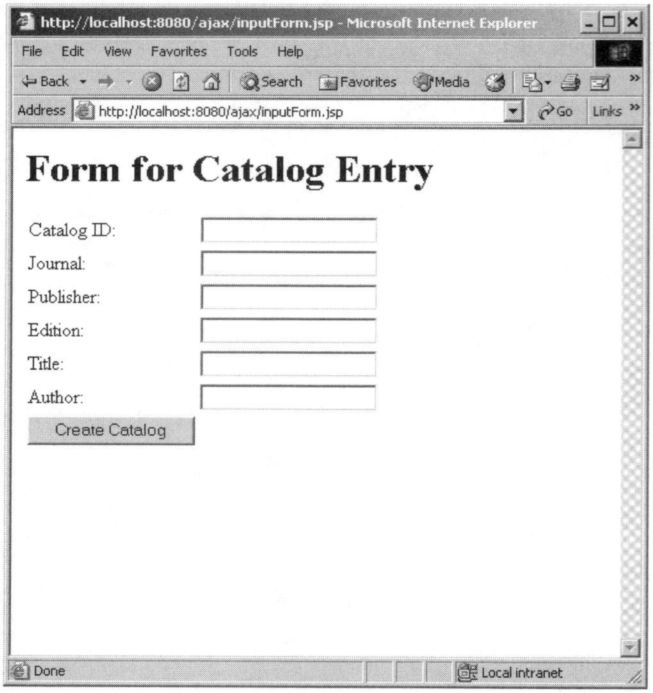

Figure 13-4. *Catalog entry input form*

To validate a catalog ID value, specify a catalog ID field value. An HTTP request gets sent to the server, and the XML response is returned to the browser-based user interface. If the catalog ID field value is valid, the message "Catalog ID is Valid" gets displayed, as shown in Figure 13-5.

If a catalog ID field value is specified that is not valid, the message "Catalog ID is not Valid" appears, and the Create Catalog button gets disabled, as shown in Figure 13-6. Also, the field values for the catalog ID appear.

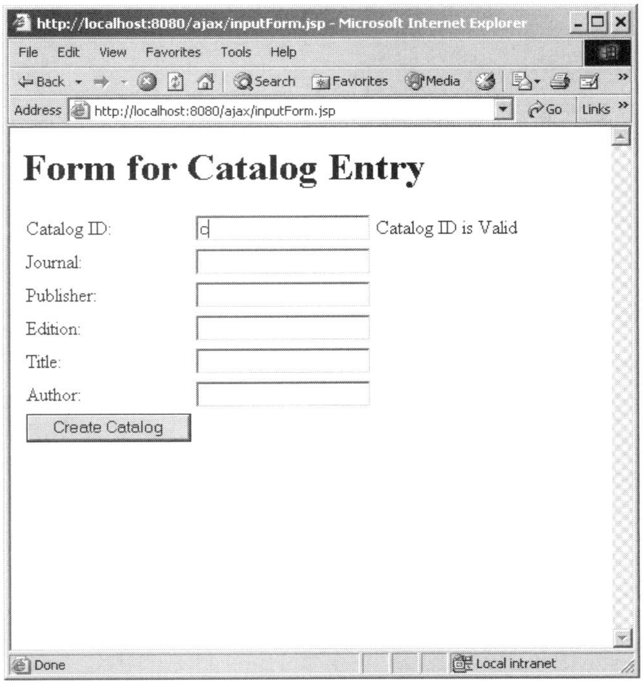

Figure 13-5. *Specifying the catalog ID field value*

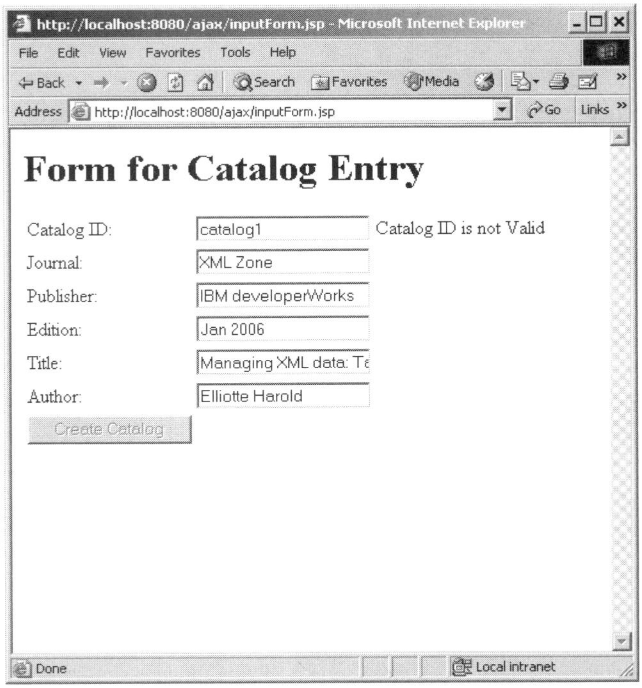

Figure 13-6. *Validating the input field catalog ID*

To create a catalog entry, enter a valid catalog ID, and click the Create Catalog button, as shown in Figure 13-7.

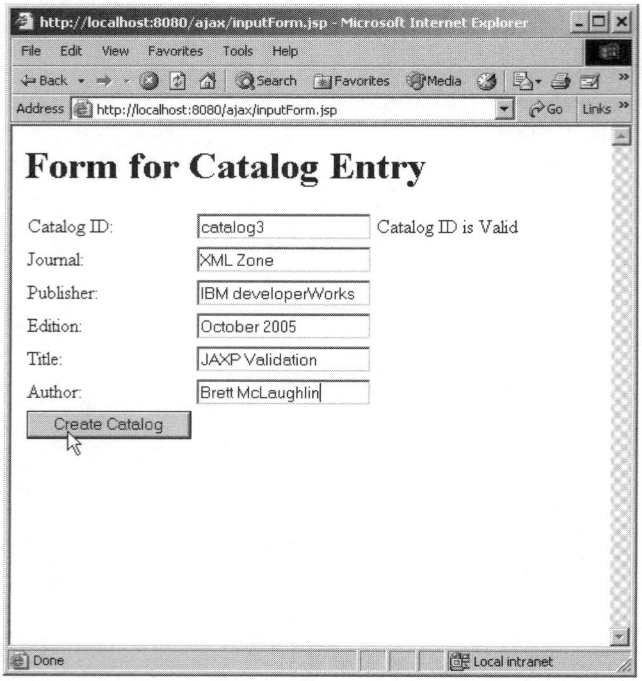

Figure 13-7. *Creating a catalog entry*

This creates a catalog entry in the database. If you retype a catalog ID value that was previously used to create a catalog entry, the message catalog ID that is not valid gets displayed dynamically, without even submitting the form, as shown in Figure 13-8. This is of course because while you are typing in the catalog ID form field, the data is being asynchronously validated with the server, and as soon as the data you type matches an existing catalog ID, the message "Catalog ID is not Valid" is displayed.

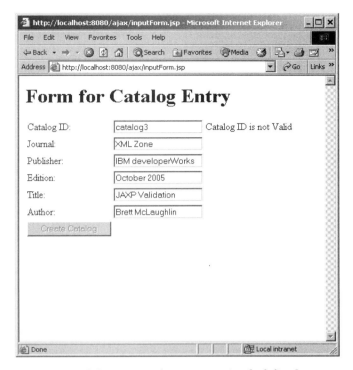

Figure 13-8. *Validating a catalog entry previously defined*

Summary

Ajax allows you to refresh the content of a web page dynamically without posting the web page to the server. You can implement Ajax web techniques by combining the XML DOM, JavaScript, and XMLHttpRequest technologies. W3C has introduced a Working Draft of the XMLHttpRequest object to standardize the technology. Ajax has various helpful uses such as form validation, autocompletion, and data refreshes on a web page periodically. You implemented one of these applications, dynamic form validation, in this chapter.

■ ■ ■

CHAPTER 14

Building XML-Based Web Services

When you want to buy a book from Amazon,[1] you go to Amazon's website, find your book, and order it. That is simple enough. Now, imagine you are an organization that orders lots of books from Amazon, such as a large university library. You could certainly do your book selection manually. However, what if Amazon offered a network service that a computer program could use to automatically search, select, and add books to a shopping cart based on your selection criteria? It turns out that Amazon indeed offers such a service!

In general, such network services are called *web services*.

The *raison d'etre* for web services is *interoperability* between loosely coupled applications. By *loosely coupled*, we mean that the interacting applications are stand-alone applications and that the interaction between applications happens via standards-based protocols.

This chapter pulls together a number of concepts from the entire book and presents a real-world web service example. One of the challenges of presenting a real-world example is that the technologies used in building it cannot be neatly circumscribed under topics covered in one book. Therefore, it should not come as a surprise that this real-world web service example is at least peripherally based on technologies beyond the scope of this book. We will, of course, let you know when we are dealing with such technologies, and offer suggestions about where you can learn more about them.

Buckle up. It is going to be a bumpy ride!

Overview of Web Services

We started this book by noting that XML is a platform-independent means of representing structured textual information, which makes it an ideal vehicle for exchanging information between loosely coupled software applications. Since web services are essentially a standards-based approach to interoperability, it is only natural that web services use XML in many aspects.

This chapter's discussion of web services is based on the following W3C Recommendations and Notes and other interoperability standards:

- XML-based technologies solve key technological issues of the web services architecture. XML 1.0, XML Schema, and XPath 1.0, all of which we covered in Part 1 of this book, play a foundational role in the web services technologies.

- SOAP 1.1[2] defines an XML-based messaging framework for web services interaction. SOAP 1.2[3] is the latest version of this messaging framework. In this chapter, we will primarily cover SOAP 1.1. However, we will note the differences between SOAP 1.1 and SOAP 1.2.

---

1. Amazon is an online seller of books and other merchandise at `http://www.amazon.com`.
2. The SOAP 1.1 W3C Note is available at `http://www.w3.org/TR/2000/NOTE-SOAP-20000508/`.
3. The SOAP 1.2 W3C Recommendation is available at `http://www.w3.org/TR/soap12`.

- SOAP Messages with Attachments[4] defines how a SOAP 1.1 message is to be carried within a Multipurpose Internet Mail Extensions (MIME) multipart-related message so that the normal SOAP 1.1 message processing is preserved. We will cover SOAP Messages with Attachments in this chapter.

- WSDL 1.1[5] is an XML-based language for formally describing web services. At the time of writing this book, WSDL 1.1 is in widespread use, and WSDL 2.0 is a Candidate Recommendation. In this chapter, we will confine our coverage to WSDL 1.1.

- Despite WSDL 1.1 and SOAP 1.1, *interoperability* between applications using web services is still a problem. To alleviate this problem, the Web Services Interoperability (WS-I) organization has defined the Basic Profile (BP)[6] 1.1 specification that attempts to clarify web services-related W3C Notes and Recommendations. We will cover WS-I BP 1.1 in this chapter.

- Universal Description, Discovery, and Integration (UDDI) is a WS-I BP 1.1–endorsed registry for web services. A UDDI registry is analogous to the telephone white pages or yellow pages. Applications can query a UDDI registry about a specific web service (like you query an online white pages website) and, in response, obtain the location of a WSDL 1.1 document (like you get a phone number from a white pages query) that formally describes the web service. Web service registration and discovery using UDDI is an advanced topic and is beyond the scope of this book. However, we will discuss UDDI in the context of the web services architecture.

All the web service–related Notes and Recommendations covered in this chapter are supported in the Java API for XML-Based Web Services (JAX-WS) 2.0[7] specification, which is implemented in Java Platform Enterprise Edition[8] (Java EE) version 5. In particular, JAX-WS 2.0 supports SOAP 1.1, SOAP Messages with Attachments, WSDL 1.1, and WS-I BP 1.1.

Understanding the Web Services Architecture

In the following sections, we will discuss the overall web services architecture, first defining basic web service concepts and then covering various web service architectural models.

Basic Web Service Concepts

You will start by looking at some basic web service concepts that will help you understand the rest of this discussion.

Web Service Client Perspective

From a client perspective, a web service has the following key aspects:

- A web service is formally described through a WSDL 1.1 document. We will cover in detail what is in a WSDL 1.1 document in the "Understanding WSDL 1.1" section, but for now, it is sufficient to understand that a WSDL document defines an interface for a web service. For example, an Amazon web service has its formal description available at `http://soap.amazon.com/schemas2/AmazonWebServices.wsdl`.

---

4. The Soap Messages with Attachments W3C Note is available at `http://www.w3.org/TR/SOAP-attachments`.
5. The WSDL 1.1 W3C Note is available at `http://www.w3.org/TR/wsdl`.
6. The WS-I Basic Profile 1.1 specification is available at `http://www.ws-i.org/Profiles/BasicProfile-1.1.html`.
7. More information about JAX-WS 2.0 is available at `http://www.jcp.org/en/jsr/detail?id=224`.
8. Java EE is available at `http://java.sun.com/javaee/`.

- The web service network address defines a location where a web service is available on the network; this location is specified as an HTTP URL. For example, the network address of an Amazon web service is `http://soap.amazon.com/onca/soap2`.

- Client applications that want to use the web service may discover the location of the WSDL 1.1 document through a UDDI registry, or through other means, such as direct input.

- Client applications interact with the web service using SOAP 1.1 messages transported within HTTP 1.0/1.1 messages.

Figure 14-1 shows web service interaction from a client perspective.

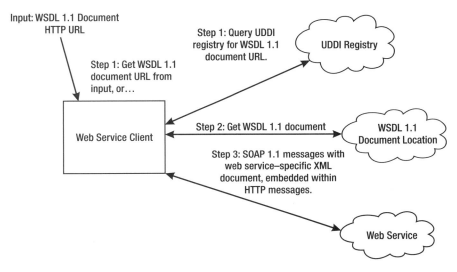

Figure 14-1. *Web service interaction from a client perspective*

Agents and Services

From a logical viewpoint, a web service endpoint can be split into two parts:

- The first part is the *service endpoint interface* (SEI). The SEI is the web service contract with its clients, analogous to a Java interface.

- The second part is the *agent*. The agent is a concrete software implementation of the SEI, analogous to a Java class implementing a Java interface.

Providers and Requestors

A web service is provided by a provider entity. A *provider entity* can be an individual or an organization. A provider entity provides the web service through a *provider agent*. A provider agent is a concrete software implementation of the web service SEI. For example, if Amazon provides a web service, Amazon is the provider entity.

A web service is used by a *requestor entity*. A requestor entity can be an individual or an organization. A requestor entity uses the web service through a *requestor agent*. A requestor agent is a software component that uses the web service's WSDL 1.1 document–based description to interact with the web service. For example, any entity using Amazon's web service would be the requestor entity.

You can implement both the provider agent and the requestor agent using the JAX-WS 2.0 APIs.

Service Description

A provider entity describes a web service through a WSDL 1.1 document. You will learn about the details of a WSDL 1.1 document in the section "Understanding WSDL 1.1." For now, it is sufficient to understand that a WSDL 1.1 document is capable of formally describing a service interface and includes the endpoint HTTP URI address of the provider agent.

Service Semantics

It is important to note that the WSDL 1.1 document does not define service semantics. Service semantics are defined either implicitly or explicitly through a verbal or written exchange between a provider entity and a requestor entity. In some cases, the service semantics may be defined as a legally binding contract between a provider entity and a requestor entity.

Web Service Architectural Models

The web services architecture is a multifaceted architecture. To simplify things, it is best to examine each facet of this architecture in the context of a separate architectural model. So, we will cover the following three web service architectural models individually:

- The message-oriented model
- The service-oriented model
- The resource-oriented model

Message-Oriented Model

All interaction between a web service and its client is based on the exchange of XML content encapsulated within SOAP 1.1 messages, which are transported inside HTTP 1.0/1.1 messages. The message-oriented model is focused on the structure, processing, and transmission of these XML-based messages. However, this model is not concerned with the web service–specific content of a SOAP 1.1 message or the semantics of a Web-based service. Looking through the prism of a message-oriented model, you can observe the following key points:

- All agent-to-agent conversations during the use of a web service are built upon a one-way exchange of a SOAP 1.1 message between a sender agent and a receiver agent. Of course, the receiver at one moment can become a sender the next moment.

- A SOAP 1.1 message is contained in an envelope. Each envelope contains an optional header and a required body.

- A SOAP 1.1 message travels between a sender and a receiver over an HTTP message transport. The reliable delivery of a message is the concern of the message transport.

- A receiver must have a unique HTTP URI address so a sender can uniquely identify the receiver.

- You can define complex web service message exchange patterns on top of the basic one-way exchange pattern.

  Figure 14-2 summarizes the message-oriented model.

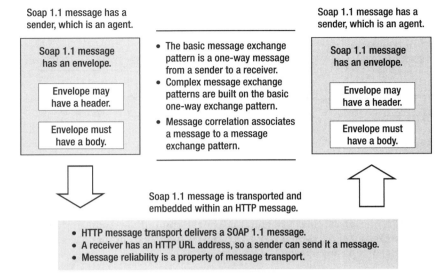

Figure 14-2. *Message-oriented model*

It is possible to build complex message exchange patterns based on the simple one-way exchange pattern described in Figure 14-2. The most obvious message exchange pattern that follows naturally from the one-way exchange pattern is the request-response pattern. Figure 14-3 shows both the one-way pattern and the request-response pattern.

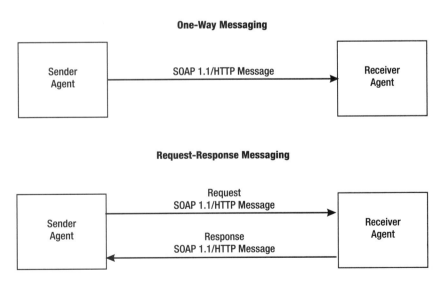

Figure 14-3. *Message exchange patterns*

The simple two-node patterns can be extended to multiple nodes, where a message travels from an initial sender to an ultimate receiver through a number of intermediate nodes, as shown in Figure 14-4.

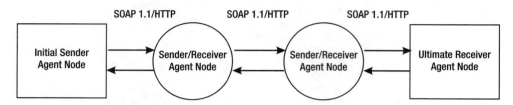

Figure 14-4. *Request-response messaging with intermediate agent nodes*

The message-oriented model is the closest abstraction of physical reality, because a web service interaction is essentially an exchange of XML documents encapsulated in SOAP 1.1 messages, which are transported inside HTTP messages. However, it may not be the appropriate model from the point of view of abstracting the essential elements of a web service interface. For that, the service-oriented model exists, which we discuss next.

The Service-Oriented Model

In the service-oriented model, the focus is on the service provided by a provider agent and used by a requestor agent. From the perspective of this model, you focus on the following aspects of a web service:

- A provider agent implements all the operations defined by the web service SEI.

- A requestor agent uses a service proxy to invoke an SEI operation, which, depending on the operation, may return nothing, a response, or one or more faults.

Figure 14-5 summarizes the service-oriented model.

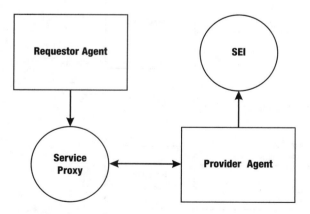

Figure 14-5. *The service-oriented model*

This model is fairly simple to understand, but from a practical point of view, it says nothing about how a requestor agent discovers or addresses the service provider agent. For that you need to focus on the resource-oriented model, which is covered next.

Resource-Oriented Model

From this model's perspective, a web service is a resource that can be consumed by a web service client. Essential aspects of this model are as follows:

- A web service is a network-based resource identifiable through an HTTP URI.
- A web service resource is described through a WSDL 1.1 document.
- A web service resource may be registered with a UDDI registry.
- A web service resource may be discovered by querying a UDDI registry, as shown in Figure 14-1.

Now, you are ready to examine the details associated with the web service messaging framework, WSDL, client-service interaction, and the JAX-WS 2.0 APIs that implement a complete web service client-side and service-side protocol stack.

However, it is best to do all this in the context of example use case scenarios. So, in the next section, we will explain the example use case scenarios that will provide a practical framework for our discussion of SOAP 1.1, SOAP Message with Attachments, WSDL 1.1, and JAX-WS 2.0.

Example Use Case Scenarios

Imagine you want to build a document storage website. Naturally, users would expect to be able to upload their documents to this website and retrieve them later, using a browser-based user interface.

However, you survey prospective and current users and find that in addition to a browser-based user interface, they want a web service that will allow computer programs to interact with this website. You give the issue some thought, and you come with the following four use case scenarios for this web service:

- Uploading documents to a project
- Downloading documents from a project
- Getting information about all the projects owned by a user
- Removing documents from a project

You'll now examine each use case in detail.

Uploading Documents to a Project

The first use case is uploading documents to a project under your account. In this use case scenario, a ZIP file and a manifest file are sent to the web service for uploading the documents in the ZIP file into a project in your account.

The motivation for this scenario is a program that could be configured to do the following:

1. Automatically select a set of documents from your desktop.
2. Zip the documents into a ZIP file.
3. Add a manifest to the ZIP file.
4. Upload the ZIP file documents into a project in your account, using the web service.

The manifest file will contain information about documents in the ZIP file that need to be put into the project. The web service will do the following:

1. Add documents specified within the manifest to the requested project in your account.

2. If no such project exists, the web service will create one automatically; the same rule applies to any folders under the project.

3. Once the documents are uploaded into a project, the web service will respond with a manifest that shows up-to-date contents of the updated project.

Downloading Documents from a Project

The second use case is downloading documents from a project. In this use case scenario, the following happens:

1. A manifest file specifying what you want to download from a project is sent to the web service.

2. The web service is expected to respond with a ZIP file that contains the requested documents.

The motivation for this scenario is a program that could be configured to automatically send a request manifest to the web service with a request for documents to be downloaded and then unzip the returned ZIP file.

Getting Information About All Projects

The third use case provides information about the contents of all the projects owned by a user. The requested information can be restricted to just a list of projects, just a list of folders within all the projects, or information about all the documents in all the projects.

Removing Documents from a Project

The fourth use case is the ability to delete documents from a project. Again, the information of what to delete is sent in a manifest file; in this case, no response is expected.

Finally, for security reasons, all requests carry your email and password.

Now you are ready to look at the SOAP 1.1 messaging framework that will convey the web service interaction messages related to the example use case scenarios.

Understanding the SOAP 1.1 Messaging Framework

We will discuss how to build the web service for the use case scenarios in the "Using JAX-WS 2.0" section. For now, imagine that a provider agent for the web service already exists and a requestor agent (web service client) that can use this web service also already exists. All web service interaction is, of course, SOAP 1.1 messaging. So, what do these SOAP 1.1 messages look like? We will go into the SOAP 1.1 messaging details shortly; for now we'll provide a simple example of the SOAP 1.1 message exchange.

Simple SOAP 1.1 Message Exchange

In this example, you will see a complete request-response message exchange pattern in the context of the third use case, getting information from all projects. We are discussing the third use case because it is complex enough that we can show a nontrivial exchange, yet it is simple enough so as to not overwhelm you.

Request Message

Imagine that the web service client requests information about all the projects owned by a user but restricts the information detail to just project names. Listing 14-1 shows the complete SOAP 1.1 request message for this use case.

Listing 14-1. *SOAP 1.1 Request Message for Third Use Case*

```
<?xml version="1.0" ?>
<soapenv:Envelope
  xmlns:ns1="http://www.apress.com/xmljava/webservices/schemas"
  xmlns:ns2="http://www.apress.com/xmljava/webservices/definitions"
  xmlns:soapenv="http://schemas.xmlsoap.org/soap/envelope/"
  xmlns:xsd="http://www.w3.org/2001/XMLSchema" >

  <soapenv:Header>
    <ns1:userInfo>
      <email>foo@acme.com</email>
      <pwd>bar</pwd>
    </ns1:userInfo>
  </soapenv:Header>

  <soapenv:Body>
    <ns1:projectsDetail>
      <folders>false</folders>
      <documents>false</documents>
    </ns1:projectsDetail>
  </soapenv:Body>

</soapenv:Envelope>
```

If you examine the message in Listing 14-1 from an intuitive standpoint, you may notice the following points:

- Apparently, the soapenv prefix associated with the http://schemas.xmlsoap.org/soap/envelope/ namespace defines SOAP 1.1 constructs.

- The root element is soapenv:Envelope, and it contains two subelements: soapenv:Header and soapenv:Body.

- You may notice that the soapenv:Header element has a single child element named ns1:userInfo, which is qualified with the ns1 prefix in the http://www.apress.com/xmljava/webservices/schemas namespace. The child elements of ns1:userInfo contain email (foo@acme.com) and password (bar) information related to the user.

- You may notice that the soapenv:Body element has a single child element named ns1:projectsDetail. The child elements of ns1:projectsDetail appear to be boolean switches that indicate you do not want any information about folders (<folders>false</folders>) or documents (<documents>false</documents>) within the projects, which conforms with your intent of getting information about project names owned by the user.

Operation

At this point you may be wondering when the provider agent receives this message, how does it know what operation this message is requesting since, apparently, nowhere in the message does it say that the requestor wants information about all projects that a user owns?

From an intuitive standpoint, the answer to this question is that the provider deciphers the operation requested by a message by looking at the content of the soapenv:Body element, which in Listing 14-1 is a single ns1:projectsDetail element.

Since the content of the soapenv:Body element implies a specific operation, the content must be unique across all types of messages received by this web service. For example, you cannot have another use case within the example web service that receives a message with a single ns1:projectsDetail element as the child element of the soapenv:Body element.

Response Message

Listing 14-2 shows the response to the request message in Listing 14-1.

Listing 14-2. *SOAP 1.1 Response Message for Third Use Case*

```
<?xml version="1.0" ?>
<soapenv:Envelope
  xmlns:ns1="http://www.apress.com/xmljava/webservices/schemas"
  xmlns:ns2="http://www.apress.com/xmljava/webservices/definitions"
  xmlns:soapenv="http://schemas.xmlsoap.org/soap/envelope/"
  xmlns:xsd="http://www.w3.org/2001/XMLSchema" >

  <soapenv:Body>
    <ns1:projects>
      <project createdOn="2006-06-27T19:00:35.046-04:00"
        email="foo@acme.com"
        lastUpdated="2006-06-27T19:00:35.187-04:00"
        name="testproject.zip" />
    </ns1:projects>
  </soapenv:Body>

</soapenv:Envelope>
```

If you examine the response message, again from an intuitive standpoint, you may notice the following points:

- The response message has no soapenv:Header element. This suggests the soapenv:Header element must be optional in a SOAP 1.1 message, which it is.

- The response message soapenv:Body has an ns1:projects child element, which presumably is a list of all the projects.

- The ns1:projects element has a single ns1:project child element with name equal to testproject.zip. It also shows additional information about when the project was created (createdOn) and last updated (lastUpdated). Presumably, foo@acme.com owns the project.

Having looked at an example SOAP 1.1 message exchange based on the request-response message pattern, you are ready to learn more about SOAP 1.1 messaging.

SOAP 1.1 Messaging (WS-I BP 1.1)

In this section, you will examine SOAP 1.1 messaging details but *filtered through WS-I BP 1.1*. In our opinion, there is no point in ignoring WS-I BP 1.1, since the whole idea behind using web services is interoperability.

SOAP 1.1 is an XML-based messaging framework for exchanging structured information between peer nodes in a network-based distributed environment. SOAP is designed to be extensible. By *extensible*, we mean that higher-level services, such as security or transactions, can be layered upon the basic SOAP messaging framework, without having to change the underlying structural rules for a SOAP message. SOAP implies no particular semantic model. Because it is XML-based, is extensible, and implies no particular semantic model, it's ideal for use in web services messaging.

For the purpose of this discussion, we will associate the soapenv prefix with the http://schemas.xmlsoap.org/soap/envelope/ namespace, keeping in mind of course that the choice of the soapenv prefix is completely arbitrary.

Basic Concepts

The most important concepts of the SOAP 1.l messaging framework are as follows:

- A SOAP 1.1 message is a one-way message, going from an initial sender to an ultimate receiver, possibly via intermediate nodes.
- A SOAP 1.1 message is contained in an envelope.
- The envelope contains an optional header and a mandatory body.
- The header child elements, also known as *header blocks*, can be targeted at anybody along the message path.
- The application data is contained as well-formed XML content within the body element.
- The body content is generally targeted at the ultimate receiver.

You'll take a closer look inside a SOAP 1.1 message.

SOAP 1.1 Envelope

A SOAP 1.1 message is an XML document with soapenv:Envelope as its root element. The structure of a SOAP 1.1 message XML document that conforms to WS-I BP 1.1 must adhere to the following rules:

- The document must not contain any processing instructions or a document type declaration. If you are not sure what these are, review the XML primer in Chapter 1.
- The soapenv:Envelope element should not contain the namespace declaration xmlns:xml="http://www.w3.org/XML/1998/namespace".
- soapenv:Envelope can have an optional soapenv:Header child element. If present, soapenv:Header must be the first immediate child of the soapenv:Envelope element. All immediate child elements of soapenv:Header must be namespace qualified.
- soapenv:Envelope must have a mandatory soapenv:Body element. It must follow the soapenv:Header element if the soapenv:Header element is present, or it must be the first immediate child of the soapenv:Envelope element. Immediate child elements of the soapenv:Body element must be namespace qualified.
- soapenv:Body must be the last child element of the soapenv:Envelope element.
- soapenv:Envelope, soapenv:Header, and soapenv:Body must not contain any attributes qualified in the http://schemas.xmlsoap.org/soap/envelope/ namespace.

The SOAP 1.1 messages shown in Listings 14-1 and 14-2 are examples of WS-I BP 1.1–conformant messages.

SOAP 1.1 Encoding Style

The header blocks and the `soapenv:Body` content can be whatever the web service requires, as long as the header blocks and the `soapenv:Body` content are namespace qualified and are, of course, well-formed XML.

This raises the obvious question, how should the header blocks and the `soapenv:Body` content be encoded? The answer, as per WS-I BP 1.1, is simple: neither the header blocks nor the `soapenv:Body` content should be encoded. WS-I BPI 1.1 prohibits the use of any encoding style, including SOAP 1.1 encoding.[9]

All header blocks and `soapenv:Body` content must be serialized literally, which means the header blocks and `soapenv:Body` content must conform to a schema definition. In case you are wondering, does this lack of an encoding style limit the ability of web services in any way? The answer, simply, is no. In fact, the only reason for the existence of SOAP 1.1 encoding is that at the time the SOAP 1.1 W3C Note was being composed, the XML Schema language was not completed.

The detailed rules related to encoding are as follows:

- Any element in the `http://schemas.xmlsoap.org/soap/envelope/` namespace must not contain the `soapenv:encodingStyle` attribute.

- Any immediate child or grandchild of the `soapenv:Body` element must not contain any `soapenv:encodingStyle` attribute.

Now you are ready to take a closer look at each of the `soapenv:Envelope` child elements.

SOAP 1.1 Header

The main purpose of the `soapenv:Header` element is extensibility. Web services need different types of capabilities that overlay the basic web services interaction. These capabilities could be services related to security,[10] transaction management, or orchestration of complex business processes based on elementary web services. Information related to these capabilities resides in the child elements of the `soapenv:Header` element; these immediate child elements are called *header blocks*.

In the following discussion, keep in mind that multiple intermediate nodes may process a SOAP 1.1 message, before it reaches the ultimate receiver, as shown in Figure 14-4. The intermediate nodes act as receivers as well as senders, switching their status as needed. In fact, these intermediate nodes and the ultimate receiver collaborate to implement capabilities such as security or transaction management.

This raises the obvious question, if the information related to these infrastructure services is carried within the `soapenv:Header` header blocks, then how is an intermediate node recipient to know what header blocks are intended for it, as opposed to some other node along the message path? This is where header attributes, which are described next, enter the picture.

Header Attributes

SOAP 1.1 defines certain attributes that can be associated only with header blocks to indicate how a recipient of this message should process the associated header blocks. These attributes are as follows:

---

9. The SOAP 1.1 encoding rules are part of SOAP 1.1 Recommendation (`http://www.w3.org/TR/2000/NOTE-SOAP-20000508/`).

10. The WS-Security 1.1 OASIS standard is an example of an extensible capability added to support all aspects of security (`http://www.oasis-open.org/committees/tc_home.php?wg_abbrev=wss`).

- The `soapenv:actor` attribute on the header block indicates the logical function or role that the recipient must play in processing this header block. If an intermediate recipient node understands the specified role, then the header block is intended for its consumption.

- The `soapenv:mustUnderstand` attribute on a header block indicates whether, assuming the recipient fits the role specified by the `soapenv:actor` attribute, the processing of a particular header child element is mandatory by a recipient.

The soapenv:actor Attribute The value of a `soapenv:actor` attribute is a URI that indicates the logical role that the recipient must assume in processing the associated header block. A special URI, `http://schemas.xmlsoap.org/soap/actor/next/`, denotes the logical role of being the `next` node along the message path. Omitting this attribute implies that this child element should be processed by the ultimate receiver.

Consider the following example `soapenv:Header` element:

```
<soapenv:Header>
    <ns1:userInfo
      soapenv:actor="http:// www.apress.com/xmljava/webservices/auth">
      <email>foo@acme.com</email>
      <pwd>bar</pwd>
    </ns1:userInfo>
  </soapenv:Header>
```

This example `soapenv:Header` element has a single header block, `ns1:userInfo`, which has a `soapenv:actor` attribute set to the `http://www.apress.com/xmljava/webservices/auth` URI. This means if a recipient fits the implied role associated with the specified URI, it is expected to process the `ns1:userInfo` header block.

An intermediate node that processes a header block must remove the header block from the `soapenv:Header` element. If an intermediate node processes a header block but also wants the header block to be processed by another node along the message path, it may modify and add the header block to the `soapenv:Header` element. You can remove and then add a header block simply by modifying the header block in place.

The soapenv:mustUnderstand Attribute This attribute can have a value of only 0 or 1. Omitting this attribute implies a value of 0. If this attribute is specified on a header block with the value 1, it means that if the recipient can assume the role implied by the `soapenv:actor` attribute of the header block, then the recipient must process the header block.

Consider the following revised example `soapenv:Header` element that you saw earlier:

```
<soapenv:Header>
    <ns1:userInfo
      soapenv:mustUnderstand="1"
      soapenv:actor="http://www.apress.com/xmljava/webservices/auth">
      <email>foo@acme.com</email>
      <pwd>bar</pwd>
    </ns1:userInfo>
  </soapenv:Header>
```

If the recipient of this message can assume the `http://www.apress.com/xmljava/webservices/auth` role (whatever that means semantically), it must process the `ns1:userInfo` header block. We will discuss in the "SOAP 1.1 Processing Model" section what must happen if a recipient is unable to live up to such an obligation.

SOAP 1.1 Body

Other than that all the immediate child elements of the soapenv:Body element must be namespace qualified and be well-formed XML elements, they can contain whatever content the web service deems appropriate; SOAP 1.1 has nothing to say on this issue. Recall that, as per WS-I BP 1.1, no encoding scheme, including SOAP 1.1 encoding, is allowed in these child elements. All soapenv:Body child elements must conform to a schema definition.

SOAP 1.1 Fault

The soapenv:Fault element, if it occurs, must be an immediate child element of the soapenv:Body element, and it must not occur more than once. It is designed to indicate error or status information related to SOAP 1.1 message processing. A soapenv:Fault element can have only the subelements shown in Table 14-1; these elements should not be namespace qualified because they are local to the soapenv:Fault element.

Table 14-1. *SOAP 1.1 Fault Subelements*

Fault Subelement	Value	Mandatory?	Description
faultcode	Namespace-qualified name	Yes	This is intended to be consumed programmatically. SOAP 1.1 defines special fault codes, which are shown in Table 14-2.
faultstring	Text	Yes	This is a human-readable description of fault, not intended for programmatic consumption.
faultfactor	URI	Mandatory for intermediate nodes	This identifies the source of fault.
detail	Element	Mandatory if fault is because of processing of the soapenv:Body element	It must contain information related only to the error in processing the soapenv:Body element; it must not contain information related to the error in processing the soapenv:Header element. It can contain zero or more subelements that may or may not be namespace qualified. It may have zero or more attributes. Subelements and attributes must not be in the http://schemas.xmlsoap.org/soap/envelope/ namespace.

Table 14-2 shows the special SOAP 1.1 fault codes; all these fault codes are in the http://schemas.xmlsoap.org/soap/envelope/ namespace.

Table 14-2. *SOAP 1.1 Fault Codes*

Name	Description
VersionMismatch	The SOAP envelope has an invalid namespace, meaning something other than `http://schemas.xmlsoap.org/soap/envelope/`.
MustUnderstand	The `soapenv:mustUnderstand` value is set to 1 on a `soapenv:Header` child element and the recipient fits the `soapenv:actor` role associated with the child element, but the recipient does not understand how to process the child element.
Client	Message processing failed because the client sent incorrect information. The client must not resend the same information again.
Server	Message processing failed because the server, for whatever reason, was not able to successfully process the message.

As an example of a SOAP 1.1 fault message, if you were to type the Amazon web service `http://soap.amazon.com/onca/soap2` URL in a browser, you would see the SOAP fault message shown in Listing 14-3 returned. Try it!

Listing 14-3. *SOAP Fault Message Example*

```
<?xml version="1.0" encoding="UTF-8" ?>
<SOAP-ENV:Envelope
    xmlns:SOAP-ENC="http://schemas.xmlsoap.org/soap/encoding/"
    SOAP-ENV:encodingStyle="http://schemas.xmlsoap.org/soap/encoding/"
    xmlns:SOAP-ENV="http://schemas.xmlsoap.org/soap/envelope/"
    xmlns:xsi="http://www.w3.org/1999/XMLSchema-instance"
    xmlns:xsd="http://www.w3.org/1999/XMLSchema">
    <SOAP-ENV:Body>
        <SOAP-ENV:Fault>
            <faultcode xsi:type="xsd:string">SOAP-ENV:Client</faultcode>
            <faultstring xsi:type="xsd:string">Bad Request</faultstring>
            <detail xsi:type="xsd:string">The request contains no SOAP message.</detail>
        </SOAP-ENV:Fault>
    </SOAP-ENV:Body>
</SOAP-ENV:Envelope>
```

The returned fault in Listing 14-3 makes perfect sense, because if you type the web service URL in a browser, all you are doing is sending a simple HTTP GET message containing no SOAP 1.1 message inside it, whereas the web service is obviously expecting to receive an appropriately formatted SOAP 1.1 message.

Now you are ready to look at the SOAP 1.1 processing model.

SOAP 1.1 Processing Model

SOAP 1.1 defines only a simple one-way message exchange pattern, going from an initial sender to an ultimate receiver, possibly via intermediate nodes. However, more complex message patterns such as the request-response pattern can be built upon the one-way pattern. The message processing rules are as follows:

- Any intermediate node must process a header block, if the intermediate node can assume the `soapenv:actor` role specified for the header block and if the `soapenv:mustUnderstand` attribute for the header block is set to 1. Failure to process such a header block must return a `soapenv:Fault` message with a `soapenv:MustUnderstand` fault code subelement.

- Any intermediate node must remove header blocks processed by it, before forwarding the message to the next node along the message path. An intermediate node may of course add back a header block after processing and removing it, if it needs to target the header block at another node along the message path.

- The generally expected convention is that only the ultimate receiver is expected to process the `soapenv:Body` element, although there is nothing to that effect in SOAP 1.1 or in WS-I BP 1.1. If you choose to violate this convention, consider its implications carefully.

- A SOAP 1.1 fault can be returned only if a response is expected. If any node returns a fault, that fault must be propagated back to the initial sender, in place of a response.

In the next section, you will look at the important differences between SOAP 1.1 and SOAP 1.2.

SOAP 1.2 and SOAP 1.1 Differences

Remember, WS-I BP 1.1 does not explicitly support SOAP 1.2, so we do not recommend it at this point. However, at some point in the near future, it will be widely adopted, so it is important to familiarize yourself with the general differences between SOAP 1.1 and SOAP 1.2.

The most notable difference between SOAP 1.1 and SOAP 1.2 is that the SOAP 1.2 processing model is much more explicit than the SOAP 1.1 processing model. In fact, SOAP 1.2 has adopted many of the processing model requirements specified in WS-I BP 1.1 to improve interoperability. So, from the point of view of improving interoperability, SOAP 1.2 is almost the same as SOAP 1.1 plus WS-I BP 1.1.

Other important differences between SOAP 1.1 and SOAP 1.2 are as follows:

- The most important difference is of course that SOAP 1.2 is associated with a new namespace: `http://www.w3.org/2003/05/soap-envelope`. This means a SOAP 1.1 node receiving a SOAP 1.2 message will generate a `VersionMismatch` SOAP fault. A SOAP 1.2 node may choose to process a SOAP 1.1 message as a SOAP 1.1 message or generate a `VersionMismatch` SOAP fault.

- SOAP 1.2 introduces the concept of SOAP *roles*. At a given point of time, a SOAP node assumes a specific SOAP 1.2 role, which is identified by a URI. Three special roles—`next`, `none`, and `ultimateReceiver`—are defined in SOAP 1.2; each of those roles is associated with a unique URI. The SOAP 1.2 `role` attribute replaces the SOAP 1.1 `actor` attribute for `Header` child elements. The importance of this change is that all along, the semantics associated with the SOAP 1.1 `actor` attribute were what one would normally ascribe to a role; SOAP 1.2 finally clarifies this issue by changing the name of the attribute to `role`.

- SOAP 1.2 introduces a `relay` attribute that can be associated with a `Header` child element. This `relay` attribute suggests rules for forwarding a `Header` child element at an intermediate node, if the `Header` child is not understood by the intermediate node and if the `mustUnderstand` attribute for the child element is not set to `true`.

Next, you will look at how SOAP 1.1 messages are carried within MIME multipart-related messages.

SOAP 1.1 Message with Attachments

You'll now revisit the use case scenarios to see what the request-response message exchange for the second use case, downloading a project, looks like. Listing 14-4 shows the request message for downloading a project.

Listing 14-4. *Downloading a Project SOAP 1.1 Request Message*

```
<?xml version="1.0" ?>
<soapenv:Envelope
  xmlns:ns1="http://www.apress.com/xmljava/webservices/schemas"
  xmlns:ns2="http://www.apress.com/xmljava/webservices/definitions"
  xmlns:soapenv="http://schemas.xmlsoap.org/soap/envelope/"
  xmlns:xsd="http://www.w3.org/2001/XMLSchema" >
  <soapenv:Header>
    <ns1:userInfo>
      <email>foo@acme.com</email>
      <pwd>bar</pwd>
    </ns1:userInfo>
  </soapenv:Header>

  <soapenv:Body>
    <ns1:project
createdOn="2006-06-28T20:51:23.937-04:00"
email="foo@acme.com"
lastUpdated="2006-06-28T20:51:23.968-04:00"
name="testproject.zip" >
    </ns1:project>
  </soapenv:Body>
</soapenv:Envelope>
```

Listing 14-5 shows the response message to the request message shown in Listing 14-4.

Listing 14-5. *Downloading a Project SOAP 1.1 Response Message*

```
------=_Part_2_16020374.1151542284234
Content-Type: text/xml; charset=utf-8

<?xml version="1.0" ?>
<soapenv:Envelope
    xmlns:soapenv="http://schemas.xmlsoap.org/soap/envelope/"
    xmlns:xsd="http://www.w3.org/2001/XMLSchema"
    xmlns:ns1="http://www.apress.com/xmljava/webservices/schemas"
    xmlns:ns2="http://www.apress.com/xmljava/webservices/definitions">
  <soapenv:Body>
    <ns1:manifest
        name="testproject.zip"
        lastUpdated="2006-06-28T20:51:23.968-04:00"
        email="ajay_vohra@yahoo.com"
        createdOn="2006-06-28T20:51:23.937-04:00">
      <folder
        location="popuptest/WEB-INF/"
        lastUpdated="2006-06-28T20:51:24.000-04:00"
        createdOn="2006-06-28T20:51:23.968-04:00">
        <document name="weblogic.xml"
        lastUpdated="2006-06-28T20:51:24.000-04:00"
        createdOn="2006-06-28T20:51:24.000-04:00">
        </document>
        <document
```

```
        name="web.xml"
        lastUpdated="2006-06-28T20:51:23.984-04:00"
        createdOn="2006-06-28T20:51:23.984-04:00">
          </document>
        </folder>
      </ns1:manifest>
    </soapenv:Body>
  </soapenv:Envelope>
  ------=_Part_2_16020374.1151542284234
  Content-Type: application/octet-stream
  Content-ID: <zip=38edc2fb-8e13-4a5d-b3cc-7452edd30ad6@jaxws.sun.com>
  Content-transfer-encoding: binary


  ------=_Part_2_16020374.1151542284234-
```

If you examine the response message in Listing 14-5, you'll notice it is a MIME multipart-related message. The first part contains a SOAP 1.1 message document, and the second part contains binary content (we have deleted the binary content from Listing 14-5) associated with downloaded ZIP file. The SOAP 1.1 message part and the related parts form a SOAP 1.1 message package. Within a SOAP 1.1 message package, a core part contains the SOAP 1.1 message, and one or more related parts contain attachments. In the "Understanding WSDL 1.1" section, you will see how an abstract WSDL 1.1 message definition is bound to a concrete MIME multipart-related message.

Understanding WSDL 1.1

Whenever you have to build a web service, the first step you need to take is to formally describe the web service in a WSDL 1.1 document. Although it is possible to reverse engineer a WSDL 1.1 document from Java classes, in our opinion, such reverse engineering is adequate only for building trivial web services, perhaps for quick prototyping. The reverse-engineering option seriously limits the flexibility you need to describe nontrivial, real-world web services. So, we will not discuss it any further in this chapter.

We describe the overall structure of a WSDL 1.1 document next.

WSDL 1.1 Document Structure

A WSDL 1.1 document is an XML document that conforms to the WSDL 1.1 schema, which is available at http://schemas.xmlsoap.org/wsdl/. The WSDL 1.1 schema location also defines the WSDL 1.1 namespace. Assuming the wsdl prefix for the WSDL 1.1 namespace, the root element of a WSDL 1.1 document is wsdl:definitions.

The wsdl:definitions element contains the following child elements:

- The wsdl:types element defines data type definitions using the XML Schema language. In other words, the XML content of wsdl:types element is a schema definition.

- The wsdl:message element defines an abstract message type used in web service interaction. Each wsdl:message consists of one or more wsdl:part elements, whereby each wsdl:part is based on either a schema element or a schema type, defined within wsdl:types. The wsdl:definitions element can contain one or more wsdl:message elements.

- The wsdl:portType element defines an abstract service interface. Each wsdl:portType element can contain one or more wsdl:operation elements. However, each wsdl:operation element within a wsdl:portType must have a unique value for its name attribute.

- A `wsdl:operation` element is an abstract definition of a service operation. Each `wsdl:operation` contains a combination of `wsdl:input`, `wsdl:output`, and `wsdl:fault` elements; each of these elements is a message component that is part of the message exchange pattern used by `wsdl:operation`.

- Each `wsdl:input`, `wsdl:output`, and `wsdl:fault` element is based on a `wsdl:message` element. If a `wsdl:operation` uses a request-response message exchange pattern, it must specify a `wsdl:input` element and a `wsdl:output` element, and possibly one or more `wsdl:fault` elements. If a `wsdl:operation` uses a one-way message exchange pattern, it must specify a single `wsdl:input` element.

- Since a `wsdl:portType` element defines an abstract service interface, it needs to be mapped to a messaging protocol and a transport protocol. Each `wsdl:portType` is recursively mapped to a messaging protocol and a transport protocol in a `wsdl:binding` element, which is a child of `wsdl:definitions`.

- Each `wsdl:portType` abstract interface is mapped to a concrete network endpoint address through a `wsdl:port` element. A `wsdl:port` element is defined within a `wsdl:service` element, which is a child of `wsdl:definitions`.

Listing 14-6 shows the basic outline of a WSDL 1.1 document.

Listing 14-6. *Basic Outline of a WSDL 1.1 Document*

```
<wsdl:definitions
  xmlns:wsdl="http://schemas.xmlsoap.org/wsdl/">

  <wsdl:types>
   <!-- schema elements or schema types -->
  </wsdl:types>

  <!-- One or more abstract message types -->
  <wsdl:message name="...">

   <!-- One or more message parts -->
   <wsdl:part element="..." name="..." type="...">
        <!-- Based on either a schema element or a schema type -->
   </wsdl:part>

  </wsdl:message>

  <!-- one or more abstract port type interfaces -->
  <wsdl:portType name="...">

   <!-- One or more abstract operations, but name should be unique -->
   <wsdl:operations name="...">
     <!-- Request must have an input -->
     <wsdl:input message="..." name="...">
     </wsdl:input>

     <!-- Optional response contains one output element
          and zero or more fault elements -->
     <wsdl:output message="..." name="...">
     </wsdl:output>
     <wsdl:fault message="..." name="...">
```

```
      </wsdl:fault>
     </wsdl:operations>

   </wsdl:portType>

   <wsdl:binding name="..." type="...">
    <!-- Maps the port type to a messaging
        and a transport protocol -->
   </wsdl:binding>

   <wsdl:service name="..." >

    <!-- One or more ports -->
    <wsdl:port binding="..." name="...">
     <!-- Binds a port type binding to a network endpoint address -->
    </wsdl:port>

   </wsdl:service>
</wsdl:definitions>
```

In the next section, you will examine an example WSDL 1.1 document.

Example WSDL 1.1 Document

In our opinion, if you are building a web service, the only way to start is to first construct a WSDL 1.1 document. To build the example web service that implements all the use case scenarios, you need to construct a WSDL 1.1 document that formally describes the example web service. We will show you how to do that step by step; we describe these steps in detail in the following sections:

1. Declare the relevant namespaces.

2. Define a schema in a separate document.

3. Import the schema into a WSDL 1.1 document.

4. Define message types used by the web service.

5. Define the web service interface (port type), including all the operations.

6. Define the binding of port type to the SOAP 1.1/HTTP messaging and transport protocols.

7. Define the port that binds the web service binding to the endpoint address.

Namespace Declarations

The first step you want to take is to declare all the namespace declarations you will need in this document:

- The WSDL 1.1 language constructs are defined in the http://schemas.xmlsoap.org/wsdl/ namespace, and you will use the wsdl prefix with this namespace.

- The target namespace for the document will be http://www.apress.com/xmljava/webservices/ definitions, which is entirely arbitrary. You will use the defs prefix with this namespace.

- The namespace for the XML Schema language is http://www.w3.org/2001/XMLSchema, and you will use the xsd prefix with this namespace.

- The namespace for MIME constructs is `http://schemas.xmlsoap.org/wsdl/mime/`, and you will use the `mime` prefix with this namespace.

- The WSDL 1.1 to SOAP binding is specified in the `http://schemas.xmlsoap.org/wsdl/soap/` namespace in the `soap` prefix.

- You will be defining your own schema types, and you will use the `http://www.apress.com/xmljava/webservices/schemas` namespace for the schema types. You will use the `types` prefix with this namespace.

The root `wsdl:definitions` element of the WSDL 1.1 document with the relevant namespace declarations is as follows:

```
<?xml version='1.0' encoding='UTF-8' ?>
<wsdl:definitions
  targetNamespace="http://www.apress.com/xmljava/webservices/definitions"
  xmlns:defs="http://www.apress.com/xmljava/webservices/definitions"
  xmlns:mime="http://schemas.xmlsoap.org/wsdl/mime/"
  xmlns:soap="http://schemas.xmlsoap.org/wsdl/soap/"
  xmlns:types="http://www.apress.com/xmljava/webservices/schemas"
  xmlns:wsdl="http://schemas.xmlsoap.org/wsdl/"
  xmlns:xsd="http://www.w3.org/2001/XMLSchema" >
 </wsdl:definitions>
```

Schema Definition

In writing any but the most trivial of WSDL 1.1 documents, you will need schema data types. Although it is not a must, it is best to define these data types within a separate schema file and the schema file imported within the WSDL 1.1 document. Separating the schema definition from the WSDL 1.1 document is highly recommended, both for maintenance and for reuse. For the example web service, define the schema definition shown in Listing 14-7 in a separate file named `types.xsd`.

Listing 14-7. *Schema Types for Example Web Service in* `types.xsd`

```
<?xml version='1.0' encoding='UTF-8' ?>
<xsd:schema
  targetNamespace="http://www.apress.com/xmljava/webservices/schemas"
  xmlns="http://www.apress.com/xmljava/webservices/schemas"
  xmlns:xsd="http://www.w3.org/2001/XMLSchema"
  xmlns:xsi="http://www.w3.org/2001/XMLSchema-instance"
  xsi:schemaLocation="http://www.w3.org/2001/XMLSchema
    http://www.nubean.com/schemas/schema.xsd" >

  <xsd:complexType name="documentInfo" >
    <xsd:attribute name="name" type="xsd:string" use="required" ></xsd:attribute>

    <xsd:attribute name="createdOn"
      type="xsd:dateTime" use="optional" >
    </xsd:attribute>
    <xsd:attribute name="lastUpdated"
      type="xsd:dateTime" use="optional" >
     </xsd:attribute>
  </xsd:complexType>
```

```
  <xsd:complexType name="folderInfo" >
    <xsd:sequence>
    <xsd:element maxOccurs="unbounded"  minOccurs="0"  name="document"
       type="documentInfo" >
     </xsd:element>
     </xsd:sequence>
    <xsd:attribute name="location"
      type="xsd:string"  use="required" >
    </xsd:attribute>
    <xsd:attribute name="createdOn"
     type="xsd:dateTime"  use="optional" >
    </xsd:attribute>
    <xsd:attribute name="lastUpdated"
       type="xsd:dateTime"  use="optional" >
    </xsd:attribute>
   </xsd:complexType>

  <xsd:complexType name="projectInfo" >
    <xsd:sequence>
    <xsd:element maxOccurs="unbounded"
       minOccurs="0"  name="folder"  type="folderInfo" >
    </xsd:element>
    </xsd:sequence>
    <xsd:attribute name="name"  type="xsd:string"  use="required" ></xsd:attribute>
    <xsd:attribute name="createdOn"
      type="xsd:dateTime"  use="optional" >
    </xsd:attribute>
    <xsd:attribute name="lastUpdated"
      type="xsd:dateTime"  use="optional" >
    </xsd:attribute>
    <xsd:attribute name="email"
      type="xsd:string"  use="required" >
    </xsd:attribute>
   </xsd:complexType>

  <xsd:element name="manifest"  type="projectInfo" ></xsd:element>
  <xsd:element name="project"  type="projectInfo" ></xsd:element>
 <xsd:element name="remove"  type="projectInfo" ></xsd:element>

 <xsd:element name="projects" >
  <xsd:complexType>
   <xsd:sequence>
      <xsd:element maxOccurs="unbounded"  minOccurs="0"
          name="project"  type="projectInfo" >
      </xsd:element>
   </xsd:sequence>
  </xsd:complexType>
</xsd:element>
```

```
 <xsd:element name="projectsDetail" >
  <xsd:complexType>
   <xsd:sequence>
     <xsd:element name="folders"  type="xsd:boolean" ></xsd:element>
     <xsd:element name="documents"  type="xsd:boolean" ></xsd:element>
   </xsd:sequence>
  </xsd:complexType>
</xsd:element>

  <xsd:element name="userInfo" >
   <xsd:complexType>
    <xsd:sequence>
      <xsd:element name="email"  type="xsd:string" ></xsd:element>
      <xsd:element name="pwd"  type="xsd:string" ></xsd:element>
     </xsd:sequence>
    </xsd:complexType>
  </xsd:element>

  <xsd:element name="authDetail" >
   <xsd:complexType>
    <xsd:sequence>
       <xsd:any></xsd:any>
     </xsd:sequence>
    </xsd:complexType>
  </xsd:element>

  <xsd:element name="authScope" >
   <xsd:complexType>
    <xsd:sequence>
       <xsd:element name="scope"  type="xsd:string" ></xsd:element>
     </xsd:sequence>
    </xsd:complexType>
  </xsd:element>

  <xsd:element name="faultDetail" >
   <xsd:complexType>
    <xsd:sequence>
      <xsd:element minOccurs="1"  name="major"  type="xsd:string" ></xsd:element>
      <xsd:element minOccurs="0"  name="minor"  type="xsd:string" ></xsd:element>
     </xsd:sequence>
    </xsd:complexType>
  </xsd:element>
 </xsd:schema>
```

We will not describe this schema definition in great detail. By now, you should be familiar with schema constructs; if you need to review this material, please refer to Chapter 1. Briefly, the schema in Listing 14-7 defines data types for use in the example WSDL 1.1 document; these data types include the following:

- The userInfo schema type contains email and password information.
- The projectInfo schema type contains information about a project.

- The project, remove, and manifest elements are all of type projectInfo.

- The projects schema element contains information about a list of projects.

- The projectsDetail schema element contains information about what type of elements should be included in returned content when getting information about all the projects.

- The folderInfo schema type contains information about folders, and they are nested within projectInfo.

- The documentInfo schema type contains information about documents, and they are nested within folderInfo.

- The authScope schema element defines the authentication scope.

- The authDetail schema element defines the arbitrary authentication data that may be sent with userInfo. This is an example of extensibility using xsd:any.

You should have no problem deciphering the structure of each of these schema elements or types by examining the schema shown in Listing 14-7.

Schema Import

You will refer to the xsd:complexType definitions and the xsd:element declarations shown in Listing 14-7 within the WSDL 1.1 document, so the first step you need to take within your WSDL 1.1 document is to import the schema definition, which is assumed to be defined in a file named types.xsd. The schema import within the WSDL document is as follows:

```
<wsdl:types>
    <xsd:schema>
      <xsd:import
namespace="http://www.apress.com/xmljava/webservices/schemas"
schemaLocation="types.xsd" >
      </xsd:import>
    </xsd:schema>
 </wsdl:types>
```

Abstract Message Definitions

As you have already seen, all web service interactions involve the exchange of messages. So, of course, in the WSDL 1.1 document, you have to define the abstract messages used by the example web service. Through the appropriate wsdl:binding definition, you will later map these abstract messages to the soapenv:Body content.

Not surprisingly, these messages are based on the schema elements defined within the schema shown in Listing 14-7; the element attribute of a wsdl:part denotes a schema element in the types namespace. For example, the abstract request message for getting all the projects for a user, GetProjects, is as follows:

```
<wsdl:message name="GetProjects" >
    <wsdl:part element="types:userInfo"  name="user" ></wsdl:part>
    <wsdl:part element="types:projectsDetail"  name="detail" ></wsdl:part>
</wsdl:message>
```

The GetProjects abstract message has two parts:

- The first part is based on the types:userInfo schema element.

- The second part is based on the types:projectsDetail schema element.

Each wsdl:message element contains one or more wsdl:part elements. The wsdl:message names and the wsdl:part names are completely arbitrary but should attempt to impart some information about web service semantics.

Some wsdl:part elements are based on schema elements defined within the schema shown in Listing 14-7, such as types:manifest; other wsdl:part elements are based on built-in schema types, such as xsd:base64Binary, as shown in the following DownloadZip message:

```
<wsdl:message name="DownloadZip" >
    <wsdl:part element="types:manifest"  name="manifest" ></wsdl:part>
    <wsdl:part name="zip"  type="xsd:base64Binary" ></wsdl:part>
</wsdl:message>
```

The xsd:base64Binary data type refers to binary data in Base 64 encoding.

Listing 14-8 shows the complete set of abstract message definitions that describe the messages for all the use case scenarios within the WSDL 1.1 document.

Listing 14-8. *WSDL 1.1 Message Definitions for Example Web Service*

```
<wsdl:message name="ProjectFault" >
    <wsdl:part element="types:faultDetail"  name="faultDetail" ></wsdl:part>
    </wsdl:message>

  <wsdl:message name="DownloadProject" >
    <wsdl:part element="types:userInfo"  name="user" ></wsdl:part>
    <wsdl:part element="types:project"  name="project" ></wsdl:part>
   </wsdl:message>

  <wsdl:message name="GetProjects" >
    <wsdl:part element="types:userInfo"  name="user" ></wsdl:part>
    <wsdl:part element="types:projectsDetail"  name="detail" ></wsdl:part>
   </wsdl:message>

  <wsdl:message name="AuthUser" >
    <wsdl:part element="types:userInfo"  name="user" ></wsdl:part>
    <wsdl:part element="types:authDetail"  name="detail" ></wsdl:part>
   </wsdl:message>

  <wsdl:message name="Project" >
    <wsdl:part element="types:project"  name="project" ></wsdl:part>
   </wsdl:message>

  <wsdl:message name="Projects" >
    <wsdl:part element="types:projects"  name="projects" ></wsdl:part>
   </wsdl:message>

 <wsdl:message name="RemoveProject" >
    <wsdl:part element="types:userInfo"  name="user" ></wsdl:part>
    <wsdl:part element="types:remove"  name="remove" ></wsdl:part>
   </wsdl:message>

  <wsdl:message name="UploadZip" >
    <wsdl:part element="types:userInfo"  name="user" ></wsdl:part>
    <wsdl:part element="types:manifest"  name="manifest" ></wsdl:part>
    <wsdl:part name="zip"  type="xsd:base64Binary" ></wsdl:part>
   </wsdl:message>
```

```
<wsdl:message name="DownloadZip" >
  <wsdl:part element="types:manifest"  name="manifest" ></wsdl:part>
  <wsdl:part name="zip"  type="xsd:base64Binary" ></wsdl:part>
</wsdl:message>
```

The abstract messages are used by wsdl:operations within wsdl:portType, as discussed in the next section.

Port Type

Just like a Java interface, the wsdl:portType element describes an abstract web service interface. Each wsdl:portType element contains one or more wsdl:operation elements, whereby each wsdl:operation element defines the message exchange pattern for that wsdl:operation.

A wsdl:operation element in the most general request-response message exchange pattern case contains a wsdl:input element, a wsdl:output element, and zero or more wsdl:fault elements, where each of these elements is associated with a wsdl:message definition through the message attribute. wsdl:input, as the name implies, defines the request message, wsdl:output defines the response message, and wsdl:fault defines the details of the SOAP fault message. An example of a request-response wsdl:operation is download, as shown here:

```
<wsdl:operation name="download" >
    <wsdl:input message="defs:DownloadProject"  name="project" >
    </wsdl:input>
    <wsdl:output message="defs:DownloadZip"  name="downloadZip" >
    </wsdl:output>
    <wsdl:fault message="defs:ProjectFault"  name="fault" >
    </wsdl:fault>
</wsdl:operation>
```

In download wsdl:operation shown previously, defs:DownloadProject, defs:DownloadZip, and defs:ProjectFault are abstract messages that are used in the request-response message exchange pattern.

For a one-way exchange pattern, only a single wsdl:input element is required, as in the case of remove wsdl:operation shown here:

```
<wsdl:operation name="remove" >
 <wsdl:input message="defs:RemoveProject"  name="project" >
 </wsdl:input>
</wsdl:operation>
```

You cannot specify a wsdl:fault message without a wsdl:output message, because a SOAP fault message is generated only if a response was expected. So, for example, you cannot add a wsdl:fault to a wsdl:operation named remove.

The wsdl:portType for the example web service is named ProjectPortType, and it defines the following wsdl:operation for the use case scenarios:

- Uploading documents to a project is defined by upload.

- Downloading documents from a project is defined by download.

- Getting information about all the projects owned by a user is defined by getProjects.

- Removing documents from a project is defined by remove.

- An authenticate operation, which is not required for these use cases, can be used to authenticate a user and keep user information in an HTTP session.

Listing 14-9 shows the complete wsdl:portType for the example web service.

Listing 14-9. *Port Types for the Example Web Service*

```
<wsdl:portType name="ProjectPortType" >

    <wsdl:operation name="download" >
      <wsdl:input message="defs:DownloadProject"  name="project" ></wsdl:input>
      <wsdl:output message="defs:DownloadZip"  name="downloadZip" ></wsdl:output>
      <wsdl:fault message="defs:ProjectFault"  name="fault" ></wsdl:fault>
    </wsdl:operation>

    <wsdl:operation name="upload" >
      <wsdl:input message="defs:UploadZip"  name="uploadZip" ></wsdl:input>
      <wsdl:output message="defs:Project"  name="project" ></wsdl:output>
      <wsdl:fault message="defs:ProjectFault"  name="fault" ></wsdl:fault>
    </wsdl:operation>

    <wsdl:operation name="remove" >
      <wsdl:input message="defs:RemoveProject"  name="project" ></wsdl:input>
    </wsdl:operation>

    <wsdl:operation name="getProjects" >
      <wsdl:input message="defs:GetProjects"  name="getprojects" ></wsdl:input>
      <wsdl:output message="defs:Projects"  name="projects" ></wsdl:output>
      <wsdl:fault message="defs:ProjectFault"  name="fault" ></wsdl:fault>
    </wsdl:operation>

    <wsdl:operation name="authenticate" >
      <wsdl:input message="defs:AuthUser"  name="authuser" ></wsdl:input>
      <wsdl:output message="defs:AuthUser"  name="authuser" ></wsdl:output>
      <wsdl:fault message="defs:ProjectFault"  name="fault" ></wsdl:fault>
    </wsdl:operation>
  </wsdl:portType>
```

As noted, `wsdl:portType` is an abstract interface. This abstract interface has to be bound to a messaging protocol and a transport protocol, which is discussed in the next section.

Port Type Bindings to SOAP 1.1/HTTP

The abstract `wsdl:portType` needs to be bound to the SOAP 1.1/HTTP messaging protocol. Therefore, you need to recursively bind the `wsdl:portType` element to SOAP 1.1/HTTP. In the following discussion, the `soap` prefix, which is associated with a WSDL 1.1 to SOAP 1.1 binding, is associated with the `http://schemas.xmlsoap.org/wsdl/soap/` namespace.

The SOAP 1.1/HTTP binding for `defs:ProjectPortType` `wsdl:portType` is named `ProjectSoapBinding`.

SOAP 1.1 to HTTP Binding

The following snippet specifies that the SOAP 1.1 messaging be bound to the HTTP (`http://schemas.xmlsoap.org/soap/http`) message transport:

```
<soap:binding style="document"
        transport="http://schemas.xmlsoap.org/soap/http" >
</soap:binding>
```

In addition, it specifies that the SOAP 1.1 messaging mode should be of type document, which is described in the next section.

SOAP 1.1 Messaging Style

SOAP 1.1 messaging style, which is a completely distinct concept from the concept of message exchange patterns (which can be request-response or one-way) and the concept of message encoding (which for us is always literal), specifies rules for the structure of the XML content in the payload of the soapenv:Body element. Two possible SOAP 1.1 messaging styles exist:

- Remote procedure call (rpc) style
- Document (document) style

You will look at each of the messaging styles next.

Remote Procedure Call Style

As the name implies, this style embodies the semantics associated with remote procedure invocations. Under this style, the following is true:

- The content of the soapenv:Body element always has a single child element whose tag name corresponds to the operation name being remotely invoked.

- The grandchild elements of the soapenv:Body element denote the parameters associated with the remote operation.

- The names and order of the grandchild elements correspond to the remote operation parameter names and their order.

- The child and grandchild elements of soapenv:Body element must be namespace qualified; the namespace is application specific.

This style is completely redundant, because the document style, which we will describe in the next section, is much more general and, more important, adheres to the fundamental tenets of keeping interacting applications as loosely coupled as possible. By contrast, the rpc style is akin to making a method call, with all the attendant implications of tight coupling between the calling application and the called application. In our opinion, the rpc style is the antithesis of loosely coupled applications and should be, as much as possible, avoided.

Document Style

The rules for the structure of soapenv:Body in the document style are simple:

- The content of soapenv:Body element should be well-formed XML, and all soapenv:Body child elements should be namespace qualified in an application-specific namespace.

- If a wsdl:part, mapped to the soapenv:Body element, corresponds to a schema element (that is, it has an element attribute), in the document-style message the schema element occurs as a child of the soapenv:Body element.

- If a wsdl:part, mapped to the soapenv:Body element, corresponds to a schema type (that is, it has a type attribute) in the document-style message, then the soapenv:Body element assumes this schema type, and the child elements of soapenv:Body conform to this schema type. This implies that in the case of a wsdl:part with a type attribute, there can be only one wsdl:part in its wsdl:message, since the soapenv:Body element can assume only a single schema type.

Listing 14-1 is an example of document-style message. You will see examples of specifying document style in the `wsdl:operation` to `soap:operation` binding in the next section.

Binding wsdl:operation to SOAP 1.1

This is where you make a `wsdl:operation` concrete by binding each `wsdl:operation` to SOAP 1.1 messaging. For example, the binding of download `wsdl:operation` to SOAP 1.1 consists of the following parts:

- Defining a `soap:operation` with a `soapAction` and SOAP 1.1 messaging `style`. A `soapAction` is a hint to message processing nodes, which, according to WS-I BP 1.1, helps improve interoperability between applications. It is transported as an HTTP header attribute. It is essentially a mechanism to infer something about a SOAP message by just looking at the HTTP header, without having to inspect the SOAP message.

- Binding a `wsdl:input` abstract message to `soap:header` and `soap:body`.

- Binding `wsdl:output` to a `mime:multipartRelated` message.

- Binding `wsdl:fault` to `soap:fault`.

We explain each of the previous steps in the following sections.

Defining soap:operation

The `soap:operation` binding for download `wsdl:operation` is defined as follows:

```
<soap:operation
        soapAction="http://www.apress.com/xmljava/webservices/download"
        style="document" >
</soap:operation>
```

Remember, each SOAP 1.1 message is transported within an HTTP message. The URI in the `soapAction` attribute of `soap:operation` is included as the value of the SOAPAction HTTP header.

Binding wsdl:input

The `wsdl:input` in a download operation is based on the `defs:DownloadProject` abstract message, which defines two `wsdl:part` elements, as shown here:

```
<wsdl:message name="DownloadProject" >
    <wsdl:part element="types:userInfo"  name="user" ></wsdl:part>
    <wsdl:part element="types:project"  name="project" ></wsdl:part>
</wsdl:message>
```

When `defs:DownloadProject` is bound to a SOAP 1.1 message, you can choose to bind the user part to the `soap:header` element and the project part to the `soap:body` element, as shown here:

```
<wsdl:input>
        <soap:header message="defs:DownloadProject"
           part="user"  use="literal" >
        </soap:header>

        <soap:body parts="project"  use="literal" ></soap:body>
</wsdl:input>
```

Binding wsdl:output

The wsdl:output in a download operation is based on the defs:DownloadZip abstract message, as shown here:

```
<wsdl:message name="DownloadZip" >
    <wsdl:part element="types:manifest"  name="manifest" ></wsdl:part>
    <wsdl:part name="zip"  type="xsd:base64Binary" ></wsdl:part>
</wsdl:message>
```

The defs:DownloadZip abstract message contains two parts. The first part is manifest, and the second part, zip, is a Base 64 binary type containing the downloaded ZIP file. The wsdl:output is bound to the SOAP 1.1 message as a MIME multipart-related message. The manifest part is bound to the soap:body contained within a mime:part, and the zip part is bound to a mime:content contained within mime:part, as shown here:

```
<wsdl:output>
  <mime:multipartRelated>
    <mime:part>
      <soap:body parts="manifest"  use="literal" ></soap:body>
    </mime:part>

    <mime:part>
      <mime:content part="zip"  type="application/zip" >
    </mime:content>
     </mime:part>
   </mime:multipartRelated>
</wsdl:output>
```

Binding wsdl:fault

The wsdl:fault is mapped to soap:fault, as shown here:

```
<wsdl:fault name="fault" >
  <soap:fault name="fault"  use="literal" ></soap:fault>
</wsdl:fault>
```

Complete Port Type Binding

Listing 14-10 shows the complete SOAP 1.1/HTTP binding for ProjectPortType.

Listing 14-10. *SOAP 1.1/HTTP Binding for ProjectPortType*

```
<wsdl:binding name="ProjectSoapBinding"  type="defs:ProjectPortType" >
    <soap:binding style="document"
        transport="http://schemas.xmlsoap.org/soap/http" >
     </soap:binding>
    <wsdl:operation name="download" >
     <soap:operation
        soapAction="http://www.apress.com/xmljava/webservices/download"
        style="document" >
     </soap:operation>
    <wsdl:input>
      <soap:header message="defs:DownloadProject"
         part="user"  use="literal" >
       </soap:header>
```

```
        <soap:body parts="project"  use="literal" ></soap:body>
      </wsdl:input>

      <wsdl:output>
        <mime:multipartRelated>
          <mime:part>
            <soap:body parts="manifest"  use="literal" ></soap:body> </mime:part>

          <mime:part>
            <mime:content part="zip"  type="application/zip" ></mime:content>
          </mime:part>
        </mime:multipartRelated>
      </wsdl:output>

      <wsdl:fault name="fault" >
        <soap:fault name="fault"  use="literal" ></soap:fault> </wsdl:fault>
    </wsdl:operation>

  <wsdl:operation name="upload" >
    <soap:operation
        soapAction="http://www.apress.com/xmlJava/webservices/upload"
        style="document" >
    </soap:operation>
    <wsdl:input>
      <soap:header message="defs:UploadZip"  part="user"  use="literal" >
        </soap:header>

      <mime:multipartRelated>
        <mime:part>
          <soap:body parts="manifest"  use="literal" ></soap:body>
        </mime:part>
        <mime:part>
          <mime:content part="zip"  type="application/zip" ></mime:content>
        </mime:part>
      </mime:multipartRelated>
    </wsdl:input>

    <wsdl:output>
      <soap:body parts="project"  use="literal" ></soap:body> </wsdl:output>

    <wsdl:fault name="fault" >
      <soap:fault name="fault"  use="literal" ></soap:fault></wsdl:fault>
    </wsdl:operation>

  <wsdl:operation name="remove" >
    <soap:operation
        soapAction="http://www.apress.com/xmlJava/webservices/remove"
        style="document" >
    </soap:operation>
    <wsdl:input>
      <soap:header message="defs:RemoveProject"
      part="user"  use="literal" >
      </soap:header>
      <soap:body parts="remove"  use="literal" >
```

```
            </soap:body>
          </wsdl:input>
      </wsdl:operation>


  <wsdl:operation name="getProjects" >
    <soap:operation
      soapAction="http://www.apress.com/xmljava/webservices/getprojects"
        style="document" >
      </soap:operation>
    <wsdl:input>
        <soap:header message="defs:GetProjects"
            part="user"  use="literal" >
        </soap:header>
        <soap:body message="defs:GetProjects"
          parts="detail"  use="literal" >
        </soap:body>
      </wsdl:input>

      <wsdl:output>
        <soap:body parts="projects"  use="literal" ></soap:body>
       </wsdl:output>

      <wsdl:fault name="fault" >
        <soap:fault name="fault"  use="literal" ></soap:fault> </wsdl:fault>
    </wsdl:operation>

  <wsdl:operation name="authenticate" >
    <soap:operation
      soapAction="http://www.apress.com/xmljava/webservices/authenticate"
      style="document" >
      </soap:operation>
    <wsdl:input>
        <soap:header message="defs:AuthUser"
        part="user"  use="literal" ></soap:header>
        <soap:body message="defs:AuthUser"
          parts="detail"  use="literal" >
        </soap:body>
      </wsdl:input>

      <wsdl:output>
        <soap:header message="defs:AuthUser"
          part="user"  use="literal" >
        </soap:header>
        <soap:body message="defs:AuthUser"
          parts="detail"  use="literal" >
        </soap:body>
      </wsdl:output>

      <wsdl:fault name="fault" >
        <soap:fault name="fault"  use="literal" ></soap:fault>
      </wsdl:fault>
    </wsdl:operation>
  </wsdl:binding>
```

Service Port

Each `wsdl:portType` binding must be attached to a `wsdl:port` within a `wsdl:service`. For example, the `defs:ProjectSoapBinding` port type binding shown in Listing 14-10 is mapped to the `ProjectPortTypeImplPort` port within the `ProjectPortTypeImplService` service, as shown here:

```
<wsdl:service name="ProjectPortTypeImplService" >
    <wsdl:port binding="defs:ProjectSoapBinding"  name="ProjectPortTypeImplPort" >
      <soap:address location="REPLACE_WITH_ACTUAL_URL" ></soap:address>
    </wsdl:port>
</wsdl:service>
```

The mapping of a concrete port type binding to a port `location` creates a network service endpoint that can be accessed by other applications using an HTTP URL. In general, although you can, you should not specify a `location` HTTP URL and leave it as it is shown in the previous example. Typically, this URL should be automatically assigned during the deployment of the web service, which is discussed in detail in the "Using JAX-WS 2.0" section.

The complete WSDL 1.1 document for the example web service is included in the project. To recap, building a WSDL document involves defining a schema definition, defining message types, defining a port type (web service interface), defining a port type binding that binds a port type to SOAP/HTTP, and, finally, defining a port that binds a port type binding to a network address.

Now that you have a WSDL 1.1 document, you are ready to build the example web service using JAX-WS 2.0, which is what you will do in the next section.

Using JAX-WS 2.0

JAX-WS 2.0 is based on JSR-224.[11] A reference implementation of the JAX-WS 2.0 specification is included in the Java EE 5 SDK.[12] In this section, we will use Java EE 5 SDK to show how to build and deploy the example web service. The steps for building the web service using the Java EE 5 SDK are as follows:

1. Use the `wsimport` tool included in the Java EE 5 SDK to automatically generate the Java code that defines the Java types corresponding to the schema types, message types, and port types defined in the `services.wsdl` document shown in Listing 14-10.

2. Implement the web service provider agent, writing whatever Java code is needed to implement the application logic. The application logic implemented by this web service corresponds to the use cases described earlier in the "Example Use Case Scenarios" section.

3. Compile generated and manually coded Java class files and package them into a Java EE enterprise application archive file.

4. Deploy the enterprise application archive file in Sun One Application Server 9.0, which is included in the Java EE 5 SDK. This makes the web service available for use at a specific HTTP URL.

5. Write web service clients (requestor agents) to interact with the web service and run the clients, and then observe the interaction.

In the following sections, you will follow the steps outlined previously.

---

11. JSR-224 is available at `http://www.jcp.org/en/jsr/detail?id=224`.
12. The Java EE 5 SDK is available at `http://java.sun.com/javaee/downloads/index.jsp`.

Installing the Software

Before you can proceed, you need to download and install the Java EE 5 SDK, which includes Sun One Application Server 9.0. The server includes the Java DB database, which is based on Apache Derby.[13]

After installing the SDK, start the included Java DB database and Sun One Application Server 9.0. On Windows,[14] you can select Start Java DB in the Sun One Application Server 9.0's Programs menu to start the database, and select Start Default Server to start the server.

After starting the database and the server, go to `http://localhost:8080/` in a browser, and verify that the server is running. When the server starts, it prints the ports it is listening on, so if `http://localhost:8080/` does not work, try the other ports listed by server, such as `http://localhost:2492/`.

After the server is running, you can go to `http://localhost:4848/` to access the Sun One Application Server 9.0 administration console. If you are asked to log in, specify the username and password you configured during the server installation. The administration console provides the Enterprise Applications link for deploying enterprise applications and the Web Services link for deploying web services.

Setting Up the Eclipse Project

You will need J2SE 5.0 to build your Eclipse project. Therefore, install J2SE 5.0, in case you have not already done so.

Next, you need to download the `Chapter14` project from `http://www.apress.com/` and import the project into Eclipse by selecting File ➤ Import. It is important that your Eclipse workspace not contain any spaces in its file system path; otherwise, you will run into problems later in this chapter, as you go through the steps for building the example web service. Figure 14-6 shows the `Chapter14` project directory structure.

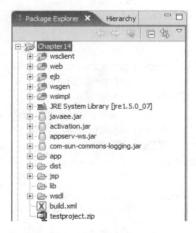

Figure 14-6. *Project directory structure*

---

13. Apache Derby is part of the Apache DB project (`http://db.apache.org/derby/`).
14. For other platforms, follow the product documentation.

The project folders are as follows:

- The wsclient folder contains Java files corresponding to the web service clients, used to interact with the example web service.

- The wsdl folder has the web service WSDL 1.1 document (services.wsdl), the WSDL 1.1 customization file (svcbindings.xml) used for customizing WSDL 1.1 to Java mappings, the schema document (types.xsd), and the JAXB 2.0 binding customization file (binding.xjb) used for customizing JAXB 2.0 object bindings.

- The web folder has Java files, XML documents, and properties files related to Java Server Faces (JSF)–based implementations of web pages. Understanding the contents of this folder is not central to understanding web services, and this content appears in this chapter solely because we wanted to show how to build a complete working example. JSF is part of Java EE 5 and is a server-based technology for constructing a web-based user interface. JSF is beyond the scope of this book. However, if you are interested in learning more about JSF, we recommend *Pro JSF and Ajax: Building Rich Internet Components.*[15]

- The ejb folder contains Java code related to application logic and database persistence, based on the Enterprise Java Beans (EJB) 3.0 technology. EJB 3.0 is part of Java EE 5 and is a technology for implementing object-relational mapping, automatic database persistence, and application logic. EJB 3.0 is beyond the scope of this chapter. For a more detailed look at EJB 3.0, we recommend *Pro EJB3: Java Persistence API.*[16]

- The wsgen folder is for Java source files generated by the wsimport tool. When you initially import the project into Eclipse, this folder will be empty. The generated Java files correspond to JAXB 2.0 object binding files and web service interfaces.

- The wsimpl folder has Java files for implementing web service interfaces. These implementation files use EJBs to implement the application logic and interact with the database.

- The app directory has the application.xml deployment descriptor in the config folder. In this project, we will show how to build an enterprise application archive, which will be deployed in the server. This archive will contain the example web service. The application.xml deployment descriptor specifies deployment directives for the enterprise application, when the application is deployed in the Sun One Application Server 9.0. For more details about this, we recommend the Java EE 5 tutorial at http://java.sun.com/javaee/5/docs/tutorial/doc/.

- The jsp directory has the JSF pages for the web services application.

- The Testproject.zip file is an example ZIP file that will be used by the web service client to upload documents to a project using the web service.

Figure 14-7 shows the Chapter14 project Java build path.

15. *Pro JSF and Ajax: Building Rich Internet Components* (Apress, 2006) by Jonas Jacobi and John Fallows.
16. *Pro EJB3: Java Persistence API* (Apress, 2006) by Mike Keith and Merrick Schincariol.

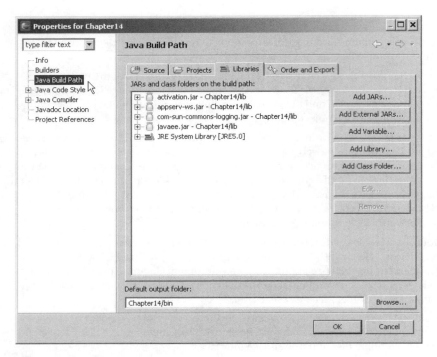

Figure 14-7. *Chapter14 project Java build path*

Setting Up the wsimport Tool

The wsimport tool processes a WSDL 1.1 document as follows:

- It generates the SEI, the service, and the JAXB 2.0 object bindings, based on the contents of the WSDL 1.1 document.

- The SEI is a Java interface corresponding to a wsdl:portType definition within a WSDL 1.1 document. The provider agent that implements the web service provides a concrete implementation for an SEI.

- The service is a class that can be used by a web service client to interact with the web service.

- The JAXB 2.0 object bindings correspond to the schema types in the WSDL 1.1 document. These object bindings are used for marshaling and unmarshaling web service data types to and from XML content encapsulated within SOAP 1.1 messages.

You will use wsimport to generate the SEI, the service, and the JAXB 2.0 object bindings for the services.wsdl WSDL 1.1 document.

To use the wsimport tool, you need to first create an external tools configuration for wsimport by selecting Run ➤ External Tools ➤ External Tools. To create an external tools configuration, go through the following steps:

1. Right-click the Program node in the External Tools area, and select New.

2. Specify a name for the configuration, such as wsimport.

3. Specify the wsimport.bat file in the Location field.

4. In the Working Directory field, specify ${project_loc}, and in the Arguments field, you need to specify the following arguments: -s wsgen -d bin -keep -verbose -b wsdl/binding.xjb -b wsdl/svcbindings.xml wsdl/${resource_name}.

5. Click the Apply button. An external tools configuration gets configured for the wsimport tool, as shown in Figure 14-8.

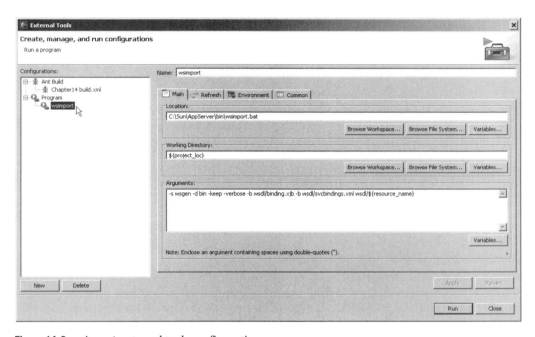

Figure 14-8. *wsimport external tools configuration*

You also need to add the environment variable JAVA_HOME by selecting the Environment tab and subsequently clicking the New button. To add the wsimport external tools configuration to the Favorites menu, select the Common tab, and select the External Tools box in the Display in Favorites menu.

WSDL 1.1 to Java Mapping

Before you run the wsimport tool to generate the WSDL 1.1 to Java mapping for services.wsdl, we will cover the general concepts of this mapping process (we refer to the concept of customizations, which we will cover later in the section "Customizing WSDL 1.1 to Java Mapping"):

- Each wsdl:portType within a WSDL 1.1 document is mapped to a Java SEI.

- Each wsdl:operation within a wsdl:portType is mapped to a Java method within the SEI.

- In the absence of customizations, the name of the mapped Java method is the same as the name of the wsdl:operation name attribute. By default, since the wsdl:operation name within a wsdl:portType is unique, there will be no overloaded methods. It is best to adhere to unique method names if you are using customizations.

- Each wsdl:operation must have one input message (wsdl:input). It may have zero or one output messages (wsdl:output) and, if an output message is present, zero or more fault messages (wsdl:fault).

- The input and output messages are mapped to Java method parameters using either the nonwrapper style or the wrapper style. For exhaustive rules governing mapping under these styles, we recommend the JAX-WS 2.0 specification. However, the following details pertaining to these styles should be sufficient for most purposes:

  - In the nonwrapper style, if the wsdl:part is part of an input message, the wsdl:part element is mapped to a Java method parameter. For output messages, the wsdl:part element is mapped to either a holder class parameter or a return type. You can never go wrong if you use the nonwrapper style—problem solved.

  - The wrapper style is applicable only if the wsdl:message referred to by a wsdl:input or a wsdl:output has only one wsdl:part. In our opinion, don't bother with it. However, if you must, read the next point.

  - In the wrapper style, the wsdl:part element is deemed to be a wrapper element (which is how the style gets its name). The children of the wrapper element are mapped to Java method parameters if the wsdl:part is part of an input message. If the wsdl:part is part of an output message and the wrapper element has more than one child, the children are mapped to Java method parameters using a holder class; for one child, it is just mapped to a Java method return type. If the wsdl:part is part of both input and output messages, the holder class method parameter is the answer.

- The fault message is mapped to a custom Java exception class.

In the next section, we will discuss how to customize the WSDL 1.1 to Java mapping.

Customizing the WSDL 1.1 to Java Mapping

You can customize the WSDL 1.1 to Java mapping for services.wsdl through an external customization file. For an exhaustive survey of all the possible customizations, we recommend the JAX-WS 2.0 specification.[17] However, we will discuss some of the more commonly used customizations in the following sections.

One quick observation: the scope of the various bindings is determined through XPath expressions addressing the WSDL 1.1 document node. For example, the node="//wsdl:portType[@name= 'ProjectPortType']" XPath expression addresses ProjectPortType wsdl:portType in services.wsdl.

Package Name

You can customize the Java bindings package name as shown here:

```
<jaxws:package name="com.apress.javaxml.ws" >
</jaxws:package>
```

MIME Content

Remember, we had some wsdl:parts in services.wsdl that were bound to SOAP 1.1 mime:content, as shown here in an excerpt from Listing 14-10:

```
<mime:part>
    <mime:content part="zip"  type="application/zip" >
            </mime:content>
 </mime:part>
```

---

17. The JAX-WS 2.0 specification is available for download at http://www.jcp.org/en/jsr/detail?id=224.

If you want to bind the `mime:content` to the most specific Java type allowed by metadata in the type attribute, then you can specify that in the customization, as shown here:

```
<jaxws:enableMIMEContent>true</jaxws:enableMIMEContent>
```

Method Name

If you want to customize the Java method name corresponding to a `wsdl:operation`, you can do so as shown here for `download wsdl:operation`:

```
<jaxws:bindings
node="//wsdl:portType[@name='ProjectPortType']/wsdl:operation[@name='download']" >
    <jaxws:method name="downloadProject" ></jaxws:method>
    </jaxws:bindings>
```

In the previous example, the `download wsdl:operation` name is mapped to the `downloadProject` Java method name.

Handler Chains

It is possible to specify a handler chain that intercedes between a web service client and an SEI for messages traveling in either direction. The following example specifies a handler chain for a logging handler:

```
<javaee:handler-chains>
  <javaee:handler-chain>
    <javaee:handler>
      <javaee:handlerclass>
        com.apress.javaxml.ws.impl.LoggingHandler
      </javaee:handler-class>
    </javaee:handler>
  </javaee:handler-chain>
 </javaee:handler-chains>
```

The `LoggingHandler.java` of course is a custom class and is included in the Eclipse project for this chapter.

Complete Customization File

The `svcbindings.xml` file, shown in Listing 14-11, contains customizations for WSDL 1.1 to Java bindings: `services.wsdl`.

Listing 14-11. *Customizations for WSDL 1.1 to Java Mapping:* `svcbindings.xml`

```
<?xml version='1.0'  encoding='UTF-8' ?>
<jaxws:bindings wsdlLocation="services.wsdl"
  xmlns:jaxws="http://java.sun.com/xml/ns/jaxws"
  xmlns:wsdl="http://schemas.xmlsoap.org/wsdl/"
  xmlns:xs="http://www.w3.org/2001/XMLSchema" >
  <jaxws:package name="com.apress.javaxml.ws" >
  </jaxws:package>
  <jaxws:enableMIMEContent>true</jaxws:enableMIMEContent>

  <jaxws:bindings node="//wsdl:portType[@name='ProjectPortType']" >
    <jaxws:enableWrapperStyle>true</jaxws:enableWrapperStyle>
```

```
    <jaxws:bindings node="//wsdl:portType
     [@name='ProjectPortType']/wsdl:operation
     [@name='download']" >
      <jaxws:method name="downloadProject" ></jaxws:method>
    </jaxws:bindings>

    <jaxws:bindings node="//wsdl:portType
      [@name='ProjectPortType']/wsdl:operation
      [@name='upload']" >
      <jaxws:method name="uploadProject" ></jaxws:method>
    </jaxws:bindings>

    <jaxws:bindings node="//wsdl:portType
      [@name='ProjectPortType']/wsdl:operation
      [@name='remove']" >
      <jaxws:method name="removeProject" ></jaxws:method>
    </jaxws:bindings>

  </jaxws:bindings>

  <jaxws:bindings node="wsdl:definitions"
      xmlns:javaee="http://java.sun.com/xml/ns/javaee" >
      <javaee:handler-chains>
          <javaee:handler-chain>
              <javaee:handler>
  <javaee:handlerclass>
   com.apress.javaxml.ws.impl.LoggingHandler
   </javaee:handler-class>
              </javaee:handler>
          </javaee:handler-chain>
      </javaee:handler-chains>
   </jaxws:bindings>
 </jaxws:bindings>
```

In the next section, we will discuss how to customize JAXB 2.0 bindings.

Customizing JAXB 2.0 Bindings

The binding.xjb shown in Listing 14-12 contains external JAXB 2.0 customizations, which are applied to the types.xsd schema. These customizations specify the Java package for the object bindings and whether to generate value classes; they should be fairly obvious, and if they are not, we recommend reviewing Chapter 6, which covers JAXB in detail.

Listing 14-12. *JAXB 2.0 Customizations: binding.xjb*

```
<?xml version='1.0' encoding='utf-8' ?>
<jxb:bindings version="2.0"
    xmlns:jxb="http://java.sun.com/xml/ns/jaxb"
    xmlns:xs="http://www.w3.org/2001/XMLSchema" >
  <jxb:bindings node="/xs:schema"
    schemaLocation="types.xsd" >
    <jxb:globalBindings generateValueClass="true" >
    </jxb:globalBindings>
```

```
  <jxb:schemaBindings>
    <jxb:package name="com.apress.javaxml.ws" ></jxb:package>
  </jxb:schemaBindings>
  </jxb:bindings>
</jxb:bindings>
```

Now, you are ready to run the wsimport tool.

Running wsimport

To run the wsimport tool, first select the services.wsdl WSDL 1.1 document, and then select Run ➤ External Tools ➤ wsimport.

Running the wsimport tool maps the services.wsdl document to the SEI and service Java types and generates JAXB 2.0 object bindings, as per the customizations passed as arguments to wsimport. Remember, the arguments to wsimport are -s wsgen -d bin -keep -verbose -b wsdl/binding.xjb -b wsdl/svcbindings.xml wsdl/${resource_name}. In the arguments, binding.xjb refers to an external customization file for the JAXB 2.0 bindings, and svcbindings.xml refers to an external customization file for the WSDL 1.1 to Java mappings.

The Java files corresponding to the SEI, the service, and the JAXB 2.0 object bindings for the services.wsdl document get generated in the wsgen folder in the com.apress.javaxml.ws package. To bring the generated files into the Eclipse project view, you need to refresh the Chapter14 project files by selecting File ➤ Refresh. Listing 14-13 shows the output from the wsimport tool.

■**Note** If you see an error at this point instead of the output shown, make sure the absolute file system path to the Eclipse project location has no spaces in it.

Listing 14-13. *Output from wsimport*

```
com\apress\javaxml\ws\AuthDetail.java
com\apress\javaxml\ws\AuthScope.java
com\apress\javaxml\ws\DocumentInfo.java
com\apress\javaxml\ws\FaultDetail.java
com\apress\javaxml\ws\FolderInfo.java
com\apress\javaxml\ws\ObjectFactory.java
com\apress\javaxml\ws\ProjectInfo.java
com\apress\javaxml\ws\ProjectPortType.java
com\apress\javaxml\ws\ProjectPortTypeImplService.java
com\apress\javaxml\ws\Projects.java
com\apress\javaxml\ws\ProjectsDetail.java
com\apress\javaxml\ws\UserInfo.java
com\apress\javaxml\ws\package-info.java
com\apress\javaxml\ws\AuthDetail.java
com\apress\javaxml\ws\AuthScope.java
com\apress\javaxml\ws\DocumentInfo.java
com\apress\javaxml\ws\FaultDetail.java
com\apress\javaxml\ws\FolderInfo.java
com\apress\javaxml\ws\ObjectFactory.java
com\apress\javaxml\ws\ProjectFault.java
com\apress\javaxml\ws\ProjectInfo.java
com\apress\javaxml\ws\ProjectPortType.java
com\apress\javaxml\ws\ProjectPortTypeImplService.java
com\apress\javaxml\ws\Projects.java
```

```
com\apress\javaxml\ws\ProjectsDetail.java
com\apress\javaxml\ws\UserInfo.java
com\apress\javaxml\ws\package-info.java
```

The generated file `ProjectPortType.java` in the `com.apress.javaxml.ws` package defines the SEI; `ProjectPortTypeImplService.java` implements the service. All the other generated files in the `com.apress.javaxml.ws` package correspond to JAXB 2.0 object bindings.

ProjectPortType SEI

The generated code for SEI in `ProjectPortType.java` uses a number of different Java annotation tags, which are explained in Table 14-3.

Table 14-3. *Annotation Tags Used in* `ProjectPortType.java`

Tag Name	Description
WebService	When used with a Java interface, it defines an SEI. The name attribute specifies the name of the web service, and the `targetNamespace` attribute defines the target namespace of the corresponding `wsdl:portType`.
HandlerChain	Associates this web service with an externally defined handler chain, and the `file` attribute defines the location of the handler chain file. The handler chain is invoked before the SEI is invoked.
SOAPBinding	Specifies how the web service is mapped to the SOAP 1.1 message body. The `paramterStyle` attribute specifies whether the parameters are directly put into the message body (`ParameterStyle.BARE`) or whether they are wrapped in an element that bears the name of the operation (`ParameterStyle.WRAPPED`). Basically, `BARE` corresponds to the document style, and `WRAPPED` corresponds to the rpc style.
WebMethod	This specifies a method that is exposed as a web service operation. The `operationName` attribute specifies the name of the `wsdl:operation`. The `action` attribute specifies the corresponding `soapAction`.
WebParam	This specifies a method parameter that is mapped to a `wsdl:part`. The `name` attribute specifies the name of this parameter. The `partName` specifies the name of the `wsdl:part`. The `header` attribute specifies whether the parameter is contained with a SOAP 1.1 header or body. The `targetNamespace` specifies the XML namespace associated with the parameter.
WebResult	This specifies a return value that is mapped to a `wsdl:part`. The `name` attribute specifies the name of this return value. The `partName` specifies the name of the `wsdl:part`. The `header` attribute specifies whether the parameter is contained with a SOAP 1.1 header or body. The `targetNamespace` specifies the XML namespace associated with the parameter.
OneWay	This specifies there is only an input message with no response.

The `ProjectPortType` SEI mapping contains the Java mapping for `ProjectPortType` `wsdl:portType`, as per the rules described in the section "WSDL 1.1 to Java Mapping." For example, the `download` `wsdl:operation` is mapped to a Java method as shown here:

```
@WebMethod(operationName = "download",
        action = "http://www.apress.com/xmljava/webservices/download")
    public void downloadProject(
        @WebParam(name = "userInfo",
            targetNamespace = "http://www.apress.com/xmljava/webservices/schemas",
            header = true, partName = "user")
        UserInfo user,
        @WebParam(name = "project",
            targetNamespace = "http://www.apress.com/xmljava/webservices/schemas",
            partName = "project")
        ProjectInfo project,
        @WebParam(name = "manifest",
            targetNamespace = "http://www.apress.com/xmljava/webservices/schemas",
            mode = Mode.OUT, partName = "manifest")
        Holder<ProjectInfo> manifest,
        @WebParam(name = "zip",
            targetNamespace = "", mode = Mode.OUT, partName = "zip")
        Holder<DataHandler> zip)
        throws ProjectFault;
```

In the previous example, the mapping of message parts to Java method parameters uses the nonwrapper style, because the input and output messages have two message parts each. The output message parts, manifest and zip, are mapped to holder classes, Holder<ProjectInfo> and Holder<DataHandler>, respectively. The fault message part is mapped to the generated ProjectFault exception.

Listing 14-14 shows the generated code for the ProjectPortType SEI in ProjectPortType.java.

Listing 14-14. *Generated Code in ProjectPortType.java*

```
package com.apress.javaxml.ws;

import javax.activation.DataHandler;
import javax.jws.HandlerChain;
import javax.jws.Oneway;
import javax.jws.WebMethod;
import javax.jws.WebParam;
import javax.jws.WebParam.Mode;
import javax.jws.WebResult;
import javax.jws.WebService;
import javax.jws.soap.SOAPBinding;
import javax.jws.soap.SOAPBinding.ParameterStyle;
import javax.xml.ws.Holder;

@WebService(name = "ProjectPortType",
    targetNamespace = "http://www.apress.com/xmljava/webservices/definitions")
@HandlerChain(file = "ProjectPortType_handler.xml")
@SOAPBinding(parameterStyle = ParameterStyle.BARE)
public interface ProjectPortType {
```

```java
    @WebMethod(operationName = "download",
        action = "http://www.apress.com/xmljava/webservices/download")
    public void downloadProject(
        @WebParam(name = "userInfo",
            targetNamespace = "http://www.apress.com/xmljava/webservices/schemas",
            header = true, partName = "user")
        UserInfo user,
        @WebParam(name = "project",
            targetNamespace = "http://www.apress.com/xmljava/webservices/schemas",
            partName = "project")
        ProjectInfo project,
        @WebParam(name = "manifest",
            targetNamespace = "http://www.apress.com/xmljava/webservices/schemas",
            mode = Mode.OUT, partName = "manifest")
        Holder<ProjectInfo> manifest,
        @WebParam(name = "zip",
            targetNamespace = "", mode = Mode.OUT, partName = "zip")
        Holder<DataHandler> zip)
        throws ProjectFault;

@WebMethod(operationName = "upload",
    action = "http://www.apress.com/xmlJava/webservices/upload")
@WebResult(name = "project",
    targetNamespace = "http://www.apress.com/xmljava/webservices/schemas",
    partName = "project")
public ProjectInfo uploadProject(
    @WebParam(name = "userInfo",
        targetNamespace = "http://www.apress.com/xmljava/webservices/schemas",
        header = true, partName = "user")
    UserInfo user,
    @WebParam(name = "manifest",
        targetNamespace = "http://www.apress.com/xmljava/webservices/schemas",
        partName = "manifest")
    ProjectInfo manifest,
    @WebParam(name = "zip", targetNamespace = "", partName = "zip")
    DataHandler zip)
    throws ProjectFault;

@WebMethod(operationName = "remove",
    action = "http://www.apress.com/xmlJava/webservices/remove")
@Oneway
public void removeProject(
    @WebParam(name = "userInfo",
        targetNamespace = "http://www.apress.com/xmljava/webservices/schemas",
        header = true, partName = "user")
    UserInfo user,
    @WebParam(name = "remove",
        targetNamespace = "http://www.apress.com/xmljava/webservices/schemas",
        partName = "remove")
    ProjectInfo remove);
```

```
    @WebMethod(action = "http://www.apress.com/xmljava/webservices/getprojects")
    @WebResult(name = "projects",
        targetNamespace = "http://www.apress.com/xmljava/webservices/schemas",
        partName = "projects")
    public Projects getProjects(
        @WebParam(name = "userInfo",
            targetNamespace = "http://www.apress.com/xmljava/webservices/schemas",
            header = true, partName = "user")
        UserInfo user,
        @WebParam(name = "projectsDetail",
            targetNamespace = "http://www.apress.com/xmljava/webservices/schemas",
            partName = "detail")
        ProjectsDetail detail)
        throws ProjectFault;

    @WebMethod(action = "http://www.apress.com/xmljava/webservices/authenticate")
    public void authenticate(
        @WebParam(name = "userInfo",
            targetNamespace = "http://www.apress.com/xmljava/webservices/schemas",
            header = true, mode = Mode.INOUT, partName = "user")
        Holder<UserInfo> user,
        @WebParam(name = "authDetail",
            targetNamespace = "http://www.apress.com/xmljava/webservices/schemas",
            mode = Mode.INOUT, partName = "detail")
        Holder<AuthDetail> detail)
        throws ProjectFault;
}
```

We will show how to implement the `ProjectPortType` SEI in the next section.

Implementing the ProjectPortType SEI

The `ProjectPortType` SEI is implemented in the `ProjectPortTypeImpl.java` file in the `com.apress.javaxml.ws.impl` package, under the `wsimpl` folder, as shown in Listing 14-15. The `javax.ejb.EJB` annotation tag in Listing 14-16 refers to an EJB interface. In the code shown in Listing 14-15, you will notice that in each of the SEI methods, you merely invoke a corresponding EJB method. This is because the application logic is all implemented within EJB classes.

Listing 14-15. *SEI Implementation in* `ProjectPortTypeImpl.java`

```
package com.apress.javaxml.ws.impl;

import javax.activation.DataHandler;
import javax.ejb.EJB;
import javax.xml.ws.Holder;

import com.apress.javaxml.ws.AuthDetail;
import com.apress.javaxml.ws.FaultDetail;
import com.apress.javaxml.ws.ProjectInfo;
import com.apress.javaXml.ws.Projects;
import com.apress.javaxml.ws.ProjectsDetail;
import com.apress.javaxml.ws.UserInfo;
import com.apress.javaxml.ws.ProjectFault;
import com.apress.javaxml.service.ProjectLocal;
import com.apress.javaxml.service.UserLocal;
```

```java
@javax.jws.WebService(
    targetNamespace = "http://www.apress.com/xmljava/webservices/definitions",
    serviceName = "ProjectPortTypeImplService",
    portName = "ProjectPortTypeImplPort",
    endpointInterface = "com.apress.javaxml.ws.ProjectPortType",
    wsdlLocation = "WEB-INF/wsdl/services.wsdl")
public class ProjectPortTypeImpl {
    @EJB
    private ProjectLocal projectLocal;

    @EJB
    private UserLocal userLocal;

    public void downloadProject(UserInfo user, ProjectInfo project,
            Holder<ProjectInfo> manifestHolder, Holder<DataHandler> dhHolder)
            throws ProjectFault {
        try {
            // download ZIP file
            manifestHolder.value = project;
            DataHandler dh = projectLocal.downloadZipFile(user,
                    manifestHolder.value);

            // put data handler in data handler holder
            dhHolder.value = dh;
        } catch (Exception e) {
            FaultDetail detail = new FaultDetail();
            detail.setMajor("DOWNLOAD");
            detail.setMinor("NONE");
            throw new ProjectFault(e.getMessage(), detail);
        }
    }

    public ProjectInfo uploadProject(UserInfo user, ProjectInfo manifest,
            DataHandler zip) throws ProjectFault {

        try {
            // upload ZIP file
            projectLocal.uploadZipFile(user, manifest, zip);
        } catch (Exception e) {
            FaultDetail detail = new FaultDetail();
            detail.setMajor("UPLOAD");
            detail.setMinor("NONE");
            throw new ProjectFault(e.getMessage(), detail);
        }
        return manifest;
    }

    public void removeProject(UserInfo user, ProjectInfo remove) {
        projectLocal.remove(user, remove);
    }

    public Projects getProjects(UserInfo user, ProjectsDetail projectsDetail)
            throws ProjectFault {
```

```java
        Projects projects = null;
        try {
            // get projects
            projects = projectLocal.getProjects(user, projectsDetail);
        } catch (Exception e) {
            FaultDetail detail = new FaultDetail();
            detail.setMajor("GETPROJECTS");
            detail.setMinor("NONE");
            throw new ProjectFault(e.getMessage(), detail);
        }
        return projects;
    }

    public void authenticate(Holder<UserInfo> userInfoHolder,
            Holder<AuthDetail> authDetailHolder) throws ProjectFault {
        try {
            UserInfo userInfo = userInfoHolder.value;
            userLocal.login(userInfo.getEmail(), userInfo.getPwd());
        } catch (Exception e) {
            FaultDetail detail = new FaultDetail();
            detail.setMajor("AUTHENTICATE");
            detail.setMinor("NONE");
            throw new ProjectFault(e.getMessage(), detail);
        }
    }

}
```

The `ProjectPortTypeImpl` class uses the `ProjectLocal` and `UserLocal` EJBs to access the application logic. Listing 14-16 shows the `ProjectLocal` EJB, which is in the `ProjectLocal.java` file in the `com.apress.javaxml.service` package in the `ejb` folder.

Listing 14-16. *ProjectLocal EJB in ProjectLocal.java*

```java
package com.apress.javaxml.service;

import javax.activation.DataHandler;
import javax.ejb.Local;

import com.apress.javaxml.ws.*;

@Local
public interface ProjectLocal {
    public ProjectInfo uploadZipFile(UserInfo user,
    ProjectInfo manifest, DataHandler zip);

    public DataHandler downloadZipFile(UserInfo user, ProjectInfo manifest);

    public void remove(UserInfo user, ProjectInfo manifest);

    public Projects getProjects(UserInfo user, ProjectsDetail detail);
}
```

The `ProjectLocal` EJB interface is implemented by the `ProjectService` class. The `ProjectService` class in the `com.apress.javaxml.service` package in the `ejb` folder provides the actual application logic associated with the use case scenarios. The `ProjectService` class is not directly relevant to understanding web services, so it is included for reference in the Eclipse project for this chapter.

Listing 14-17 shows the `UserLocal` EJB, which is in the `UserLocal.java` file in the `com.apress.javaxml.service` package in the ejb folder.

Listing 14-17. *UserLocal EJB in UserLocal.java*

```
package com.apress.javaxml.service;

import javax.ejb.Local;

@Local
public interface UserLocal {
    public void login(String email, String pwd);
    public void register(String email, String pwd);

    public void changePwd(String email, String cpwd, String npwd);

    public void unregister(String email, String pwd);
}
```

The `UserLocal` interface is implemented by the `UserService` class. The `UserService` class in the `com.apress.javaxml.service` package in the ejb folder provides the actual application logic for use cases associated with registering a new user, logging in a user, changing a password for an existing user, and unregistering a user. The `UserService` class is not directly relevant to understanding web services, so it is included for reference in the Eclipse project for this chapter.

Building the Web Service

Here are the steps for building and deploying the web service application to Sun One Application Server 9.0:

1. Build the `Chapter14` project by selecting the `Chapter14` project node in Package Explorer and selecting Project ➤ Build Project.

2. Build the enterprise application archive using the `build.xml` Ant file. To invoke Ant on the `build.xml` file, right-click the `build.xml` file, and select Run As ➤ Ant Build.

The `build.xml` file has three targets: jar, war, and ear. The jar target creates an EJB 3.0-compliant archive module: `projectejb.jar`. Listing 14-18 shows the contents of `projectejb.jar`. The source code corresponding to these classes is included in the project.

Listing 14-18. *Contents of projectejb.jar*

```
META-INF/MANIFEST.MF
com/apress/javaxml/persistence/Document.class
com/apress/javaxml/persistence/DocumentKey.class
com/apress/javaxml/persistence/Folder.class
com/apress/javaxml/persistence/FolderKey.class
com/apress/javaxml/persistence/Project.class
com/apress/javaxml/persistence/ProjectKey.class
com/apress/javaxml/persistence/User.class
```

```
com/apress/javaxml/service/ProjectLocal.class
com/apress/javaxml/service/ProjectService.class
com/apress/javaxml/service/UserLocal.class
com/apress/javaxml/service/UserService.class
com/apress/javaxml/ws/DocumentInfo.class
com/apress/javaxml/ws/FolderInfo.class
com/apress/javaxml/ws/ProjectInfo.class
com/apress/javaxml/ws/UserInfo.class
META-INF/persistence.xml
```

The war target creates a web application archive module: projectservice.war. Listing 14-19 shows the contents of projectservice.war. The jsp files and the XML documents under WEB-INF are included in the project.

Listing 14-19. *Contents of projectservice.war*

```
META-INF/MANIFEST.MF
WEB-INF/classes/com/apress/javaxml/beans/UserBean.class
WEB-INF/classes/com/apress/javaxml/i18n/messages.properties
WEB-INF/classes/com/apress/javaxml/service/ProjectLocal.class
WEB-INF/classes/com/apress/javaxml/service/UserLocal.class
WEB-INF/classes/com/apress/javaxml/ws/AuthDetail.class
WEB-INF/classes/com/apress/javaxml/ws/AuthScope.class
WEB-INF/classes/com/apress/javaxml/ws/DocumentInfo.class
WEB-INF/classes/com/apress/javaxml/ws/FaultDetail.class
WEB-INF/classes/com/apress/javaxml/ws/FolderInfo.class
WEB-INF/classes/com/apress/javaxml/ws/ObjectFactory.class
WEB-INF/classes/com/apress/javaxml/ws/ProjectFault.class
WEB-INF/classes/com/apress/javaxml/ws/ProjectInfo.class
WEB-INF/classes/com/apress/javaxml/ws/ProjectPortType.class
WEB-INF/classes/com/apress/javaxml/ws/ProjectPortTypeImplService_handler.xml
WEB-INF/classes/com/apress/javaxml/ws/ProjectPortType_handler.xml
WEB-INF/classes/com/apress/javaxml/ws/Projects.class
WEB-INF/classes/com/apress/javaxml/ws/ProjectsDetail.class
WEB-INF/classes/com/apress/javaxml/ws/UserInfo.class
WEB-INF/classes/com/apress/javaxml/ws/impl/LoggingHandler.class
WEB-INF/classes/com/apress/javaxml/ws/impl/ProjectPortTypeImpl.class
WEB-INF/classes/com/apress/javaxml/ws/package-info.class
WEB-INF/classes/types.xsd
WEB-INF/wsdl/services.wsdl
WEB-INF/wsdl/types.xsd
WEB-INF/faces-config.xml
chgpwd.jsp
home.jsp
index.jsp
register.jsp
styles.css
WEB-INF/web.xml
```

The ear target creates an enterprise application archive: project.ear. Listing 14-20 shows the contents of project.ear. The META-INF/application.xml file is included in the project.

Listing 14-20. *Contents of project.ear*

```
META-INF/MANIFEST.MF
projectejb.jar
projectservice.war
META-INF/application.xml
```

The ear target triggers the war target; the war target triggers the jar target. All module archives are created under the dist folder. The default target is ear. Listing 14-21 shows the output from building build.xml.

Listing 14-21. *Output from build.xml*

```
Buildfile: C:\workspace\Chapter14\build.xml
jar:
   [delete] Deleting: C:\workspace\Chapter14\dist\projectejb.jar
      [jar] Building jar: C:\workspace\Chapter14\dist\projectejb.jar
war:
   [delete] Deleting: C:\workspace\Chapter14\dist\projectservice.war
      [war] Building war: C:\workspace\Chapter14\dist\projectservice.war
ear:
   [delete] Deleting: C:\workspace\Chapter14\dist\project.ear
      [ear] Building ear: C:\workspace\Chapter14\dist\project.ear
BUILD SUCCESSFUL
```

Deploying the Web Service

You need to deploy the project.ear file in the administration console of Sun One Application Server 9.0. You need to start the default server, start the Java DB server, and then open the administration console for Sun One Application Server 9.0. To deploy the project.ear application, select the Applications ➤ Enterprise Applications node in the administration console. Click the Deploy button. Select the project.ear file with the Browse button in the File to Upload, and click Next, as shown in Figure 14-9.

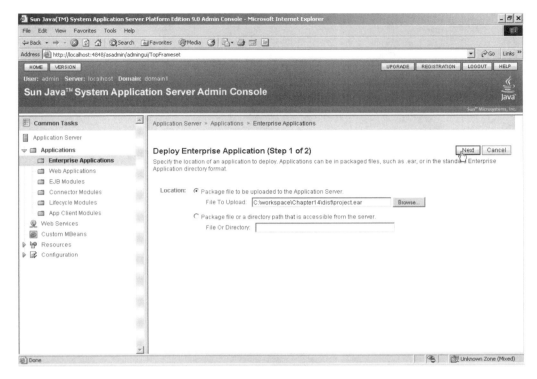

Figure 14-9. *Deploying the* `project.ear` *application*

To run the verifier on the application and precompile the JSPs, select the check boxes for Run Verifier and Precompile JSPs. To deploy the web service application, click the Finish button, as shown in Figure 14-10.

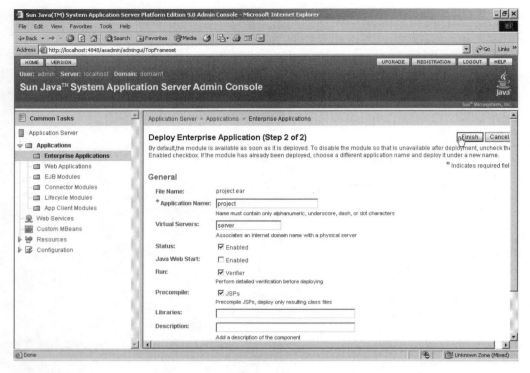

Figure 14-10. *Configuring settings for and deploying the* `project.ear` *application*

The `project.ear` enterprise application gets deployed and appears under Enterprise Applications in the Application Server tree.

You can test the web service deployment by selecting the Web Services ➤ ProjectPortTypeImpl node and clicking the Test button, as shown in Figure 14-11.

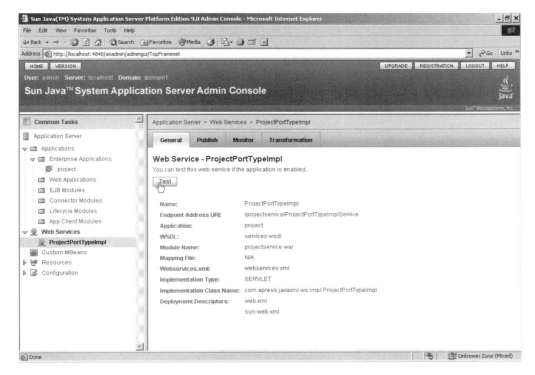

Figure 14-11. *Testing web service*

A form to test web service implementation appears, as shown in Figure 14-12. This form is not useful for actually testing the web service, but it does verify a successful deployment. We will not use this form to test the web service.

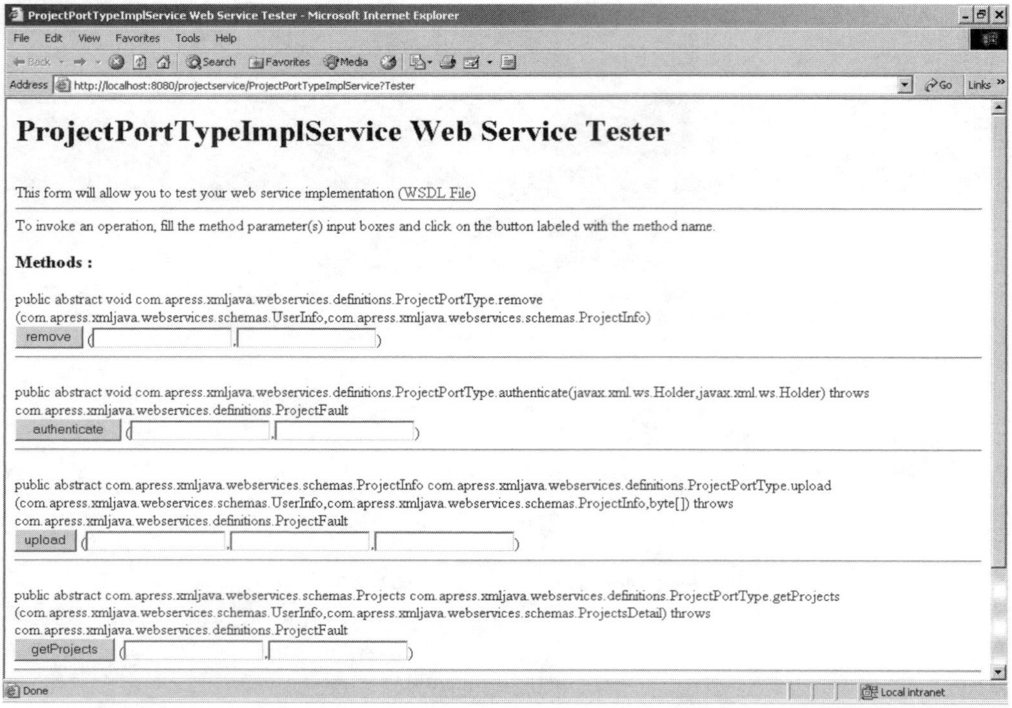

Figure 14-12. *Output from testing the web service*

Registering a New User

You need to register a user with the web service so you can connect as a client for the web service. Using the URL http://localhost:8080/projectservice/index.faces, display the form to register a user. Click the Register link, specify a user email and password, and click Register button, as shown in Figure 14-13.

Figure 14-13. *Registering a new user*

The specified user email gets registered.

Web Service Client

The web service client uses a generated service proxy class,
com.apress.javaxml.ws.ProjectPortTypeImpl.java, as shown in Listing 14-22, to interact with the
web service. The key method of this class that you will use is the ProjectPortTypeImplService(URL
wsdlLocation, QName serviceName) constructor to create a service proxy instance. You will invoke
the getProjectPortTypeImplPort() method on the service proxy instance to get an instance of the
ProjectPortType service interface.

Listing 14-22. *Service:* ProjectPortTypeImpl.java

```
package com.apress.javaxml.ws;

import java.net.MalformedURLException;
import java.net.URL;
import javax.jws.HandlerChain;
import javax.xml.namespace.QName;
import javax.xml.ws.Service;
import javax.xml.ws.WebEndpoint;
import javax.xml.ws.WebServiceClient;


@WebServiceClient(name = "ProjectPortTypeImplService",
    targetNamespace = "http://www.apress.com/xmljava/webservices/definitions",
    wsdlLocation = "wsdl/services.wsdl")
@HandlerChain(file = "ProjectPortTypeImplService_handler.xml")
public class ProjectPortTypeImplService
    extends Service {

    private final static URL PROJECTPORTTYPEIMPLSERVICE_WSDL_LOCATION;

    static {
        URL url = null;
        try {
            url = new URL
              ("file:/C:/eclipse-workspaces/xmlbook/Chapter14/wsdl/services.wsdl");
        } catch (MalformedURLException e) {
            e.printStackTrace();
        }
        PROJECTPORTTYPEIMPLSERVICE_WSDL_LOCATION = url;
    }

    public ProjectPortTypeImplService(URL wsdlLocation, QName serviceName) {
        super(wsdlLocation, serviceName);
    }

    public ProjectPortTypeImplService() {
        super(PROJECTPORTTYPEIMPLSERVICE_WSDL_LOCATION,
            new QName("http://www.apress.com/xmljava/webservices/definitions",
            "ProjectPortTypeImplService"));
    }
```

```
    @WebEndpoint(name = "ProjectPortTypeImplPort")
    public ProjectPortType getProjectPortTypeImplPort() {
        return (ProjectPortType)super.getPort(new
          QName("http://www.apress.com/xmljava/webservices/definitions",
            "ProjectPortTypeImplPort"),
            ProjectPortType.class);
    }

}
```

The example web service application includes a web service client, ProjectClient, that can be used to test all the use case scenarios defined by the web service. Listing 14-23 shows the code for com.apress.javaxml.ws.client.ProjectClient.

Listing 14-23. *Web Service Client: ProjectClient.java*

```java
package com.apress.javaxml.ws.client;
import javax.xml.namespace.QName;
import javax.xml.ws.Holder;

import java.io.File;
import java.io.FileOutputStream;
import java.net.*;
import java.util.*;
import java.util.logging.Logger;
import java.util.zip.ZipEntry;
import java.util.zip.ZipFile;

import javax.activation.*;

import com.apress.javaxml.ws.*;

public class ProjectClient {
    private static ProjectPortTypeImplService service;

    private static final Logger logger = Logger.getLogger(ProjectClient.class
            .getName());

    private static File zfile;

    private static String email, pwd;

    private static URL wsdlUrl;

    private final static QName PROJECTSERVICE = new QName(
            "http://www.apress.com/xmljava/webservices/definitions",
            "ProjectPortTypeImplService");

    /**
     * @param args
     *              the command line arguments
     */
    public static void main(String[] args) {
      try {
```

```
        if (args.length == 4) {
        email = args[0];
        pwd = args[1];
        wsdlUrl = new URL(args[2]);
        zfile = new File(args[3]);
        } else {
        System.out
          .println("Usage: <email> <password> <wsdl URL> <zipfile>");
        System.exit(1);
        }

        doProjectServiceTests();

    } catch (Exception e) {
        logger.severe(e.toString());
    }
}

private static void log(DocumentInfo dinfo) {
    logger.info("Document Name:" + dinfo.getName());
    logger.info("Document Created On:" + dinfo.getCreatedOn());
    logger.info("Document Last Updated On:" + dinfo.getLastUpdated());
}

private static void log(FolderInfo finfo) {
    logger.info("Folder Location:" + finfo.getLocation());
    logger.info("Folder Created On:" + finfo.getCreatedOn());
    logger.info("Folder Last Updated On:" + finfo.getLastUpdated());
    List<DocumentInfo> docs = finfo.getDocument();

    Iterator<DocumentInfo> it = docs.iterator();
    while (it.hasNext()) {
        DocumentInfo docInfo = it.next();
        log(docInfo);
    }
}

private static void log(ProjectInfo pinfo) {
    logger.info("Project Name:" + pinfo.getName());
    logger.info("Project Created On:" + pinfo.getCreatedOn());
    logger.info("Project Last Updated On:" + pinfo.getLastUpdated());
    List<FolderInfo> folders = pinfo.getFolder();

    Iterator<FolderInfo> it = folders.iterator();
    while (it.hasNext()) {
        FolderInfo folderInfo = it.next();
        log(folderInfo);
    }
}

private static void doProjectServiceTests() {
    try {
        logger.info("\nBegin ProjectService Tests\n");
```

```java
            logger.info("Create service for:" + wsdlUrl);
            service =
                                        new ProjectPortTypeImplService(wsdlUrl,
                                                PROJECTSERVICE);

            ProjectPortType port = service.getProjectPortTypeImplPort();

            UserInfo userInfo = new UserInfo();
            userInfo.setEmail(email);
            userInfo.setPwd(pwd);

            Holder<UserInfo> userInfoHolder = new Holder<UserInfo>();
            userInfoHolder.value = userInfo;
            logger.info("Authenticate user:" +
        userInfo.getEmail()+":"+userInfo.getPwd());

            AuthScope scope = new AuthScope();
            scope.setScope("session");

            AuthDetail authDetail = new AuthDetail();
            authDetail.setAny(scope);

            Holder<AuthDetail> authDetailHolder = new Holder<AuthDetail>();
            authDetailHolder.value = authDetail;

            try {//Web Service Call - Authentication
                port.authenticate(userInfoHolder, authDetailHolder);
            } catch(Exception e) {
                e.printStackTrace();
                logger.info("User is not authorized");
                System.exit(1);
            }
            logger.info("User is authorized");

            ProjectInfo projectInfo = new ProjectInfo();

            projectInfo.setName(zfile.getName());
            projectInfo.setEmail(email);

            ZipFile zipFile = new ZipFile(zfile);
            Enumeration entries = zipFile.entries();
            HashMap<String, FolderInfo>
            folderMap = new HashMap<String, FolderInfo>();

            while (entries.hasMoreElements()) {
                ZipEntry zipEntry = (ZipEntry) entries.nextElement();
                String entryName = zipEntry.getName();
                if (!zipEntry.isDirectory()) {
                    String location = entryName.substring(0, entryName
                            .lastIndexOf("/") + 1);
                    String name = entryName.substring(entryName
                            .lastIndexOf("/") + 1);
                    FolderInfo folderInfo = (FolderInfo) folderMap
                            .get(location);
```

```
        if (folderInfo == null) {
            folderInfo = new FolderInfo();
            folderMap.put(location, folderInfo);
            folderInfo.setLocation(location);
            projectInfo.getFolder().add(folderInfo);
        }
        DocumentInfo docInfo = new DocumentInfo();
        docInfo.setName(name);
        folderInfo.getDocument().add(docInfo);
    }
}
DataHandler dh = new DataHandler(new FileDataSource(zfile));

logger.info("Uploading zip file:" + zfile.getName());
                        //Web Service Call-Upload
ProjectInfo retProjectInfo = port.uploadProject(userInfo,
        projectInfo, dh);
logger.info("Begin Upload Project Status");
log(retProjectInfo);
logger.info("End Upload Project Status");

logger.info("Get All Projects:" + userInfo.getEmail());
ProjectsDetail detail = new ProjectsDetail();
detail.setFolders(false);
detail.setDocuments(false);

Projects projects = port.getProjects(userInfo, detail);
List<ProjectInfo> projectList = projects.getProject();
Iterator<ProjectInfo> itp = projectList.iterator();
while (itp.hasNext()) {
    projectInfo = itp.next();
    logger.info("Downloading Project:" + userInfo.getEmail() + ":"
            + projectInfo.getName());
    Holder<ProjectInfo> mf = new Holder<ProjectInfo>();
    Holder<DataHandler> zip = new Holder<DataHandler>();
                        //Web Service Call-Download
    port.downloadProject(userInfo, projectInfo, mf, zip);

    dh = zip.value;

    if (dh != null) {
        File temp = File.createTempFile(projectInfo.getName(),
                ".zip");
        FileOutputStream fos = new FileOutputStream(temp);
        dh.writeTo(fos);
        fos.close();
        zipFile = new ZipFile(temp);
        entries = zipFile.entries();
```

```
                    logger.info(("Begin Zip Entries:"));
                    while (entries.hasMoreElements()) {
                        ZipEntry zipEntry = (ZipEntry) entries.nextElement();
                        String entryName = zipEntry.getName();
                        logger.info("Zip entry:" + entryName);
                    }
                    logger.info(("End Zip Entries"));
                    temp.delete();
                }

                ProjectInfo pinfo = new ProjectInfo();
                pinfo.setEmail(projectInfo.getEmail());
                pinfo.setName(projectInfo.getName());

                logger.info("Remove Project:"+
                 userInfo.getEmail()+":"+pinfo.getName());
                port.removeProject(userInfo, pinfo);
            }
            logger.info("\nEnd ProjectService Tests\n");
        } catch (Exception ex) {
            logger.severe(ex.toString());
        }
    }
}
```

Running the ProjectClient Client

To run the ProjectClient client in Eclipse, you need to configure a Java application configuration for ProjectClient by selecting Run ➤ Run.

ProjectClient needs to know about the location of the WSDL document for the web service. You obtain the location of the WSDL document from the web service deployed in Sun One Application Server 9.0 by selecting the Web Services ➤ ProjectPortTypeImpl node and clicking the services.wsdl link, as shown in Figure 14-14.

In the services.wsdl file, the soap:address element's location attribute, suffixed with ?WSDL, specifies the WSDL URL.

In the Program Arguments field of the ProjectClient application configuration, specify the user email, password, WSDL URL, and the testproject.zip file, as shown here:

```
useremail password <WSDL URL> testproject.zip
```

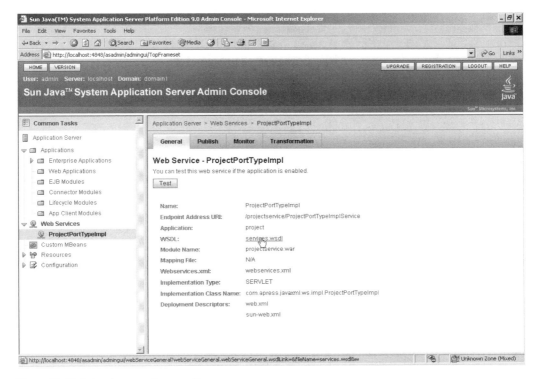

Figure 14-14. *Selecting* services.wsdl

Run the ProjectClient application by selecting Run As ➤ Run. Listing 14-24 shows the output from running ProjectClient.java.

Listing 14-24. *Output from* ProjectClient.java

```
com.apress.javaxml.ws.client.ProjectClient doProjectServ
iceTests
INFO:
Begin ProjectService Tests

com.apress.javaxml.ws.client.ProjectClient doProjectServ
iceTests
INFO: Create service for:http://d207-6-39-2.bchsia.telus.net:8080/projectservice
/ProjectPortTypeImplService?WSDL
com.apress.javaxml.ws.client.ProjectClient doProjectServ
```

```
iceTests
INFO: Authenticate user:dvohra09@yahoo.com:administrator
com.apress.javaxml.ws.impl.LoggingHandler log
INFO: <?xml version="1.0" ?><soapenv:Envelope xmlns:soapenv="http://schemas.xmls
oap.org/soap/envelope/" xmlns:xsd="http://www.w3.org/2001/XMLSchema" xmlns:ns1="
http://www.apress.com/xmljava/webservices/schemas" xmlns:ns2="http://www.apress.
com/xmljava/webservices/definitions"><soapenv:Header><ns1:userInfo><email>dvohra
@yahoo.com</email><pwd>administrator</pwd></ns1:userInfo></soapenv:Header><soape
nv:Body><ns1:authDetail><ns1:authScope><scope>session</scope></ns1:authScope></n
s1:authDetail></soapenv:Body></soapenv:Envelope>
com.apress.javaxml.ws.impl.LoggingHandler log
INFO: <?xml version="1.0" ?><soapenv:Envelope xmlns:soapenv="http://schemas.xmls
oap.org/soap/envelope/" xmlns:xsd="http://www.w3.org/2001/XMLSchema" xmlns:ns1="
http://www.apress.com/xmljava/webservices/schemas" xmlns:ns2="http://www.apress.
com/xmljava/webservices/definitions"><soapenv:Header><ns1:userInfo><email>dvohra
@yahoo.com</email><pwd>administrator</pwd></ns1:userInfo></soapenv:Header><soape
nv:Body><ns1:authDetail><ns1:authScope><scope>session</scope></ns1:authScope></n
s1:authDetail></soapenv:Body></soapenv:Envelope>
com.apress.javaxml.ws.client.ProjectClient doProjectServ
iceTests
INFO: User is authorized
com.apress.javaxml.ws.client.ProjectClient doProjectServ
iceTests
INFO: Uploading zip file:testproject.zip
com.apress.javaxml.ws.impl.LoggingHandler log
INFO: ------=_Part_0_26171428.1151199877220
Content-Type: text/xml; charset=utf-8

<?xml version="1.0" ?><soapenv:Envelope xmlns:soapenv="http://schemas.xmlsoap.or
g/soap/envelope/" xmlns:xsd="http://www.w3.org/2001/XMLSchema" xmlns:ns1="http:/
/www.apress.com/xmljava/webservices/schemas" xmlns:ns2="http://www.apress.com/xm
ljava/webservices/definitions"><soapenv:Header><ns1:userInfo><email>dvohra09@yahoo
.com</email><pwd>administrator</pwd></ns1:userInfo></soapenv:Header><soapenv:Bod
y><ns1:manifest name="testproject.zip" email="dvohra09@yahoo.com"><folder location
="popuptest/"><document name="error.html"></document><document name="index.jsp">
</document><document name="login.html"></document></folder><folder location="pop
uptest/WEB-INF/"><document name="web.xml"></document><document name="weblogic.xm
l"></document></folder></ns1:manifest></soapenv:Body></soapenv:Envelope>
------=_Part_0_26171428.1151199877220
Content-Type: application/octet-stream
Content-ID: <zip=7c8243a2-3223-4891-9336-11ab17a7e926@jaxws.sun.com>
Content-transfer-encoding: binary

PK____

------=_Part_2_24166053.1151199960199--
com.apress.javaxml.ws.client.ProjectClient doProjectServ
iceTests
INFO: Begin Zip Entries:
com.apress.javaxml.ws.client.ProjectClient doProjectServ
iceTests
INFO: Zip entry:popuptest/WEB-INF/web.xml
com.apress.javaxml.ws.client.ProjectClient doProjectServ
```

```
iceTests
INFO: Zip entry:popuptest/WEB-INF/weblogic.xml
 com.apress.javaxml.ws.client.ProjectClient doProjectServ
iceTests
INFO: Zip entry:popuptest/error.html
com.apress.javaxml.ws.client.ProjectClient doProjectServ
iceTests
INFO: Zip entry:popuptest/index.jsp
com.apress.javaxml.ws.client.ProjectClient doProjectServ
iceTests
INFO: Zip entry:popuptest/login.html
com.apress.javaxml.ws.client.ProjectClient doProjectServ
iceTests
INFO: End Zip Entries
com.apress.javaxml.ws.client.ProjectClient doProjectServ
iceTests
INFO: Remove Project:dvohra09@yahoo.com:testproject.zip
com.apress.javaxml.ws.impl.LoggingHandler log
INFO: <?xml version="1.0" ?><soapenv:Envelope xmlns:soapenv="http://schemas.xmls
oap.org/soap/envelope/" xmlns:xsd="http://www.w3.org/2001/XMLSchema" xmlns:ns1="
http://www.apress.com/xmljava/webservices/schemas" xmlns:ns2="http://www.apress.
com/xmljava/webservices/definitions"><soapenv:Header><ns1:userInfo><email>dvohra
@yahoo.com</email><pwd>administrator</pwd></ns1:userInfo></soapenv:Header><soape
nv:Body><ns1:remove name="testproject.zip" email="dvohra09@yahoo.com"></ns1:remove
></soapenv:Body></soapenv:Envelope>
com.apress.javaxml.ws.client.ProjectClient doProjectServ
iceTests
INFO:
End ProjectService Tests
```

Summary

This was a capstone chapter that drew from many concepts covered in this book.

Building a XML-based web service starts with formally describing a web service in a WSDL document. Specifying a WSDL document starts with describing user-defined data types in a schema definition. The user-defined data types are the basic building blocks for defining various messages types required by the web service use cases. The message types are then used in defining a port type, which defines a web service interface.

The web service message types and port types are abstract types. To make these types concrete, you need to bind these types to the SOAP messaging framework and the HTTP transport protocol. Finally, the concrete binding of the port type is bound to an HTTP URL, which defines a web service port. We covered all these concepts in this chapter in the context of a complete web service example.

A WSDL document contains enough information that code generation tools can easily generate the Java code associated with implementing a web service provider agent. In addition, code generation tools can use a WSDL document to generate a service proxy that can be used by a web service requestor agent to interact with the web service. In this chapter, we used Sun One Application Server 9.0 tools to generate Java code corresponding to an example web service and then build and deploy the web service in Sun One Application Server 9.0. Finally, we showed how to build a web service client that can interact with the web service.

Index

Find it faster at http://superindex.apress.com

You Need the Companion eBook

Your purchase of this book entitles you to buy the companion PDF-version eBook for only $10. Take the weightless companion with you anywhere.

We believe this Apress title will prove so indispensable that you'll want to carry it with you everywhere, which is why we are offering the companion eBook (in PDF format) for $10 to customers who purchase this book now. Convenient and fully searchable, the PDF version of any content-rich, page-heavy Apress book makes a valuable addition to your programming library. You can easily find and copy code—or perform examples by quickly toggling between instructions and the application. Even simultaneously tackling a donut, diet soda, and complex code becomes simplified with hands-free eBooks!

Once you purchase your book, getting the $10 companion eBook is simple:

❶ Visit **www.apress.com/promo/tendollars/**.

❷ Complete a basic registration form to receive a randomly generated question about this title.

❸ Answer the question correctly in 60 seconds, and you will receive a promotional code to redeem for the $10.00 eBook.

2560 Ninth Street • Suite 219 • Berkeley, CA 94710

eBookshop

THE EXPERT'S VOICE™

Offer valid through 3/07.